THE PSYCHOLOGY OF
ETHNIC GROUPS
IN THE UNITED STATES

THE PSYCHOLOGY OF
ETHNIC GROUPS
IN THE UNITED STATES

Pamela Balls Organista | Gerardo Marín | Kevin M. Chun
University of San Francisco

Los Angeles | London | New Delhi
Singapore | Washington DC

For information:

SAGE Publications, Inc.
2455 Teller Road
Thousand Oaks, California 91320
E-mail: order@sagepub.com

SAGE Publications Ltd.
1 Oliver's Yard
55 City Road
London EC1Y 1SP
United Kingdom

SAGE Publications India Pvt. Ltd.
B 1/I 1 Mohan Cooperative Industrial Area
Mathura Road, New Delhi 110 044
India

SAGE Publications Asia-Pacific Pte. Ltd.
33 Pekin Street #02-01
Far East Square
Singapore 048763

Printed in the United States of America.

Library of Congress Cataloging-in-Publication Data

Balls Organista, Pamela.
The psychology of ethnic groups in the United States/Pamela Balls Organista, Gerardo Marín, Kevin M. Chun.
 p. cm.
Includes bibliographical references and index.
ISBN 978-1-4129-1540-3 (pbk.)

 1. Minorities—Mental health—United States. 2. Minorities—United States—Psychology. I. Marín, Gerardo. II. Chun, Kevin M. III. Title.

RC451.5.A2O74 2010
616.890089—dc22   2009002549

Printed on acid-free paper.

09 10 11 12 13 10 9 8 7 6 5 4 3 2 1

Acquiring Editor:	Lisa Cuevas Shaw
Associate Editor:	Lindsay Dutro
Editorial Assistant:	Sarita Sarak
Production Editor:	Sarah K. Quesenberry
Copy Editor:	Taryn Bigelow
Proofreader:	Andrea Martin
Indexer:	Jeanne Busemeyer
Typesetter:	C&M Digitals (P) Ltd.
Cover Designer:	Gail Buschman
Marketing Manager:	Christy Guilbault

BRIEF CONTENTS

DETAILED CONTENTS

PREFACE

In the same fashion as most software manuals, this book should probably begin by stating, "Congratulations . . ." not just because you bought this book but because you have acknowledged the fact that in our multicultural society, we need to better understand the relationship between ethnicity and culture and psychology. Indeed, in the 21st century it is practically impossible not to encounter cultural and ethnic diversity among one's friends, neighbors, and colleagues, at school and on the street. Interestingly, the same is true of many other nations across the globe, including in the Americas, Europe, Asia, and Africa.

In writing this book we wanted to acknowledge that the ethnic and cultural diversity that we encounter in our lives is a central reason for our nation's richness and strength. We hope that by reading this book you will become an informed member of our ethnically diverse community.

This book will help you to become familiar with some of the most pressing issues that need to be understood when we study the psychology of all the people who reside in the United States—European Americans and people of color. For many of the questions raised in this book, the final answers are not yet available, but the joint efforts of current and future researchers will provide some new parameters and guidelines to follow. Our hope is that this book will help you to be a conscientious and critical consumer of psychological research. We also hope that the book may interest you in contributing to this important enterprise of building an ethnic psychology.

Contemporary psychological research in the United States includes de facto the presence of a variety of members of ethnic groups. One reason for this situation is the high proportion of the country's population that belongs to one of the four major ethnic groups (African Americans, American Indians and Alaska Natives, Asian Americans, and Hispanics/Latinos). But, as we implied above, demographics is just one argument for the need to study a culturally appropriate psychology. More important is the need to obtain an appropriate understanding of what are accurate and valid scientific findings and what information is tainted by poor methodologies or faulty interpretations. Indeed, it is difficult to accept the implicit premise of some social science research that would propose that members of one culture or ethnic group (usually non-Hispanic Whites) are representative of all humanity. This is what happens when researchers fail to include sufficient numbers of members of appropriate ethnic and cultural groups in their research projects. Just as psychologists have questioned the validity of behavioral rules derived from research with college undergraduates, social and behavioral scientists must question the validity and reliability of findings based on a select and unique group of individuals from one ethnic group.

This book is not intended to replace basic psychological books and textbooks. Rather, the book provides a survey of essential issues that need to be understood when studying the behavior of all peoples. We invite you to join us in this exploration of the relationship of ethnicity and psychology as you read the pages that follow. The introductory section to the book presents an overview of the book including how it is organized and also how to make best use of its various sections. Although most readers tend to overlook the Introduction section in textbooks, we urge you to take a look at this section because it will help you to understand the book and to better learn the principles and facts we are presenting. But first, we would like to tell you a little about how the book came to be and who we are.

THE ROAD WE HAVE TRAVELED

This book is the third joint book publication we have produced in the last few years. More than 10 years ago, we started the search for a textbook that could be used in courses on ethnic psychology. There were a few books on the market, but they did not quite fit our understanding of ethnic psychology as a field that was continuously evolving yet also mature enough to offer important contributions to the analysis of diverse human behaviors. Our early disappointment with available texts led us to edit a book of classic and contemporary readings that was published in 1998 by Routledge, titled *Readings in Ethnic Psychology*. That book was one of the first to use the label "ethnic psychology" to talk about the psychology of ethnic/racial minority groups in the United States. A few years later, we realized that acculturation was one of the key principles in ethnic psychology and that it was time to update the early work in the field, to identify theoretical developments as well as new applications of this construct. We held a conference at the University of San Francisco centered on acculturation, and some of the presentations from that conference were later collected in the book *Acculturation: Advances in Theory, Measurement, and Applied Research,* published in 2003 by the American Psychological Association.

We would like to tell you something about ourselves so that you see how our experiences and lives have shaped what you will read.

Pamela Balls Organista was born in St. Louis, Missouri. She attended Washington University in St. Louis where she obtained a B.A. in Psychology and Black Studies. She attended Arizona State University for graduate studies in clinical psychology, obtaining her Ph.D., and then the University of California, San Francisco, where she completed a postdoctorate in clinical psychology with an emphasis in public service and minorities. She has been at the University of San Francisco (USF) since 1992 and currently serves as Professor and Chair in the Department of Psychology and the founding and current director of Ethnic Studies in the College of Arts and Sciences. Her research interests have centered on health risks and protective factors in primarily underserved populations including poor medical patients, Mexican migrants, and ethnic minority youth.

Gerardo Marín was born in Pereira, Colombia, and raised in Cali, Colombia. His family immigrated to the United States when he was 17 years old. He attended Miami Dade Community College for two years and then transferred to Loyola University in Chicago where he obtained a B.S. in Psychology in 1970. He attended graduate school at DePaul University obtaining an M.S. in Psychology in 1972 and his Ph.D. in 1979. Gerardo has been at USF since 1982 and currently holds the position of Professor of Psychology and Vice Provost for Academic Affairs. He has published over 125 articles, chapters, and books mostly on topics such as acculturation, culturally appropriate research methods, AIDS, and tobacco and alcohol use among ethnic minority groups. He was involved in developing two of the most widely used acculturation scales for Latinos and served as the scientific editor for the Surgeon General's report on tobacco use among ethnic minorities. He also has been interested in cross-cultural psychology and in international activities and has been an active member of various international psychological associations including the Interamerican Society of Psychology (SIP). He has been honored by various psychological associations and nongovernmental organizations and was awarded a doctorate honoris causa by the Catholic university in Hungary (Pázmany Péter Katolikus Egyetem). Gerardo has a granddaughter (Sienna M. Lindamood) and two children, Melisa (married to Kevin Lindamood) and Andrés Daniel (married to Kathleen Broderick).

Kevin M. Chun is a fifth generation Chinese American with long-standing family roots in San Francisco. He received a B.S. in Psychology from Santa Clara University in 1990 and his Ph.D. in Clinical Psychology from the

University of California, Los Angeles, in 1995. While at UCLA, he worked with his mentor and adviser, Dr. Stanley Sue, at the National Research Center on Asian American Mental Health. He completed a psychology internship at Palo Alto VA Medical Center and received an Irvine Scholar Dissertation Fellowship at USF in 1995. Soon after, Kevin joined USF as a full-time faculty member and is currently Professor of Psychology and Director of Asian American Studies. His research focuses on family acculturation processes and health issues for Chinese American immigrants. Kevin and his University of California, San Francisco, colleague Dr. Catherine Chesla received two consecutive R01 grants from the National Institutes of Health to investigate cultural issues in diabetes management for Chinese American immigrant families, and to develop the first empirically supported diabetes management intervention for this ethnic group. Kevin is a contributing author to a number of scholarly works, including *Handbook of Asian American Psychology* (first and second editions), *Acculturation and Parent-Child Relationships: Measurement and Development,* and *Handbook of Mental Health and Acculturation in Asian American Families.* He was a recipient of the Early Career Award for Distinguished Contributions from the Asian American Psychological Association in 2005.

ACKNOWLEDGMENTS

The writing of this book has been "in process" for approximately four years, at times delayed by other pressing deadlines or by competitive demands on our time. Nevertheless, we are proud of the final product and thankful for all the support we received from a number of individuals. Jointly, we wish to thank our dean, Jennifer Turpin (Dean of Arts and Sciences at USF), who has always shown interest in our research and who encouraged us to complete the book. We also wish to thank our President, Fr. Stephen A. Privett, S. J., and our Provost, James L. Wiser, who have created the institutional climate necessary to make this book a reality. We also wish to thank our colleagues in the Psychology Department at USF who by their example and encouragement made it possible for us to work on our three books that were born of our collegial search for what is best for our students (the search for the *Magis* that characterizes Jesuit education). We also wish to thank the staff at Sage who from the beginning have been enthusiastic, supportive, and helpful and who gently prodded us to move on and complete the book. We have been fortunate to work with an excellent editorial staff over the years including Jim Brace-Thompson, Cheri Dellelo, Deya Saoud, Lindsay Dutro, and Erik Evans who assisted us through the completion of this project.

Thanks are also due to the anonymous reviewers who provided thoughtful and thorough critiques of our manuscript.

Individually, we also wish to express special thanks to a number of people who have supported us while writing the book. We hope they feel proud of their contributions and share in our joy to have completed an important task.

Pamela is eternally grateful to work collaboratively with her esteemed friends and colleagues, Gerardo and Kevin. Together, they have had the opportunity to work on several projects (articles, presentations, books, and grants) that reflect the mission of the University of San Francisco and their values—namely, to continually create, through their scholarship and service, a more just and inclusive world. As a multicultural team, they are able to address issues through a variety of cultural lenses and provide a complex understanding of the psychosocial challenges, promises, and questions that still remain for ethnic minorities living in the United States. Taking on the writing of this manuscript has been a daunting process, and without the passion and support of others, its completion would have been dubious. In particular, she is grateful for her close family and friends. They are upbeat, bright, and good people that never cease to amaze her with their work and commitment to others. She wants to express her thanks to her two sisters, Zoneice and Tunderleauh, and nephews, Demerrio and Tory. She gives special thanks to her husband, Kurt Organista, who continually provides a rich source of inspiration, intellectual collaboration, and loving support. Their beautiful and beloved children, Zena Laura and Zara Luz, never fail to make her think and care more deeply, laugh/play, and recognize that they hold a special place of importance in one another's lives as "Momma" and "Daughters." Finally, she wants to express her heartfelt gratitude to her parents, Zevonzell and Cynthia Balls, who provided a good upbringing, home, and a strong education to sustain her. Throughout her life, they love her, encourage her, and believe in her. These gifts are meaningful and invaluable and she would like to dedicate this book to them.

Gerardo wishes to express a special appreciation to Pamela and Kevin, his respected colleagues who have been part of many "crazy" ideas and who have sustained his interest in these issues and taught him much. His daughter, Melisa, and his son, Andrés, have been instrumental in shaping the book and in making it a reality and he needs to thank them for their ever so gentle "Papi, how is the book coming?" questioning. In particular, he wishes to thank Lois Ann Lorentzen for her constant and caring companionship, her love, her emotional support, her example, and her disappointed face when other things stole time away from writing. As the book was being written, a little princess was born, his granddaughter Sienna M. Lindamood who has brought much happiness and hope to her family and especially to her "Ato."

She exemplifies in her background the realities of a multiethnic society and he would like to dedicate this book to her.

Kevin also wishes to thank his dear friends and colleagues, Gerardo and Pamela, for their continued friendship and support throughout the years. He continues to be inspired by their professional expertise, intellectual curiosity, and abiding commitment to social justice. Kevin is also grateful for the generous and unconditional support of his partner, Anthony Ng; his family, Cynthia and Henry Lum Wilfred Chun, and Annett, Shaun, Garrett, and Harrison Wright; and his many caring friends and extended family members in the San Francisco Bay Area. He dedicates this book to his late grand aunt, Frances Chun Kan, a former singer and entertainer at the Forbidden City Nightclub in San Francisco's Chinatown, who was a loving family member, bon vivant, civil rights pioneer, and inspirational role model to all.

Pamela Balls Organista
Gerardo Marín
Kevin Chun

INTRODUCTION

You are reading this book in exciting and challenging times. The country and the rest of the world are experiencing great mobility across borders, bringing people from different cultures into contact with each other. Financial problems in the United States at the end of 2008 have brought economic challenges and difficulties not just to the United States but also to many other countries. The U.S. Census Bureau is predicting that within a generation, the country will be so ethnically diverse that European Americans will no longer be the majority. In 2009, we welcomed the inauguration of the first ethnic minority president in the more than 200 years of history of the country. These and many other momentous events support the need for all of us to become more informed about our multicultural society. That is a key reason for this book.

Before you start reading Chapter 1, there are a few things we would like to point out that will make your reading more productive.

INTENDED AUDIENCE

This is a textbook intended for undergraduate and beginning graduate students interested in ethnic psychology. As such, we envision it will be assigned in classes as diverse as those exploring ethnicity, race, culture, class, gender, sexual orientation, minority status, ethnic diversity, and multiculturalism. For a more detailed coverage of the various topics, we recommend a series of journals, handbooks, and other books at the end of Chapter 1 that will help you gain a comprehensive understanding of the field.

GOAL

We wrote this book with the aim of offering a comprehensive overview of the best-quality research in psychology and in other social sciences regarding *ethnic minorities in the United States*. This text focuses on four ethnic minority groups: African Americans, American Indians and Alaska Natives, Asian Americans, and Hispanics/Latinos. Our selection of these four ethnic minority groups is not intended to ignore the fact that there are many other ethnic minorities in the country. Instead, these four ethnic minorities have received the most attention in the ethnic psychology literature, allowing for in-depth analyses of their psychological experiences. Furthermore, we are focusing our analysis of the four ethnic minority groups to research conducted in the United States. There is important research conducted with ethnic minorities in other countries. For example, research with individuals of Asian background living in Canada or Australia, Latinos living in Scandinavia, or Northern Africans living in Southern Europe and in Germany. Nevertheless, this book does not cover these studies because analyzing the contributions of different national contexts, including the effects of their different sociopolitical environments and historical forces, to the psychology of their residents and citizens is beyond the scope of this book. For the sake of clarity and consistency, we thus decided to focus our analysis on an American national context.

A WORD ABOUT LABELS

We realize that during the last few decades ethnic and racial labels have evolved that reflect changes in sociopolitical beliefs and attitudes in the United States. In writing this book, we tried to reflect the most commonly used labels in the social sciences literature at the beginning of the 21st century. As such, we frequently use "African American" instead of "Black" to denote individuals who trace their background to Africa or certain areas of the Caribbean. Likewise, we tend to use "Latino" rather than "Hispanic" or the older label "Spanish American" to denote individuals who trace their background to Latin America. We use "Latino" as an English-language label that includes women and men rather than as a Spanish-language label that would require two different words (Latino and Latina or the newer forms of Latin@ or Latino/a). We made this choice for convenience and appearance and not as a way of ignoring a very important part of the Latino population. We use "Asian American" to denote individuals who trace their background to Asia. The label "American Indian" is used to denote those who trace their background to the first peoples of the country and it replaces "Native American." Most likely, by the second edition of this book, we will change some of these labels as sociopolitical attitudes and beliefs about ethnicity and race continue to evolve.

THE BOOK'S ORGANIZATION

We have tried to write the book in a way that is inviting and easy to read by including a number of helpful features. Every chapter begins with a *Vignette,* a short story that illustrates practical applications of key topics and issues that are presented in the chapter. Likewise, you will find *boxes* throughout the chapters that expand coverage of certain topics by providing added examples of relevant research, and extended data and commentary. Do not skip these features because they will help to contextualize and punctuate key ideas in the main text of the chapter.

At the end of each chapter you will find three sections that will help you study and remember what the chapter has covered. First, a section called *Key Terms* presents a list of the concepts covered in the chapter that deserve special consideration. These terms also are shown in bold type when they are discussed in the text of the chapter. You will want to make sure that you can define each of these terms and explain why they are important to the chapter topics.

Also, at the end of each chapter you will find a section called *Learning by Doing* where we suggest exercises that you can do to help improve your understanding of the implications of the theoretical concepts that were included in the chapter. These mini-studies will take a little time and effort but will make concrete the abstract ideas you have studied. Finally, each chapter includes a section labeled *Suggested Further Readings* where we list books that you may want to consult to gain a deeper understanding of the topics presented in the chapter.

***

We hope that you will enjoy reading this book and that you will gain more comprehensive and nuanced perspectives on our multiethnic society. Furthermore, we hope that you will be able to see the relevance of ethnicity, race, culture, and other important identity dimensions to core psychology principles and theories, and learn how to work and live more effectively in an ethnically diverse world.

We would enjoy hearing your thoughts and opinions about our book as well as any suggestions for future revisions. Feel free to contact us by e-mail: Pamela Balls Organista (organistap@usfca.edu), Gerardo Marín (marin@usfca.edu), or Kevin Chun (chunk@usfca.edu).

CHAPTER 1

ETHNIC DIVERSITY AND PSYCHOLOGY

VIGNETTE

Learning About Ethnic Diversity in Psychology

Lee started his undergraduate studies in biology at a private university in Chicago. His parents were born in New York and his grandparents came from China in the early 20th century. They were all very proud of Lee's academic accomplishments. Lee's acceptance into college validated their years of sacrifice and hard work to provide Lee the best possible education. Moreover, his plan to later pursue

(Continued)

(Continued)

a medical degree was a "dream come true" to his mother. Lee studied hard to obtain the best grades in his courses, but college seemed markedly different from his high school years. For one, he was living away from his home in Southern California. Two, he no longer had his group of friends—most of Asian descent—for hanging out and socializing. Indeed, he felt somewhat different from his peers since most of the students in his classes were White Americans. Nevertheless, he managed to pass his freshman year courses and was determined to pull his grades up higher during his second year. He also needed to take other courses to fulfill his core requirements. He decided that introductory psychology was a good choice since it dealt with the study of human behavior—and as a future doctor, it might have some relevance to his career. Although he aced the course, he was unhappy with the almost total absence of information about Asian Americans—it almost seemed as if he and other students of color were being ignored by psychology (at least the psychology described in the textbook and in lectures). He also thought that some of the psychological principles mentioned in class were not part of his experience as an Asian American—a feeling that was shared by his roommate Dwayne, an African American computer science major from St. Louis, Missouri. Looking for an elective to take, Lee chose a relatively new course in the curriculum, Psychology of Ethnic Groups in the United States. The title captured his attention because he hoped to hear about his culture and people like himself and like Dwayne. On the first day of class, the instructor, Dr. Gonzalez, introduced the course by saying, "The purpose of this course is to educate and sensitize you about the major psychological issues facing individuals from different ethnic or racial groups with special attention focused on African Americans, Latinos, Asian Americans, and American Indians. We are going to explore what psychology says about this emerging majority in the country and also what psychology has failed to address." As Lee listened, he got more and more excited. He thought, "Finally, this is a course about me and Dr. Gonzalez is an Asian American like myself—the first Asian American professor I've seen here."

The United States can easily be defined as a rich and complex cultural and ethnic mosaic that is a work in progress. With each passing decade, residents and immigrants and their children and grandchildren add to its color and energy, sustaining our historical self-portrait as a diverse nation enriched by the contributions of many different peoples. Yet, this vision and its underlying beliefs of unlimited opportunity, equality, and freedom have been challenged by a long and complicated history centered on our difficulties in understanding and accepting people's differences. Ever since the founding of this country, skin color, national origin, and cultural differences have been used to restrict the rights and freedoms of certain groups or have been allowed to shape the nature of our personal interactions.

Psychologists have made important contributions to our understanding of ethnic and cultural differences but we are still struggling to find ways to cogently discuss and examine ethnicity and culture and their influences on people's behavior. This book is an attempt to summarize the most significant knowledge and information we have about the psychology of ethnic minority groups, and in doing so we hope to contribute to the development of a new and respectful scientific language to discuss these concepts in an informed and balanced manner. Furthermore, the book should help you identify ways in which you can contribute to building an ethnically diverse country that respects differences and benefits from what people with different perspectives and experiences contribute.

At this point, it is important to briefly explain the use of certain key words throughout the book. As mentioned in greater detail in Chapter 2, the book uses the word "ethnicity" rather than race in order to avoid using a poorly defined term and to better reflect the differences across groups of individuals who have been exposed to varying cultures, traditions, and experiences. Furthermore, ethnicity has generally not been associated with faulty perceptions of superiority of one group over another as has been the case for race. Box 1.1 briefly defines key concepts such as **culture, ethnicity,** and **ancestry** that are mentioned in this and the other chapters of the book. The next chapter includes a comprehensive discussion of the various terms and their applicability in psychological research.

BOX 1.1

Some Basic Terms

Ancestry: A person's origin, heritage, or descent that is associated with birthplace of self or ancestors.

Culture: A set of attitudes, values, beliefs, and norms that are shared within a group and transmitted across generations.

Ethnicity: A social group's distinct sense of belongingness as a result of common culture and descent.

Nationality: A person's country of birth or descent.

Race: A socially constructed concept based on prevailing social and political attitudes. Often used to express ambiguous distinctions, promote dominance of certain privileged groups, and oppress groups that are deemed inferior.

The United States has a population that is quite diverse in a number of ways beyond ethnicity or culture. For example, we differ in terms of gender, sexuality, age, socioeconomic status, religious belief, physical ability, nationality, ancestry, educational level, employment, place of residence, and so on. All of these areas of diversity are important since they affect the way we think and act. For example, Mary, who was raised on a farm in rural Illinois, may exhibit attitudes or behaviors that are different from her cousin Samantha, who was raised in the heart of

Chicago, or from another cousin who lives on a farm in rural Northern California. This book is dedicated to exploring differences due to people's ethnicity and this emphasis on ethnicity does not negate the important role that the other diversity variables can have on people's attitudes and behaviors. Indeed, many psychology departments recognize this fact by offering not just a course on the Psychology of Ethnic Groups but also courses such as the Psychology of Women, the Psychology of Men, Poverty and Psychology, and so on.

THE UNITED STATES AS AN ETHNICALLY DIVERSE SOCIETY

The United States is, and has been since its creation, a country that frequently takes pride in its ethnic and cultural diversity. A short overview of our history shows how European immigrants joined the first Americans in sharing a bountiful land full of promise. Later years brought to our shores more Europeans, many of them fleeing poverty or political and religious persecution. Africans were forced to come to our land under inhumane conditions and to sacrifice their lives at the service of those whose families had arrived a few years before them. Other ethnic and cultural groups were brought together under one flag and one nation through land purchases (as in the case of the Cajuns in Louisiana) or through political agreements (as in the case of Mexicans living in what is now the southwestern United States).

In the 19th and 20th centuries, large groups of Italians, Jews, Irish, Chinese, and Mexicans, among others, came to the United States to contribute to the country's economic growth by performing manual and skilled labor jobs that few people wanted at the wages offered or under the conditions in which the jobs needed to be performed. The latter part of the 20th century and the beginnings of the 21st century have witnessed the continued arrival of individuals from all over the world who eagerly wish to contribute to the welfare of the nation and to enjoy its economic and educational opportunities and freedoms. The end result of these migrations over the course of three centuries is a distinctly diverse society that witnesses the presence on its shores of individuals with multiple cultural traditions and pursues the goal, in many respects unrealized, of considering all women and men as having been created equal.

The cultural and ethnic diversity that characterizes the United States can easily be experienced in our large cities where people of all cultures interact with each other even if not with perfect comfort. Our traditions and our foods celebrate that diversity and our laws endeavor to support the richness it contributes. Indeed, many of us live in ethnically diverse settings where we feel comfortable eating foods from diverse cultures, dancing to a variety of rhythms, or playing or watching sports that come from many cultures.

Nevertheless, a truly culturally diverse country is defined by national policies that support, and individual behaviors that demonstrate, an understanding, appreciation, and respect of ethnic and cultural differences.

A truly diverse society is not created by the mere presence of individuals who look, act, or think differently from each other because of the color of their skin, the shape of their eyes, their national origin, or their fluency in speaking English. The mere presence of ethnically or culturally diverse individuals constitutes what can be called **facial diversity,** that is, variations in people's physical characteristics such as skin color, eye shape, national origin, or hair texture. But facial diversity by itself does not support the existence of a truly multicultural society. What is needed to develop a functioning multicultural society is the presence of positive interpersonal relationships among diverse individuals and the sharing of power and resources and mutual collaboration and dialogue. Facial diversity, for example, can be seen when politicians claim cultural diversity when a token number of ethnic minorities are appointed to government posts. Facial diversity can also be seen when university officials claim cultural diversity on their campuses yet students from different ethnic groups never have meaningful and shared experiences with one another such as collaborative classroom relationships or shared extracurricular activities.

A Multicultural Society

The words "multicultural" and "pluralistic" have often been used to mean different things by politicians, scholars, and the public. In this book, we argue that **multiculturalism** requires an abiding and respectful concern and interest in the lived experiences and human conditions of diverse groups of people. It involves "stepping into another person's shoes" to understand how she or he experiences and views the world. This understanding becomes possible when we delve into a group's psychosocial experiences and when we learn to appreciate and respect what makes us different and unique. Multiculturalism also requires a personal commitment to critically evaluate one's own **privilege** or preferential standing in the world, and one's own cultural biases and stereotypes. Lastly, multiculturalism rests on a fundamental belief in the common good and a willingness to contribute to it.

Going beyond facial diversity into building a functioning multicultural community allows individuals to benefit from interacting with people of diverse backgrounds and cultures. For example, research on ethnically diverse school settings has shown that classrooms where individuals of different ethnicities interact produce not only greater cultural awareness and interest in studying ethnic groups but also higher levels of academic development and satisfaction and an enhancement of student retention rates (Gurin, Dey, Hurtado, & Gurin, 2002; G. E. Lopez, 2004).

Research conducted at the University of Michigan by Gurin and colleagues (2002) showed that ethnic diversity produced a number of positive results not only for ethnic minority students but also for Whites. Those students who experienced diversity in classroom settings and in informal interactions showed high levels of civic and interpersonal engagement with diverse others. Interestingly, the research showed that these effects continued well after the students graduated from the university. In an analysis of research findings on the effects of ethnically diverse environments, Gurin and colleagues (2002) found improvements in critical thinking, ability to manage complex and conflictual situations, and preparedness for participating in an ethnically diverse democracy by showing respect for differences across groups.

Furthermore, Antonio (2004) has found that diverse social groups enhance the intellectual self-confidence of their members, increase people's ability to integrate different perspectives, and help improve the educational aspirations of ethnic minority students. Indeed, Anthony Marsella (1998), a psychologist from Hawai'i, recently argued that "ethnocultural diversity is as important for human survival as is biological diversity because it provides social and psychological options and choices in the face of powerful unpredictable environmental demands" (p. 1288).

THE ETHNIC DIVERSITY OF THE UNITED STATES

The most recent national census (conducted in the year 2000) showed that a large percentage of the total population of the country considered themselves as belonging to at least one ethnic group regardless of the length of time they and their families had resided in the United States. For example, a substantial percentage of the country's population considered themselves to have German ancestry (15.2%), where ancestry is defined by the Census Bureau as "a person's ethnic origin, heritage, descent, or 'roots,' which may reflect [his or her] place of birth, place of birth of parents or ancestors, and ethnic identities that have evolved within the United States" (Brittingham & de la Cruz, 2004). As shown in Table 1.1, other ancestries claimed by large percentages of the population of the United States included Irish (10.8%), English (8.7%), Mexican (6.5%), Italian (5.6%), Polish (3.2%), and French (3.0%). While the actual numbers and their percentages in the total population will necessarily change during the 2010 census, the significance of a person's ancestry and the rank order of the major ancestries will probably not change radically from what is presented in Table 1.1.

This book summarizes the knowledge that psychologists have contributed to our understanding of the various ethnic or cultural groups in the United States. Particular attention is given to individuals who self-identify as African

Table 1.1 Ethnic Backgrounds of U.S. Population (selected ancestries), Census 2000

Ethnic Background	Number	Proportion of Total Population (%)
African American	24,903,412	8.8
American Indian	7,876,568	2.8
Arab	205,822	0.1
Asian Indian	1,546,703	0.5
Chinese	2,271,562	0.8
Cuban	1,097,594	0.4
English	24,509,692	8.7
Filipino	2,116,478	0.8
French	8,309,666	3.0
German	42,841,569	15.2
Irish	30,524,799	10.8
Italian	15,638,348	5.6
Japanese	1,103,325	0.4
Korean	1,190,353	0.4
Mexican	18,382,291	6.5
Norwegian	4,477,725	1.6
Polish	8,977,235	3.2
Portuguese	1,173,691	0.4
Puerto Rican	2,652,598	0.9
Russian	2,652,214	0.9
Scotch-Irish	4,319,232	1.5
Scottish	4,890,581	1.7
Swedish	3,998,310	1.4
Vietnamese	1,029,420	0.4
Welsh	1,753,794	0.6

SOURCE: Brittingham & de la Cruz (2004).

Americans or Blacks, American Indians or Native Americans, Asian Americans, and Hispanics or Latinos (see Box 1.2 for definitions of various ethnic groups). This does not mean that other ethnic groups (e.g., Irish American, Italian American, German American, Polish American) are not important or have not been studied by psychologists. Instead, the emphasis on the four major groups is a way of making the discussion manageable and controlling the length of the book. Furthermore, many of the concepts mentioned in the book (e.g., acculturation, ethnic identity, family structure) are also applicable to other ethnic groups. The same is true of the analysis of the role of culture and ethnicity on people's attitudes and behaviors. As you read the book, reflect on how the concepts or ideas being presented are similar to or different from what has been your own experience.

BOX 1.2

Definitions of Ethnic Groups
(according to the U.S. Census Bureau)

African Americans or Blacks: "People having origins in any of the Black racial groups of Africa."

American Indians and Alaska Natives: Individuals "having origins in any of the original peoples of North and South America (including Central America), and who maintain tribal affiliation or community attachment."

Asian Americans and Pacific Islanders: "People having origins in any of the original peoples of the Far East, Southeast Asia, or the Indian subcontinent."

Hispanics or Latinos: "A person of Cuban, Mexican, Puerto Rican, South or Central American, or other Spanish culture or origin regardless of race."

Native Hawai'ian or Pacific Islander: "People having origins in any of the original peoples of Hawai'i, Guam, Samoa, or other Pacific Islands."

White [at times referred to as "non-Hispanic Whites"]: "People having origins in any of the original peoples of Europe, the Middle East, or North Africa."

SOURCE: Grieco & Cassidy (2001).

According to the 2000 decennial census, approximately 30.6% of the population of the United States belonged to one of the four major ethnic minority groups (see Table 1.2). These groups are expected to experience rapid growth rates in the next few years. Indeed, the 2006 American Community Survey conducted by the U.S. Census Bureau showed that

Table 1.2 Proportional Representation of Ethnic Minority Groups

	2000 Census	2006 American Community Survey	Estimated for 2050
African Americans	12.7%	12.4%	14.6%
American Indians or Alaska Natives	1.5%	0.8%	1.1%
Asian Americans	3.8%	4.4%	8.0%
Hispanics	12.6%	14.8%	24.4%

SOURCE: U.S. Census Bureau (2008).

approximately 32.5% of the total population of the country belonged to one of the four major ethnic groups (U.S. Census Bureau, 2008). By the year 2050, it is estimated that approximately half of the population of the country will be made up of individuals who identify wholly or partially as African American, American Indian, Asian American, or Latino (U.S. Census Bureau, 2008).

Within-Group Diversity

It is important to remember that the labels used in the census reports (such as "Hispanics" or "Asian Americans") as well as in this book and in much of research, are labels of convenience that mask or hide important **within-group differences.** These differences among the members of the group ("within-group") are the product of variations in origin, socioeconomic status, educational level, employment, and many other variables that affect people's behavior. As such, it is possible to see how Asian Americans differ in terms of ancestry since some trace their ancestry to Japan while others to China and others to Vietnam, Laos, Cambodia, Philippines, or one of the other nations of Asia.

Ancestry

National origin or ancestry has significant impact on the characteristics or behavior of members of a given group that may differentiate them from other closely related ethnic groups with whom they may share values, attitudes, or behaviors. For example, Hispanics or Latinos in the United States differ in terms of a number of variables, including national ancestry or origin and length of residence in the United States. Nevertheless, research

(Sabogal, Marín, Otero-Sabogal, Marín, & Pérez-Stable, 1987) shows that they tend to share, for example, the importance assigned to members of the family in making important decisions.

A fairly large number of Latinos, for example, trace their heritage to the early Californians or Mexicans who lived in New Mexico and California before their annexation to the United States. Many of them became part of this country as a result of the Guadalupe Hidalgo treaty in 1848 that ended the war between the United States and Mexico. Other Latinos are more recent immigrants who have come to the United States in search of better economic or educational opportunities. Some have come as immigrants, others as part of special visa agreements to work the fields or in specialized industries (e.g., information technology, farming, food processing), while others have arrived as undocumented residents (without a visa or a work permit). At the same time, Latinos have a variety of national heritages or ancestries with a large percentage tracing their family ancestry to Mexico (Mexican Americans), Puerto Rico, and Cuba, followed by those whose heritage can be traced to Central and South America.

Within-group variability in terms of national origin or ancestry is also found among the other major ethnic groups. For example, there are over 220 Native American nations in the United States (Champagne, 1994). Most of these Native nations differ significantly from each other in their history and traditions as well as in their current demographic and socioeconomic status. Likewise, the label "African American" denotes those who are descendants of the slave trade and whose families therefore have been in the United States for generations as well as more recent African or Caribbean immigrants. The label "Asian American" includes individuals who trace their family's background to countries as diverse as China, India, Japan, Philippines, Korea, and Vietnam.

This heterogeneity or diversity in ancestry is just one of a number of variables that produce within-group variability. Aspects such as educational achievement, social class, civic incorporation, acculturation, and health status also affect the within-group variability in the various ethnic groups.

An important corollary of this within-group heterogeneity is the need to analyze information by breaking down the groups in terms of important or relevant variables or characteristics. This process is called **disaggregation** of information and it allows researchers to better understand the characteristics of a given group. While, at times, considering a group of Asian Americans of various national backgrounds can be informative, often it is more important to differentiate groups that are subsumed in these larger categories. For example, wide disparities exist in educational attainment, health status, and employment between Chinese and Japanese Americans (two groups with long histories in the United States) and the relatively newer Southeast Asian immigrant and refugee groups, such as the Hmong and Mien. In general, Chinese and Japanese Americans show higher educational and income levels than the Hmong and the Mien. Additionally, the Hmong and the Mien show greater adjustment problems due to their exposure to severe wartime trauma and migration-related stress.

While disaggregation by national heritage or ancestry is important to better understand the characteristics of an ethnic group, few researchers carry it out in their studies because of the difficulties involved in gathering large enough representative samples from one national heritage. Indeed, this lack of appropriate disaggregation by national origin is probably one of the most important limitations of research on ethnic groups in the United States (see Chapter 3).

Multiracial or Multiple Ethnicities

It is also important to consider the role of dual or multiple ethnicities when studying minority ethnic groups in the United States. The 2000 census was the first to allow respondents to indicate if they identified with more than one "race." The data showed that approximately 6.8 million people, or 2.4% of the total population, considered themselves to belong to two or more "races" (N. A. Jones & Smith, 2003). The majority of these multiracial individuals (40%) lived in the western part of the United States with an additional 27% living in the South. Overall, California, New York, Texas, Florida, Hawai'i, Illinois, New Jersey, Washington, Michigan, and Ohio showed the largest proportions of multiracial individuals.

The 2000 census (N. A. Jones & Smith, 2003) also showed that 39.9% of American Indians and Alaska Natives reported belonging to two or more races compared to 13.9% of Asian Americans, and 4.8% of African Americans. A very significant finding of the 2000 census is the fact that a large proportion of children under the age of 18 were reported to be multiracial. Overall, 7.7% of Latinos under the age of 18 were reported as belonging to two or more races. Among those not Hispanic or Latino, the equivalent proportion was 3.2%. Research with the 1980 and 1990 censuses has shown that the reporting of multiple ancestries tends to be more frequent among the young and the better educated. In general, therefore, younger generations are exhibiting a large proportion of multiple ethnicities, a factor that further enriches our country as a multicultural society and that places particular demands on service providers and policy-makers as well as educators.

Language Use and Proficiency

Language proficiency is another characteristic that varies within ethnic groups. The 2000 census showed that approximately 18% of people age 5 years or older spoke a language other than English at home. The corresponding figure for the 1990 census was 14% and 11% for the 1980 census (Shin & Bruno, 2003). In the year 2000, approximately 28.1 million people spoke Spanish at home. Other frequently spoken languages, other than English and Spanish, are Chinese (2.0 million), French (1.6 million), German (1.4 million), Tagalog (language of Philippines; 1.2 million), Vietnamese (1.0 million), and Italian (1.0 million) (Shin & Bruno, 2003).

A phenomenon of particular importance among recent immigrants and particularly among Latinos is the level of language maintenance that occurs across extended periods of time of residence in the United States and even across generations. Research with Latinos has shown that immigrants maintain proficiency in Spanish even after 50 years of residence in the country and after having achieved proficiency in the use of English (Bahrick, Hall, Goggin, Bahrick, & Berger, 1994). An earlier study with Cuban American youths (Garcia & Diaz, 1992) showed that while Spanish was preferred by children in preschool, a mixture of English and Spanish was the preferred pattern during the last years of high school although the social setting (e.g., school, home) and the participants in the verbal exchange (e.g., among friends, siblings, parents) moderated which language was used.

Educational Attainment

Historically, the United States has been improving the level of educational attainment of its population by supporting compulsory education in primary and secondary schooling and helping to finance tertiary (college) education. The 2000 census showed that 80.4% of those individuals age 25 or older had at least finished secondary (high school) education and 24.4% had completed at least a bachelor's degree. Nevertheless, there are important differences in educational attainment across ethnic groups. As shown in Figure 1.1, among those individuals who are 25 years or older, Asian Americans show the highest levels of educational attainment in terms of achieving at least a bachelor's degree as well as an advanced degree. Latinos, on the other hand, show the lowest percentages in educational achievement. Educational attainment therefore is another variable that may be relevant to disaggregate in research being conducted among ethnic minority groups.

Figure 1.1   Educational Attainment, 2000 Census (adults 25 years or older)

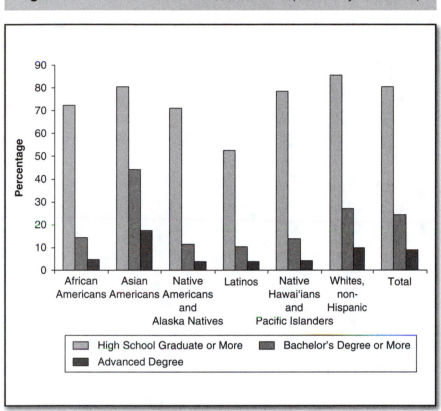

SOURCE: Bauman & Graf (2003).

Socioeconomic Status and Poverty

Poverty rates in the United States have been declining over the years although members of minority ethnic groups continue to exhibit higher rates of poverty than Whites. In the 2000 census, a total of 33.9 million people in the United States (12.4% of the total population) reported incomes that were below the poverty level. Ten years earlier (1990), 13.1% had been classified as living below the poverty line. As shown in Figure 1.2, the 2006 American Community Survey conducted by the U.S. Census Bureau also showed that poverty rates differed across ethnic minority groups.

There are some social variables that differentiate poverty rates across individuals and families. Overall, the poverty rate of foreign-born individuals is higher (16.1%) than that of the native born (11.1%) while

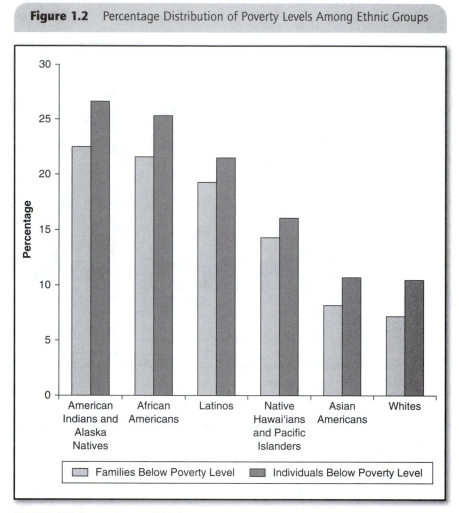

Figure 1.2 Percentage Distribution of Poverty Levels Among Ethnic Groups

SOURCE: U.S. Census Bureau (2006).

naturalized foreign-born citizens show a lower poverty rate (9.9%) (Proctor & Dalaker, 2002). Also relevant is the fact that a significant number of ethnic minority households are multifamily or multigenerational in nature, which artificially influences average household income figures. Other factors that are relevant in analyzing the poverty levels of ethnic minorities include the fact that some ethnic groups (e.g., Latinos, African Americans) are relatively young and tend to have lower levels of educational attainment. In addition, large proportions of members of ethnic groups reside in costly areas of the country such as

California, New York, and large metropolitan areas such as Chicago, where costs are higher and home ownership is more difficult. Also important in the case of Latinos and Asian Americans is the fact that large amounts of income are sent as remittances to their country of origin in order to help house, feed, and educate children, parents, and other relatives. The Pew Hispanic Center (2006) estimates that remittances to Latin America exceeded $30 billion per year or an average of $2,500 per Latino household per year.

The fact that high levels of poverty exist among members of ethnic groups is a troubling finding not only because it implies that there is no disposable income for entertainment and savings but more important because it means that there are daily needs that are not being properly met (nutrition, educational stimulation, proper housing). Furthermore, experiences of poverty have significant effects on people's behavior (American Psychological Association Task Force on Socioeconomic Status, 2007) and particularly on a child's intellectual and emotional development (G. W. Evans, 2004). For example, a large-scale study on the effects of economic deprivation on early development (Duncan, Brooks-Gunn, & Klebanov, 1994) showed that low family income and poverty status correlated with the levels of children's cognitive development and their social maturity. Furthermore, poverty can be related to a person's psychological well-being (Saéz-Santiago & Bernal, 2003), overall level of depression (Downey & Coyne, 1990), and inferior parenting skills (Rainwater, 1970). All of these are factors that significantly affect an individual's well-being and functioning in society.

WHY STUDY THE PSYCHOLOGY OF ETHNIC DIVERSITY?

This book is part of recent efforts in psychology where researchers and practitioners struggle to better understand and appreciate ethnic diversity and its effects on people's behavior. In a sense, the book tries to answer many of the questions that Lee and Dwayne (the two students in the vignette at the beginning of the chapter) had regarding what psychology has to say about their own experiences and their own culture. The information included in this book will also help students of all ethnic groups learn how psychology has tried to better understand the effects of a person's culture on behavior. As such, the book explores how being raised in one ethnic or cultural community influences such characteristics as the way individuals think about the world, or the value they place on family interactions, or the expectations people have of personal relationships.

Providing a Context

What is the relevance of our country's ethnic diversity to psychology? Simply, our knowledge of human behavior only makes sense when properly contextualized in terms of the characteristics of the population. As Trickett (1996) has argued, psychological theory, research, and interventions need to be located in the sociocultural context where individuals and communities reside. As a matter of fact, much research in ethnic psychology and in cross-cultural psychology suggests that what is appropriate or even valued in one culture may be rejected in others (Sternberg, 2004). For example, Okagaki and Sternberg (1993) found that Latino parents tended to define intelligence in their school-age children in terms of skills in social competence while Asian American and White parents tended to emphasize cognitive skills. At the same time, teachers, reflecting the values of the White parents, placed emphasis on cognitive skills and rewarded children in terms of the development of those skills rather than social competence. Not surprisingly, Latino children were ranked as less intelligent by those teachers since their conceptions of intelligence differed from what the culture of the parents valued the most. Indeed, many researchers argue that "the concept-ualization, assessment, and development of intelligence [or any other psychological construct] cannot be fully or even meaningfully understood outside their cultural context" (Sternberg, 2004, p. 325). The same statement can be made regarding psychological research and theorizing with members of ethnic groups in a diverse society.

Improving the Validity of Psychology

One other important reason for studying the psychology of ethnic minority groups is contributing to its validity and usefulness. Ignoring cultural values and expectancies as well as using inappropriate methodological approaches to measurement can produce terribly false information and conclusions with limited external validity (Helms, 2006; S. Sue, 1999).

The area of intelligence measurement is one where psychology has frequently made embarrassingly erroneous statements based on improper conceptualization of the constructs, ignorance of group-specific values, or invalid measurements. It is widely known, for example, that during the infancy of intelligence measurement in the early part of the 20th century, intelligence tests were given to recently landed immigrants as a way of detecting would-be immigrants who showed mental deficiencies. Some immigrants were excluded by simple observation on the part of immigration officials or through examinations and tests that suffered from untrained translators, elimination of items from the original version, or changes to the wording of questions. Not surprisingly, data showed that many immigrants with limited English abilities often scored fairly low in intelligence. For example, early researchers considered that the majority of Italian, Hungarian, and Russian immigrants who they tested should be considered as "morons" or "feeble-minded" although they failed to consider the fact that many of them did not speak English and had been asked to answer an intelligence test in a language they did not understand or speak. A more recent example is the argument of the heritability of intelligence as an explanation for lower IQ scores among African Americans (Herrnstein & Murray, 1994), where the effects of culture-specific definitions of intelligence and the pervasive influence of socioeconomic status were ignored while using measuring instruments that were not culturally appropriate since they were not normed or standardized for the populations tested. Proper attention to cultural and ethnic differences would have allowed those psychologists to properly contextualize their findings and to make scientifically valid observations.

Attention to ethnic variations in psychological theory and instrumentation, of course, does not imply an absolute relativism that would reject all that psychology has produced. It is indeed quite possible that some of the theories and behavioral principles that have evolved over the last 100 years or so of scientific psychology are generalizable or applicable to all ethnic populations and across cultures. In that sense, we should be able to use certain psychological principles to explain the behavior of people from different cultures and ethnicities. What is important is to question the a priori assumption of generalizability across ethnicities or cultures. That generalizability needs to be demonstrated. That goal becomes the guiding principle of ethnic psychology as presented throughout this book.

Advancing Culturally Diverse Societies

A number of issues are of relevance when we try to understand how culturally diverse societies can function better by supporting the incorporation of individuals of varying cultural and ethnic backgrounds and by respecting and celebrating those differences. As shown at the beginning of this chapter, a diverse environment helps individuals improve their learning and performance. For psychologists, therefore, a key concern is how our science can best contribute to those goals of understanding cultures and ethnic differences and promoting individual growth in ethnically and culturally diverse environments.

Unfortunately, much of psychological research has assumed that findings obtained in the United States (mostly among White college students) actually represent human behavior across all cultures (Fowers & Davidov, 2006). This assumption of universality is questionable and has done much damage to the science and profession by supporting a **Eurocentric bias.** Such bias refers to the overemphasis given by some individuals to the experiences and characteristics of White individuals who trace their ancestry to Europe and that are considered as "normal" or "ideal." This bias has often been characterized as "cultural imperialism" (Jahoda, 1988; U. Kim & Berry 1993).

The overreliance on White college students in psychological research and the lack of non-White researchers have produced this Eurocentric science that may have limited generalizability or applicability when individuals from other ethnic groups are considered. Indeed, attention to ethnic psychology will help the development of diverse societies that respect and support the ethnic and cultural characteristics of its members and provides them with culturally appropriate services (Berry, 2003). Unfortunately, many individual members of ethnic minority groups, like Lee (the student mentioned at the beginning of the chapter), find that much of psychological research does not reflect their experiences because it has been based on research that for the most part has excluded non-Whites.

The proper understanding of contemporary ethnically and culturally diverse societies requires input from various disciplines to provide a more appropriate and comprehensive picture of a nation. Berry (2003) has argued that an understanding of diverse societies requires at a minimum the interaction of psychology, sociology, anthropology, and political science that together provide an understanding of three key aspects of a diverse society: (1) its sociocultural factors (e.g., discrimination, prejudice), (2) public policies (such as health care policy, social welfare policy), and (3) the behavior of individuals (e.g., psychological adjustment, coping behavior).

While the emphasis in this book is on psychological research, we have added at times findings and theories from sociology and other social sciences in order to provide a more comprehensive perspective. Indeed, a significant amount of research in the social sciences has helped psychologists develop better research with ethnic minority communities. Anthropologists, for example, have provided a nuanced understanding of culture functioning by researching how primary social units (such as the family) function and how they influence people's values, beliefs, attitudes, and social behaviors. Sociologists have helped psychologists understand the role played by groups and other social entities in supporting an individual's development of values and norms as well as expectations for the way they and others should behave.

Research with ethnic minority communities also helps scientists and service providers (such as counselors, therapists) to properly support the social, personal, and psychological development of members of ethnic communities as well as to prevent illness and other problems. To be useful to these communities, psychological research, as well as that of other social and behavioral sciences, must adhere to standards of scientific integrity and validity including external or ecological validity in research studies (D. W. Sue & Sue, 2008; S. Sue, 1999). Preventive and therapeutic services in psychology as well as in medicine and public health must likewise reflect the needs of those individuals being served rather than the characteristics of the providers (Rossa, Dumka, Gonzales, & Knight, 2002).

In short, understanding and contributing to a diverse society requires a comprehensive analysis of its members and institutions where issues such as ethnicity, minority status, class differences, cultural values, immigration experiences, acculturation, dominant group attitudes and policies, and other concepts need to be considered as the background against which societies function. These constructs and social characteristics are discussed in greater detail later on in the rest of the book, particularly in Chapter 2.

ETHNIC PSYCHOLOGY AS DIFFERENT FROM CROSS-CULTURAL PSYCHOLOGY

It is important to differentiate between cross-cultural psychology and ethnic psychology. While both areas are concerned with the effects of culture and cultural differences on people's behavior, they differ in terms of their cultural or geographic area of emphasis. **Cross-cultural psychology** emphasizes differences in cultural influences across nations or regions of the world. **Ethnic psychology,** on the other hand, tends to focus on ethnic and cultural group differences within a single nation or community (Segall, Lonner, & Berry, 1998). As such, cross-cultural psychology would focus, for example, on studying differences and similarities in moral development in children in the United States and in Mexico while ethnic psychology would concentrate on studying moral development among Mexican Americans and/or African Americans. While both areas share some of the same methodological concerns (see Chapter 3) and areas of scientific interest (e.g., values, intergroup relations, cognition, psychopathology), they differ in their unit of analysis (who is studied) and location of research (within-country/nation for ethnic psychology or across countries or cultures for cross-cultural psychology).

As mentioned above, there are topical areas that overlap in cross-cultural and ethnic psychology and these similarities in interests actually enrich their development by cross-fertilizing theoretical advances and empirical discoveries. Nevertheless, care should be taken not to make inappropriate generalizations. Indeed, findings from cross-cultural research must be carefully analyzed before they are generalized to an ethnic population and vice versa. For example, research on the development of a child's value structure among children in Beijing cannot be generalized to Chinese Americans in San Francisco since both groups of children have been exposed to a number of important differences in child rearing including family size (usually one child in Beijing), schooling (usually public, government subsidized schools in Beijing), and ethnic diversity of the social environment (greater in San Francisco).

Another important difference between cross-cultural psychology and ethnic psychology is the centrality of the recognition given to the role played by differences in culture learning (usually called "acculturation") on an individual's beliefs, values, attitudes, and behaviors. Research in ethnic psychology must take into consideration how acculturation affects people's behavior if not directly at least indirectly (see Chapter 4 for a more thorough discussion of acculturation and its effects).

Also essential to ethnic psychology is the recognition of the significance of certain social conditions that affect the attitudes and behaviors of ethnic groups such as often being part of statistical minorities and experiencing the results of social and economic stratification. At the same time, both cross-cultural psychology and ethnic psychology share the belief that in order for psychology to be valid and useful it must consider the mutual influences that exist between culture and people's behavior (Segall et al., 1998).

THE GROWTH OF ETHNIC PSYCHOLOGY

The overlap between ethnic psychology and cross-cultural psychology will be seen throughout this book as principles, and even authors and research findings, from cross-cultural psychology are mentioned. Nevertheless, an examination of cross-cultural psychology and of ethnic psychology text-books or even research articles will easily show the differences in perspective, individuals studied, and theories or hypotheses. Indeed, the last few years have seen a significant growth in ethnic psychology publications including the *Handbook of Ethnic & Minority Psychology* (Bernal, Trimble, Burlew, & Leong, 2003), the collection of articles in *Readings in Ethnic Psychology* (Balls Organista, Chun, & Marín, 1998), handbooks or texts directed at practitioners or clinicians such as the *Handbook of Multicultural Counseling* (Ponterotto, Casas, Suzuki, & Alexander, 2001), as well as the recently published *Encyclopedia of Race, Ethnicity, and Society* (Schaefer, 2008). These publications join a number of textbooks (e.g., Organista, 2007; D. W. Sue & Sue, 2008) as well as books dealing with methodological concerns in social science research with ethnic populations such as *Research With Hispanic Populations* (Marín & VanOss Marín, 1991) and *Race and Ethnicity in Research Methods* (Stanfield & Dennis, 1993). There are also a number of journals that emphasize ethnic psychological research (see Box 1.3). In addition, most scientific journals in the social and behavioral sciences are now publishing an increasing number of articles dealing with ethnic psychology.

BOX 1.3

Examples of Journals Publishing Ethnic Psychology

Cultural Diversity & Ethnic Minority Psychology
Equity and Excellence in Education
Ethnic and Racial Studies
Ethnicities
Ethnicity & Health
Hispanic Journal of Behavioral Sciences
Identities
Identity
International Journal of Intercultural Relations
International Migration Review
The Journal of Black Psychology
The Journal of Educational Issues of Language Minority Students
Journal of Immigrant and Minority Health
Minority Health

The field of ethnic psychology is rapidly growing in significance and scientific importance as a result of the realization that a psychology based on members of one group alone (usually Whites) does not validly represent the variety and richness of the country. Indeed, significant advances in ethnic psychology have been made in other diverse societies such as Canada and Israel as well as in francophone countries (France, Belgium) where the field is often called *psychologie interculturelle* (intercultural psychology).

Nevertheless, attention to ethnic psychology in the United States is a somewhat recent phenomenon. Only as recently as 2002, the American

Psychological Association (APA) issued a series of guidelines for the training and professional practice of psychologists (see Box 1.4). These principles respond to the need for psychologists to be knowledgeable and proficient in understanding the members of various ethnic groups and to be culturally competent in their professional practice whether teaching, conducting research, or applying psychological knowledge. The guidelines are fairly broad but are based on the belief that as social beings we all have attitudes and expectancies that can affect how we treat other individuals, particularly those who differ from ourselves. Furthermore, the guidelines support the notion that much of psychological research may be limited in its usefulness and appropriateness by the monocultural perspectives of researchers and the lack of diversity (ethnic, gender, socioeconomic status, sexual orientation, etc.) in subject pools, research teams, and peer reviewers. According to the APA (2002), the guidelines "reflect the continuing evolution of the study of psychology, changes in society-at-large, and emerging data about the different needs for particular individuals and groups historically marginalized or disenfranchised within and by psychology based on their ethnic/racial heritage and social group identity or membership" (p. 1).

BOX 1.4

A Selection of APA Guidelines on Multicultural Education, Training, Research, Practice, and Organizational Change for Psychologists

- Psychologists are encouraged to recognize that, as cultural beings, they may hold attitudes and beliefs that can detrimentally influence their perceptions of and interactions with individuals who are ethnically and racially different from themselves
- Psychologists are encouraged to recognize the importance of multicultural sensitivity/responsiveness, knowledge, and understanding about ethnically and racially different individuals
- As educators, psychologists are encouraged to employ the constructs of multiculturalism and diversity in psychological education
- Culturally sensitive psychological researchers are encouraged to recognize the importance of conducting culture-centered and ethical psychological research among persons from ethnic, linguistic, and racial minority backgrounds
- Psychologists strive to apply culturally appropriate skills in clinical and other applied psychological practices
- Psychologists are encouraged to use organizational change processes to support culturally informed organizational (policy) development and practices

SOURCE: American Psychological Association (2002).

The achievements and developments we currently witness in ethnic psychology are the result of the efforts of a number of individuals who for decades advocated the development of a psychology that reflected the social realities of the country. This history of slow but certain achievements is well documented by B. G. Holliday and Holmes (2003), and Box 1.5 highlights some of those key developments as identified by both psychologists.

BOX 1.5

Some Key Moments in the Development of Ethnic Psychology

1885	Opening of first mental hospital for the exclusive treatment of African Americans near Petersburg, Virginia
1899	Howard University in Washington, D.C., offers its first psychology course
1920	Francis C. Sumner is first African American awarded a Ph.D. in Psychology (Clark University)
1920	J. Henry Alston is first African American to publish a psychological research article
1928	Howard University establishes a Department of Psychology
1937	Alberta B. Turner is first African American woman to receive a Ph.D. in Psychology (Ohio State University)
1943	Robert Chin is first Chinese American to receive a Ph.D. in Psychology (Columbia University)
1951	Efrain Sanchez-Hidalgo is first Puerto Rican to receive a Ph.D. in Psychology (Columbia University)
1962	Martha Bernal is first Mexican American woman to be awarded a Ph.D. in Psychology (Indiana University)
1963	The APA establishes a committee to analyze problems in training and employment due to race (Ad Hoc Committee on Equality of Opportunity in Psychology)
1968	The Association of Black Psychologists (ABPsi) is founded
1970	The Association of Psychologists Por La Raza is founded
1970	Kenneth B. Clark becomes the first person of color to be president of the APA
1971	The National Institute of Mental Health (NIMH) establishes the Center for Minority Group Mental Health Programs
1972	The Asian American Psychological Association is founded
1974	The APA Minority Fellowship Program is founded
1974	Founding of the *Journal of Black Psychology*
1975	The Society of Indian Psychologists is founded
1978	The APA establishes an Ad Hoc Committee on Minority Affairs
1979	The APA founds the Office of Ethnic Minority Affairs with Esteban Olmedo as its first director
1979	Founding of the National Hispanic Psychological Association
1979	Amado Padilla founds the *Hispanic Journal of Behavioral Sciences*
1979	The first issue of the *Journal of the Asian American Psychological Association* is published

(Continued)

(Continued)

1980	The APA establishes the Board of Ethnic Minority Affairs
1985	First convention of the Asian American Psychological Association
1986	The APA's Division 45 (The Society for the Psychological Study of Ethnic Minority Issues) is established
1986	Logan Wright is the first individual of American Indian heritage to become president of the APA
1999	First issue of the journal *Cultural Diversity & Ethnic Minority Psychology*
1999	The APA passes a resolution supporting affirmative action and equal opportunity
1999	Richard M. Suinn is first Asian American to be elected APA president
2002	Norman B. Anderson becomes first African American to serve as APA's chief executive officer
2002	The APA issues its "Guidelines on Multicultural Education, Training, Research, Practice, and Organizational Change for Psychologists"
2003	Publication of the *Handbook of Racial & Ethnic Minority Psychology*

SOURCE: Based on a chapter by B. G. Holliday & Holmes (2003).

The growth of ethnic psychology also supported the exploration of ethnic identity and culture and their psychological implications among individuals commonly considered as White (the study of **Whiteness**). This research recognizes that individuals whose skin color is light ("White") share experiences and attitudes that differentiate them from others whose skin color is darker. These shared experiences go beyond the social and economic privileges that historically have been awarded to lighter-skinned individuals in this country. Hattam (2001) argues that research on Whiteness has produced some important results that allow for a more complete understanding of the major ethnic groups "of color" (African Americans, American Indians and Alaska Natives, Asian Americans, and Latinos). In particular, Hattam argues that research on Whiteness has allowed U.S. social scientists to validate the role of class and social privilege in people's ethnic identification. Chapter 2 presents a more comprehensive discussion of the study of Whiteness in the United States and its implications for ethnic psychology.

Chapter Summary

This chapter has briefly presented an overview of the field of ethnic psychology and its importance in contemporary American society. While there are many other very diverse societies in the world (Canada, Belgium, Hong Kong, Singapore, Israel), the historical, demographic, political, and economic characteristics of the United States require the development of a unique or, at least, distinctive body of knowledge that addresses the conditions of ethnic groups in this country. Ethnic psychology contributes to the development of psychology as a science and as a profession by properly contextualizing theories and findings in terms of ethnicity. Furthermore, the work of ethnic psychologists, as reflected in this book, allows all psychologists to understand the limits in the generalizability of our findings and, in doing so, improve the validity of scientific research. While most of the literature reviewed in this book emphasizes four ethnic groups (African Americans, American Indians, Asian Americans, and Latinos), the overall findings can be applicable to other ethnic groups in the country. In this sense, ethnic psychology supports the development of scientific behavioral knowledge about the diverse society that is the United States.

Key Terms

Ancestry (page 7)

Cross-Cultural Psychology (page 23)

Culture (page 7)

Disaggregation (page 14)

Ethnicity (page 7)

Ethnic Psychology (page 23)

Eurocentric Bias (page 22)

Facial Diversity (page 9)

Multiculturalism (page 9)

Nationality (page 7)

Privilege (page 9)

Race (page 7)

Whiteness (page 28)

Within-Group Differences (page 13)

Learning by Doing

- Interview, if possible, your parents, guardians, or caregivers, uncles and aunts, and grandparents and ask them to self-identify in terms of their ethnic background. Then draw a diagram or family tree where you indicate the relationship (who is a parent to whom, for example) and the ethnic label that they apply to themselves (use the Census Bureau terms in Box 1.2 as well as the label actually used by the individuals). Then, analyze how labels or ethnicities have changed over time, how some people prefer very specific labels rather than those used by the Census Bureau, and indicate how you would define yourself.
- Interview your parents' or caregivers' siblings (your aunts and uncles) and your grandparents and identify their highest academic achievement and that of their children (your aunts and uncles and your cousins). Indicate, for example, if they have graduated from high school, or have completed two years of college, a master's degree, or a doctorate. Note how academic achievement may have changed over generations and identify how many college graduates have children who also have gone to college.
- Talk to various members of your family (e.g., parents, guardians, and/or their siblings) and draw a diagram that traces who migrated to the United States and from where. Use this information to identify how many generations removed you are from the various cultural groups represented in your family.

Suggested Further Readings

Balls Organista, P., Chun, K. M., & Marín, G. (Eds.). (1998). *Readings in ethnic psychology.* New York: Routledge.
   A collection of classic and contemporary research reports on ethnic psychology. The book covers methodological areas as well as topics related to applied fields including risk behaviors, identity, and psychological interventions.

Belgrave, F. Z., & Allison, K. W. (2006). *African American psychology: From Africa to America.* Thousand Oaks, CA: Sage.
   An excellent overview of psychological research with African Americans that incorporates the migration experience of early and recent ancestors.

Bernal, G., Trimble, J. E., Burlew, A. K., & Leong, F. T. L. (Eds.). (2003). *Handbook of racial & ethnic minority psychology.* Thousand Oaks, CA: Sage.
   A comprehensive book analyzing most areas of research and practice with ethnic minority groups. The authors represent many leaders in the field and the various chapters are excellent overviews of theories and research findings.

Bolaffi, G., Bracalenti, R., Braham, P., & Gindro, S. (2003). *Dictionary of race, ethnicity & culture.* London: Sage.
   A very complete dictionary of terms, topics, and issues related to the study of ethnicity and culture. The majority of the writers are European and contribute perspectives often ignored or unknown in the United States.

Fong, T. P., & Shinagawa, L. H. (2000). *Asian Americans: Experiences and perspectives.* Upper Saddle River, NJ: Prentice Hall.
   This book was one of the first to summarize major areas of research with Asian Americans. It is a very important source of early material on the topic.

Franklin, J. H., & Moss, A. A. (2003). *From slavery to freedom: A history of African Americans* (8th ed.). New York: Knopf.
   An important resource on the history of African Americans. This book is a comprehensive overview of what has characterized the experiences of African Americans from the early times in the Americas up to their recent more contemporary history.

Ifekwunigwe, J. O. (Ed.). (2004). *'Mixed race' studies: A reader.* London: Routledge.
   An important overview of research with biracial and multiethnic individuals, including European perspectives. This is an excellent companion to Root's book (see below).

Jackson, Y. K. (Ed.). (2006). *Encyclopedia of multicultural psychology.* Thousand Oaks, CA: Sage.
   A useful compilation of research in ethnic psychology with emphasis on all ethnic groups and helpful in gaining a perspective on the types of research psychologists have conducted among ethnic groups.

Neville, H. A., Tynes, B. M., & Utsey, S. O. (Eds.). (2008). *Handbook of African American psychology* (2nd ed.). Thousand Oaks, CA: Sage.
   A very well researched summary of research among African Americans by some of the best known and active psychologists in the field. An essential resource for students and professionals.

Padilla, A. M. (Ed.). (1995). *Hispanic psychology: Critical issues in theory and research.* Thousand Oaks, CA: Sage.
   A compilation of key articles from the *Hispanic Journal of Behavioral Sciences* by one of the pioneers in the field.

Root, M. P. P. (Ed.). (1996). *The multiracial experience: Racial borders as the new frontier.* Thousand Oaks, CA: Sage.
   This book summarizes basic and applied psychological and sociological research on multiracial individuals. Very useful for understanding early research on the topic.

Schaefer, R. T. (Ed.). (2008). *Encyclopedia of race, ethnicity, and society* (Vols. 1–3). Thousand Oaks, CA: Sage.
   A recently published encyclopedia that addresses research with ethnic minority groups from the perspectives of the various social sciences. An excellent resource for students and researchers.

Velasquez, R. J., Arellano, L. M., & McNeill, B. W. (Eds.). (2004). *The handbook of Chicana/o psychology and mental health.* Mahwah, NJ: Lawrence Erlbaum.
   The book is a collection of chapters analyzing psychological issues among Mexican Americans and serves as an introduction to the study of all Latinos.

CHAPTER 2

BASIC THEORETICAL CONCEPTS

VIGNETTE

"Mommy, what color are you?"

At the end of Sheila's workday, she left to pick up her 2-year-old daughter, Laura, at her day care center. As Sheila positioned Laura into her car seat, she detected a very inquisitive look on her daughter's face. Once Sheila strapped on her seat belt, she noticed through her rearview mirror that

(Continued)

(Continued)

Laura still looked somewhat puzzled. Laura then asked, "Mommy, what color are you?" What a question, Sheila thought! How could it be that at the mere age of 2 Laura was even aware of the idea of color in people? Sheila then wondered, is this question about my ethnicity or a question about my race? She started to feel a moment of discomfort as she stalled for the "correct" answer to her daughter's inquiry . . . should she respond that she is Black . . . African American . . . a person of color? Sheila even started to think that perhaps Laura was asking this question because she was confused by her own sense of identity as a multiethnic person, part African American and part Latino (or is it better to say Mexican American . . . Chicano . . . Hispanic?). As Sheila's pause in her response became more pregnant, she suddenly had an insight: Why sweat it trying to come up with the perfect answer? I am the parent—I should be the one asking the questions. So Sheila turned to Laura and asked, "Well, what color do you think I am?" Without hesitation, Laura replied, "Mommy, you're beige!" Sheila laughed and looked at herself in the rearview mirror. Sure enough, her daughter possessed a precocious knack for identifying colors. At a very early age, Laura could discern among various shades of blue—aqua versus turquoise versus navy blue. Indeed, Sheila's "color" is beige. Like many African Americans, Sheila's ancestry is diverse and consists of family members of African, American Indian, and European descent. In addition, Laura is at a developmental age that is more concrete. Had Sheila responded that she was "Black," Laura probably would have looked incredulously at her for failing to recognize that her skin was not even close to that color. Laura even held up her stuffed doggie, Gromit, and noted that he too was beige.

The moment of confusion described in this vignette is not unusual in discussions centered on topics of ethnicity and race. Yet, it is important to gain a basic understanding of concepts that are pertinent to the study of ethnic psychology—and sensitivity toward the complexity involved in defining these concepts. This chapter will begin with a discussion centered on culture—its definition, components, and effects on human behavior. Contemporary definitions of ethnicity and race will be presented together with a discussion of the controversies surrounding the use of race as a biological construct, as opposed to a social construct. In addition, we will define social orientations (collectivism and individualism) and cultural views of the self (interdependent and independent self-construals) and their effects on major psychological processes that are presented in later chapters. The chapter will conclude by identifying and describing important social conditions that affect the behavior of ethnic minority groups in the United States such as the process of racialization that underlies social stratification and the intersection between race, socioeconomic class, gender, and other dimensions of stratification.

Throughout this book, we would like to provide a basic understanding of certain constructs that are central to the study of ethnic minority populations in the United States. A **construct** is a term that is frequently used in the field of psychology and refers to a concept or idea based on theory and/or empirical observation. For example, "clinical depression," "attachment," and "intelligence" are all constructs that have been studied extensively by psychologists, psychiatrists, and other scientists and professionals (e.g., Ainsworth, 1989; Blatt, 2004; Sternberg, 1985). Although certain constructs are widely discussed for European Americans, they may not be entirely applicable to the psychological experiences of other ethnic groups. In the case of depression, currently, we have theories about the causes and manifestations of major depression that have been formulated, assessed, and tested through empirical or scientific observations (Blatt, 2004). Ethnic psychologists have discovered that this construct may have very different meanings and manifestations in different cultural groups, particularly for new Asian American and Latino immigrants (Balls Organista, Organista, & Kurasaki, 2003; S. Sue, Sue, Sue, & Takeuchi, 1998). Many of the constructs in the field of ethnic psychology have spawned wide-ranging debates in terms of their validity. Throughout this book, we have tried to briefly summarize the most important of these debates and the varying interpretations of various constructs used in ethnic psychology.

UNDERSTANDING CULTURE

Although most of us can readily think of what culture might entail, the task of developing a definition that clearly distinguishes culture is very difficult. Much of the difficulty in defining culture lies in the fact that it is a **multidimensional construct,** meaning that it consists of many different elements or components. Although there are many different definitions of culture, many ethnic psychologists view **culture** as a set of attitudes, values, beliefs, and norms that are shared within a group and transmitted across generations (Matsumoto & Juang, 2004; Triandis, 1994). As a multidimensional construct, culture has been viewed as consisting of both internal dimensions and external dimensions. Internal dimensions include attitudes, beliefs, and values. For example, culture can be expressed through the belief in the importance of the family above all other social relationships, or the value placed on personal independence or a person's positive or negative attitudes regarding behaviors such as abstinence, celibacy until marriage, or children's obedience to parents. External dimensions of culture include those social structures and institutions in which culture is expressed within societies. For example, culture can be exhibited through formal, organized social structures and social organizations such as government, education, religion, and political and economic systems. Culture can also be displayed through social relationship patterns or kinship networks. It is also expressed through individuals' ability to satisfy their psychological needs for affiliation, problem solving, stress reduction, and adaptation to their social environment through adherence to **social norms.** Social norms are explicit and implicit rules regarding the formation and engagement of social relationships and behaviors (Comer, 2007). For instance, in patriarchal cultures there is an established hierarchy of power that influences how members relate to the male authority figure in the family—in particular, female family members are socialized to defer to the males' authority in decision making and rules of the family.

Culture is also dynamic because it constantly changes and develops over time. For example, contemporary American culture is quite different from American culture when this nation was founded. Whether it is musical, clothing and food preferences, or social and political attitudes, culture is a living entity that is reconstructed and reenacted by different generations across history. Cultural transformations are due to a number of factors, including increasing globalization in trade and commerce, mass media, and transportation that facilitate and expand the exchange of information, materials, and even peoples. As a result, there are many characterizations of culture as a construct. While a complete catalog of definitions is beyond the scope of this chapter, it is instructive to briefly review the various ways in which culture has been defined by social and behavioral scientists.

Dimensions of Culture

According to Bolaffi, Bracalenti, Braham, and Gindro (2003), culture has always been considered to represent what is learned and taught with emphasis being placed on what differentiates one group from another and on the fact that culture has an existence predicated by the group's own reality. Bolaffi et al. (2003) further suggest that the construct of culture has often been defined by emphasis of the researchers involved in writing the definition. For example, from a sociological perspective, Lévi-Strauss (1966) defined culture as a normative construct while psychoanalytic perspectives usually emphasize culture as a more subconscious process that influences dreams (as Freud suggested [E. Jones, 1953]), or myths and symbols (as proposed by Jung [1967]), or language (as mentioned by Lacan [Dor, 2001]).

From a more psychosocial perspective, Triandis (1994) defines culture as "a set of human-made objective and subjective elements that in the past have increased the probability of survival and resulted in satisfaction for participants in an ecological niche, and thus became shared among those who could communicate with each other because they had a common language and they lived in the same time and place" (p. 22). Examples of objective elements of culture include materials that a group may use such as machinery, foods, shelter, tools, and dress (Triandis, 2002). Subjective elements of culture are the ways in which a group understands and makes sense of its social environment, including ideas about beauty, spirituality, philosophy, values, money management, and child-rearing principles (Triandis, 2002).

A somewhat different perspective in defining culture is taken by U. Kim (2001) by arguing that "culture is the collective utilization of natural and human resources to achieve desired outcomes" (p. 58). Thus, culture is viewed as a process that allows a group to effectively share its resources to accomplish goals that reflect the values, beliefs, and/or behaviors of the members.

More recently, a fairly comprehensive definition of culture was proposed by J. M. Jones (2003). He suggests that culture can be considered as including a variety of elements categorized as "*psychological* (patterns of thinking, feeling, behaving, and valuing); *symbolic* (representations of meaningful psychological patterns); *historical* (cultural elements selectively derived and transmitted over time); [and] *dynamic* (cultural elements that both shape meaning and are transformed by events and actions)" (p. 223). Regardless of the definition, culture has been considered by many researchers as an important construct that helps define the characteristics of a human group including its psychosocial and behavioral norms and expectancies. In this sense, culture is an important construct in ethnic psychology that allows us to better understand what influences people's behaviors and attitudes.

It is important to note that culture differs from **nationality** or **ancestry** that defines a person's country of birth or descent. We do not automatically assume that a person's birth or citizenship in a particular country will mean that he or she will adopt the country's prominent cultural norms (Matsumoto & Juang, 2004). However, in general there may be a strong relationship between nationality and culture simply through exposure to common behaviors, customs, beliefs, attitudes, and so on.

"Culture" is often used interchangeably with "ethnicity" (H. Betancourt & Lopez, 1993); however, culture is a more general construct that influences ethnicity and ethnic identification by shaping our meaning of ideals and values (Rohner, 1984, as cited in H. Betancourt & Lopez, 1993) as well as views about our self and about others (Markus & Kitayama, 1991) and the behaviors that are associated with those thoughts (Nisbett, Peng, Choi, & Norenzayan, 2001; Peng & Nisbett, 1999).

Cultural Influences on Psychological Processes

As mentioned in Chapter 1, a significant amount of research has been conducted by cross-cultural psychologists trying to identify how culture influences people's behavior and how individuals from various cultures differ from each other. Such studies, for example, have found that cultures tend to differ in the way in which they process cognitive information (Markus & Kitayama, 1991). East Asians, for instance, tend to make judgments of causality by attending to all details while Westerners tend to concentrate on specific objects and categories (Nisbett et al., 2001). Other studies have suggested that cultures differ in the way the self is understood in relation to others; some cultures value mutual support and reliance on the family while other cultures promote personal independence (Markus & Kitayama, 1991).

Cross-cultural and ethnic psychologists consider cultural differences and preference for certain values to be important in predicting physical and psychological health. For example, Maria Cecilia Zea and colleagues (Zea, Quezada, & Belgrave, 1994) suggest that the cultural values of *allocentrism* (an individual's concern for the group to which he/she belongs) and *familialism* (strong devotion to family) play important roles in Latino patients' recovery from disabilities in terms of the emotional and social support received. Sociologists Ronald Angel and Marta Tienda (1982) and Elena Bastida (2001) state that extended family households found among some cultures are particularly important in the early adjustment of immigrants to a foreign country. Susan Savage and Mary Gauvain (1998) report that responsibilities assigned to children are influenced by culture-specific expectancies of children's ability to plan at certain ages. Finally, other researchers (e.g., Damron-Rodriguez, Wallace, & Kington, 1994) suggest that the quality of medical care received by ethnic minorities is affected, in part, by cultural values. Issues related to the physical and psychological health of ethnic minority groups are further discussed in Chapters 8 and 9.

UNDERSTANDING ETHNICITY

The term **ethnicity** derives from the Greek word *ethnos* meaning a people as well as a nation or a crowd (Bhopal, 2003; Bolaffi et al., 2003). Ethnicity refers to a social group's distinct sense of belongingness as a result of common culture and descent (Al-Issa, 1997; J. M. Jones, 1992). Max Weber, the sociologist, considered ethnicity as being derived from the belief in shared origins that members of a group hold without a direct correspondence to a nation or a race and that manifests itself through commonly practiced customs and memories of the group's history (Bolaffi et al., 2003).

Similar to culture, ethnicity can reflect several different dimensions that can be used in defining the construct. For example, some authors consider ethnicity as including three components: (1) group membership either by choice or externally imposed that allows a differentiation of **in-groups** (i.e., groups that maintain respect, esteem, loyalty, and, consequently, are more desirable) and **out-groups** (i.e., groups that are subjected to disapproval, contempt, competition, and, consequently, are less desirable); (2) emphasis on a common identity; and (3) the assignment of specific beliefs or behaviors (stereotypes) to members of the group by individuals who belong to other ethnic groups (Bolaffi et al., 2003). At the same time, Jean Phinney (1996) suggests that "[t]here are at least three aspects of ethnicity that may account for its psychological importance. These include (a) the cultural values, attitudes, and behaviors that distinguish ethnic groups; (b) the subjective sense of ethnic group membership (i.e., ethnic identity) that is held by group members; and (c) the experiences associated with minority status, including powerlessness, discrimination, and prejudice" (p. 919). "Ethnic identity" is a relatively new construct that grew out of the ethnic consciousness movements (of the early 1970s) in reaction to historically oppressive racial typologies. Ethnicity nonetheless is a social construction similar to "race."

Marger (2000) states that ethnic groups possess unique cultural traits. Ethnic groups exist within a larger cultural and social system, but maintain behavior characteristics that distinguish them from other groups within a given society. For example, the practice of Kwanzaa by some African Americans can highlight their distinctive African-based values from those reflected in the traditional Christian holiday celebration of Christmas. Common traditions also support a sense of community among members of ethnic groups. There is also a sense of communion primarily derived from a shared ancestry or heritage. Ethnic group membership is acquired at birth by virtue of one's parents and the culture in which one is raised. Membership is reinforced by the cultural values, symbols, beliefs, and practices that people are exposed to as they grow up as well as by the distinctions that members of other ethnic groups make as they ascribe group membership based on commonly held beliefs and attitudes, physical characteristics (phenotype), group-valued practices, and personal identification.

Members of an ethnic group can have the potential to interpret what occurs in their group as being correct and "best" compared to other ethnic groups. They may perceive their customs, traditions, values, and so on as being more universal and thus they might believe that everyone should embrace them. They may favor those from their own ethnic group and/or feel negative toward others outside their group. All of these descriptions are related to the concept of **ethnocentrism,** the bias of viewing one's own ethnic group as superior to others (Brewer & Campbell, 1976). As discussed more thoroughly in Chapter 7, this ethnocentrism is closely related to negative stereotyping (prejudice) of members of other ethnic groups and to discriminatory practices against them. Our earlier history as a nation saw the curtailment of basic rights and benefits based on many of those prejudicial attitudes borne out of ethnocentric thinking. As such, during the first years of our nation, voting rights to women and Blacks and to those without land were not granted. Chinese Americans were not allowed to own property or to live in European American neighborhoods in many major cities until the mid-1950s. Blacks brought to the country as enslaved laborers were not given the care that sometimes was freely accorded to animals. More recently, Blacks and other ethnic minority groups were not allowed admission to certain institutions of higher learning and, even when granted, they were excluded from certain social clubs or fraternities/sororities. In addition, Mexican Americans were forbidden to use Spanish in school. All of these inhumanities were institutionalized and supported by ethnocentric beliefs.

The Problems of Ethnic Assessment and Labels

The assessment of ethnicity is often problematic. As reviewed in the next chapter, many people often are dismayed by the limitation of "checking the one box" that best describes one's ethnicity. Most measures rely on self-definitions of ethnicity where the person is given the "choice" of which box to check; but this self-assessment ignores the fact that sometimes ethnicity cannot be limited to broad categories such as Asian or Hispanic because the boxes do not reflect the heterogeneity that may exist within any one group, nor will they reflect the multiple ethnicities that may exist within any one individual. The option of marking "Other" in response to these categories is wholly unsatisfying for those who embrace their multiple ethnicities and wish to explicitly identify their ethnicities when asked.

There can also be uncertainty about the "correct" label when choices are provided. In the vignette, Sheila wonders which ethnic label, "African American" or "Black," she should use to appropriately identify her ethnicity to her daughter. The African American label reflects contemporary usage and recognition of her ethnocultural roots rather than skin color characteristics. However, others with black skin would agree with then Illinois senator Barack Obama in saying that "some of the patterns of struggle and degradation that Blacks here in the United States experienced aren't that different from the colonial experiences in the Caribbean or the African Continent" (quoted by Swarns, 2004, p. 1). Indeed, a number of African Americans prefer to be called "Black," particularly those recently migrated (from Africa or the Caribbean) or some of their children (Swarns, 2004). Also, some individuals believe that positively affirming one's "Blackness" is a political statement that neutralizes historically negative representations of "dark" racial skin color or phenotype.

As a further example, the use of the labels "Latino" and "Hispanic" interchangeably reflects contemporary usage in the literature. Despite continuing debate and arguments to favor one term over the other (Marín & VanOss Marín, 1991), current usage patterns in psychology do not necessarily show any particular preference. Ethnic identity, the sense of one's self as belonging to a particular ethnic group (or groups), as well as assessment of ethnicity are addressed in detail in Chapter 5.

Some authors have criticized the use of the construct of ethnicity in social science research because they feel that it represents a "construction of Western colonial culture" (Bolaffi et al., 2003) and that it carries the assumption of culture that is primitive, simplistic, and strikingly unusual. As such, ethnicity is sometimes used to describe a sort of exoticism often represented in words such as "ethnic music," "ethnic art," or "ethnic food," which can best be described by emphasizing their place in a group's folklore. Other researchers favor the use of ethnicity because it supports the development of a supportive "collective ego" (Comaroff, 1987) for members of groups who share common histories or characteristics. In this book, we use ethnicity as a way to identify those groups that share not only a history but also social structures and psychosocial characteristics such as attitudes, beliefs, and values. Ethnicity, as used in this book, does not refer to underdevelopment or to exotic groups and, as mentioned above, the construct can also be applied to individuals whose skin color is light ("Whites").

UNDERSTANDING RACE

Ethnicity is often used interchangeably with the term **race;** however, these terms are different. Although all humans belong to one species, *Homo sapiens,* biologists and anthropologists have attempted to classify and categorize physical/biological traits that may differ among populations. We often observe others and inquire or make assumptions (not necessarily accurate) about their racial background. Sheila initially thought that Laura's question of "What color are you?" was an inquiry about her race.

Historically, studying race based on contrived or visible physical differences between groups of people was particularly popular during the

18th, 19th, and early 20th centuries. The inherent flaws with discerning reliable and valid physical and biological indicators of racial distinctions are illustrated by early research in physical and cultural anthropology (Guthrie, 1998). Researchers used a variety of dubious strategies to classify racial groups, including assessment of cranium or brain size, skeletal structures, and behavioral observation. Robert Guthrie (1998) reviewed the work of several prominent anthropologists who developed race measurement methods such as Ales Hrdlicka, who described precise instructions for using a spinning color top to measure skin pigment, and Felix von Luschan, who invented a porcelain scale of skin color that required holding up various colored blocks next to the skin until a match was made between the shade and the subject's skin color. Similarly, other scientists developed methods and instruments to measure observable anatomical features (i.e., phenotypes) such as hair texture (distinguish between "straight," "curly or wavy," "frizzy," or "woolly" forms of hair), hair color (use of a color wheel to distinguish color variations from blond, red, to brunette/black), and differences in thickness of lips, length of head, height of nose, and other body features (Guthrie, 1998). However, there was no consensus about which of these types of characteristics, phenotypes, genotypes (measurements based on genetic traits inherited from one's parents), and/or anatomical traits would be used consistently in defining race.

Many of the earliest racial categories included distinct categories for Caucasoid, Mongoloid, and Negroid people. However, some systems also included separate categories for certain indigenous groups (e.g., aborigines, Bushmen). These systems were based on oversimplified and stereotypical physical markers that exist at least to some degree among groups. However, clearly this classification is imprecise and ignores large segments within populations that do not fit neatly into narrow and fixed categories. For example, where do you place groups that have mixed ancestry, like many from Indonesia or mestizo (mixture of indigenous tribes and Spanish ancestry) groups from Latin America?

Although scientific studies on racial differences flourished particularly during the 19th century, the classification of race has perhaps spawned the greatest level of controversy and argument among psychologists and those in related disciplines. Racial categories are arbitrary and contingent upon the goals and theories of the classifier (Marger, 2000). Generally, most recent analyses yield the conclusion that it is difficult at best or nearly impossible to distinguish clear-cut "pure" races with consistent physical features, genetic markers, and other biological indicators that separate one group from another (H. Betancourt & Lopez, 1993; A. H. Yee, Fairchild, Weizmann, & Wyatt, 1993; Zuckerman, 1998). Despite some differences between groups, the relative proximity and mobility of diverse groups over the past centuries, the high level of mixing (also known as genetic interchangeability) of groups, and adaptations to changing environments have led to more complex phenotypic traits. Indeed, F. L. Jackson (1992) concluded that "the zoological definition of race, based on significant genetic differences, cannot be legitimately applied to contemporary humans" (p. 120). Moreover, many agree that a greater level of diversity can be found within any one "racial" group than between various racial groups (J. Marks, 1995; Okazaki & Sue, 1998; Zuckerman, 1998).

Race is socially constructed based on prevailing social and political attitudes. As a social-political construct, race is used to express ambiguous racial distinctions, promote dominance of certain privileged groups, and oppress groups that are deemed "inferior." History shows us that "race" is often used to promote racism and prejudice. Labeling racial groups can create negative stereotypes and myths about the nature of different groups—hence, the individuality of the person is suppressed and, consequently, his or her humanity can become less salient. As noted later on in this text (e.g., Chapter 7), criticism of racial labels does not negate the terrible impact of racism and racial distinctions in the history of the United States and the suffering of many individuals that has resulted because of the color of their skin or of traits perceived to be associated with genetic or biological characteristics. The random and abhorrent killings of American Indians, the perversity of slavery of African Americans, and the unfairness of policies discriminating or segregating access or services to African Americans and Asian Americans are examples of how "racial differences" have been used to partly justify the destruction of the goals of equity and justice enshrined in the U.S. Constitution. The reality of these social and political consequences leads researchers to argue that race and racial identity, specifically, can be important constructs for study when we want to understand the psychological effects of social marginalization, discrimination, and prejudice for certain groups that have been racialized (Helms, 1990).

Whiteness

Research in the social sciences has recently begun to give more attention to **Whiteness** and to Whites as a "cultural" group (Twine & Gallagher, 2008). This research recognizes that individuals whose skin color is light ("white") share experiences and attitudes that differentiate them from others whose skin color is darker. Similar to other cultures, these shared experiences go beyond the social and economic privileges that historically have been awarded to lighter-skinned individuals, and include the assumption of commonly held or generalized attitudes and values among Whites. Twine and Gallagher (2008) note that since the 1990s, the number of scholarly works on the study of Whiteness and White identity has surged, particularly in the United States. In a recent overview of the interdisciplinary field of Whiteness Studies, a newly emerging body of research is described that builds upon earlier writings on racial identity development. In these contemporary studies, the formation, destabilization, and maintenance of White identity, culture, and privilege are explored through inventive methodologies, for example, critical analyses of "racial consciousness biographies" (written accounts of how Whites perceive and negotiate their Whiteness in their everyday private and public lives), Internet sites, newspapers, music, and other popular media (Twine & Gallagher, 2008).

The study of Whiteness has not been without its critics, both within academic circles and the popular media. For example, in a *New York Times* article, Talbot (1997) charged that this represents the "academic trend du jour," a trendy exploration of an ill-defined concept that makes racial categories necessary and absolute. In contrast, Twine and Gallagher (2008) note the steady proliferation of empirical work has produced hundreds of books, qualitative studies, and scholarly articles that challenge our current racial categories and social hierarchies. Similarly, Hattam (2001) states that research on Whiteness has produced some important results that allow for a more complete cultural understanding of the major ethnic groups "of color" (African Americans, American Indians and Alaska Natives, Asian Americans, and Latinos). In particular, Hattam (2001) argues that research on Whiteness has allowed U.S. social scientists to validate a historical perspective on the construct of "race" as well as emphasize the role of class and social privilege in people's ethnic identification. Helfand and Lippin (2002) further suggest that "Whiteness is an historical, cultural, social and political category" created in part by the fact that "Whiteness is so often invisible to White people, but not invisible to people of color" (p. 12).

SOCIAL ORIENTATIONS OR WAYS OF BEING

Hofstede (1980), in his influential book on cultural values, defines **cultural dimensions** as "a broad tendency to prefer certain states of affairs over others" (p. 19). It is in that sense that cultural dimensions are discussed here. They are perceived to be frequently found (modal) preferences for certain behaviors or beliefs or worldviews held by members of a human group, defined by culture, nationality, or ethnicity, that vary in terms of intensity (i.e., personal relevance) and direction (e.g., certain outcomes are positive while others are evaluated as negative) or modality (Hofstede, 1980; Kluckhohn, 1961) and serve to differentiate members of one ethnic group from those of another. These constructs have received names as varied as "value structures" (Hofstede, 1980), "cultural dimensions" or value orientations (Kluckhohn & Strodtbeck, 1961), and "cultural syndromes" (Triandis, 1994). Researchers working with members of ethnic groups often use these basic cultural dimensions to explain behavioral or cognitive differences across ethnic groups identified in their studies.

Characterizing societies or ethnic groups by using certain general dimensions or cultural dimensions is obviously a process of simplification and of blurring of individual differences. Nevertheless, the use of cultural dimensions allows the prediction and explanation of the normative (or modal) behaviors of certain cultural or ethnic groups. While at times these efforts have been fraught with methodological limitations, the overall result has been heuristically and practically important.

Research in psychology and anthropology has produced a large number of social orientations that are perceived as being related to people's preferred orientation or ways of being. Many of these dimensions are perceived to be specific to a given culture while others are more general. For example, Latin Americans and Latinos are described in the literature as valuing positive interpersonal relations, a social script defined as *simpatía* (Triandis, Bontempo, Villareal, Asai, & Lucca, 1988) that is somewhat related to the Japanese social script of *amae* or the Filipino *delicadeza*. In addition, Asian cultures are often described as placing special value on "face saving," protection of one's integrity, within close interpersonal relationships (Zane & Mak, 2003). Researchers also have identified social dimensions that seem to be central to a large number of cultures and ethnic groups. Among these are familialism, allocentrism, and interdependence. We review some of these dimensions below and others are summarized in later chapters.

Views of the Self Across Cultures

It is proposed that individuals from cultures that emphasize responsibility toward others are more likely to make **interdependent construals of the self** in which they tend to value interpersonal relationships and see others as integral to their self-conceptualization. According to Markus and Kitayama (1991), interdependent persons view their behavior as greatly influenced by the thoughts, actions, and beliefs of others in their community. Interdependent construals are more commonly associated with societies such as those of Africa, Asia, and Latin America (Constantine, Gainor, Ahluwalia, &

Berkel, 2003; Markus & Kitayama, 1991). **Independent construals of the self,** in which individuality and one's unique thoughts, emotions, and behaviors are distinguished from those of others, tend to be best exemplified by societies such as the United States, Canada, and Germany (Constantine et al., 2003; Markus & Kitayama, 1991). As expected, data from cross-cultural studies indicate that **collectivistic cultures** (cultures focused on the community as a whole) are more highly correlated with interdependent self-construals, while **individualistic cultures** (cultures focused on individual autonomy) are more associated with independent self-construals (e.g., Chia, Allred, Cheng, & Chuang, 1999; Morling & Fiske, 1999; Singelis, 1994).

However, in other recent empirical studies and critical analyses, psychologists question the clear dichotomy between interdependent versus independent and collectivistic versus individualistic constructs. Several argue that these constructs should be more accurately conceptualized and measured as complex phenomena that can even coexist within many individuals and social relationships (e.g., Emde & Buchsbaum, 1990; Grotevant, 1998; Guisenger & Blatt, 1994; Neff, 2003; Triandis, 1995; Triandis & Gelfand, 1998). For example, Neff (2003) notes that many of the classic studies that explored infant attachment to caregiver (e.g., Ainsworth, 1967; Bowlby, 1969) suggest that a secure, stable, interdependent relationship between the caregiver and child facilitates the infant's autonomous exploration of the world. Furthermore, research on parenting styles indicates that an authoritative style (i.e., supportive and warm, yet with firm limits and adaptable to the child's needs) actually stimulates greater independence and self-confidence as well as social adaptability and skills in children (e.g., Steinberg, 2001). Neff and her colleagues (Neff & Harter, 2002a, 2002b, 2003) as well as others propose that a balance between independence and interdependence is needed for positive self-development and harmonious personal relationships. However, while this balance may be desirable in several instances, it is also important to consider that an individual's self-construal or social orientation may be more adaptive in certain cultural contexts but less so in others.

Researchers suggest that closely associated with the social dimension of individualism are personal values such as autonomy, privacy, self-reliance, and competition as well as societal institutions that are person-centered and individually oriented. Collectivism, on the other hand, has been associated with such behaviors and attitudes as (1) holding group-centered values where members of a given society or group are concerned about how their actions impact others; (2) greater valuing of the views and needs of the members of the in-group even if it means personal sacrifices; (3) the sharing of resources without concern for individual utilitarian considerations; (4) holding beliefs that are similar to those of the members of the in-group; (5) the acceptance of the group's norms; as well as (6) accepting values such as interdependence, cooperation, and sociability (Hui & Triandis, 1986; Triandis, 1990, 1994).

A newer trend in research is to study how these self-constructs may be composed of differing components or subtypes. Triandis and his associates (Triandis, 1995; Triandis & Gelfand, 1998), for example, describe two types of individualism, **horizontal individualism** and **vertical individualism.** Horizontal individualism refers to cultures that value the individual but not necessarily a societal hierarchical structure. Vertical individualism refers to a cultural orientation that values the individual but also societal competitiveness that leads to upward mobility. According to Triandis and Gelfand (1998), a capitalist society like the United States might best exemplify vertical individualism. Likewise, collectivism can be conceptualized as running along horizontal and vertical axes: **Horizontal collectivism** represents a cultural orientation that favors commonality among individuals and interdependence—but not with the control of authoritarian force. **Vertical collectivism** represents a cultural orientation that also values interdependence and deference to the common needs of the community, but deference or submission to a higher authority is also supported. Although this is an influential multidimensional model, studies designed to demonstrate the applicability of these constructs across a variety of cultures have been limited in number (Gouveia, Clemente, & Espinosa, 2003).

According to recent studies, the importance placed on independence or interdependence can vary in hierarchical social structures. For instance, Neff (2001) studied rights and responsibilities within marital relationships among lower-middle-class Hindu Indians. She found that support for characteristics/behaviors consistent with independence was much more emphasized for husbands while support for interdependence was more emphasized for wives. Interestingly, however, many within the group were critical of this imbalance and restraint placed on women's autonomy.

Future chapters include a more thorough discussion of other social scripts and of the way in which people's behaviors and attitudes are influenced by these social orientations or cultural dimensions. For example, we describe the role of familialism in supporting individuals' actions in Chapter 6 and discuss the relationship of culture-specific patterns to ethnic, racial, and gender identities in Chapter 5. Nevertheless, it is important to mention here that acculturation (the culture learning process described in Chapter 4) differentially affects these social dimensions. Specific components or aspects of these dimensions that are central to a culture are less affected by the process of acculturation and assimilation than more peripheral aspects.

An important caveat to the literature on social dimensions is the danger of assuming a "damaging culture" perspective (Buriel, 1984; Ramirez & Castaneda, 1974) or a victim blaming approach (Ryan, 1972). This perspective would explain problems being experienced by members of an ethnic group (e.g., poverty, unemployment, crime) by referencing the group's culture or the relevant cultural syndrome or social script rather than the political, social, and economic conditions that are more directly related to the problems. The cultural dimensions discussed here are of help in describing general cultural patterns, in helping individuals to better comprehend how cultures differ, in developing research protocols and intervention strategies that are culturally appropriate, as well as in training professionals who will be culturally sensitive and capable (Marín, 1993).

Nevertheless, the social conditions experienced by many members of the major ethnic groups should not be construed to be the direct result of the cultural dimensions described in this book. Such an approach to the social sciences would be not only simplistic but also naive and prejudicial.

SOCIAL STRATIFICATION

As noted earlier, many "differences" do not fully represent innate or biological distinctions; instead, they more strongly represent social constructions that are formed within a social context. Hence, it is important to look at the way in which societies are designed to empower or disenfranchise individuals or groups. **Social stratification** describes a system of how society's resources and rewards are distributed among various groups. The question becomes, in any given society, who receives the rewards (e.g., wealth, power, freedom, prestige)? When a social system is stratified, there is a structured hierarchy in which groups receive differential access to society's rewards. Because this text is focused on ethnicity, it is important to consider how our society determines social stratification based on people's ethnicity—but there are also other dimensions such as age, gender, socioeconomic standing, and sexual orientation that are interrelated and simultaneously impact social systems.

Stratification systems are not unique to the United States or other industrialized countries; they occur in many different countries and can change over time. Social stratification can be illustrated by slave, caste, or class systems (Rothman, 2002). Slave systems consist of those in bondage (slaves) and those that are free (masters or free men). In the United States, we tend to think of slavery as being a thing of the past, something that ended roughly two centuries ago. Yet, modern slavery is very much a part of our world. There are millions of cases of children and adults who are held against their will and must work hard labor in inhumane working conditions to pay their "debt" owed to their masters—or they are sold or forced into slavery systems. Slave industry can take the form of forced labor on farms or plantations, in factories, or within the sex trade industry. This form of stratification is particularly evident in poor, less-industrialized countries where women and children and sometimes men are forced to labor long hours in component factories or sewing industries in order to save enough money to pay the owners for their housing and sustenance with little recourse to other sorts of employment. Sex workers in many countries also face similar conditions where prostitution is one of very few options for avoiding extreme poverty and where the proceeds are seldom enough for these individuals to gain independence from their masters. Caste systems are social strata determined by fixed family patterns in which children are born into the caste of their parents. Caste systems have existed for centuries in certain countries although, currently, in certain areas they have lessened in their rigidity due to the introduction of more democratic ideals, modernization, and exposure to other cultures' alternative religions and media.

Within more industrialized countries like the United States, **class systems** have been the most popular form of social stratification. One of the best known models of a class system is the one proposed by Karl Marx. His model emphasizes economics as the basis for stratification. Two groups are distinguished, the ruling class and the working class. This two-tier model states that the "haves" are members of the ruling class that have ownership and authority over production and resources (e.g., commerce, transportation, food production, media). The "have nots" are members of the working class who can only provide labor in order to obtain any type of resource.

In general, social classes are constituted of individuals that share an equal likelihood of acquiring society's rewards. Rothman (2002) describes a contemporary class typology that is based on society's economic system. In this system, many of the difficulties faced by members of society are directly linked to their place in the social class hierarchy. Groups are categorized as "the elite," "upper middle class," "lower middle class," "working class," and "the poor." At the top of the stratification system is the elite class that exercises a potent level of power over economic, political, and social entities. The elite are made up of some of the wealthiest individuals who have derived their power from wealth and property. Sometimes this wealth is inherited over generations within families (e.g., the Bush, Getty, Heinz, or

Kennedy families). In other cases, the wealth that characterizes the elite is acquired through innovation, investments, or the development of industries (as in the case of the founders of McDonald's, Walmart, or Microsoft). Interestingly, the elite class in the United States constitutes only about 1% of the total population, and yet it holds approximately 38% of the total national wealth. The top 20% of households (those with incomes of $180,000 a year or more) hold more than 80% of the nation's wealth (Mantsios, 2004; Mishel, Bernstein, & Boushey, 2003). In contrast, the bottom 60% of the American population holds less than 6% of the national wealth. The relationship between these classes inevitability leads to conflict and struggle over this inequitable system.

Another classic model is offered by Max Weber (as described by Gerth & Mills, 1946). Similar to Marx and others, Weber acknowledges the significant role of economic factors in establishing a social hierarchy. In addition, Weber notes the role of social classes that express lifestyle group differences in terms of their ability to acquire material possessions, property, and access to education among other resources. **Socio-economic status (SES)** is often highly correlated with social class because economic status usually relates to social opportunities and lifestyle, at least in the United States. Weber's model also gives attention to political parties that wield authority within the system. Political parties are any groups that assert influence toward community change—contemporary examples would include labor unions, consumer and environmental protection agencies, organizations for professional groups (e.g., psychologists, social workers, teachers), ethnic organizations (e.g., National Association for the Advancement of Colored People), and formal political parties (e.g., Democrat, Republican, Green, Independent). Membership in a powerful party that wields authority can influence one's ability to reap consequent benefits from social and political changes that support an individual. Conversely, members of weak political parties may be unable to move ahead within society due to failure to effectively change the social and political climate or laws that can protect their interests.

An alternative model of social stratification is described by Marger (2000) and adapted from a **distributive system model** developed by Gerhard Lenski (1966). This multidimensional model is based on parallel class systems where each system represents a social dimension such as political force, wealth and property acquisition, and occupation. And, pertinent to our purposes, ethnicity is also included as a particular class system within the model (see Figure 2.1). Marger notes that there is remarkable consistency across class systems especially within a multiethnic society. As such, individuals in a particular class will exert a similar level of

Figure 2.1 The Distributive System of American Society. *A, B,* and *C* represent three individuals.

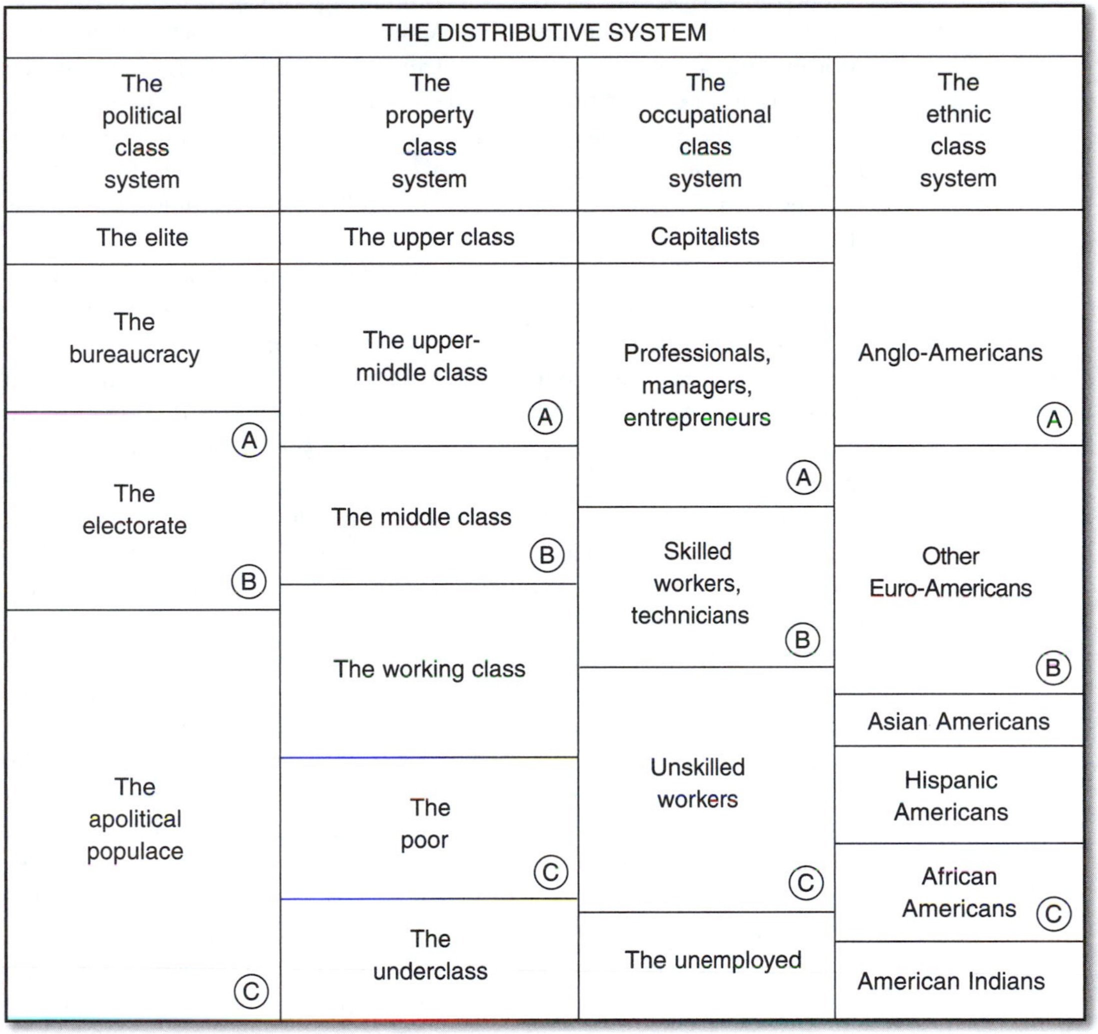

THE DISTRIBUTIVE SYSTEM			
The political class system	The property class system	The occupational class system	The ethnic class system
The elite	The upper class	Capitalists	
The bureaucracy	The upper-middle class	Professionals, managers, entrepreneurs	Anglo-Americans
(A)	(A)		(A)
The electorate	The middle class	(A)	Other Euro-Americans
(B)	(B)	Skilled workers, technicians	
	The working class	(B)	(B)
			Asian Americans
The apolitical populace	The poor	Unskilled workers	Hispanic Americans
	(C)		African Americans (C)
	The underclass	(C)	
(C)		The unemployed	American Indians

SOURCE: Marger (2000), adapted from Lenski (1966).

power and benefit from relevant levels of privilege no matter what social dimension is examined. For example, those who are ranked high within the ethnic class system (e.g., European Americans) will similarly rank high on the hierarchies of the other class systems—economic wealth, professional occupation, and so on—whereas those who are ranked low within the ethnic class system (e.g., African Americans and American Indians) will rank low on other social strata. However, there are problems inherent in ranking ethnic minority groups as though certain groups are worse off than other groups. For instance, ranking Asian Americans above Hispanic Americans, African Americans, or American Indians in the ethnic class system can inadvertently perpetuate the "model minority stereotype," that is, that Asians are the ideal of all ethnic minority groups, and it overlooks the continuing stratification experiences of certain groups (e.g., Southeast Asian refugees) that fall under the broad umbrella of this ethnic category as discussed in the previous chapter.

It is important to note that many, including Marger (2000), acknowledge that these patterns are not immune to exceptions. There are, for example, White Americans who do not enjoy authority and high rank across all social dimensions and certain members of ethnic groups who are generally ranked lower on the ethnic class hierarchy that nonetheless succeed in other social dimensions. Marger (2000) notes, however, that such exceptions tend to be infrequent due to institutionalized forms of discrimination that make it difficult for certain groups to gain upward mobility. This is most apparent when considering how many ethnic minorities have been elected to the U.S. presidency. Is this simply a matter of character or interest in politics or real differences in access and power that make upward mobility possible?

Missing from Marger's (2000) model is the inclusion of gender as another social dimension that intersects the class systems that shape our society. **Gender** refers to the socially and psychologically defined and acquired characteristics that distinguish being male from being female, whereas **sex** describes the biological/physiological characteristics of men and women (Santrock, 2005). Although this may sound like a straightforward distinction, some social scientists argue that in order to understand gender in our society, one must look at the complex interaction of biological, psychosocial, and cognitive influences on gender (Deaux, 1999; Santrock, 2005). Moreover, gender definitions and expectations can change within any historical point in time—thus, gender has evolved over the course of civilizations and across cultures.

Within a stratified system, we can see that there are differences between the ranking of men and women within particular class systems. Perhaps an area where this is most salient is in the occupational class system. The disparity between payment for the work of women and men has been well documented (Rothman, 2002). Despite working more hours than men and doing more than their fair share of work worldwide, only roughly one third of women receive payment for labor compared to three fourths of men (Rothman, 2002). Even now, in contemporary U.S. society, women (no matter what their overall class status including racial/ethnic class) perform more unpaid work (e.g., housework, child care, elder care) than men (Rothman, 2002). Power or wealth can help reduce these unpaid hours, however, because the affluent can afford to hire others to do domestic chores and dependent care services. Clearly, unpaid work is essential to the survival of families and homes, but the fact that much of the work is unpaid testifies to the inequity of value and reward that are placed on "real work" (i.e., paid labor) versus "responsibilities" (i.e., work that supports the house and dependents) that may be restricted based on gender roles.

Likewise, sexual orientation is another form of social stratification. This is perhaps most poignantly illustrated by continuing discrimination and hate crimes that are directed toward gays and lesbians. Also, homophobic political rhetoric in the ongoing debate on same-sex marriage echoes discriminatory attitudes that fueled antimiscegenation laws, making interracial marriage a crime. Such instances of discrimination and hate are often pronounced for gays and lesbians of color because they can be considered minorities within a minority community. Indeed, the terms "double jeopardy," "triple jeopardy," and even "multiple jeopardy" are used to refer to multiple minority statuses that may characterize an individual (Lindsay, 1979). For example, a woman who is an ethnic minority and lesbian may be considered at increased risk for stress related to experiences as a member of all three groups (Bowleg, Huang, Brooks, Black, & Burkholder, 2003). These and other related issues pertaining to experiences of ethnic minority gays and lesbians are discussed in detail in Chapter 5.

No matter what theoretical model of stratification is examined, it is clear that social class status can have a powerful influence on individuals' and families' access to resources that benefit adjustment such as those related to health, education, and living in a safe environment. As such, any stratification system will ultimately impact the psychological and physical well-being of its members. As reported in Chapter 1, members of ethnic groups show a disproportionately high level of poverty relative to Whites. This is especially true for American Indians and Alaska Natives, African Americans, Latinos, and Southeast Asian refugee groups. Of additional concern is the toll of poverty on children and their development that is associated with limits in the level and type of social and cultural stimulation and the quality and quantity of nutritional intake (V. L. Allen, 1970).

Low SES children are more likely to be exposed to violence, environmental toxins, poor quality of food, and improper housing or homelessness than higher-level SES children (Santrock, 2004). When poverty becomes long term, these dangerous conditions predictably lead to a host of negative outcomes for children into middle adulthood including lower functioning in terms of behavioral, psychological, and medical problems (Schoon et al., 2002). (See Chapters 8 and 9 for more information on physical and psychosocial adjustment of ethnic groups.)

Many stratification systems exist for many years and even centuries in certain societies. Sustaining a system of inequality is contingent upon having an **ideology** or set of beliefs that supports and justifies the imbalance. Social scientists point to many ideologies that may support our U.S. stratified structure. The most popular include racism, sexism, and **meritocracy**—the perception that those who receive the rewards (e.g., the upper class) have done so based solely on the strength of their own efforts. If you work hard enough, you can make it in our society. Implicit (and often explicit) in this rationale is that those who have not made it (e.g., the lower class or the underclass) failed because of a lack of ability and/or character.

MINORITY STATUS

Minority status can be defined in a number of ways. On a broad social level, the term **minority** has been used to refer to groups that lack power and access to society's resources resulting from discrimination and subjugation by the dominant society (Alvidrez, Azocar, & Miranda, 1996). Hence, being deemed an ethnic person is not necessarily interchangeable with being deemed a minority person. For instance, there are currently people in the United States, like Italian Americans or Irish Americans, who are members of ethnic groups but—due to assimilation processes—are not typically considered minorities. Berry (1998) notes that minorities' disempowerment and discrimination are often determined by the characteristics of the dominant groups such as their openness to share privilege and status, the nature of relationships between groups (e.g., positive or tension-filled), and level of tolerance or embracement of difference or diversity.

Regardless of the rationale for the label of "minority"—ethnicity, sexuality, religious beliefs, or cultural traditions—continued discrimination in the United States not only is countercultural but also cannot be part of a truly diverse society. The minority label has received its share of criticism as the result of its implication of subordination to a dominant group, rather than emphasizing the unique characteristics of a group that make it distinct and vibrant. Members of the **dominant group** are advantaged socially, politically, and economically within society. Because of these advantages, the cultural norms and values of the dominant group become the standard. In this context, some believe that minority groups become defined in terms of their deficits in relation to dominant groups, blurring their strengths in the process (Berry, 1998). Obviously, many authors who use "minorities" to refer to African Americans or Asian Americans or other ethnic groups are using the term as a shorthand descriptor devoid (at least partly) of negative connotations.

POWER AND PRIVILEGE

Some researchers have begun addressing the conditions under which **privilege** ensues. Privilege is usually defined as the unfair advantages and benefits afforded people who hold a dominant position within a social stratification system. While equity in access and opportunities are valued goals of our society as we strive to follow Martin Luther King, Jr.'s dictum that people should "not be judged by the color of their skin but by the content of their character" (1963), equality of opportunities and the elimination of prejudice are still to be achieved (Crosby, Iyer, Clayton, & Downing, 2003; D. W. Sue, 2003). Some individuals are assigned privileges and benefits or entitlements as a by-product of their skin color.

Peggy McIntosh (2004) popularized the concept of "White privilege" in her often-cited work based on her experiences teaching women's studies courses. She noted that while several men were willing to acknowledge that women were disadvantaged in many situations (e.g., job upward mobility), they had difficulty admitting that they themselves were privileged in many situations as a consequence of sexism. In a sense, we are taught that it is important to recognize the painful consequences of bigotry, yet we are not taught to look at ourselves as possible beneficiaries of someone's oppression. McIntosh applied this analysis to a self-examination on race and found that she too, as a White woman living in the United States, was privileged by the simple fact of living in a society where racism and ethnic discrimination exist. She listed a large number of privileges she receives on a daily basis because of her White racial/ethnic status in the United States (see Box 2.1).

BOX 2.1

Daily Effects of White Privilege

1. I can, if I wish, arrange to be in the company of people of my race most of the time.

2. If I should need to move, I can be pretty sure of renting or purchasing housing in an area which I can afford and which I would want to live.

3. I can be reasonably sure that my neighbors in such a location will be neutral or pleasant to me.

4. I can go shopping alone most of the time fairly well assured that I will not be followed or harassed by store detectives.

5. I can turn on my television or open to the front page of the paper and see people of my race widely and positively represented.

(Continued)

(Continued)

6. When I am told about our national heritage or about "civilization," I am shown that people of my color made it what it is.

7. I can be sure that my children will be given curricular materials that testify to the existence of their race.

8. If I want to, I can be pretty sure of finding a publisher for this piece on White privilege.

9. I can go into a music shop and count on finding the music of my race represented, into a supermarket and find the staple foods that fit with my cultural traditions, into a hairdresser's shop and find someone who can cut my hair.

10. Whether I use checks, credit cards, or cash, I can count on my skin color not to work against the appearance that I am financially reliable.

11. I can arrange to protect my children most of the time from people who might not like them.

12. I can swear, or dress in secondhand clothes, or not answer letters, without having people attribute these choices to the bad morals, the poverty, or the illiteracy of my race.

13. I can speak in public to a powerful male group without putting my race on trial.

14. I can do well in a challenging situation without being called a credit to my race.

15. I am never asked to speak for all the people of my racial group.

16. I can remain oblivious to the language and customs of persons of color who constitute the world's majority without feeling in my culture any penalty for such oblivion.

17. I can criticize our government and talk about how much I fear its policies and behavior without being seen as a cultural outsider.

18. I can be reasonably sure that if I ask to talk to "the person in charge," I will be facing a person of my race.

19. If a traffic cop pulls me over or if the IRS audits my tax return, I can be sure I haven't been singled out because of my race.

20. I can easily buy posters, postcards, picture books, greeting cards, dolls, toys, and children's magazines featuring people of my race.

21. I can go home from most meetings of organizations I belong to feeling somehow tied in, rather than isolated, out-of-place, outnumbered, unheard, held at a distance, or feared.

22. I can take a job with an affirmative action employer without having my co-workers on the job suspect that I got it because of my race.

23. I can choose public accommodations without fearing that people of my race cannot get in or will be mistreated in the places I have chosen.

24. I can be sure that if I need legal or medical help, my race will not work against me.

25. If my day, week, or year is going badly, I need not ask of each negative episode or situation whether it has racial overtones.

26. I can choose blemish cover or bandages in "flesh" color and have them more or less match my skin.

SOURCE: McIntosh (2004).

The Asian American psychologist Derald Wing Sue (2004) further acknowledges that not only is there disproportioned access to society's rewards, but these advantages are unearned and accrued to "White people by virtue of a system normed on the experiences, values, and perceptions of their group" (D. W. Sue, 2004, p. 764). In addition, White privilege can influence and limit racial interactions (Lucal, 1996) since individuals may choose not to interact with others who are perceived to be less worthy or less accomplished since they lack some of the benefits that the privileged received.

Privilege is not only exhibited in race and gender matters; there are other privilege statuses including heterosexual privilege, middle- and upper-class privilege, physically- and mentally-abled privilege, and so on (McIntosh, 2004; Rosenblum & Travis, 2003). While the idea of privilege can be seemingly simple and straightforward, the reactions of those that are "privileged" can be complex. Consistent with McIntosh's male colleagues' reaction, a limited number of studies conducted typically with students such as counselor trainees or undergraduates support that there is resistance to acknowledging privileged status (Hays & Chang, 2003). Often there is difficulty in recognizing gains that are received on the backs of others who are less privileged. One hardly wants to adopt the title of "oppressor," and there is the associated guilt that may accompany any acknowledgment of unfair advantage over others. Moreover, one of the basic ways that privilege statuses are maintained is by ideologies—many of which are similar to those that support social stratification. If we believe that life is fair and we live in an unbiased society that truly rewards the best and brightest, these ideals will alleviate our discomfort over inequality. Similarly, the **just-world hypothesis** states that our thoughts about experiences are influenced by our need to believe that the world is a just place in which good people are rewarded for their positive deeds and bad people are punished for their wicked ways (Lerner, 1980). Adhering to this sort of viewpoint can provide at least an illusion of safety (if one has a positive sense of self) and an explanation for meaningless tragedies. Yet, the risk of a just-world view is that it can lead to a *blaming the victim* mentality in which one reasons that if bad things happen to a person, then he or she must have done something wrong to trigger this outcome—hence, they got what they deserved.

One final matter on privilege is that as a social construct it is possible that individuals can simultaneously be members of groups that are oppressed *and* oppressive in their power. For example, a middle-class, heterosexual Alaska Native woman may be privileged in terms of her class and sexual orientation, but be subjugated due to her ethnicity and gender status. Because the acceptance or recognition of the existence of privilege is likely to be suppressed, she will be more likely to be aware of the ways in which being Alaska Native and a woman are likely to hamper her chances of equality in society. Yet, she will have to deal with the privileges and challenges experienced within the context of her self and social environment. Rosenblum and Travis (2003) argue that despite the coexistence of both privilege and oppression within any one person, stigma is so pervasive and strong in our society, that oppression can often trump privileges that one's other statuses might offer. They present a number of examples of health, housing, economic, hiring, and promotion disparities that offer evidence that inequality is a strong and persistent force that must be continually addressed. Consequently, we need to look at the intersection of ethnicity, class, gender, and other dimensions that may converge to place particular groups at high risk for disempowerment and disadvantage.

Chapter Summary

This chapter reviewed a number of constructs that are important in the field of ethnic psychology and related fields of study. Many of the constructs such as race, ethnicity, and culture share similar challenges: They have multiple dimensions that define them, and these multiple meanings can often prove to be controversial and lead to misunderstandings and poor science. Nevertheless, at their best, they provide fruitful insights into the nature of human beings—those aspects that serve to join us together as a human race and those that distinguish our unique behaviors, thoughts, values, and histories that enrich our diversity. These are some of the basic constructs that will be revisited throughout the text. In addition, other constructs such as acculturation and ethnic identity will be examined in depth in later chapters of this book. We have also sought to provide a social context to the study of ethnic groups in the United States by discussing societal stratification and the nature of privilege that impact the quality of life of ethnic groups.

Key Terms

Ancestry (page 35)

Class Systems (page 47)

Collectivistic Cultures (page 44)

Construct (page 33)

Cultural Dimensions (page 42)

Culture (page 33)

Distributive System Model (page 48)

Dominant Group (page 52)

Ethnicity (page 36)

Ethnocentrism (page 38)

Gender (page 50)

Horizontal Collectivism (page 45)

Horizontal Individualism (page 45)

Ideology (page 52)

Independent Construals of the Self (page 44)

Individualistic Cultures (page 44)

In-Groups (page 37)

Interdependent Construals of the Self (page 43)

Just-World Hypothesis (page 55)

Meritocracy (page 52)

Minority (page 52)

Multidimensional Construct (page 33)

Nationality (page 35)

Out-Groups (page 37)

Privilege (page 53)

Race (page 39)

Sex (page 50)

Social Norms (page 34)

Social Stratification (page 46)

Socioeconomic Status (page 48)

Vertical Collectivism (page 45)

Vertical Individualism (page 45)

Whiteness (page 41)

Learning by Doing

- Respond to the following three questions:
  1. What is your ethnicity?
  2. What is your culture?
  3. What is your race?

Was there any overlap in your answers? How were you able to distinguish among ethnicity versus culture versus race?

- Think of the various ways in which you are "privileged." Generate a list of at least 10 activities or behaviors that you can engage in without question because of who you are as a person with certain statuses (e.g., status afforded your gender, ethnicity, SES, age). Now imagine that one of your statuses changed: For example, you and your parents (or significant other) lose all financial resources and housing due to a natural disaster and a crash in the stock market. How would the list of privileges change now that you are at a lower level of economic stability? Would some of the privileges disappear? Would new privileges appear? Alter the list accordingly.

Suggested Further Readings

Guthrie, R. V. (1998). *Even the rat was white: A historical view of psychology* (2nd ed.). Needham Heights, MA: Allyn & Bacon.
    Classic historical overview and critique of the measurement of race and racial differences. It also provides an account of the early contributions of African Americans to the field of psychology.

Jacobson, M. F. (1998). *Whiteness of a different color: European immigrants and the alchemy of race.* Cambridge, MA: Harvard University Press.
    Provides a historical analysis of "Whiteness" as a racial identity that has undergone various conceptualizations over time.

Marger, M. N. (2000). *Race and ethnic relations: American and global perspectives* (5th ed.). Belmont, CA: Thomson Wadsworth.
    Explores social stratification patterns of race and ethnic relations in the United States and abroad (e.g., South Africa, Brazil, Canada, Northern Ireland).

Montagu, A. (1974). *Man's most dangerous myth: The fallacy of race* (5th ed.). New York: Oxford University Press.
    Classic analysis of the "myth" of race. Provides evidence that many alleged racial differences are illusory or insignificant.

Omi, M., & Winant, H. (1994). *Racial formation in the United States: From the 1960s to the 1990s* (2nd ed.). New York: Routledge.
    A scholarly contribution to the argument that race is more accurately defined as a social construct as opposed to a biological construct. Documents the changing conceptualizations of race in the United States and the influence of political factors on our views of race.

Rosenblum, K. E., & Travis, T.-M. C. (2003). *The meaning of difference: American constructions of race, sex and gender, social class, and sexual orientation.* New York: McGraw-Hill.
    Textbook reader of the construction, experience, and sociological meaning of difference across the dimensions of race, sex, gender, social class, and sexual orientation. Writings include works by noted scholars, journalists, artists, and activists.

Rothman, R. A. (2002). *Inequality and stratification: Race, class, and gender* (4th ed.). Upper Saddle River, NJ: Prentice Hall.
    A straightforward analysis of how the intersection of race, ethnicity, class, and gender relates to social, political, and economic inequality.

Tatum, B. D. (2003). *"Why are all the Black kids sitting together in the cafeteria?" and other conversations about race.* New York: Basic Books.
    A psychologist's examination of the development of racial identity in Blacks and how to address issues of racism within a multicultural context. The text manages to be both analytical and readable through the use of personal anecdotes and reflections, thus making it a good choice for a wide audience, from high school youths to scholars, interested in these topics.

CHAPTER 3

METHODOLOGICAL ISSUES IN ETHNIC PSYCHOLOGY RESEARCH

VIGNETTE

"That is not me!!"

While reading a psychology textbook, Bobby, a Filipino American nursing student, was surprised to read that the authors talked about Asian Americans as a single group and made generalizations that

(Continued)

(Continued)

did not reflect her family or herself. The authors talked about how Asian Americans were a "model minority" that had achieved great academic and economic success in the country. The authors suggested that this level of success was due to their long history of living in the United States and to their proficiency in speaking English. They concluded that due to these circumstances, traditional cultural values such as the significance of the family in decision making had become less relevant. Bobby was confused with those statements. She was an immigrant to the United States and so were all of her close relatives. Having arrived in the United States four years earlier, she was still trying to master English since the family spoke Tagalog in the Philippines as well as after their arrival in this country. Working overtime and at times two jobs, her parents were able to help her pay for the portion of college tuition not covered by scholarships and federal and state aid. She felt that she didn't fit the description in the textbook and none of her Filipino American high school friends were that different from herself. In class the next day, she asked two Asian American friends how accurate they thought the textbook description was. Sophia, a Vietnamese American born in the United States, said that her parents were still working two shifts and that she was the only sibling in her family who was attending college. Ronald, a Chinese American also born in the United States, reported that his father had gone to college while his mother worked at the shop set up by his grandfather and preferred to speak Cantonese to English. After a long discussion at the campus juice bar, the three concluded that the authors had failed to realize that there were many differences among Asian Americans based not just on their ancestral countries but also on how long they had lived in the United States, the opportunities they had had for employment and education, the level and types of prejudice experienced, and many other additional variables. While Bobby, Sophia, and Ronald shared some cultural values that made them comfortable interacting with each other, they also agreed that their lives and experiences were so different that, at times, the label "Asian American" was of little value.

As a science, psychology relies on the findings of research to better understand human behavior. Ethnic psychology, like all other fields of psychology, must also rely on the results of research to better understand and predict the behavior of members of the various ethnic minority communities in the United States. Unfortunately, much of the early findings in ethnic minority psychology were the result of projects carried out by psychologists and other social scientists who were either unaware of or ignored the special requirements involved in conducting research with special populations. For example, researchers (like the authors of Bobby's psychology textbook) assumed that all members of an ethnic group were similar **(intragroup homogeneity)** and grouped diverse individuals into one single group even though they differed significantly from each other.

Furthermore, it is not unusual to find early research projects where African Americans, Asian Americans, and Hispanics are all grouped together as "minorities" when analyzing their behaviors or attitudes. In other cases, researchers have ignored methodological developments and innovations that would guarantee the validity and usefulness of the results. Proper translation procedures, for example, were seldom followed when adapting a test for use with individuals who did not speak English fluently. The end result of these situations was the production of research findings that are of limited use. Fortunately, we have made significant strides in improving our research methodology in the last few decades and we are now able to rapidly build a better science of ethnic psychology.

The main purpose of this chapter is to provide you with an understanding of the methodological issues that need to be addressed when conducting research with ethnic populations and make you aware of potential limitations in the research available in the literature. The methodological issues covered in this chapter will allow you to better analyze what you read in textbooks and scientific journals or even the popular press regarding ethnic minority groups. This chapter does not replace methodological handbooks that explain basic research methodologies and books specifically written to guide researchers working with ethnic populations. Rather, we hope to provide you with an overview of the challenges that researchers face when studying ethnic groups that in turn will guide you in reflecting on the usefulness of research findings.

This chapter begins with a description of what is involved in conducting research that is sensitive and responsive to the characteristics of the groups being studied, what we call culturally appropriate research. A second section summarizes some of the most serious methodological problems that researchers need to address when investigating ethnic populations including threats to the validity of some psychological instruments and the difficulties involved in obtaining an appropriate translation. A later section covers topics that can affect participation in research or the accuracy of people's responses such as perceptions of exploitation and abuse by earlier researchers. A final section of the chapter addresses ethical concerns that are particularly relevant to ethnic minority research such as improper informed consent, perceived limitations in the free participation in the research project, fear of loss of privacy and confidentiality, and the high personal cost of participation. It should be noted that these issues are relevant to quantitative research as well as to methods that are qualitative in nature. Obviously, some problems or concerns, because of their nature, are more relevant to either quantitative or qualitative methods.

Throughout the chapter, we have included questions that you can ask yourself as you read reports of scientific research dealing with ethnic minority populations. These questions will guide your understanding of the research process and help you evaluate the validity and usefulness of the research findings. Keeping those questions in mind will help you to better understand how a research study was conducted and to reflect on how helpful the findings are.

CULTURALLY APPROPRIATE RESEARCH

In general, the goal of researchers working with ethnic populations should be to conduct **culturally appropriate research** or what other researchers have called "culturally sensitive research" (Rogler, 1999a). We prefer to use the term "culturally appropriate research" to indicate that there are specific requirements that should be met in order to have valid and reliable research with ethnic populations that go beyond being aware and respectful of cultural or ethnic differences.

As shown in Box 3.1, culturally appropriate research involves, first, developing and testing theories and hypotheses that are sensitive to and respectful of cultural variations and that appropriately reflect the possible role of culture and ethnicity in shaping behavior. A second requirement is the use of research methods that are appropriate, familiar, and relevant to the question being researched as well as to the members of the ethnic group being studied. Third, culturally appropriate research implies that the analysis and interpretation of data and other results of a research project must take into consideration not only the culture that characterizes participants but also other relevant variables such as their gender, socioeconomic conditions, educational level, and migration history. Obviously, conducting culturally appropriate research does not mean ignoring the more common requirements for good research, such as being grounded in theory or testing properly derived hypotheses or utilizing methods that produce valid and reliable observations. Rather, the requirements of culturally appropriate research must be added to those of otherwise valid investigations.

BOX 3.1

Characteristics of Culturally Appropriate Research Include

- theories that are sensitive to cultural variations
- methods that are appropriate, familiar, and relevant to the ethnic group
- analyses that take into consideration culture and other relevant characteristics of the population
- adherence to widely accepted principles for ethical, valid, and reliable research

As with all human products, psychological theories, hypotheses, and research methods not only reflect the scientific and professional concerns and interests of the researchers but are heavily influenced by the investigator's own culture and worldviews. The development of culturally appropriate hypotheses, instruments, and research procedures requires the recognition on the part of researchers that often without realizing it, their words and their actions reflect the social context in which they have lived and the cultures to which they belong. It is therefore essential that all of the components of a culturally appropriate research project be contextualized.

Contextualization

The development of culturally appropriate research involves the proper cultural contextualization of the issues to be studied and the way in which information is to be obtained, analyzed, and interpreted. **Contextualization** can be defined as the recognition of the role that social and cultural contexts (situations or characteristics) have in shaping human behavior.

The need to consider the historical and social context in which human artifacts (e.g., books, paintings, scientific theories) were produced has been quite common among scholars in literary criticism and comparative literature but notably absent among social and behavioral scientists. For example, it is not difficult to find the influence of the American South in Mark Twain's writings. The analysis of those influences is part of the work of literary critics and researchers and becomes a central component of their writings. Your American literature instructors have probably talked about how books such as *Huckleberry Finn* or *The Kite Runner* or movies such as *Gone With the Wind* or *Supersize Me* can best be understood when we consider the history and politics of the times as well as the social and economic conditions of the people who lived during the period when the book was being written or the movie was being produced.

Like poets and novelists, social scientists of necessity reflect the culture to which they belong and the social conditions in which they live. For example, Freud's work was heavily influenced by the prude Viennese culture in which he was born and Skinner's understanding of behavior was shaped by the individualistic Anglo-Saxon culture in which he was raised. Their cultural experiences significantly shaped the theories they developed to explain human behavior.

The development of culturally appropriate research procedures requires therefore that researchers recognize the role that their culture plays in the development of their view of human behavior and that the theories and methods to be used properly reflect the culture of the group or groups being studied. As Gardiner (2001) suggests, this contextualization implies that "behavior cannot be studied meaningfully or fully understood independent of the (cultural) context in which it takes place" (p. 102). Indeed, one of the strengths of qualitative research (ethnographies, structured observations, focus groups, interviews of informers, etc.) is the emphasis that researchers place on understanding the meaning and nature of people's action by defining the context in which they take place (Chun, Morera, Andal, & Skewes, 2008).

As you read psychological research concerning ethnic minority groups, you may want to reflect on questions such as the following: (1) Was the topic of the research project relevant to the ethnic populations included in the project? (2) Did the researchers consult members of the ethnic group when interpreting the results? (3) Were the researchers sensitive to the social, cultural, and political context in which the ethnic group lives?

IMPLEMENTING CULTURALLY APPROPRIATE RESEARCH

There are four major areas involved in producing culturally appropriate research that are of particular importance to readers and consumers of psychological research. First, is the need to determine if the researchers used culturally appropriate research methods and instrumentation. Second, students of ethnic psychology need to find out if the researchers were able to properly communicate with the research participants. A third central concern is how well the researchers identified the participants so that biases and overgeneralizations were controlled or eliminated. Finally, there is a need to establish the validity and cultural appropriateness of the interpretation of the results. These four areas are covered next.

Culturally Appropriate Methods

An important component of culturally appropriate research is the use of methods that are relevant to the ethnic or cultural group being studied. This implies that all research instruments or questions must be appropriately familiar to the respondents and include behaviors that the participants can produce. For example, it would be inappropriate to ask a mute person to verbally say "yes" or "no" to a series of questions. Equally inappropriate would be to ask individuals with limited fluency in English to answer questions in an interview that are in English or to take college entrance exams in a language that they do not fully control. Unfortunately, the psychological literature includes studies where people are asked to perform tasks that are beyond their capacity or experience or to answer tests and surveys in languages they do not fully understand. Indeed, as mentioned in Chapter 1, a number of immigrants coming to the United States through Ellis Island were required to take an intelligence test in English even if they were unable to speak the language. This procedure led to the exclusion of a number of individuals who were poorly educated or did not speak English or a language with linguistic roots similar to English.

To understand the importance of using culturally relevant methods, assume for a moment that you are not familiar with the rules of soccer. Your mathematics teacher decides to make a quiz fun and uses soccer-related questions to check on your ability to add and subtract. One question says: "How many players will finish the game with the Panthers team if they lose two players during the first half and are allowed to replace them with only one player?" If you are not familiar with soccer rules (and don't know how many players are allowed on the field at the start of a game), you most likely will be unable to properly answer the question although you are quite capable of adding and subtracting. The same situation can happen when culturally inappropriate methods or instruments are used in psychological research. The individuals may very well be able to perform a task or to report an attitude or value but the approach used to elicit their responses is unknown to them or inappropriate to their culture.

The need for culturally appropriate research procedures can be seen in a study of family dynamics and decision making among Puerto Ricans (Rogler, 1999b). In the original plan, the respondents would be asked to identify who in the family decides such significant issues as where to vacation, which school the children should attend, and the type of insurance to purchase. During pretesting, the researchers found that these concerns were irrelevant to poor Puerto Rican families since they seldom if ever had those choices. Family decision making revolved instead around more basic survival issues and did not resemble the issues facing middle-class families in the United States. As such, the study, in order to be culturally appropriate, needed to address decision making about issues relevant to family survival rather than about such irrelevant issues as where to vacation or which type of insurance to buy. As Rogler (1999b) states, "the concept of decision-making presupposed a situation in which families made choices in an open, companionate relationship between spouses. . . . Just as poverty severely constricted choices, it severely constricted decision-making" (p. 430).

The choice of psychological instruments used in research is probably one of the most difficult decisions made by researchers. At a minimum, there is a need to identify instruments that properly and accurately measure the variable or variables being investigated. This is usually referred to as the **validity** of the instrument. In addition, researchers working with ethnic populations must address the need for the **cultural appropriateness of the instruments.** This means that the instrument (e.g., observation guides, interview questions, tasks to be performed, surveys, tests) must properly reflect the characteristics and experiences of the population in which it is being used. For example, as we noted earlier, it is essential that an instrument be in a language in which the respondent is fluent so that questions are fully understood and answered. If not, the results are invalid because the test is not culturally appropriate. The same can be said about the instrument's reading level, which may not be appropriate to the abilities of the intended participants because it is too difficult or too complex.

The difficulties with establishing the cultural appropriateness of various tests or paper-and-pencil instruments (such as surveys) go beyond the language used in the test or questionnaire. How appropriately an instrument reflects a concept as defined within the culture of a group is also relevant here. This type of validity has been called **construct validity.** It is important therefore to analyze this type of validity whenever a research instrument is used in groups different from those for which it was originally developed. The concern of the researcher must be to use instruments that validly measure a concept or behavior in a way that is relevant to the group in which it is being used. For example, research with Latinos has shown that, in many cases, distant relatives (aunts, uncles, second cousins) are considered to be family members for whom one should feel not only respect but also a sense of responsibility and admiration and whose advice should be considered (Sabogal et al., 1987). Interviewers or researchers using questionnaires or tests analyzing family relations where Latinos are included in the sample should therefore go beyond asking questions about how the respondent interacts with parents and siblings to include other members of the family such as grandparents, godparents, uncles, aunts, and second cousins.

Psychological Tests

The American Psychological Association (Turner, DeMersr, Fox, & Reed, 2001) has stated that consideration of ethnic, racial, and cultural variables may be of importance in the selection of tests to be used. The American Psychological Association further supports the notion that there are a number of issues associated with the use of tests among diverse populations that should be of concern to researchers. These include the need for identifying construct equivalence (or construct validity as defined above), controlling the possible presence of test bias, and using proper procedures for examining between-group differences. While an analysis of these issues is beyond the scope of this book, students of ethnic psychology should be aware of the fact that tests, even well-known and often-used tests, may produce invalid results when utilized with populations that were not included in the development of the instrument, or when the instrument was not properly adapted. Indeed, Padilla (2001) suggests that "the reliability and validity of a test used with individuals of different cultural or linguistic groups who were not included in the standardization group are questionable" (p. 6).

As you read studies in ethnic psychology, you will want to pay particular attention to the cultural appropriateness of the instruments by reflecting on such questions as (1) Do the instruments used in the research project reflect the experiences and abilities of the group being studied? (2) Can the participants be expected to properly understand what is being asked of them as part of participating in the study? (3) If the response required of research participants is the performance of a behavior, is that behavior part of the regular repertoire of behaviors of the group?

Communicating Across Ethnic Groups

Communication difficulties across cultures or ethnic groups are another problematic area when conducting research with ethnic populations. These difficulties can be the product of differential linguistic abilities (such as when one person is not fully fluent in the language that is being used in the study) as well as culture-mandated differences in communication styles (e.g., preferences for deferential styles, gaze-avoiding patterns, differences in talkativeness). Respect, for example, is demonstrated in some cultures by avoiding the gaze of persons with social power as when a student avoids looking at a teacher directly in the eye. In other cultures, this gaze avoidance can possibly be interpreted as deviousness or demonstrating lack of respect or engagement in the conversation. Differential familiarity with communication styles and response procedures is a particularly problematic aspect of research across cultures and can lead to inappropriate or invalid interpretations of research findings.

There are a number of issues related to the use of language that can affect the validity and usefulness of information gathered through interviews or paper-and-pencil tests. These range from differences in preference for using a given language **(linguistic preference)** to variations in the ability to speak a language **(fluency).**

Linguistic Preferences

It is not uncommon for individuals who are fluent in various languages to choose the use of one over the other in specific contexts. For example, Bobby, in our vignette, may prefer speaking Tagalog when talking to her siblings but use English when writing a letter to her high school friends. These preferences have important implications for the language used in research. Regardless of fluency or the ability to speak two or more languages, individuals may feel more confident expressing certain thoughts or feelings in one specific language and not in another. Researchers therefore need to offer bilinguals the opportunity to choose the language they will use in answering paper-and-pencil instruments or when participating in an interview or when explaining behaviors or concepts as part of observational or participatory research.

There are numerous research findings that show how bilinguals, even proficient bilinguals, have different ways of expressing themselves in each language so that they are better able to express emotion in one language and not in the other (Marín, Triandis, Betancourt, & Kashima, 1983). Indeed, for individuals familiar with various languages, certain words or expressions may not carry the same connotation or meaning. For example, the phrase "I love you" may have a different emotional meaning compared to saying "*Te amo*" in Spanish or "*Je t'aime*" in French, even if the person is familiar with the three languages.

Language Preference and Fluidity

There are other frequently ignored considerations that are necessary as researchers plan the analysis of communities with special linguistic needs. For example, sociolinguistic research has shown that bilingual youth seem to prefer the use of English in formal situations (as research settings may be perceived by some) and to use the other language in informal and family environments. Indeed, Garcia and Diaz (1992) found that Hispanic youth in South Florida (an environment that can be expected to support bilingualism because of its ethnic diversity) reported that while most youths started speaking only Spanish or mostly Spanish during their elementary school years, they had shifted to equal use of both languages by the time they reached high school. Furthermore, the study showed that in intimate settings (with parents, with family members, while praying) the preferred language of use was Spanish except when talking with siblings where there was almost an even split between English and Spanish. In summary, when interacting in informal settings (e.g., with friends) both languages were fairly equally used but in formal settings (at school, work, government office), English was the most frequently used language. In general, studies have shown that preference for the mother or initial tongue is based on the perception that it is a better channel to communicate psychological and physical states and feelings (Reichman, 1997).

Likewise, researchers should not assume that all respondents have the same linguistic preference or fluidity because some members of a given ethnic community are generally proficient in a language or prefer to speak a tongue other than English. For example, investigators should never assume that all Hispanics speak Spanish fluently or that all Chinese Americans speak Cantonese or Mandarin. The diversity in preferred languages and in associated meanings makes it necessary for researchers to be very familiar with the characteristics of the communities that are going to be included in the research project. Unfortunately, this requirement of culturally appropriate research has received little attention on the part of some researchers and has limited the validity of the research. As you read research reports with ethnic groups, you may want therefore to pay particular attention to the languages used in the interviews or in the instruments.

Difference in preferred modes of expression (or ways in which information is organized) can be another often-ignored methodological concern that affects the validity of research findings. American Indians, for example, have been reported as preferring to provide a historical context when talking about their health or some other aspect of their lives, which may be perceived as irrelevant information by individuals not trained in properly understanding their culture. Likewise, American Indians tend to prefer placing the summary of a statement or its conclusion in the middle of a statement or paragraph while some Asian cultures would place it at the beginning. Latinos' preference for the passive tense of a verb (e.g., "it broke" rather than "I broke it") may also provide inappropriate perceptions of assumed responsibility to the unaware researcher or therapist.

Language concordance or the similarity between the language spoken by the research participant and the language used by observers, researchers, or interviewers is an important issue that also has received little attention by investigators conducting research with ethnic groups. Research, mostly in medical settings, has shown that language concordance between patient and doctor is related to increased reports of better well-being by patients (Pérez-Stable, Nápoles-Springer, & Miramontes, 1997). Other studies have found that ethnic similarity between researcher and participant produces better-quality findings and a higher rate of complete answers (Webster, 1996). Indeed, it is not surprising that participants in a research project would feel not only a sense of connection but possibly even of trust with a researcher who speaks the language of preference of the respondents. This linguistic and ethnic concordance can affect therefore the validity of the responses and the actual usefulness of the results in shaping science or confirming the predictions of a hypothesis.

One important implication of the findings mentioned in this section is the need to consider language use (particularly when the respondent chooses it) as one of the variables to be researched in terms of its effects on the variables being measured. Language used may indeed provide a more comprehensive and complete perspective on many behaviors and perceptions that are part of a study, particularly those related to physical and mental health (Kirkman-Liff & Mondragón, 1991).

Culture Specific Meanings of Words

As mentioned above, there seems to be some support in the literature for differential affect or intensity being assigned to the meaning or evaluation of certain words or constructs across ethnic groups. There is evidence, for example, that members of ethnic minority groups differ in their comfort when discussing certain behaviors (e.g., drug use or sex) and even when using the words associated with them. A study with urban Latino and African American adolescents (K. Ford & Norris, 1991) found that adolescents of both groups were uncomfortable discussing sexual behaviors and that Hispanic women were particularly uncomfortable discussing menstruation. Cultural variations in level of comfort when using or hearing certain words can also be expected when investigating topics that are of particular significance to an individual's life or experiences (e.g., religion, sexual behavior, alcohol or drug use). For example, topics related to politics and political activities can produce significant emotional reactions from respondents who have escaped repressive political regimes or who have been tortured, exiled, or persecuted by a given political organization or entity as is the case with many Latin Americans, Africans, and Middle Easterners.

There is also the need to consider specific vocabularies that are used by certain subgroups and that may vary across or within ethnic groups. For example, Mays and her colleagues (Mays, Flora, Schooler, & Cochran, 1992) have argued that African American gay men use a group-specific vocabulary to talk about sexual practices that includes words that are not common outside the group. These group- or subgroup-specific vocabularies make it essential for researchers and practitioners to properly understand those words in order to interact with members of the group. The same is true among small adolescent groups (gangs and affinity or friends groups) and among other individuals who may use special words to define territory or enhance their self-protection or to define themselves even if the words are not socially acceptable or widely understood.

In addition, measuring procedures in research must take into account cultural or religious norms that may make specific stimuli or response instruments invalid or even insulting. For example, some ethnic or cultural groups disapprove of using images of God or of religious figures while other groups associate certain colors or numbers with good or bad outcomes. For example, many Asian cultures associate red with good luck and white with death and many individuals in the United States associate the number 13 with bad luck to the point that many buildings do not have a floor designated with the number 13. These cultural values must be taken into consideration by researchers in order to avoid offending the individuals who will be asked to participate in a research project. As a consumer of ethnic research, therefore, you need to reflect on whether the instruments and activities used in a study were culturally appropriate. The use of inappropriate words, images, or behaviors in a research project will produce results of limited validity and usefulness. Indeed, early cross-cultural research in psychology often showed how groups not familiar with certain stimuli or measuring procedures (e.g., tracing of figures, making objects from plasticine or wire) usually obtained lower scores than individuals who were familiar with the objects or procedures (Serpell, 1979).

Translation

The difficulties encountered by investigators interested in studying individuals who are not fluent speakers of the researchers' language led many of them to use translated research instruments. Nevertheless, as you will see below, translation is a complex and difficult process that may not necessarily control for the problems mentioned above in communication across cultures and languages.

In an important article, Vijver and Hambleton (1996) described three types of bias in cross-cultural research that are of relevance when considering the translation of instruments: (1) **construct bias,** where the concept or construct being analyzed (e.g., need for achievement, independence) has different meaning or implications in each culture and these variations lead to differential aspects being emphasized when defining or understanding the construct within one culture; (2) **method bias,** which relates to factors associated with the application of the instrument and the type of response individuals provide or factors that influence those responses (e.g., the tendency to agree with the statements being presented by the researcher, what is often called **acquiescent response**); and (3) **item bias,** which refers to aspects of the question or item (e.g., wording, content) that have different meanings or implications across cultures. Obviously, the best way to avoid all these biases is to have the interview, test, or instrument undergo a process that is more complex than just translating it from one language to another so as to make sure that the items are relevant to the culture (avoiding construct bias), as well as presented in an appropriate fashion (avoiding method bias), and are properly worded (avoiding item bias).

One of the problems related to the translation of instruments that have undergone lengthy psychometric analysis (often referred to as **standardized instruments**) is the possibility of responses being partially produced by the new wording. For example, a number of studies have looked at a well-known measure of depression (Center for Epidemiological Studies-Depression Scale or CES-D) and its translation and adaptation to Spanish. These studies are indicative of the problems associated with using instruments developed for one culture in another group even after proper translation procedures have been followed, and they apply not just to tests but also to questions used in interviews or in observational studies. One problem faced by researchers using the CES-D in their investigations was how to properly translate items that use informal or colloquial statements such as "shaking the blues," which do not have proper equivalents in other languages and are meaningless if literally translated ("moving the blue colors" if literally translated into Spanish).

A second possible problem with the translation of a psychological test is related to the internal structure of the instrument. Although some research (e.g., Roberts, Vernon, & Rhoades, 1989) showed that translation of the CES-D did not affect the statistical characteristics of the test, specifically its dimensionality and reliability, other studies (e.g., Golding & Aneshensel, 1989; Guarnaccia, Angel, & Worobey, 1989; Posner, Stewart, Marín, & Pérez-Stable, 2001) have shown that indeed the internal dimensionality of the instrument is different in English and in Spanish. These results could mean that while the wording of the items is similar in both languages, the way the items are being interpreted by respondents in English and in Spanish is so different that they could be answering to what in practice amounts to two different tests. Furthermore, responses to at least some items seem to differ based on the birthplace (abroad or in the United States) of the respondents, indicating that acculturation (see Chapter 4) or generational history had an effect on the way they interpreted the various questions (Golding, Aneshensel, & Hough, 1991).

The Translation Process

As suggested by Sperber, Devellis, and Boehlecke (1994), the goal in translating is "to adapt the instrument in a culturally relevant and comprehensible form while maintaining the meaning of the original items" (p. 502). Suggestions for conducting translation of questionnaires, interviews, and other instruments have been in existence in the research literature for many years, particularly in the works of cross-cultural investigators and ethnic psychologists (e.g., Brislin, 1980; Brislin, Lonner, & Thorndike, 1973; Marín & VanOss Marín, 1991).

The simplest and less valid translation process uses one language as the standard while the instrument is translated into the target language by an experienced or volunteer translator. The translator creates a new version of the instrument in the target language, usually adopting a fairly "literal" approach to translation, and the process ends at that point. For example, a researcher asks Thuan, her Vietnamese American student, to translate a survey from English into Vietnamese and takes the result of the process as the final version to be used for interviewing other Vietnamese Americans. This approach is of limited use since it does not consider linguistic limitations of the translator and variability in culture-specific meaning of words or concepts that may be unfamiliar to the translator. Unfortunately, this translation approach was used in much early research.

An alternative translation approach has been called **double translation** (Marín & VanOss Marín, 1991) or **back translation** by other authors (e.g., Brislin, 1980). This approach, which is often considered one of the best procedures currently available for translating instruments, involves the use of at least two bilingual translators and a significant level of consultation within the research team and across translators. This translation procedure has a number of possible variations but it involves going back and forth across languages trying to obtain versions that are appropriate to the language and the culture of the respondents and that do not differ significantly in meaning from the intended goal of the project. For example, one translator (Translator A) takes the original version of the instrument written in the Original Language (e.g., French) and translates it into the Target Language (e.g., Mandarin) producing Mandarin Version 1. A second translator (Translator B) then takes the Target Language version of the instrument (Mandarin Version 1) and translates it into the Original Language without consulting with Translator A and producing French Version 2. Once the two Original Language versions (French Version 1 and French Version 2) are ready, the researchers compare the instruments in order to identify problems with the translations (odd wording, improper meaning, incomplete sentences, etc.). At this stage, the researchers can engage the translators in discussions as to what was done and how to resolve any discrepancies. A repetition of the process is often recommended (from French Version 2 to Mandarin Version 2 to French Version 3) with the same or with different translators. The process of consultation and modification continues until researchers and translators are satisfied that the two linguistic versions are similar and equally useful in each language. See Box 3.2 for an example of the double translation procedure.

BOX 3.2

Example of Double Translation

Original Language Version 1
"I often feel hungry when studying"

Target Language Version 1
"Frecuentemente, siento hambre cuando estudio"

Original Language Version 2
"Frequently, I feel hunger when I study"

Target Language Version 2
"Frecuentemente me siento con hambre cuando estoy estudiando"

Original Language Version 3
"Often I feel hungry when studying"

Erkut and colleagues (Erkut, Alarcon, Coll, Tropp, & Garcia, 1999) have suggested an approach they call the **dual focus approach to translation** whereby bilingual and bicultural research teams work together to plan the research project and to develop the instruments that will be used. During the initial stage, members of the team become familiar with the literature and make sure that the concepts and constructs to be used in the research project are equally valid in all cultures. Development of the instrument follows that initial stage whereby all members of the research team work to guarantee that the words to be used in both versions are equivalent in their emotional meaning (affect), familiarity, and ease of comprehension (clarity). Focus groups made up of indigenous informants review the instrument and provide feedback as to its linguistic and cultural appropriateness. Psychometric and statistical analyses are then conducted to establish the usefulness and internal consistency of the instruments in the research enterprise.

Use of Interpreters

In some situations or research projects, there is a need to utilize interpreters who translate instructions or questions to the respondents as they are being verbalized by the researcher or therapist. This approach, while not ideal, may become necessary for certain qualitative research projects such as when conducting field studies, ethnographies, interviews, and focus groups or while carrying out initial exploratory visits to communities to be studied. The use of interpreters, however, is fraught with difficulties and problems. Research on the use of interpreters in medical settings, for example, has shown that interpreters usually do not properly transmit information to patients or to health personnel mostly because they don't understand what is being said, they lack enough cultural and/or personal sensitivity, fail to understand street expressions or dialects, don't pay attention to nonverbal communication, or inappropriately translate words that have various meanings (Brooks, 1992).

In general, the use of interpreters should be avoided or used sparingly. When reviewing research where interpreters have been used to collect information, you should be careful to identify situations or topics that may be subject to misinterpretation or mistranslation and pay particular attention to how those problems may affect the validity of the information.

Properly Identifying and Describing Participants

The proper identification and description of the participants in a research project is important in helping students and other researchers understand the implications of the results. This concern is of particular importance when conducting research with ethnic groups since there are a number of approaches that can be taken when describing those individuals who form an ethnic group in the United States. For example, basic demographic information provides an understanding of the group's size (usually based on self-identification) and such socioeconomic characteristics as median age, average income, and mean level of formal education. At the same time, historical information can be used to understand the reasons for the group's presence in the country, its level of involvement with the dominant culture(s), or its current social and political status.

The overriding principle in defining the members of an ethnic group is the belief that what may unite these individuals is the shared culture and traditions that are valued and/or defended and that have survived migrations, the passing of time, and the onslaught of a massive globalizing culture. Many of these characteristics are partially subsumed in the ethnic label used to identify members of the group and those labels can be self-assigned (e.g., African American or Latino) or imposed by other groups (e.g., Black or Hispanic).

It is indeed common in the United States to use labels such as Asian Americans, Hispanics, African Americans, Latinos, American Indians, Mexican Americans, Vietnamese Americans, Chinese Americans, Cuban

Americans, Puerto Ricans, Filipino Americans, or Laotian Americans. These labels and others, as mentioned in Chapter 1, imply that there are a number of characteristics that define or are shared by individuals who are members of those groups. Nevertheless, there is a need to understand that ethnic or cultural labels are **labels of convenience** that allow researchers, politicians, care providers, and others to identify individuals who share some general characteristics. Those ethnic labels do not necessarily reflect intragroup homogeneity or similarity nor do they necessarily imply common psychological characteristics (Okazaki & Sue, 1995; Weiss & Weiss, 2002).

It is important, therefore, to remember that there is great variability within the various ethnic groups that are found in the United States. They vary in terms of their migration history, their socioeconomic characteristics (educational level, income, average age), as well as in terms of psychological variables. The various ethnic labels are convenient ways to talk about a group of individuals who share some characteristics.

Those ethnic labels nevertheless stand for groups that include significant intragroup variability and are not equivalent to the grouping used in the natural sciences such as when botanists group plants or zoologists group animal families or when biologists categorize blood types. For example, individuals who consider themselves Chinese Americans vary in terms of numerous variables including their immigration history. Some came to the United States to work on the construction of the railroads while others migrated to join those early relatives. Another group of Chinese Americans came escaping the Communist revolution and the war with Japan while others came to the United States when Hong Kong was ceded back to the People's Republic of China. Recently, Chinese from the southern provinces of the People's Republic are coming to the United States in search of economic advancement.

These differences in immigration history of various Chinese Americans can also be found in terms of the average educational level of the various groups as well as in terms of their average income, English-language fluency, and other variables. While all of these groups can be described as Chinese Americans who share certain cultural values, they also differ in terms of a number of variables. The same variability can be found among other Asian American groups as well as among African Americans, American Indians, and Latinos. These differences require that researchers and consumers of research pay attention to the variability that exists not only within the larger labels used to identify ethnic groups (Asian Americans, Latinos, African Americans, American Indians, etc.) but also within the more specific labels (e.g., Chinese Americans, Cuban Americans, Filipino Americans, Mexican

Americans). The examination of this intragroup variability is often called **disaggregation** of results.

Disaggregating Participants

You may recall how in the vignette at the beginning of this chapter, Bobby and her friends were unhappy with what they read in their textbooks because they could not fully identify with the ethnic groups being described. What explains those differences in people's behaviors and attitudes is the variability mentioned in the previous paragraphs. It is necessary therefore for researchers to properly define their respondents or research participants by describing those individual characteristics that differentiate members of the group.

Culturally appropriate research demands proper disaggregation or sampling and reporting of relevant characteristics that produce differences within and across ethnic groups. This process of disaggregation implies that together with including information on typical sociodemographic parameters (gender, education, age), researchers must study participants who are members of ethnic groups in terms of other relevant variables such as immigration status, country of birth, literacy, acculturation level, and language preference and use (Baluja, Park, & Myers, 2003). The description of respondents and analysis of the information or data must address each of these items in order to more properly identify research participants (Okazaki & Sue, 1995) and produce better results.

The proper disaggregation of research participants allows students of ethnic psychology to better understand a social phenomenon. For example, separating the responses of male African Americans from those of women will allow the researcher to better define the possible role that gender plays in shaping people's behavior. A study on rates of tobacco use (or prevalence) among Latinos is a good example of the need to properly disaggregate research findings. The study (Marín, Pérez-Stable, & Marín, 1989) showed that acculturation (or rate of learning of a new culture—see Chapter 4) affected differentially the rate at which male and female Latinos smoked cigarettes. Highest rates of cigarette smoking were found among the less acculturated men while among women, the highest rates of cigarette smoking were found among the highly acculturated. Ignoring the need to differentiate respondents by gender and acculturation could have led researchers to propose erroneous conclusions about the rates of cigarette smoking among Latinos.

Unfortunately, at times researchers have not been sensitive to the need to properly identify respondents and to appropriately disaggregate information. While by now most researchers are aware of the need to define ethnic groups at least by the five major categories used by the

U.S. Department of Commerce in the 2000 census (African Americans, Asian Americans and Pacific Islanders, Hispanics, American Indians and Alaska Natives, White non-Hispanics), we must keep in mind that there are over 300 distinct ethnic groups and approximately 500 American Indian tribes that were identified in the 1990 census.

As mentioned throughout this book, it is essential for researchers to differentiate within-group communities so that among Asian Americans, for example, Chinese Americans are differentiated from Laotian or Korean or Vietnamese or Filipino Americans. This within-group variability is also found among Latinos (Mexican Americans as different from Salvadoran or Cuban or Puerto Rican or Colombian Americans) as well as among African Americans (Haitians as different from Jamaican or third generation African Americans). For example, the category "Asian American and Pacific Islanders" includes over 57 national heritages as well as people who, as a group, use more than 100 languages. The category "Latinos" includes individuals who trace their roots to over 34 different countries and while most (but not all) speak Spanish or Portuguese, there are variations in lilt, accent, and voice inflection as well as vocabulary. To better understand this complexity, check Box 3.3 to see the great intragroup variability in national background or ancestry that exists among Asian Americans and Latinos in the United States.

While the argument can be made that the use of labels identifying the larger ethnic groups is valid and relevant to some extent (e.g., Latinos irrespective of national origin do share some basic common values such as familialism or the value placed on relatives for emotional and social support), in many cases the differences within an ethnic group are as large as they are across ethnic groups (e.g., dietary habits, academic achievement, school persistence, prevalence of certain diseases). As a matter of fact, members of a given ethnic group often are very sensitive to ways in which the various subgroups differ and within-group variability may often be invoked by respondents as a way of differentiating themselves from other subgroups (e.g., Cuban Americans as different from Puerto Rican or Mexican Americans). Researchers must therefore precisely report how they identified and selected research participants in order to present information that is useful and valid to the student of ethnic psychology.

Parenting by individuals from different ethnic or cultural backgrounds is also generating an interesting and important phenomenon in the country that has implications for our research and for understanding our contemporary culture. Parenting by individuals of diverse ethnic backgrounds and ethnic intermarriage are producing a noticeable increase in the number of individuals who trace their ethnic background to more

BOX 3.3

Diversity Within Ancestries

Asian Americans

Includes individuals who trace their ancestry to countries or areas of the world such as

Bangladesh	Japan	Philippines
Bhutan	Korea	Singapore
Cambodia	Laos	Sri Lanka
China	Malaysia	Taiwan
Hong Kong	Myanmar (Burma)	Thailand
India	Nepal	Vietnam
Indonesia	Pakistan	

Latinos/Hispanics

Includes individuals who trace their ancestry to countries such as

Argentina	Dominican Republic	Panama
Bolivia	Ecuador	Paraguay
Brazil	El Salvador	Peru
Chile	Guatemala	Puerto Rico
Colombia	Honduras	Spain
Costa Rica	Mexico	Uruguay
Cuba	Nicaragua	Venezuela

than one ethnic or ancestral group. While this is not a new phenomenon, it was the 2000 decennial census that first allowed respondents to indicate that they belonged to more than one race. Indeed, the 2000 census showed that approximately 2.6% of the total population indicated belonging to two or more races and 5.4% of adults married and living with a spouse indicated having married someone of a different race/ethnicity compared with 4.5% in 1990 (Farley, 2002). These figures indicate that the probability of encountering multiethnic respondents is rapidly increasing and that researchers need to be aware of this possibility not just in terms of drafting appropriate identifiers but also in deciding how to properly treat their responses.

Unfortunately, few researchers sample ethnic individuals who represent the diversity present in the various communities and even fewer report the results of disaggregating or separating for each of the values or dimensions of each variable. As educated consumers of psychological research, ethnic psychology students should keep these variables in mind and investigate how researchers included them or failed to consider these types of within-group variability. Variables where significant within-group variability exists among ethnic communities include the following:

Gender. It is now fairly common for researchers in the social and behavioral sciences to always include gender as a variable to consider when selecting a sample and to analyze and interpret the results of the study according to the gender of the participants. Indeed, a large number of publications have supported the need for this approach and various funding agencies (e.g., the U.S. Public Health Service) require the inclusion of men and women in all studies (except when not possible, such as in the case of studies of cervical or prostate cancer). The inclusion of men and women is of obvious importance since their development and social experiences vary and these differences can produce a diversity of behaviors, attitudes, and values. For example, researchers polling peoples' opinions about welfare reform would want to analyze differences in opinions among men and women, and among adults of childbearing age and among older individuals. Failure to include those gender- and age-specific groups could provide biased perspectives on the issues being studied.

Rural/Urban Residence. Much research tends to ignore differences that may exist between those raised or who reside in small towns and rural communities and those from large metropolitan areas. Nevertheless, research is available that shows important differences between residents of rural and urban areas including their mental health (Marsella, 1998), levels of resiliency or psychological strength, and risk levels. These rural/urban differences are of particular significance when studying ethnic groups where large proportions were raised or currently reside in small towns. Indeed, this is a pattern that is true for African Americans and other U.S.-born ethnic minorities who have worked in agriculture as well as for individuals who have recently migrated from rural Asia or Latin America. Growing up in small rural areas can influence people's vision of the world, making it different from those individuals who have been raised in large metropolitan areas such as New York, Chicago, or Los Angeles.

Social Class. It is not uncommon for social and behavioral researchers to consider social class variables as important modifiers of a person's attitudes, norms, values, and behaviors. Whether measured by complex indices or by indicators (e.g., educational level, employment category, family income), social class or socioeconomic status can be a powerful modifier of a person's worldview and behavior (American Psychological Association Task Force on Socioeconomic Status, 2007; G. W. Evans, 2004). For members of ethnic groups, the experiences of belonging to a given ethnic or cultural group interact with their social class so that the latter may in some cases powerfully override certain ethnic-specific characteristics. As such, Korean Americans living in poverty may experience specific attitudes and behaviors that are more closely related to their social class (and therefore found among Whites or African Americans of the same social class status) than to the fact that they are Korean Americans. Researchers must therefore be careful to differentiate as much as possible the effects of social class and socioeconomic conditions from those of ethnic group membership.

Poverty has indeed been shown to have an effect on people's lives, development, and attitudes that goes beyond simple lifestyle deprivations. For example, research has shown that poverty status affects not only children's development (Duncan, Brooks-Gunn, & Klebanov, 1994) but also psychosocial adjustment as in the case of Hmong refugees (Westermeyer, Callies, & Neider, 1990), as well as overall health status (Stein, Nyamathi, & Kington, 1997). In these and other studies, experiencing poverty has been found to produce long-term effects on people's health and psychological well-being (American Psychological Association Task Force on Socioeconomic Status, 2007).

Generational Status. There is a substantial body of research that suggests that the generational status of respondents produces important behavioral and attitudinal differences across groups. As could be expected, the experiences of immigrants are rather different from those of their children and grandchildren. Language use and proficiency, for example, can be expected to vary across generations as well as their level of familiarity with cultural products (meals, music, literature, holidays), expectations, and other relevant concepts and experiences.

While the generational level of ethnic participants may not have been as important for those groups that came to the United States at the end of the 19th century and beginning of the 20th century (where assimilationist perspectives were strong and fairly well accepted by immigrants), the same is not true for the national/cultural groups that have recently arrived in the country. Many of these latter immigrants try to maintain language proficiency and cultural traditions as a way of defining their self-concept and personal identity as well as that of their children. Moreover, the "melting pot" phenomenon in immigrant assimilation may have been true for some groups (possibly Italians, Irish, Jews of the early 20th century) but may be less true for other immigrants (Glazer & Moynihan, 1963). As such, it becomes important for researchers and readers alike to properly understand the generational history of those individuals being studied.

Indeed, various analyses have shown that considering a respondent's generation provides better and more complex description of various psychological phenomena than when generational status is ignored. For example, Baluja, Park, and Myers (2003) found that differentiating between first and second generation Asian Americans allowed them to better understand differences in cigarette smoking whereby first generation Asian Americans showed a lower proportion of individuals who smoked (prevalence) than what was found among second generation Asian Americans. The data from that study also showed that there were differences across countries of origin, supporting the need to disaggregate results by more than one variable.

Box 3.4 describes the most commonly used **generation** labels found in the literature of the social sciences. While these labels and their definitions are useful to better understand the history of individuals and their families, they are labels of convenience that may not properly address the characteristics of all members of ethnic groups. For example, estimates (Perlmann, 2002) drawn from the decennial census show that third generation individuals (grandchildren of immigrants) are normally born within 40 years of the time of arrival of the immigrants themselves (generally around age 20 at immigration time). Fourth generation individuals are usually born around 70 years after the arrival of the immigrants. At the same time, analysis of census information of Italian immigrants shows that third generation Italians tended to intermarry (that is, marrying outside their ethnic group) in fairly large proportions (62%) and the same was true for fourth generation Italian Americans (89%). Therefore, our immigration experiences in the 20th century would show that within a window of less than 70 years, intermarriage (or outmarriage) is highly likely to occur, generating a large number of multiethnic individuals.

BOX 3.4

Defining Generational Histories

First Generation: Individual has immigrated to the United States and expects to remain in the country permanently or for a very long time.

Second Generation: Individual is born in the United States of parents who were both first generation.

Mixed Second Generation: Individual is born in the United States with one parent being born in the United States and the other being a first generation (also called 1.5 generation).

Third Generation: Individual born in the United States whose grandparents were all first generation.

Mixed Third Generation: Individual born in the United States where at least one grandparent was a first generation immigrant.

Typically, generational levels are defined as being based on place of birth and familial history but not on the age of the respondents. As shown in Box 3.4, first generation members of ethnic groups are considered to be those who immigrate into a new culture, for example, a Vietnamese refugee who arrived in the United States after the U.S.-Vietnam war or a Russian first coming to the United States after the collapse of the Soviet Union.

Alejandro Portes and his colleagues (Rumbaut & Portes, 2001) have frequently advocated the need to separately analyze individuals from various generations (disaggregating by generation) since the experiences of a first generation individual can differ across a number of situations from those of a second generation person. Indeed, generational differences can be expected in terms of level of education, language proficiency, and employment status. All of these variables are relevant in defining socioeconomic status, acculturation, and level of involvement with a majority culture and will probably impact the characteristics of the participants in a study. Indeed, generational levels have been found to influence variables such as English-language proficiency (Sodowsky, Lai, & Plake, 1991), mental health status (Vega, Gil, & Kolody, 2002), alcohol drinking patterns (Golding, Burnam, Benjamin, & Wells, 1992), and cigarette smoking (Markides, Coreil, & Ray, 1987).

Migration Rationale and History. Some researchers (e.g., Ogbu, 1978) have argued that people's behaviors in a new environment or culture can be significantly influenced by the reason for their migration experience. Ogbu suggests that the voluntary or involuntary nature of the migration experience can affect people's education and overall socioeconomic success in the new country. **Voluntary immigrants** for Ogbu are those who choose to migrate searching for economic and educational improvements. **Involuntary immigrants,** on the other hand, are those individuals who have been enslaved or colonized and may have experienced difficulties assimilating (e.g., American Indians, African Americans, Native Hawai'ians) or those who were forced to leave their country of origin because of political conditions (e.g., refugees). While the data supporting these assumptions are not very conclusive, involuntary immigrants are usually characterized as faring poorly in academic settings, having school adjustment difficulties, and experiencing scholarly failure. Ogbu further argues that in part this is due to their refusal to accept the values of the "host" culture, which in turn can be expected to lead to failure in academic pursuits and poorer future employment opportunities.

Ogbu's hypothesis is of interest in that it provides insights into certain attitudinal conflicts experienced by various ethnic groups that may in turn affect their performance and generalized willingness to adapt to or learn the new culture. Of particular importance is the distinction that can be drawn from Ogbu's (1978) typology when applied to individuals from various generations who are members of the same family unit. For example, immigrant parents who choose to migrate in search of economic advancement can be considered to be "voluntary immigrants." At the same time, their small children who are forced to relocate because of their parents' decision can be considered to be "involuntary immigrants." Differences in attitudes and in the ease of acculturation can be expected in these two groups of individuals.

This section of the chapter has emphasized the need for researchers to properly define the characteristics of their respondents by going beyond large and usually uninformative labels such as "Asian Americans" or "Latinos." As a student of ethnic psychology, you should be aware of the differences that exist within each ethnic group in terms of generation or factors such as gender, age, economic and educational status, acculturation (see Chapter 4), and experiences of prejudice and discrimination (see Chapter 7). As mentioned in the vignette that introduced this chapter, Bobby could not recognize herself as an Asian American when reading her textbooks since the authors had failed to indicate the differences that exist within and across various Asian American groups. One key lesson from this chapter is that it is difficult to properly understand ethnic groups unless the data and information are properly disaggregated by other relevant variables such as gender, generational history, and educational status.

Culturally Appropriate Analysis of Information or Data

In carrying out culturally appropriate research, there is a need for researchers to be aware of their own cultural background and social status and the effects those variables can have on their interpretation of the results of a study. Often, we tend to misinterpret behaviors that are different from those that are familiar or frequent among our friends and relatives. Indeed, an African American psychologist by the name of Robert Guthrie (2004) properly pointed out in his famous book, *Even the Rat Was White,* how much of psychological research had ignored the nuances and variability produced by differences in ethnicity, race, and other variables. This one-sided perspective of human behavior (when in extreme cases researchers, subjects, and even laboratory rats were white) challenges the generalizability of our findings. One extreme manifestation, as noted by Padilla (2001), is the fact that any deviation from White middle-class norms is often interpreted as a deficit or as a problem that requires alleviation or intervention.

A related problem is the assumption that research in ethnic psychology must include a comparison of the ethnic group with a "control" or "comparison" group of White participants. These comparisons often have an implied gradation of goodness or appropriateness where the group-specific characteristics of a dominant group are set as the standard (the "gold standard") that other groups must meet and against which deficits are identified. This approach has two limitations. First, it fails to acknowledge not only cultural variations but also the important effects of such social conditions as discrimination, poverty, unemployment, and malnutrition on people's lives. Second, setting one group as a "control" group ignores the fact that the comparison of one group against another is not necessarily more informative than research that explores an issue or tests a hypothesis within members of one ethnic group alone.

The expectation of Whites serving as the "control" or "comparison" group is an example of biases inherent in the research process that promotes the assumption of a deficit model to describe the behavior of ethnic groups (Bernal & Scharrón Del Rio, 2001). Generally, **deficit models** assume that any behavior that is different from what is found among Whites can be explained by invoking social, cultural, intellectual, or psychological limitations on the part of the members of the ethnic group. An equally absurd approach would be to set the behavior of residents of the United States as the standard against which the behavior of people from other countries should be compared. Comparative research has its value but it should not be the norm against which research relevant to ethnic minority groups is measured. For example, the developmental study of friendship patterns among African American children is as valuable as the same analysis conducted among Asian Americans or Whites. Likewise, the comparison across groups of those findings is valuable but the standard against which the findings are compared should not be the African American pattern of development or that of the White children. Using one pattern as the "gold standard" against which the others are compared in effect introduces biases in the interpretation of the results: the belief in the supremacy of one culture over another.

THE PROBLEM OF LIMITED PARTICIPATION IN RESEARCH

One of the serious issues limiting the usefulness and generalizability of much ethnic psychology research is the fact that in a number of cases, participation by ethnic community members is not as large or as continuous as could be expected. These limitations in the size or representativeness of the samples used in research limit the potential usefulness of the results for advancing theory or psychological applications.

In general, there are a number of variables that have produced concerns or outright refusals to participate in research by ethnic minority individuals. On the one hand, there are research procedures that have been designed without paying attention to the needs and characteristics of the group. Another possible explanation for why participation rates are low in some ethnic communities is a history of negative interactions between researchers and community members or a legacy of carelessness and outright abuse of the community. This problem is particularly important when conducting qualitative research where the number of participants is usually small and where self-selection biases in participation can lead to serious misinterpretations or faulty generalizations (Chun et al., 2008). This section of the chapter reviews some of these difficulties in obtaining research participants.

One frequently mentioned concern about psychological research among ethnic communities is their need to know the ultimate purpose of the study or the reasons for the collection of data and personal information. There is fear, often well founded, that information is being collected by unscrupulous individuals for dubious commercial goals (e.g., to sell products or for some form of identity theft) or by government agencies interested in tax collection or ascertaining the immigration status of the respondents. Appropriately designed and user-friendly recruitment materials and informed consent documents can help alleviate some of the doubts about the real purpose of the study (Chun et al., 2008). Proper and complete description of the study's sponsorship and the role of research institutions or universities or clinics in the research can solve fears of the future use of the information and of the nature of sponsoring institutions.

Another common problem in much research with ethnic populations is the difficulties respondents encounter in reporting to research sites (e.g., hospitals, clinics, universities) in order to participate in a research project. Transportation subsidies and on-premises child care make it easier for low-income respondents as well as those who provide child care for their own children or the children of relatives to be part of a study. Ease of access to research sites (located in communities as opposed to large universities or hospital complexes that are removed from ethnic communities) is another factor that usually enhances participation and that provides a sense of support to the participants. Lack of these support systems for participation in a research project may make it difficult for members of ethnic communities to participate in research projects and this limited participation can in turn bias the results of the study.

A recent analysis (Brown, Fouad, Basen-Engquist, & Tortolero-Luna, 2000) of perceived barriers to participation in a clinical trial for cervical cancer showed that African American and Hispanic women reported the presence of a number of barriers that would prevent them from participating in the program. Among the most frequently mentioned barriers were problems with transportation, interference with job or housework, and problems with child and elder care. Also of relevance in preventing participation or continuation in a research project was the lack of information as to the purpose of the study, the required procedures, and its usefulness.

Many of these issues also are of relevance to research that is less intrusive than medical clinical trials and to men as well as women. As a matter of fact, participation by members of ethnic minority groups in biomedical research is often made difficult by structural, cultural, and linguistic factors. Among the structural factors are problems such as poverty and low socioeconomic status, the length of the study, the schedule of activities, cost, number of follow-ups, and possible side effects. Cultural variables such as attitudes toward medical care, beliefs about the origins and treatment of certain illnesses, and cultural expectancies such as modesty can of course be expected to influence willingness to participate in a study. Finally, linguistic factors such as language proficiency and skills can be barriers to participation in a project where proper accommodations have not been made.

Researchers studying some sensitive topics (drug use, HIV/AIDS, religiosity, sexual behavior) have additional difficulties in obtaining participation. For example, involvement in AIDS research by ethnic groups can be affected by cultural, normative, and political attitudes held by members of specific groups. Researchers have argued, for example, that some African Americans refuse to participate in AIDS research and interventions due to variables such as negative attitudes toward homo-sexuality, the perception by some that AIDS is racial genocide, distrust of medical research (Shavers-Hornaday, Lynch, Burmeister, & Torner, 1997), and viewing illness as a punishment for sins (Icard, Zamora-Hernandez, Spencer, & Catalano, 1996).

There are other aspects of the research process that affect the willingness of individuals to participate in research projects. It is not uncommon in ethnic minority communities to question the actual benefit to the participants or to the community that can be derived from the research procedure. Some American Indian communities have developed their own review process whereby researchers are expected to properly and completely explain the purpose of the study and to "give back" to the community by, at a minimum, providing progress reports and data files. While the formal procedures in other ethnic communities may not necessarily match the organizational structure of American Indian tribes, they may informally exist through the roles played by ministers and priests, local government officials (ward chairs, council members, mayors), and community organizers. In the end, full participation benefits the community but, unfortunately, a number of researchers have treated ethnic minority communities without respect for their autonomy and personal integrity and more like "laboratory rats" than human beings. Exploitative situations view participants as research subjects to be observed and measured as objects rather than as individuals (Chaudhary, 2004).

The usefulness of a research project is heavily dependent on the level of participation and representativeness of the participants. The limited participation of participants, respondents, interviewees, or experimental subjects will seriously threaten the validity of the findings as well as how much can be generalized. These problems affect quantitative and experimental studies as well as research projects that are qualitative in nature.

ETHICAL CONSIDERATIONS

Research with ethnic communities must be conducted within the constraints of ethical procedures for research with human populations. These, of course, include informed consent, freedom to discontinue participation, respect for an individual's privacy and confidentiality, and appropriate balance between risk and benefit. Nevertheless, research with ethnic populations also raises the need to consider special circumstances associated with projects that involve communities that generally have limited social, economic, or political power. These special concerns include the often-limited level of involvement of community members in planning and implementation of a research project and the potential for bias and ethnocentric interpretation of results. These issues are addressed briefly in the paragraphs that follow. Studying these concerns will sensitize you as future researchers or consumers of psychological research to the complexities involved in ethnic psychology research.

Informed Consent

Basic to research with human participants is the need to obtain **informed consent** for participation. The concept of informed consent implies that the participants are properly informed as to the purpose of the study, its procedures, its potential benefits and risks, the voluntary nature of their participation, and their ability to ask questions of the researchers. Often, participants are asked to sign a form that indicates that they understand the procedures, risks, and potential benefits, and that they acknowledge their ability to discontinue participation. Unfortunately, many informed consent forms are drafted in legalistic wording that is difficult to understand for the majority of the people and certainly by individuals with limited linguistic fluency or educational achievement. Having consent forms available in the respondents' preferred language (a requirement with most human subjects protection boards) is often not enough to guarantee comprehension and appropriateness of the forms or the procedures. The need for full disclosure in informed consent has been supported by national and international codes of behavior including the Helsinki agreements on participation of human subjects in biomedical research (Macklin, 2000). There are, of course, some situations where informed consent is difficult to obtain (e.g., when conducting large-scale observational studies such as the behavior of soccer fans in a stadium) and researchers are required to ensure that individual and personal information is protected.

As you read the results of psychological research with ethnic minority communities, you may want to pay attention to a number of issues that researchers should report in their books and articles such as (1) Was informed consent obtained? (2) Was the study properly described to participants? (3) Was the informed consent form or procedure written or conducted in the participants' own or preferred language? (4) Was the description of the project and the informed consent form written in a way that was understood by the participants? Failure to meet these goals on the part of the researchers may lead you to question the validity of the results of the study.

Freedom to Discontinue Participation

Research conducted with human beings must guarantee participants the **freedom to discontinue participation** in the research project whenever they wish. This assurance allows individuals to stop participation in a research project when they feel uncomfortable or feel that the project does not meet their expectations. A problem of course arises when participants feel they cannot or should not discontinue participation or when they are not aware of being part of a research project. This ethical difficulty often arises when there are social or cultural pressures that make it difficult for individuals to stop participation. For example, members of ethnic minority communities may feel that they "should" or "must" continue participation in a research project for reasons as varied as the fear of damaging the relationship between researcher and participant, or because of fear of retribution or concerns about insulting the researcher or the institution sponsoring the study, or because of fear of losing health or psychological or educational benefits that the study was providing. Also relevant here is the situation where research participants are provided a stipend to cover transportation costs or the time spent in the study and they may feel that a contractual relationship has been established that does not "really" allow them to stop participation.

While the situations mentioned above are not necessarily unique to ethnic minority participants in research projects, cultural expectancies and social conditions (such as poverty or welfare needs) may make it more difficult for ethnic minority research participants to stop their involvement with the project. It is quite possible, for example, that participants with limited financial resources may feel that they cannot afford to lose the promised stipend even when it is handed to the participants ahead of their participation in the project. Likewise, a mother may feel that she or her children can be "blacklisted" for medical care or educational programs at school if she or someone in her family refuses to participate in a research project. Refusal to become involved in a study can also be a reality in cultures where authority figures such as teachers, lawyers, physicians, or religious or community leaders are given special status and where community members are expected to comply with their wishes or ideas.

In analyzing research projects conducted with ethnic communities, you may want to question how free the participants were to stop participation. You may want to carefully read the report in order to find answers to questions such as (1) Was freedom to discontinue participation properly explained to the participants? (2) Were there financial pressures placed on respondents to continue participation (e.g., withholding payment or stipends until the end of the study)? (3) Was there a real or implied threat of withdrawal of services or benefits if the participants stopped participation in the project? (4) Were payments or stipends large enough to force a low-income individual to continue participation?

Respect for Privacy and Confidentiality

Most researchers, particularly those conducting qualitative research such as ethnographies and community interviews, spend a considerable amount of time and effort preserving the confidentiality of the research communities and participants by deleting identifying information from research protocols, assigning pseudonyms to participants, and using invented names for communities. Nevertheless, sometimes efforts at maintaining confidentiality are not sufficient to reduce discomfort among research participants. C. Allen (1997), for example, describes the reaction of shock and unhappiness when members of a small community in the Chesapeake Bay found out that the sociologist who had visited them and whom they had welcomed into their own homes was "using" them for her research. While the name of the community was disguised in the report of the study, it was not difficult for its members to find out that they were the community involved in the study, which included descriptions of some of its members in less than positive ways.

There are, of course, other situations that can potentially create problems in this area of the need to protect privacy. Large-scale studies that identify communities or members of ethnic groups as having certain characteristics run the risk of failing to protect required confidentiality of the findings. In these cases, specific communities can be improperly identified in research reports or press releases as "violent," or "drug ridden," "involving unwed mothers," or "abusive husbands." These large-scale characterizations perpetuate myths and improperly characterize communities and their members.

Another related problem is when vulnerable respondents are asked to provide information that they do not have and cannot provide or where disclosure of certain facts can bring embarrassment and distress to the respondents. A good example of this situation is when children at school are asked to provide information about their parents and grandparents without attention being given to the fact that, in many cases, they may not have the information being asked for or that that type of disclosure may bring embarrassment to the children. Such is the case when adopted or foster children are asked to report the culture or background of their unknown parents and grandparents. A similar situation occurs with children in single-parent or same-gender households when asked about behaviors by a particular member of what some consider a "typical" household where there is a married heterosexual couple who have children of their own. Having to report that there is no "Dad" at home or that the male head-of-household is an adoptive or stepfather can bring about embarrassment and distress. Likewise, children and adults may find it difficult and embarrassing to report personal information such as parental use of tobacco or alcoholic beverages, food preferences, time spent away from home, or even level of use of television or the Internet.

The issue here, of course, is that researchers should never assume that certain behaviors that are normative in their own culture also are in another group—a central principle of culturally appropriate research. Knowledge of the culture and the involvement of community researchers is a good procedure to avoid embarrassing questions based on religious, cultural, or traditional differences. A seemingly innocent question (e.g., "What did Santa bring you?" or "How often do you go to church?") can produce emotional discomfort to the participants where those beliefs or behaviors are not normative in their own culture or family.

As you review psychological literature with ethnic minority communities, you may want to ascertain how successful the researchers were at guaranteeing and maintaining the confidentiality of the findings and the respondents' privacy. You may want to analyze the following: (1) Is the community where the research was conducted improperly identified? (2) Were participants asked to report on information they did not readily have or that brought personal embarrassment? (3) Were questions asked about values or behaviors that were foreign or not normative to a given group? (4) Did the research report provide enough detail about individuals to enable community members to identify the respondents? Unsatisfactory answers to these questions should lead you to question the validity of the research findings since the researchers did not properly guarantee the confidentiality of the research process.

Appropriate Balance Between Risks or Costs and Benefits

Ethical research procedures require that a proper balance be reached in terms of the costs incurred by the participants and the risks associated with participation in comparison to the benefits that they or the community will receive. Costs to the individual include time spent in participating, lost wages, physical or psychological effort, embarrassment suffered when disclosing attitudes or behaviors, threats to health or well-being implied in the research procedures, as well as other relevant considerations.

The argument has been made that the **cost** or **risk/benefit balance** has not been present in numerous research projects with ethnic minority populations. For example, some ethnic community members perceive social science research as a form of exploitation in which individuals from the dominant culture reap the benefits of the data collection effort through publications, presentations, grants, and awards (Blauner & Wellman, 1973; Hirsch, 1973). These gains are often obtained at the expense (time, effort, stigmatization, significant disclosure demands) of members of ethnic communities who are improperly rewarded, or who feel obligated to participate by high-pressure recruitment techniques including large payments for participation.

Furthermore, in many cases, members of ethnic communities never see the results of the study since reports are usually not presented to the community or benefits in improved health or education are seldom or never made available to the community studied. This situation has led some individuals to advocate that only minority scientists should have access to minority communities (Baca Zinn, 1979; Moore, 1973; Wilson, 1974) so that at least one or a few members of the group reap some benefits from the research process.

Particularly problematic are situations where the cost/benefit ratio involves significant levels of deception of the participants or when the study involves the use of placebos or the withholding of medical treatment.

Wheeler (1997), for example, reports on 15 studies of HIV-infected women in Africa, Thailand, and the Dominican Republic who were being provided placebos instead of appropriate medication. Obviously, this type of research presents serious ethical concerns when individuals are being prevented from receiving life-saving treatment in order to have a "better" or more controlled research project that includes the use of placebos or control conditions that require withholding of treatment.

A notorious example of improper risk/benefit balance is the study of the progression of syphilis conducted among African American men in Tuskegee, Alabama, without their knowledge of the effects of their involvement in the study (Gray, 1998) (see Box 3.5). In that research project, African American patients were purposely not given the proper treatment to alleviate syphilis in order to study the natural progression of the illness. Although an effective treatment for syphilis was available at the time, this group of men was deprived of the treatment by officials from the U.S. Public Health Service. In a book describing the project, Fred Gray (1998) summarizes the study as follows: "The government used 623 men as human guinea pigs in a misguided forty-year medical experiment. That in itself would have been bad enough. The moral and ethical injury was compounded by the fact that all of these men were African American, predominantly poor and uneducated, and were deliberately kept in the dark about what was happening to them" (p. 14). That lack of sensitivity and respect for these individuals still affects the credibility of biobehavioral and medical research among certain ethnic groups (Shavers-Hornaday et al., 1997).

BOX 3.5

The Tuskegee Syphilis Study

In 1932, officials from the U.S. Public Health Service designed a study to analyze the effects of untreated syphilis, a sexually transmitted disease that can ultimately cause death. A total of 623 African American men from Macon County, Alabama, were involved in the study that became known as the "Tuskegee Syphilis Study." Approximately half of the men who participated in the study had been diagnosed as having untreated syphilis and the other half served as a control group. During the study, the men were given physical exams, vitamins, and some free meals. Some syphilitics were told (without explanation) that they had "bad blood" while others were told nothing. The men were not told they were part of a study and they never gave consent to participate in a research project. Researchers followed the men through free physical exams and autopsies on those who had died in order to measure the progression of the illness. While penicillin was available during the period of the study, none of the men with syphilis was offered or given that life-saving treatment.

(Continued)

(Continued)

In 1972 (40 years after the beginning of the study), the media disclosed the existence of the research project and the men who were still alive learned, many for the first time, of what had happened to them. In 1973, a lawsuit was filed on behalf of the Tuskegee men for violations of the U.S. and Alabama constitutions, civil rights law, and the federal common law. The study was officially terminated by the Centers for Disease Control in 1972. It was not until 1997, however, that President Clinton addressed survivors and relatives of the study by saying, "The United States government did something that was wrong—deeply, profoundly, morally wrong. It was an outrage to our commitment to integrity and equality for all our citizens.... The American people are sorry—for the loss, for the years of hurt" (Gray, 1998, p. 13).

The conditions under which this study was conducted showed complete disregard for the human rights of the research participants. Not surprisingly, this study as well as others conducted with minority populations or prisoners or individuals in developing countries, led to distrust of much biomedical research on the part of many ethnic minority communities.

In any study with ethnic communities, efforts must be made to properly balance the ratio of cost and benefits to the members of the community as compared to those of the researchers and of the scientific community in general. Part of that cost/benefit ratio is the level of stigmatization that participation in a study may bring to the respondents (e.g., for visiting a mobile health unit or clinic, being identified as an individual with a psychological or addictive problem, being removed from a classroom for "special" activities, or receiving visits at home from people from the local university). Also relevant is the personal and psychological cost incurred by members of ethnic communities where displacement to a research site may involve more costs than the transport fare and may include changes in work schedule and difficulties with child care or the care of ailing adults.

As you review reports of research projects with ethnic minority communities, you will want to ascertain if the project properly balanced the costs and risks incurred by the participants with the benefits that they or their community received. Consider questions such as (1) Were the participants properly informed of the costs or risks they would face for their participation in the study? (2) Were the costs or risks necessary and unavoidable? (3) Did the participants benefit from the project? (4) Was the community or humanity at large a beneficiary of the project? (5) Was there an alternate less costly or risky procedure available to find answers to the research questions?

Potential for Bias in Interpretation

Another important ethical concern when conducting research with ethnic communities is the approach taken by the researchers in analyzing and interpreting the results of the study. It is essential that the interpretation of research findings take into consideration the historical, social, and political conditions of the community where the study was conducted (Chun et al., 2008; Marín & VanOss Marín, 1991). As was mentioned at the beginning of the chapter, there is a need to contextualize not only the design of the project but also the analysis of the results.

Avoiding inappropriate and discriminatory interpretations of research findings is of particular importance in research with ethnic minority communities. In many cases, it is easy for researchers to assume that the results of the study can be explained in terms of the ethnicity of the respondents when in reality they can be more properly explained in terms of certain social conditions shared by the participants. For example, high arrest indices among ethnic minority youth cannot be interpreted to mean greater aggressiveness and higher patterns of violation of the law since racial profiling and differential arrest patterns are quite common in many ethnic minority communities in the United States. Likewise, ethnicity should not be assumed to be the best explanation for poor performance in school by children who have been underserved and poorly trained in primary or secondary school. Unfortunately, much research is available that explains differences in behavior or attitudes in terms of ethnicity without considering social and structural characteristics that may be responsible for the conditions being investigated. Poverty, discrimination, low education levels, unemployment or underemployment, poor health or limited access to health care, segregation, limited linguistic fluency, and poor housing conditions are some of the many variables and social conditions that may properly explain the findings of research projects as alternatives to ethnicity or ethnic group membership.

As you read ethnic minority research you will want to analyze if the results of the study were interpreted in a biased way. You will want to find answers to questions such as (1) Were all alternative explanations investigated or mentioned? (2) What makes ethnicity or membership in an ethnic group the best possible explanation for the research findings? (3) Were members of the community involved in interpreting the results?

Chapter Summary

This chapter has addressed a number of concerns related to conducting research with ethnic populations in order to produce valid and reliable findings while guaranteeing and respecting the personal and emotional integrity of the participants. We have argued for the need to develop culturally appropriate research that respects the culture of the research participants and that includes methods and analyses that are sensitive to a culture's characteristics. Developing culturally appropriate research is a complex and time-consuming activity. It goes beyond the proper translation and adaptation of questions, tests, and questionnaires. Culturally appropriate methodologies include such additional steps as using culturally relevant theories, developing and testing culturally appropriate hypotheses, properly disaggregating the participants, and implementing appropriate interpretation of results. In analyzing the research findings, it becomes essential to consider a number of contextual variables that may moderate the significance and direction of the results. Researchers and analysts must be willing to explore alternative explanations to their findings that go beyond simply assigning causality to ethnic group membership. The possible influence of factors such as poverty, discrimination, segregation, limited academic preparation, migration history, and other such factors must be considered as being relevant to the phenomenon being studied before explaining it as due to cultural or ethnic differences.

Key Terms

Learning by Doing

- Review a recent research article in a psychology journal that includes members of at least one ethnic group. Summarize how well the researchers identified the participants (e.g., ethnic group and subgroup membership, gender, educational level, socioeconomic status, generational history, acculturation level). For each of the variables that the researchers failed to use in disaggregating the participants, indicate how the results or the findings may have been different.
- Interview members of your family or your friend's family and build a generation history tree where you place the respondent at the bottom of the "generational tree" and then identify the "tree branches" based on the national origin of each individual. In this sense, identify where the respondent's parents or guardians, grandparents, and great-grandparents were born. Then indicate the generation of each level of the tree (e.g., first generation, second generation) and the ethnic labels used by each generation.

Suggested Further Readings

Dunbar, G. (2005). *Evaluating research methods in psychology: A case study approach.* New York: Wiley-Blackwell.

This book presents an overview of classic and contemporary research in psychology from different fields and varying theoretical perspectives. The book encourages readers to question the choices made by researchers and to analyze the appropriateness of the methodological components of studies as well as the interpretation of results.

Jason, L. A., Keys, C. B., Suarez-Balcazar, Y., Taylor, R. R., & Davis, M. I. (2003). *Participatory community research: Theories and methods in action.* Washington, DC: American Psychological Association.

A comprehensive analysis of participatory community research by some of the pioneers in the field. Their experience conducting this type of research permeates the book's content and serves as a guide to those interested in not only reading but also conducting participatory community research.

Marín, G., & VanOss Marín, B. (1991). *Research with Hispanic populations.* Newbury Park, CA: Sage.

A practical and easy-to-read book on the difficulties of conducting culturally appropriate research with Latinos. The contents of the book are also relevant to research with other ethnic minority groups. The book serves as important background for those researching ethnic minority groups as well as for those reading the research reports.

Ratner, C. (1997). *Cultural psychology and qualitative methodology.* New York: Plenum.

A classic book exploring the intersection of culture and research within the perspectives of qualitative methodologies. The book explores culture from different perspectives and using different theoretical backgrounds.

Smith, J. A. (2008). *Qualitative psychology: A practical guide.* Thousand Oaks, CA: Sage.

An excellent source of practical information for students and researchers interested in understanding or conducting qualitative research.

Stanfield, J. H., II, & Dennis, R. M. (Eds.). (1993). *Race and ethnicity in research methods.* Newbury Park, CA: Sage.

A classic book introducing the concerns social science researchers (primarily sociologists and anthropologists) need to address when studying ethnic minority individuals. The authors' recommendations continue to be useful despite the passing of time since the book was first published.

Suzuki, L. A., Ponterotto, J. G., & Meller, P. J. (Eds.). (2001). *Handbook of multicultural assessment.* San Francisco: Jossey-Bass.

An all-inclusive overview of issues related to the psychological assessment of ethnic minority individuals and communities. Of particular importance in understanding issues related to measures of basic psychological processes as well as abnormal behavior.

CHAPTER 4

ACCULTURATION

VIGNETTE

"Call me 'Jessie,' not 'Josefina!'"

Josefina was born in Chicago's heavily Latino Little Pilsen neighborhood. Carlos and Maria, her parents, left Puerto Rico in their early 20s and met in Chicago while working at a factory. Carlos and Maria miss the island and their relatives and Puerto Rican food. Fortunately, Little Pilsen had a good number of markets that sold all the food staples that Carlos and Maria missed including plantains

(Continued)

(Continued)

and gandules. Carlos often expresses concern for how his kids are not as respectful and courteous as he had been as a teen and blames the American culture for having spoiled his children. He always speaks in Spanish to them and he is often accused by the children of being old-fashioned. Maria speaks English more fluently than her husband and feels perfectly comfortable among her White friends as well as among her Latino neighbors. Josefina is fully bilingual, having learned Spanish at home and English while attending school. She is as comfortable eating rice with gandules as a hamburger at the fast food outlet. She loves rock and rap music and is quite at ease dancing salsa. Her best friends during high school included a non-Latino White boy (to whom she was "Jessie") and two Latinas (one from Puerto Rico and the other a Mexican American). As a junior in high school, Josefina met Robert, a White teen who shared many of Josefina's interests in the arts and in music. Robert often walked Josefina home from school and at times they would listen to music in the living room within view of the kitchen where Maria prepared the evening meal. In April, Robert asked Josefina to the junior prom. She ran home and yelled at the door: "Mami, guess what? Robert asked me to the prom." From the back of the apartment, Carlos shouted back, "Tienes que llevar un chaperón [You have to bring a chaperone]." "I'll die if you force me to do that. Nobody brings chaperones, this is the United States. Papi, olvídate de Puerto Rico, *[Dad, forget Puerto Rico]" retorted Josefina. The discussions lasted many days, and in the end, Josefina did not go to the junior prom because her father never gave up on the idea of a chaperone. Josefina's senior year in high school was a stressful one for the Martinez family. Josefina was intent on getting good grades and a good SAT score that would allow her to get a scholarship to one of the private Catholic universities in the North Shore of Chicago (close enough to the family home but yet far enough to justify staying in the residence halls). She insisted on being addressed as Jessie rather than Josefina and would only speak English at home. She often smoked a cigarette before and after school and spent long hours on the phone speaking in English to all her friends. When the time came for the senior prom, Carlos again insisted that a chaperone was required but relented after talking with his neighbors who assured him that in the United States it was appropriate for a girl to go to a dance without a chaperone.*

Acculturation is, arguably, one of the most frequently mentioned constructs or concepts in ethnic psychology. Indeed, researchers often include some measure of acculturation in their research to analyze differences within ethnic groups and to understand the relationship of acculturation to psychosocial adjustment and health. It is not unusual therefore to read in the psychological literature how acculturation is related to a person's level of adaptability to new social situations or to depression, cigarette smoking, or alcohol use. Likewise, acculturation has been associated with phenomena as varied as intergenerational family conflict, academic performance, and utilization of mental health services. This chapter examines acculturation and the related construct of biculturalism, their definitions as well as issues related to their measurement and their effects on people's lives.

Despite growing attention to acculturation in the psychological literature, the life of this construct or concept has experienced a history of benign neglect. Since the beginnings of the 20th century, a select group of social scientists, primarily anthropologists and sociologists, has been advocating for more studies of acculturation. These early social scientists initially defined **acculturation** as a process of change that occurs when individuals from different cultures interact and share a common geographical space following migration, political conquest, or forced relocation.

Acculturation has such theoretical and practical significance in ethnic psychology that much of the rest of this book will refer to its influence in the same fashion as culture and ethnicity. Indeed, much of the behavior of Carlos, Maria, and Josefina as described in the story that begins this chapter reflects differences in their levels of acculturation. As is often found among first generation individuals who show low levels of acculturation, Carlos struggles to maintain not only the language of his country of origin, but also its cultural practices and values. Maria, on the other hand, also a first generation individual, has learned English, has a number of friends who are not Latinos, and feels comfortable interacting with people of diverse ethnic backgrounds. Josefina, as a more acculturated second generation Latina, often finds herself in conflict with the traditional practices of her parents' country of origin. While bilingual, she prefers to speak in English; she changes her name to "Jessie," and considers some practices that were normative in Puerto Rico to be old-fashioned although she enjoys its food, music, and other cultural expressions.

Much of the early research on acculturation suffered severe conceptual limitations including a simplistic assumption that acculturation inevitably leads to a weakening of one's original cultural identity and practices. This assumption reflects a **unidirectional model of acculturation** in which culture change is thought to occur in one direction—people *move away* from their culture of origin and *toward* the dominant group during resettlement in a new country. This unidirectional model of acculturation, which is discussed in greater detail below, was predominant in the United States at the beginning of the 20th century and reflected such ideas as the "melting pot" paradigm where newcomers were expected to mimic as much as possible the members of the "host" or dominant group.

This assumption about the unidirectionality of the acculturation process has been criticized by a number of researchers (see Chun, Balls Organista, & Marín, 2003) who prefer to think of acculturation as a more complex phenomenon that considers at least two cultural dimensions where, like

Josefina, an individual may retain some aspects of the culture of origin and also learn and favor aspects of the new culture. This more complex understanding of acculturation is often perceived as promoting a society characterized by individuals who are comfortable in various cultural settings, producing what is often termed a "cultural mosaic" rather than a melting pot soup. Before analyzing these differences in the way acculturation has been conceptualized, it is important to better define the term.

DEFINING ACCULTURATION

In the simplest terms, acculturation can be defined as a culture learning process experienced by individuals who are exposed to a new culture or ethnic group. While this process can occur among tourists and individuals who travel briefly abroad, in this chapter we are concerned primarily with acculturation as experienced by individuals who are exposed and learn a new culture over lengthier periods of time.

As such, we are interested in studying individuals who experience a new culture due to permanent or long-term resettlement and relocation. For example, when a large part of the southwestern United States was ceded by Mexico after the U.S.-Mexico war in the 1840s, the Mexicans who resided in what is now Texas, Arizona, New Mexico, Nevada, Utah, and California were exposed to the European American culture of the eastern United States. Consequently, the Mexicans had to undergo an imposed process of culture learning. The European American newcomers also had to undergo a process of acculturation to the Mexican and Spanish culture of the residents in the area. At a fairly superficial level, we could argue that this process of culture learning forced the original residents (the Mexicans) to learn to speak English and eat hot dogs while the newly arrived (eastern U.S. citizens) learned some Spanish and began to appreciate tacos and tortillas. As psychologists, we are interested in understanding the extent of these changes in behavior as well as trying to determine how exposure to one culture affects the values, attitudes, and psychological well-being of the new and old residents of a given area.

The process of acculturation is not limited to individuals who are forced to change their nationality because of political events such as the ones described above. Immigrants and short-term "foreign workers" or "guest workers" also experience the acculturation process as they change their residence and are exposed to a new culture. Forced relocation and enslavement, as happened with Africans to the United States and to other countries in the Americas, also produce the process of culture learning that we call acculturation. Also important to remember is the fact that the receiving or "host" ethnic or cultural group undergoes the process of acculturation as its members are exposed to new ways of thinking and acting. In that fashion, we can talk about acculturation promoting the development of bicultural individuals in nations or cultures where two or more cultures come in contact with each other and where their residents learn the attitudes, values, behavior, and other cultural aspects of the ethnic groups with whom they interact. Multicultural societies like the United States that have been created by the contributions of immigrants from many places are enriched by the presence of multiple cultures where diverse groups share their beliefs, values, attitudes, and ways of behaving.

Also important is the fact that the process of acculturation can be a long-term phenomenon affecting various generations. Indeed, acculturation is not limited to immigrants but it also takes place among their children and grandchildren. In fact, individuals are changing and learning new values, attitudes, and behaviors whenever two or more cultures come in contact with each other.

Before delving more deeply into the meaning of acculturation and its implications in psychological research, it is important to mention that other social scientists often use different terms to refer to what we call acculturation. It is not uncommon, for example, to read sociological and anthropological literature that uses terms such as "incorporation" or "assimilation" to refer to concepts fairly similar to what psychologists address as "acculturation." Indeed, much contemporary research in sociology and anthropology uses words such as **"cultural assimilation"** and "cultural integration" to define the acculturation process. This variability in terminology lends itself to confusion not only based on the possible differing meanings but also because there is a difference in emphasis. By using terms such as "incorporation" and "assimilation," sociologists and anthropologists tend to emphasize the characteristics of the larger groups such as when studies address the characteristics of an ethnic group that facilitate or promote its "civic incorporation" by becoming citizens, voting, participating in town hall meetings, and so on. Psychologists, on the other hand, tend to emphasize the more personal characteristics of the process demonstrated through changes in personal values or beliefs or behavior generally analyzed from a more individualized perspective.

Unfortunately, these variations in terminology and emphasis have undermined the advancement of the field and of our understanding of the acculturation process when there is little cross-fertilization between fields. While most of the literature cited in this chapter comes from psychologists, we have endeavored to include relevant works by sociologists and anthropologists since their perspectives enrich our understanding of what is a very complicated human activity.

Early Definitions

One of the earliest and most useful definitions of acculturation emphasized direct contact across ethnic groups and the fact that both groups would undergo changes:

Acculturation comprehends those phenomena which result when groups of individuals having different cultures come into continuous first-hand contact, with subsequent changes in the original culture patterns of either or both groups. (Redfield, Linton, & Herskovits, 1936, p. 149)

A subsequent definition proposed the idea that there could be multiple causes for acculturation and that its effects could be not only varied but also observed and measured over varying amounts of time:

[Acculturation is] culture change that is initiated by the conjunction of two or more autonomous cultural systems. Acculturative change may be the consequence of direct cultural transmission; it may be derived from non-cultural causes, such as ecological or demographic modification induced by an impinging culture; it may be delayed, as with internal adjustments following upon the acceptance of alien traits or patterns; or it may be a reactive adaptation of transitional modes of life. (Social Science Research Council, 1954, p. 974)

In his influential analysis of assimilation in the United States, the sociologist Milton Gordon (1964) suggested that acculturation needed to be differentiated from **structural assimilation** whereby the latter is defined as the incorporation of members of ethnic groups into primary relationships (e.g., social clubs, marriage) with individuals from the majority group. At the same time, Gordon defined acculturation as the adoption of the cultural norms and behavioral patterns of the majority group (often called the "core culture"), a process he considered as an essential component of the experiences of ethnic groups. Gordon's definition of acculturation influenced social science literature for many decades and determined our understanding of acculturation as those changes occurring in the immigrant group as it tries to emulate or imitate the majority group. Gordon also suggested that the changes implied in the acculturation process were more rapid among external traits (such as clothing, language, outward expression of emotions) while the more intrinsic personal characteristics (such as values, norms, or religious beliefs) would take longer to change if at all.

More recently, the sociologist Herbert Gans (1999) has defined acculturation as "the newcomers' adoption of the culture, that is, the behavior patterns or practices, values, rules, symbols, and so forth, of the host society (or rather an overly homogenized and reified conception of it)" (p. 162). This definition is significant because it moves closer to a psychosocial understanding of the concept and it acknowledges that a group's culture is an abstraction that is considered as something concrete (what he calls a "reified conception"). At the same time, Gans defines **assimilation** as an interactive process (that may not require changes in the person's values or beliefs as acculturation does) and that can best be characterized by behaviors where "the newcomers move out of formal and informal ethnic associations and other social institutions and into the host society's non-ethnic ones" (p. 162). Gans suggests that this distinction allows for the assimilation and acculturation processes to proceed at different speeds. This perspective is particularly important because it reflects the realities of assimilation being driven externally by social stratification or socioeconomic class as well as by prejudice and discrimination that may speed or slow down the ethnic group's assimilation (or incorporation as some other researchers would call it) into the social and civic fabric of the majority group or of the receiving country. It is important to remember that these processes are not unique to immigrants but that their children and grandchildren also may experience them.

In this book, we define **acculturation** as

a dynamic and multidimensional process of adaptation that occurs when distinct cultures come into sustained contact. It involves different degrees and instances of culture learning and maintenance that are contingent upon individual, group, and environmental factors. Acculturation is dynamic because it is a continuous and fluctuating process and it is multidimensional because it transpires across numerous indices of psychosocial functioning and can result in multiple adaptation outcomes.

This definition reflects our current understanding of acculturation as a continuous and dynamic process that takes place in different aspects of a person's life (what we call "multidimensional") and that is affected by the personal and social experiences of the individuals undergoing acculturation.

In general, researchers have emphasized the acculturational experiences of individuals who migrate or whose families migrated in the recent past. These studies have analyzed how individuals learn a new culture and its related attitudes, values, and behaviors. Unfortunately, little attention has been given to the changes that these groups produce in the "host" or receiving society. As can be seen in most of the definitions of acculturation reviewed above, there is the assumption that immigrants and their descendants learn about the new culture but little is said about the fact that the new culture is in turn modified by their presence. Likewise, little attention has been given to the acculturation process of the children and grandchildren of immigrants who also are exposed to this multidimensional process of personal development.

ACCULTURATION, ASSIMILATION, AND SEGMENTED ASSIMILATION

Countries such as the United States that saw significant migratory waves during the 19th and early 20th centuries experienced calls from politicians and social scientists who supported the goal of trying to create a common culture made up of many—a concept enshrined in its national ethos as *E Pluribus Unum* [Out of Many, One]. This push toward assimilation generally implied that immigrants would need to subdue or reject those values, attitudes, and behaviors that had characterized their cultures of origin as they learned and internalized the cultural characteristics perceived to define White Anglo-Saxon Protestants. At the same time that a variety of social forces and institutions (e.g., schools, churches) were pushing for cultural and behavioral assimilation, various early migrant groups established strong communities (e.g., Little Italy, Chinatown) that reinforced their ties to the culture of origin while supporting a process of biculturalism that would allow them to work effectively in both cultural communities.

In many cases, assimilation in the early 19th and 20th centuries was also promoted through indirect methods such as what the sociologist Alejandro Portes (1999) calls "symbolic violence," which is exemplified by immigrants in Ellis Island and in Angel Island being forced to assume anglicized names whenever immigration officers did not know or care to properly spell the names of members of minority groups. For example, Portes reports how a German Jew experiencing stressful reactions to the questioning of immigration officers said, *"Schoyn vergessen"* (Yiddish for "I forget") and was thereafter known as "Sean Ferguson."

It should be noted that acculturation is not a phenomenon unique to the United States or to countries that have experienced significant migratory waves. Many nations around the world include a variety of ethnic or cultural groups within their boundaries that have shared a given geographical space for centuries as in the case of Spain where Basques, Catalans, Galicians, and other cultural groups have shared parts of the Iberian Peninsula. The current phenomenon of **globalization** also can be seen as promoting some type of acculturation around the world by facilitating personal mobility across borders and the sharing of cultures and values through music, electronic and print media, and education. For example, the values reflected in songs by American rappers, Icelandic singer Bjork, or the Irish group U2 are heard throughout the world in the same way that the British magazine *The Economist* or *Newsweek* can be found in magazine kiosks almost everywhere.

The contributions of ethnic psychology researchers have produced an evaluation of the usefulness of the construct of assimilation. Indeed, Alba and Nee (1999) noted that "assimilation has come to be viewed by social scientists as a worn-out theory that imposes ethnocentric and patronizing demands on minority peoples struggling to retain their cultural and ethnic integrity" (p. 137). While Alba and Nee argue that assimilation as a construct in the social sciences is still useful, the term has been misused to imply the assumed inevitable outcome of absorption of minorities into a more homogeneous or common culture. In this sense, assimilation is a problematic term.

As a matter of fact, the anthropologist Nancy Foner (1999) has argued that the traditional concept of assimilation is an inaccurate description of the lives of immigrants and of those undergoing processes of culture learning. Foner proposes that assimilation is too simplistic a concept to analyze people's lives in this country since there is "no undifferentiated, monolithic 'American' culture" (p. 260). This criticism of traditional assimilationist thinking in the social sciences has given birth to the new construct of "segmented assimilation," which more appropriately defines the changes in social behavior that take place as people acculturate (Portes, 1999).

Segmented assimilation is defined by Foner (1999) as a process of assimilation into a particular social segment ranging from the middle to the lower classes. Indeed, sociologists (Rumbaut & Portes, 2001; M. Zhou, 1999) argue that the path taken in segmented assimilation depends on factors such as varying economic opportunity and other structural constraints, the pervasiveness of racial discrimination, as well as the segment of American society to which the immigrants are exposed more frequently. In that sense, Rumbaut and Portes suggest that

> one path may follow the so-called straight line theory . . . of assimilation into the middle-class majority; an opposite type of adaptation may lead to downward mobility and assimilation into the inner-city underclass; yet another may combine upward mobility and heightened ethnic aware-ness within solidaristic immigrant enclaves. (p. 188)

Foner (1999) further argues that the process of segmented assimilation does not necessarily imply the complete internalization of the new values and behaviors. In this sense, we could expect behavioral changes that reflect or resemble those of members of the majority (segmented assimilation) although the individual may not have completely internalized their values or attitudes (acculturation). This is indeed an important differentiation in terms and in processes that helps to better understand the changes that immigrants and those of later generations undergo as they learn new cultures. The end result of these two processes is that the cultures of immigrant minority ethnic groups can very well differ from those of the dominant culture as well as from the culture of origin. We could then witness a process of the creation of what practically could be considered a new ethnicity (a hyphenated ethnicity such as "Filipino-Americans" or "Mexican-Americans") that benefits from multiple perspectives and cultures. Foner quotes the groundbreaking works of William Thomas and Florian Znaniecki (1918) on Polish Americans at the beginning of the 20th century when they conclude that there has been the "creation of a society in which structure and prevalent attitudes is neither Polish nor American but constitutes a specific new product whose raw materials have been partly drawn from Polish traditions, partly from the new conditions in which the immigrants live, and partly from American social values as the immigrant sees and interprets them" (p. 108).

MODELS OF ACCULTURATION

The fact that acculturation has been of interest to a variety of social scientists including anthropologists, sociologists, and psychologists is reflected in the different models and definitions of the term as seen above as well as in the type of acculturation effects that are studied as reviewed in this section of the chapter.

Ethnogenesis

Within a more macrosocial perspective, sociologists and anthropologists generally have argued for the study of how acculturation allows individuals to not just learn the new culture but also integrate themselves into different "subcultures" of the majority group based on factors as complex as social class and experiences of discrimination and privilege. This process, called **ethnogenesis,** can be expected to produce a mixed set of values and behaviors that characterize the specific ethnic group and that are somewhat different from those of the original culture or of those of the dominant group.

Ethnogenesis produces changes in certain values and attitudes and their related behaviors that affect not only clothing styles, musical preferences, or speech patterns but also religious beliefs and basic cultural values. For example, Foner (1999) describes how Jamaican immigrants to the United

States change their gender role expectations of men by making them more responsible for home duties without giving up the perception of the home as the woman's domain. Other studies have shown changes among Vietnamese Americans in the definition of kinship (i.e., who is considered a relative) and the perception of who belongs to the extended family (Kibria, 1993), or differentiations in the meaning of basic cultural values such as familialism among Latinos (Sabogal et al., 1987).

Returning to our story at the beginning of the chapter, we could very well expect that the experiences of Latinos in Chicago's Little Pilsen where Latinos with heritage roots in Puerto Rico and Mexico interact with immigrants from Central and South America as well as with African Americans have created a mixed culture for each of those groups. We could hypothesize that the Puerto Rican American "culture" in which Josefina was raised was a combination of traditional Puerto Rican attitudes and values (such as the need for chaperones), together with the cultural characteristics of the groups that shared the neighborhood or the larger Chicago metropolitan area (which may not adhere to the usefulness of chaperones), as well as a Puerto Rican American component that may have evolved over the years as more second and third generation individuals inhabit the area. Examples of popular culture manifestations of this ethnogenesis can be seen in bilingual rock and rap music or the recent emergence of music mixing reggae and rap rhythms and sung in mixtures of English and Spanish such as can be found in the music of Orishas, who mixes Cuban and Caribbean rhythms with rap, or other popular contemporary artists such as Gwen Stefani.

Emphasis on the Individual

For over three decades, the Canadian psychologist John Berry (2003) has advocated a comprehensive framework for understanding the process and changes implied in the acculturation process as they affect the individual. While Berry's model is not the only one available in the literature that explains the effects of acculturation on the individual, it is very useful in understanding the varieties of possible responses to exposure to new cultures.

Berry (2003) suggests that as a result of exposure to two or more cultures, an individual experiences at least two types of changes. At one level are behavioral shifts that affect the way the individual acts in areas as diverse as speech patterns, eating habits, clothing styles, or even self-identity. A second level covers acculturative stress that includes emotional reactions on the part of the individual that can include anxiety and depression (Berry, 1980; Sam & Berry, 2006). A later section in this chapter explores acculturative stress in greater detail but at this point it is important to consider that acculturative stress is related to factors as varied as the need to learn new behaviors, beliefs, and attitudes and the realization of how different or even incompatible two cultures can be. For example, an immigrant from India may, after residing for a while in the United States, start wearing saris less frequently and to self-identify as an "Asian American" rather than as "Indian." At the same time, these acculturative experiences may produce personal and interpersonal conflicts regarding deeply ingrained cultural practices or values (e.g., arranged marriages or vegetarian diets) that may in turn promote feelings of anxiety or even psychological depression.

One of Berry's most important contributions to the study of acculturation has been his insistence on the need to consider the multiple types of responses that an individual can have to acculturation. While initially Berry (1980) talked about "varieties of acculturation," the term he currently prefers is "acculturation strategies" or "acculturation modes" (Berry, 2003). An individual's choice of a strategy depends on such previous circumstances as the person's level of involvement with each culture as well as specific attitudinal and behavioral preferences and characteristics. The choice of a particular **acculturative strategy** would reflect the attitudes or orientation that an individual assumes toward the culture of origin (or "heritage culture") and toward the other group or groups. This model therefore requires considering two dimensions. One reflects the individual's positive or negative attitude toward maintenance of the heritage culture and identity. The second dimension (also from a negative to positive continuum) classifies the individual in terms of the preferred level and type of interaction with another group or groups.

For Berry (2003), an individual's acculturation can therefore be described as approaching one of four different strategies (see Table 4.1) that are the product of the interaction of the dimensions mentioned above:

1. *Assimilation*. When an individual wishes to diminish or decrease the significance of the culture of origin and desires to identify and interact primarily with the other culture, typically with the dominant culture if one comes from an ethnic minority group.

2. *Separation*. Whenever the individual wishes to hold on to the original culture and avoids interacting or learning about the other culture(s).

3. *Marginalization*. Individuals show little involvement in maintaining the culture of origin or in learning about the other culture(s).

4. *Integration*. When a person shows an interest in maintaining the original culture and in learning and participating in the other culture(s).

Table 4.1 Acculturation Strategies Based on Attitudes Toward Learning a New
Culture and Keeping the Heritage Culture

		Attitude Toward Keeping Heritage Culture and Identity	
		Positive	**Negative**
Attitude Toward Learning and Interacting With New Culture	**Positive**	Integration	Assimilation
	Negative	Separation	Marginalization

SOURCE: Based on Berry (2003).

In general, the fewest behavioral and attitudinal changes on the part of
the individual can be found among individuals who have chosen the
separation strategy and the largest number among those using the
assimilation strategy (Berry, 2003). *Integration,* and to some extent
marginalization, implies a selective process of maintenance and rejection
that involves a moderate level of behavioral changes. In terms of acculturative stress, Berry (2003) suggests that integration implies the lowest
levels of stress while marginalization would be associated with the highest
levels of stress. By choosing an integration strategy, acculturating
individuals can be expected to experience lower levels of personal stress
since they are able to acquire the cultural characteristics of the new culture
(as expected by members of the new culture or group) while continuing to
value the culture of heritage (as possibly expected by parents, siblings, and
friends). At the same time, assimilation and separation strategies would be
associated with moderate levels of stress since they imply a selection
process that may not be supported or appreciated by the individual's
relatives or friends.

As can be seen from the above description of Berry's (2003) strategies
for acculturation, marginalization can result in serious psychological
problems for individuals resorting to or being forced to assume such a
strategy. As a matter of fact, Berry suggests that marginalization is likely to
be the result of failed attempts at assimilation combined with experiences
of discrimination. Furthermore, Berry argues that individuals can choose
integration as an acculturation strategy primarily in societies that have
open and inclusive orientations toward ethnic and cultural diversity
indicated by the value placed on multiculturalism, relatively low levels of
ethnic prejudice and discrimination, absence of intergroup hatred, and a
generalized sense of identification with the culture of the larger society

(Berry, 2003). The actual level of choice of an acculturation strategy that individuals experience (e.g., if it is imposed or if it is freely chosen) can also affect the level of stress associated with the acculturation process. For example, separation as a strategy can be less stressful if it is chosen rather than forced on individuals, as could be the case in examples of group segregation.

The members of the Martinez family as described at the beginning of the chapter can be considered to exhibit at least three of Berry's acculturation strategies. Carlos, through his emphasis on maintaining the Puerto Rican culture in his life and in his family, could be considered to have primarily adopted a separation strategy. His wife's behavior could be an example of an integration strategy, given her emphasis on enacting behaviors and espousing attitudes and values that are more closely related to the dominant U.S. culture. Their daughter Jessie could be considered as an example of an assimilation strategy, particularly during her senior year where she chose to separate herself as much as possible from the Puerto Rican heritage of her family.

In general, Berry's model of acculturation has been found useful in a variety of settings (see, e.g., Sam & Berry, 2006). While measuring the four strategies is at times difficult, the Bidimensional Acculturation Scale for Hispanics or BAS (Marín & Gamba, 1996) produces scores that can be easily related to Berry's four acculturational strategies. Studies with Korean Americans (S.-K. Lee, Sobal, & Frongillo, 2003) and with Vietnamese Americans (Pham & Harris, 2001) have found that the model was applicable to describing the acculturational experiences of the groups being studied.

Nevertheless, some authors (Del Pilar & Udasco, 2004) have questioned the practical possibility of marginalization where individuals show little interest in maintaining the culture of origin or learning a new culture. These authors argue that even in cases of colonization and discrimination, individuals reframe or reformulate their culture of origin rather than losing the culture and being left "cultureless." Another possible limitation to Berry's model is its applicability to individuals who belong to more than two ethnicities or cultures. While the model does not intrinsically ignore persons who have more than two ethnic heritages, it is much more difficult to apply in those conditions. For example, a child born of Chinese and Latino parents can choose an integration strategy into the dominant White culture while maintaining the Chinese and Latino heritage learned from the parents. The difficulties for the model's usefulness ensue when the hypothetical individual wishes to diminish the significance of one of the cultures of origin while maintaining the other. In these types of cases, the model is more difficult to use since it does not provide a predicted outcome.

The Role of Social Context

A different model of the acculturation process has been suggested by Rumbaut and Portes (2001). Reflecting its sociological roots, the model emphasizes the social context in which acculturation takes place rather than individual processes that are the basis of psychological models of acculturation. Rumbaut and Portes suggest that the results of the acculturation process, particularly for second generation individuals, are dependent on background factors of the immigrant parents such as their personal characteristics (or "human capital"), the structure of the family, parental levels of civic incorporation, experiences with discrimination, and the presence of ethnic subcultures in which the second generation individuals are raised.

This model of acculturation (Rumbaut & Portes, 2001) that emphasizes the social context in acculturation suggests two possible extreme outcomes. At one end is a process of **downward assimilation** that is the result of divergent levels of acculturation between parents and children (see the section below on generational differences in acculturation) as well as the experiences of racial and ethnic discrimination and negative experiences in the labor market and residential environments. At the other end of the continuum is a process of engagement with and acceptance of two cultures or biculturalism (as discussed below) that is produced by the selective acculturation of the parents, the presence of supportive ethnic networks, and the presence of community resources and strong familial and community networks. This process of selective acculturation characterized by biculturalism is defined as leading to "better psychosocial and achievement outcomes because it preserves bonds across immigrant generations and gives children a clear reference point to guide their future lives" (Rumbaut & Portes, 2001, p. 309).

A study with Soviet Jewish refugees in the United States (Birman & Trickett, 2001) showed that indeed there were generational differences in civic incorporation and acculturation with the older first generation refugees maintaining Russian language proficiency to a greater extent than their children regardless of their length of residence in the United States. The children, probably due to the support system they encountered, exhibited a greater sense of Russian identity than the parents although behaviorally they showed the greatest level of acculturation, probably exhibiting the biculturalism proposed by the Rumbaut and Portes model and reinforcing the importance of the social context in promoting acculturation and adaptation to a new culture (Birman, Trickett, & Buchanan, 2005).

Biculturalism

Biculturalism is one of the outcomes of the acculturation process that is mentioned in most acculturative models. Individuals choosing the integration strategy in Berry's acculturation model (described above) can be considered to be bicultural. Indeed, some researchers (e.g., Buriel & Saenz, 1980; LaFromboise, Coleman, & Gerton, 1993; Szapocznik & Kurtines, 1980) have suggested that special attention should be given to understanding those individuals who are knowledgeable about two cultures and who feel perfectly comfortable interacting in either culture group or among members of either ethnic group. For example, an immigrant from Vietnam to the United States can become a truly bicultural Vietnamese American after not just learning English but incorporating values and behaviors that define the "mainstream" U.S culture while maintaining a significant proportion of the values and behaviors that characterize Vietnam.

Biculturalism is present not just among immigrants or members of a majority or dominant culture but also among the children of ethnically mixed households or families. Households where one parent is a member of one ethnic or cultural group (e.g., White non-Hispanic) and the other parent belongs to a different ethnic group (e.g., an African American) are likely to raise children who exhibit the characteristics of biculturalism by engagement with both cultures. Parents can choose to foster a home environment that allows their children to learn both cultures and to feel comfortable in either one. The 2000 census of the United States showed that 6.8 million people (or 2.4% of the total population) considered themselves to belong to more than one race (N. A. Jones & Smith, 2003). The largest proportion involved mixtures of White and American Indian (15.9%) followed by Whites and Asians (12.7%) and Whites and Blacks (11.5%). As suggested by the various acculturation models, the external conditions of exposure to more than one culture (whether in society or in the family) alone do not necessarily produce truly bicultural individuals. There is a need for the presence of family and social conditions that reinforce bicultural identity and behavior and for the individual's active acceptance of the cultures (Root, 2003).

Although psychological research on the adaptiveness of bicultural individuals is limited (Rudmin, 2003), the literature shows that bicultural individuals have some special characteristics that distinguish them from others (e.g., LaFromboise et al., 1993). Generally, bicultural individuals are proficient not just at using the language of both cultural groups (if they differ) but, more important, in understanding the values of both groups and the associated behavioral expectancies. Bicultural individuals have been shown to have significant cognitive flexibility by easily switching from one cultural framework to the other when exposed to culture-specific symbols or to cultural stimuli that are present in the social environment (Hong, Morris, Chiu, & Benet-Martinez, 2000). Other studies (A. O. Miranda & Umhoefer, 1998) have found that when compared to monoculturals, bicultural individuals tend to show psychological well-being that includes lower levels of depression and greater sense of self-worth (Birman, 1998). LaFromboise et al. (1993) suggest that among bicultural individuals "in addition to having a strong and stable sense of personal identity, another affective element of bicultural competence is the ability to develop and maintain positive attitudes toward one's culture of origin and the second culture in which he or she is attempting to acquire competence" (p. 408). In addition, LaFromboise and colleagues argue that people who develop bicultural competencies exhibit better physical and mental health and "outperform their monoculturally competent peers in vocational and academic endeavors" (p. 409). Nevertheless, much of this research measures associations among variables since it is correlational in nature and causality or the direction of the biculturalism–well-being relationship remains a matter of conjecture.

Enculturation

Individuals who endeavor to learn or affirm their culture of origin are often described as undergoing a process of **enculturation** (Soldier, 1985). This phenomenon, which can also be considered as another model of acculturation, is often found among individuals who are three or four generations removed from a particular ethnic or cultural group and who wish now to rediscover those cultural and ethnic roots and make them part of their attitudinal and behavioral repertoire (Hansen, 1952). For example, Goering (1971) found that ethnicity and the sense of belonging to an ethnic group was of greater importance to third generation Irish Americans and Italian Americans than to first generation immigrants.

As suggested by various acculturation models, certain behaviors or attitudes and even values tend to become less salient or less personally important from one generation to the next (Rumbaut & Portes, 2001). Even by the second generation (that is, individuals who were born in the United States to immigrants), some behaviors and some cultural characteristics start to disappear. These changes usually occur at what Marín (1992) calls the superficial and intermediate levels of cultural change that often involve changes in eating habits, variations in preference for ethnic media, and less frequent use of ethnic social scripts (a culture's mores or preferred behavioral patterns). On the other hand, individuals who wish to enculturate would try to recover those practices and beliefs that were lost in previous generations and make them more central to their own (Soldier, 1985; Wilbert, 1976).

Research with American Indians (Zimmerman, Ramirez-Valles, Washienko, Walter, & Dyer, 1996) has shown that enculturation can be measured by evaluating individuals' sense of pride and interest in their culture including the importance assigned to maintaining American Indian practices and values, the level of knowledge of traditional culture that they are able to report, and their overall sense of pride in being a Native American. Also relevant in this enculturation process of American Indians was the level of involvement in ethnic activities such as sweat lodges, powwows, learning lodges, and fastings. A study with Louisiana Cajuns (Henry & Bankston, 1999) found that while significant acculturation had taken place across generations, there was a recent resurgence in enculturation focused on their Cajun identity and Acadian heritage that included such behaviors as learning French (even if they seldom used it) and a sense of ethnic pride that went beyond their social status.

Unfortunately, enculturation has received little attention from researchers. Nevertheless, there is evidence of renewed interest in "one's own roots" on the part of individuals who are third or higher generation or who had stopped considering themselves as a "hyphenated American" (as in "Italian-American" or "Irish-American"). This concern is being shown in terms of increased interest in genealogies, visiting ancestral homes, and learning the language and culture of those relatives who first migrated to the United States.

GENERATIONAL DIFFERENCES AND ACCULTURATION

Much research on acculturation has emphasized the fact that across generations, members of ethnic groups differ in their level and speed of acculturation.

In general, second and third generation individuals tend to exhibit greater levels of acculturation to the host culture than first generation members of an ethnic group (W. Perez & Padilla, 2000). These variations in level and speed of acculturation are not surprising since they tend to be related to length of residence in the "host" country as well as to the greater exposure to acculturating institutions (schools, churches, social groups) often experienced by second and higher generation members.

The phenomenon of generational differences in acculturation is best exemplified when the first generation adults have migrated as adults and either have brought young children along or had children after arriving in the United States. In some cases, the first generation adult immigrants experience difficulties in becoming proficient in the language or in understanding the requirements of the civil society for full incorporation (e.g., passing driving tests, becoming citizens) while their children because of their upbringing in schools are more proficient in English and are better able, in some cases, to navigate the requirements of a bureaucracy. Some researchers have indeed noted how the children of immigrants (even when first generation themselves) become their "parents' parents" by being translators and information brokers in the family. These differential patterns of acculturation, labeled **dissonant acculturation** by Portes (1999), often produce conflict in the family and in some cases have been associated with behavioral problems in second generation children including abuse of drugs, truancy, and disciplinary problems (Szapocznik & Kurtines, 1980).

The role reversals (as when children take on responsibilities usually assigned to parents in the family) are often perceived as undercutting parental authority and limiting the role of parents in controlling adolescents. The acculturation process and a renewed sense of independence probably also contribute to these difficulties in the behavior of second generation adolescents. Nevertheless, we should keep in mind that intergenerational conflict is not an exclusive phenomenon among immigrants (Berrol, 1995) but something that seems to be central to the value that American society places on independence. A study by Carola Suárez-Orozco and Marcelo Suárez-Orozco (1995) showed that while intergenerational conflict was present among Latinos and Whites, it was more common and more extended among the latter. At the same time, M. Zhou (1999) has suggested that immigrant children who live in inner cities and who rebel against parental values and their mobility expectations are likely to experience downward mobility and to develop an adversarial outlook as a response to the discrimination they experience and the limited opportunities to move upwardly in social class. Chapter 6 presents a more comprehensive analysis of the role of acculturation in family dynamics particularly when intergenerational conflict occurs.

ACCULTURATIVE STRESS

The challenges and difficulties experienced by acculturating individuals have been labeled by many authors as **acculturative stress** (or acculturational stress). The constellation of pressures to change and the presence of unfamiliar external social and physical environmental conditions are hypothesized as producing stressful conditions on acculturating individuals. The personal success at coping with those stressful conditions is related to an overall sense of well-being and to physical and mental health correlates. For example, an immigrant arriving in the United States will need in many cases to learn a new language; master new social conventions related to group and interpersonal behavior (e.g., when to shake hands, how to address superiors, how much interpersonal distance to keep); gain skills at dealing with government bureaucracies and civic entities (e.g., how to get a social security card, how to obtain a driver's license, how to enroll children in school); learn to perform job skills that may be very different from those used in the past (e.g., how to use an English-language keyboard, how to use a machine at work); learn daily logistics (e.g., how to use public transport, where to get stamps, how to get a telephone), as well as learning and respecting new cultural values (e.g., individualism, competition, sense of fair play, trust in civic institutions). In many cases, these situations must be handled with little previous preparation and over a short period of time. While all geographic dislocation is difficult (even when a New Yorker moves to Los Angeles), crossing cultures can be even more complex given the variety and intricacy of changes that are implied in such a move. Furthermore, the conditions that are related to acculturative stress do not disappear after a few months but may be present over a period of many years.

Acculturative stress can also occur at a family level where varying levels of acculturation when parents are compared to their children increase the likelihood for parent-child conflict and marital discord. Nevertheless, certain personal traits (e.g., being a younger versus an older adult), abilities and skills (such as being bicultural, having a high level of formal education), acculturation strategies chosen (e.g., integration versus marginalization), and goals and motives (feeling "pulled" toward a host country by greater economic and educational opportunities versus being "pushed" out of one's country of origin due to war, poverty, unemployment) may serve as protective or causal factors for acculturative stress.

Acculturative stress is related to a number of variables. For example, research with Latino adults (A. O. Miranda & Matheny, 2000) showed that acculturative stress was related to low levels of cohesion of the family, poor English language ability, and the length of residence in the United States. Subsequent research (Rodriguez, Myers, Mira, Flores, & Garcia-Hernandez, 2002) has shown that acculturative stress is related to linguistic competence (e.g., perceived pressures to learn a language, speaking with an accent), pressures to assimilate, and pressures against acculturation (e.g., people's rejection for the individual espousing majority cultural values). This last study found that the language competency variables seem to be the most important sources of acculturative stress. Not surprisingly, the significance of language competency in promoting acculturative stress is more marked among recent immigrants (Gil & Vega, 1996) and often produced by the presence of members of the same ethnic group who are already proficient in the majority language (Holleran, 2003).

A study with Cambodian and Vietnamese refugees (Nwadiora & McAdoo, 1996) also showed the significant impact of English-language deficiencies in producing acculturative stress together with unemployment and limited levels of formal education. Also relevant in producing acculturative stress is the presence of negative reactions individuals get from members of the majority group. Studies with Latinos (Sanchez & Fernandez, 1993) and with Arab Americans (Faragallah, Schumm, & Webb, 1997) have shown that experiences of discrimination or social rejection are related to acculturative stress.

Both women and men seem to experience fairly similar levels of acculturative stress at least among refugees (Nwadiora & McAdoo, 1996) and it seems to be more likely among those who emigrate after 12 years of age (Mena, Padilla, & Maldonado, 1987). Recently, Padilla and Perez (2003) have argued that acculturation is most difficult for those individuals who are visibly different from the majority group in terms of factors such as the color of their skin and language spoken. Among immigrants, the realization that relatives and friends left behind are no longer a source of emotional, personal, and financial support can also be the product of acculturative stress. Likewise, a type of "survivor guilt" may be associated with the acculturation process where stress is felt by acculturating individuals who realize that their friends and relatives back home will not have the same experiences and opportunities that they are able to enjoy in the new country.

It should be noted that the acculturation process is not necessarily always stressful. As Rogler, Cortes, and Malgady (1991) have noted, acculturating individuals also have positive experiences including feeling safer and better off than those in their country of origin. In addition, immigrants experience in many cases positive incidents in their new culture with new friends and coworkers and may enjoy the newly discovered foods, entertainment, sights, and conveniences that balance to some extent the impact of the acculturative stressors. Nevertheless, the positive effects of these new experiences may decrease after the novelty wears off and acculturating individuals often need to cope with experiences of prejudice and discrimination and the realization that, in many cases, their socioeconomic status is not rapidly improving, that only a few drive fancy cars, or that not everybody in the country lives in the homes portrayed in Hollywood movies. Indeed, the shattering of numerous myths about the United States, such as the ability to improve one's life if only you work hard or the more improbable images of "streets being paved with gold" or "dollars hanging from trees," can be particularly stressful to immigrants as they acculturate. Likewise, acculturative stress is generated as individuals must cope with the stratification processes of society in the United States where, in many cases, the color of their skin or the culture of origin or the use of accented speech determines the type of societal rewards and opportunities a person is able to receive. The poor quality of schools in many ethnic neighborhoods, for example, limits the potential for social advancement of many first and second generation individuals who experience limitations in the kind of employment they can obtain or the possibility of attending college.

Acculturative Stress and Reason for Migration

An important consideration when analyzing acculturative stress is the reason or the causes for migration. The nature of the migration experience (e.g., whether it was voluntary or forced) can be expected to affect the disposition of the immigrant toward the new culture and its people. Ogbu (1978) argued that voluntary migrants, that is, those who choose to migrate for employment or for educational or economic improvement, will react differently to the new experiences than those who have been enslaved, colonized, or forced to migrate or relocate for political reasons such as American Indians, African Americans, or Puerto Ricans. For Ogbu, involuntary migrants (and by extension their children and grandchildren) have greater difficulty in accepting the values of the mainstream or "host" culture, which in turn leads to failure in academic activities and to low-status employment.

M. Zhou (1999) suggests that indeed immigrants who reside in an ethnic inner-city enclave tend to have children who face an adversarial outlook within the community and this situation can lead first and second generation children to perform less well in school (so as to not be labeled "Whites" or "turncoats") and to avoid stigmatization of being considered foreigners in their own world. These children not only reject "nerdy" and "uncool" attitudes toward school (Gibson, 1989), but also adopt linguistic patterns and behaviors of the inner city. In addition, hostile and unwelcoming environments may lead observers (teachers, community leaders, other adults) to assume that these children will "naturally" fail and in this fashion support a self-fulfilling prophesy where the students receive less constructive feedback and less attention from the teachers.

Some authors (e.g., Burnam, Hough, Karno, Escobar, & Telles, 1987) have suggested that there is a process of selective migration among voluntary immigrants whereby the strongest ("migration of the fittest"), or the most creative and healthiest, or the risk takers or the youngest, tend to choose to migrate. This is known as the **selective migration hypothesis.** This hypothesis, if true, would argue that members of a first generation cohort would be less likely to exhibit adjustment and health problems than those belonging to a second or higher generation. Mental health research (Vega, Warheit, Buhl-Autg, & Meinhardt, 1984) shows that Mexican American immigrants have a mental health status that is similar to that of Mexicans (in Mexico) while U.S.-born Mexican Americans (second generation) exhibited poorer mental health conditions. A related **social stress hypothesis** suggests that the members of second and higher generation groups exhibit poorer mental and physical health not because they are less strong or less able to withstand acculturative stress but rather because they bear the brunt of discrimination and prejudice in our society. In addition, the social stress hypothesis endorses the assumption that immigrants are better able to maintain and use the protective cultural traditions of origin that in turn support better physical health and stronger mental health (Escobar, 1998).

Research on physical health (Nguyen, 2006; Sam, 2006) seems to shed some light on the complexity of this phenomenon. Early research (e.g., J. C. Kleinman, Fingerhut, & Prager, 1991) found that immigrant Mexican American women had rates of children with low and very low birth weight comparable to those found among White women. Furthermore, Guendelman and colleagues (Guendelman, Gould, Hudes, & Eskenazi, 1990) found that second generation Mexican American women were more likely to have low birth weight babies than first generation mothers. These results (sometimes referred to as the "Hispanic paradox" or the **"immigrant health paradox"**) seemed contradictory since immigrant mothers tended to be less educated, poorer, and to have less access to medical care. Nevertheless, subsequent research found that the improved health status does not necessarily remain consistent over time (Guendelman & English, 1995). Furthermore, more sensitive analysis of the data showed that the low birth weight phenomenon was related to a complex interaction of predictor variables such as the language ability of the mothers, their socioeconomic conditions, and their reason for migration. We could assume therefore that the explanation is more complex than at first suggested by the selective migration hypothesis or the social stress hypothesis and that the results of the acculturation process can best be explained as an interaction of multiple variables including at a minimum the preexisting conditions (physical as well as mental status) of the immigrants, their reasons for migrating, their ability to cope with acculturative stresses, access and patterns of use of support systems, experiences of prejudice and discrimination, and characteristics of their living environment. Furthermore, as argued by Nguyen (2006), most studies have failed to properly measure the role of acculturation in explaining these findings and instead have used indicators or correlates of acculturation that may have different effects on people's behavior.

MEASURING ACCULTURATION

An understanding of the approaches used to measure acculturation is important because, in some instances, theoretical or methodological characteristics of the various measures become confounding factors when trying to analyze the findings of studies exploring the relevance of acculturation. Indeed, some of the discrepancies across studies that are found in the literature can often be explained by the limited validity in the way acculturation was defined or conceptualized by the researchers or to such methodological limitations as poorly constructed instrumentation.

The majority of procedures developed for measuring acculturation have relied on self-report paper-and-pencil instruments where individuals are asked to indicate their attitudes, norms, or values or to report on the frequency or presence of certain behaviors. For example, a large number of acculturation scales ask respondents to report how well they speak, write, or understand English and/or the language of origin. A Korean American, for example, would be asked to indicate how well she speaks Korean, usually on a Likert-type scale where responses can range from "Very Well" to "Very Poorly" or "Not at All." Another item or question could ask the respondents to report on their proficiency in English. Other acculturation scales use a single item to determine the person's proficiency in English and in Korean going from one extreme to another such as "Speak Only Korean at Home" to "Speak Only English at Home."

Most acculturation scales include a wide range of behaviors and attitudes or values and frequently are designed for one major ethnic group (e.g., Asian Americans) or for a subgroup (e.g., Vietnamese Americans or Chinese Americans). Among the behaviors often included in acculturation scales are the following: language use, preference, and fluidity; media usage patterns; ethnic friendship preferences; food consumption patterns; knowledge of cultural traditions and values; ethnic self-identification; perceived prejudice and discrimination; and cultural values or scripts such as familialism (family orientation and devotion) or time orientation (personal significance of time), or group-specific cultural scripts such as *simpatía* (value placed on positive social relations).

As Zane and Mak (2003) and others (e.g., Marín & Gamba, 1996) suggest, the measurement of acculturation in psychological research has varied in terms of conceptual approaches, domains measured, psychometric characteristics of the acculturation construct, and populations sampled. While some scales consider acculturation as a unidirectional process with possible responses going in one direction from the culture of origin to the new culture, others consider the process to be bidirectional and taking place in two different fields (one related to the culture of origin and another to the new culture). An acculturation scale for Chinese Americans based on a unidirectional conceptualization of acculturation, for example, would ask respondents to indicate the ethnicity of close friends in a Likert-type scale that goes from "Only White Americans" to "Only Chinese," including a midpoint of "Half White Americans and Half Chinese" (see Figure 4.1).

Figure 4.1 Acculturation as a Unidirectional Process

Chinese Orientation   White Orientation

The unidirectional approach to the measurement of acculturation has fallen into disfavor because it implies a zero-sum approach to culture learning (Rogler et al., 1991) whereby gains in one aspect of a culture imply losses in the related aspect of the culture of origin. For example, gains in English proficiency would imply losses in proficiency in the language of origin or, in the above example, increases in friends who are White would imply decreases in the number of Chinese friends.

Most recent research favors a multidirectional conceptualization of acculturation whereby the acculturating individual is free to move from one end to the other of each culture or "cultural field." The most significant contribution of this bidirectional or multidirectional conceptualization is that it recognizes that individuals can learn a new culture's behaviors or values without having to give up aspects of the culture of origin. For example, an Iranian American can self-report knowledge of English that can vary from "Not at All" at one extreme to "Excellent" at the other. This rating is independent of the respondent's self-reported knowledge of Farsi that also can vary from "Not at All" to "Excellent." In a 5-point Likert-type scale, the Iranian American could mark a 5 ("Excellent") for knowledge of Farsi and a 3 ("Average") for knowledge of English. In a few months, the same individual could indicate a 4 ("Good") for knowledge of English without necessarily having to indicate a lowering in his knowledge of Farsi. Figure 4.2 shows how two cultures or cultural fields would intercept each

Figure 4.2 Acculturation as a Bidirectional Process

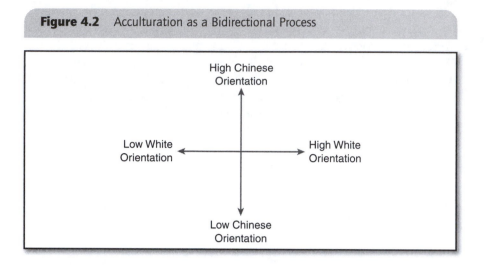

other in an acculturating individual while Figure 4.3 shows the case of an Iranian American acculturating in an English-speaking environment.

As mentioned above, acculturation scales also vary in terms of the behavioral areas or domains that they measure. Probably the most frequently used domain is related to language proficiency, preference, and use and sometimes specifying the social context in which the language is used (Zane & Mak, 2003). Often, respondents are asked to report on linguistic preferences

Figure 4.3 Hypothetical Acculturation of an Iranian American

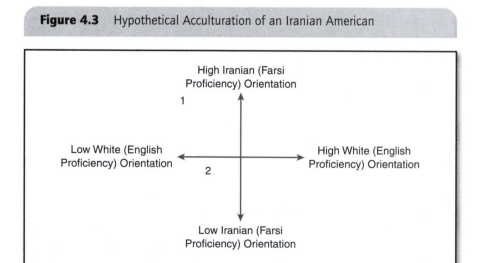

NOTE: The number 1 indicates an individual who speaks Farsi quite well but whose English is poor. The number 2 shows an Iranian American whose level of proficiency in Farsi is a little less than average and the same is true for her proficiency in English.

and proficiency in selected situations and for English as well as for the language of origin. For example, the Bidimensional Acculturation Scale for Hispanics (Marín & Gamba, 1996) asks respondents to report proficiency in English and in Spanish separately while speaking, reading, writing, listening to the radio, listening to music, and watching television (see Box 4.1).

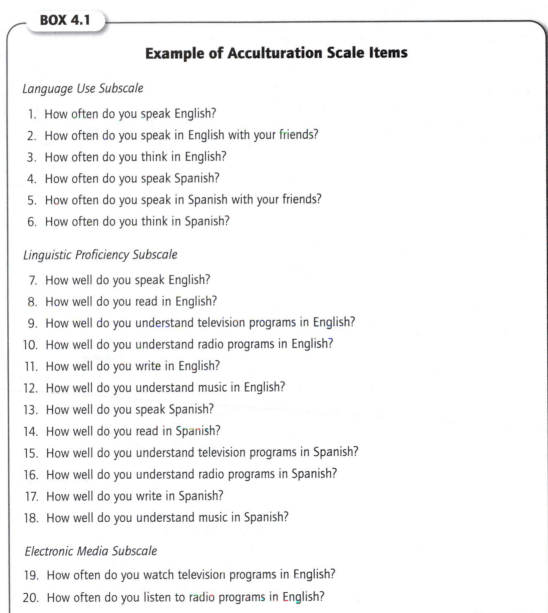

BOX 4.1

Example of Acculturation Scale Items

Language Use Subscale

1. How often do you speak English?
2. How often do you speak in English with your friends?
3. How often do you think in English?
4. How often do you speak Spanish?
5. How often do you speak in Spanish with your friends?
6. How often do you think in Spanish?

Linguistic Proficiency Subscale

7. How well do you speak English?
8. How well do you read in English?
9. How well do you understand television programs in English?
10. How well do you understand radio programs in English?
11. How well do you write in English?
12. How well do you understand music in English?
13. How well do you speak Spanish?
14. How well do you read in Spanish?
15. How well do you understand television programs in Spanish?
16. How well do you understand radio programs in Spanish?
17. How well do you write in Spanish?
18. How well do you understand music in Spanish?

Electronic Media Subscale

19. How often do you watch television programs in English?
20. How often do you listen to radio programs in English?

(Continued)

(Continued)

21. How often do you listen to music in English?

22. How often do you watch television programs in Spanish?

23. How often do you listen to radio programs in Spanish?

24. How often do you listen to music in Spanish?

The response categories for items 1 through 6 and items 19 through 24 are Almost Always (scored as 4), Often (scored as 3), Sometimes (scored as 2), and Almost Never (scored as 1).

The response categories for items 7 through 18 are Very Well (scored as 4), Well (scored as 3), Poorly (scored as 2), and Very Poorly (scored as 1).

SOURCE: Bidimensional Acculturation Scale for Hispanics (Marín & Gamba, 1996).

Another frequently used behavioral domain involves preferences for the ethnicity of the individuals with whom one socializes. For example, the original African American Acculturation Scale (Landrine & Klonoff, 1996) included items measuring the ethnicity of friends, of people individuals feel comfortable having around them, of the person they admire the most, of the people they trust, of the members of their church, and of the neighborhood while growing up. One other type of question frequently used in acculturation scales is related to the preference that individuals report for media use including printed media such as newspapers or magazines, television programming, and radio stations (English language or mainstream outlets or ethnic-specific). Other types of questions often used to measure acculturation are knowledge of culture-specific symbols or events (e.g., the meaning of the Fourth of July holiday or the colors of the flag) or familiarity with religious or patriotic figures (e.g., who were Gandhi, Bolivar, Buddha?).

The reliance on language use and proficiency items in most acculturation scales has been criticized for a number of reasons. First is the concern that linguistic abilities or preferences are just a small, if not insignificant, aspect of a person's life and that changes may reflect the effects of various circumstances that may or may not properly measure psychological acculturation (Chiriboga, 2004). For example, schooling and job requirements may externally modify linguistic practices of immigrants and second generation individuals without necessarily reflecting internal or more personal acculturation changes. At the same time, the ethnic composition of certain neighborhoods in large urban environments (such as Miami, New York, Los Angeles, San Francisco) may make it possible for older individuals to function in their language of origin without having to learn much English.

Likewise, prohibitions against use of languages other than English as those that existed in the past (and currently exist in some places of employment) may also spuriously contribute to acculturation scores that do not reflect psychological acculturation.

Furthermore, generational differences in language use have been well documented, which could reflect behavioral preferences that are not related to acculturational changes at the more basic level of values and attitudes. For example, Fishman (2000) suggested that adult immigrants continue to use the mother tongue in the majority of settings while second generation individuals tend to use it only at home with parents and other relatives who may continue to use the mother tongue. The majority of third generation individuals generally exhibit little proficiency in the heritage tongue, using the dominant language for most interactions. These patterns can therefore produce spurious correlations in acculturation scales that rely on language proficiency or preference items to measure such a fairly complex construct since there are external factors that may moderate the choice of language used. An additional limitation of most acculturation scales is the fact that they fail to ascertain or measure if the behavioral or attitudinal choices have been freely made by the individual or if they have been imposed by environmental conditions or pressures from others. For example, the choice of English-language television may be the result of an individual's personal choice or of pressures from parents to avoid television in other languages or due to the fact that there are no ethnic stations available in the place of residence. Each of these situations could have varying implications for the measurement of the individual's acculturation level.

These differences in domains, theoretical conceptualizations, and directionality contribute to the difficulties in understanding inconsistencies in psychological research dealing with acculturation among ethnic groups in the United States. Cabassa (2003) has suggested that measures of acculturation need to become more complex by increasing the number of areas that are measured so that the whole range of experiences lived by an acculturating individual can be evaluated (e.g., at home, school, work, while shopping, when accompanied by friends or alone). This is indeed a very important issue that has plagued researchers as they try to balance the need for comprehensiveness in the measure and the need for controlling the length of the instrument for practical reasons (Serrano & Anderson, 2003; Wallen, Feldman, & Anliker, 2002). Nguyen (2006) also has criticized much of current research on acculturation in the United States because of the lack of strong theoretical conceptual frameworks and the frequent lack of attention to social and structural contexts.

Despite the theoretical and methodological advantages of some approaches or scales over others, we can expect that the problem of limited comparability across measures will continue. Indeed, the last decade has seen the creation of a substantial number of acculturation scales as well as the revision of scales that had been in existence for a few years. There are acculturation scales for the major ethnic groups including African Americans, Asian Americans, and Latinos as well as for specific subgroups such as Japanese Americans (Meredith, Wenger, Liu, Harada, & Kahn, 2000), Puerto Ricans (Tropp, Erkut, Coll, Alarcón, & Garcia, 1999), Khmer (Lim, Heiby, Brislin, & Griffin, 2002), Vietnamese (Nguyen & von Eye, 2002), East Asians (Barry, 2001), Southeast Asians (J. Anderson et al., 1993), Chinese Americans (Gupta & Yick, 2001), as well as Greek Americans (A. C. Harris & Verven, 1996, 1998). Also, there are some scales that have tried to measure acculturation within multicultural groups by using items that do not explicitly address a given language (e.g., Vietnamese, Spanish) or values and attitudes related to a particular culture. These scales are meant to be used in situations where it is difficult to develop group-specific acculturation scales or where the group being studied includes individuals from multiple ethnicities. Examples of these multicultural acculturation scales include the Stephenson Multigroup Acculturation Scale (Stephenson, 2000) and one developed specifically for adolescents (Unger et al., 2002). Some of the most frequently used scales are listed in Box 4.2.

BOX 4.2

Frequently Used Acculturation Scales

African American Acculturation Scales

African American Acculturation Scale (AAAS). (Landrine & Klonoff, 1994, 1995, 1996)

- Measures eight dimensions with 74 items: family structures and practices (e.g., child taking, extended family, informal adoption); socialization practices; preference for things African American (e.g., music, magazines); consumption of traditional foods (e.g., collard greens, ham hocks); health beliefs; religious beliefs and practices; belief in superstitions; and attitudes of cultural mistrust.

African American Acculturation Scale. (Snowden & Hines, 1999)

- Includes 10 items related to media preferences, ethnic/racial characteristics of friends, church congregation, neighborhood, attitudes toward interracial marriage and familial dependence, and comfort interacting with Whites.

Asian American Acculturation Scales

Suinn-Lew Asian Self-Identity Acculturation Scale. (Suinn, Rickard-Figueroa, Lew, & Vigil, 1987)

- A unidimensional 21-item scale measuring language use, friendship patterns, and ethnic identity.

Asian American Values Scale Multidimensional. (B. S. Kim, Li, & Ng, 2005)

- An instrument of 36 items that measures various Asian values (e.g., collectivism, humility, emotional self-control, filial piety).

Asian American Multidimensional Acculturation Scale. (Chung, Kim, & Abreu, 2004)

- A multidimensional scale with 45 items measuring cultural behavior, identity, and knowledge.

Latino Acculturation Scales

Acculturation Rating Scale for Mexican Americans-Revised (ARSMA-R). (Cuellar, Arnold, & Gonzalez, 1995)

- A bidimensional scale that measures language proficiency, linguistic preference, and ethnic identification and allows researchers to classify respondents in terms of Berry's four acculturative strategies.

Short Acculturation Scale for Hispanics (SASH). (Marín, Sabogal, Marín, Otero-Sabogal, & Pérez-Stable, 1987)

- A 12-item unidimensional scale that asks respondents to identify their level of involvement with Latino and White cultures. A language use/preference factor allows researchers to quickly classify individuals as Latino-oriented or White-oriented.

Bidimensional Acculturation Scale for Hispanics (BAS). (Marín & Gamba, 1996)

- The BAS includes 12 items for each cultural domain—Hispanic versus non-Hispanic White—that measure three acculturative areas: language use, linguistic proficiency, and patterns of use of electronic media.

Native American Acculturation Scale

Native American Acculturation Scale. (Garrett & Pichette, 2000)

- The scale includes 20 multiple-choice items addressing identity, language use, ethnicity of friends, attitudes, and behaviors.

LEVELS OF ACCULTURATION

Various authors have expressed concern regarding the fact that the literature on acculturation tends to confuse central or core aspects of acculturation from those that are less important or even peripheral to the process (Chiriboga, 2004; Marín, 1992; Zane & Mak, 2003). Indeed, changes in behavior and attitudes produced by exposure to a new culture can be observed at three different levels (Marín, 1992) depending on the length of exposure and the personal significance of the behaviors or values. Probably the most superficial level, and therefore most easily changed, involves learning and/or forgetting facts and behaviors that are characteristic of an ethnic group or culture but have generally lower personal significance (e.g., meanings of holidays, food, and media preferences). A second more intermediate level involves changes in frequently performed behaviors that are of relative or moderate personal value or significance (e.g., language preference, ethnicity of friends). Finally, the third and most basic level involves modifications in an individual's core values (beliefs in justice, the value of the family).

For example, among Latinos, length of residence in the United States is related to changes at the superficial level such as patterns of media use. As such, Latinos who have lived the longest period of time in the United States show an increased preference for mass media in English rather than in Spanish (Alcalay et al., 1987–1988). Other studies have shown that as acculturation proceeds in terms of increased length of residence and personal involvement with a new culture, changes in areas such as linguistic proficiency as well as ethnic preferences for friends also occur (Cuellar, Arnold, & Gonzalez, 1995; Cuellar, Harris, & Jasso, 1980; Marín et al., 1987). Finally, research has shown that while changes at the more basic level of cultural and personal values occur as a result of acculturation among Latinos, they tend to be less frequent and to take more time (Cuellar et al., 1995; Sabogal et al., 1987).

Most research on acculturation has been concentrated on the first two levels, probably because of the difficulty in identifying operational definitions and developing culturally appropriate measures for basic cultural values. Indeed, the analysis by Zane and Mak (2003) of 22 frequently used acculturation scales found that only 5 included the measurement of cultural values.

It is important to note that in this age of globalization and internationalized mass media, changes related to the most superficial levels of acculturation can be the product of circumstances that have little to do with psychological acculturation. As many international travelers can note, the influence of Hollywood films and of international mass media such as the BBC, MTV, or CNN can be seen everywhere including the most remote of places. This internationalization of electronic and print mass media makes it possible for some aspects of the culture of the United States to be transmitted via movies, radio, and television programs. As such, recent immigrants to the United States can easily report familiarity with our cultural icons and events (Coca-Cola, McDonald's, KFC, Pepsi, rap music, movie actors, the Fourth of July) immediately upon arriving and before being exposed to the acculturational process of living in a new culture. This familiarity with certain cultural products may potentially modify or buffer acculturative stress among certain individuals who may find a supportive image in the product or idea that is not totally unfamiliar to them.

Chapter Summary

This chapter has presented an overview of acculturation as one of the most significant concepts in ethnic psychology. Acculturation has received a considerable amount of attention on the part of many researchers and is a concept or construct often mentioned when trying to predict or explain the behavior of individuals who are exposed to a new culture. Despite its relatively short history, important changes have occurred in the ways in which acculturation is defined, how it is measured, and how its effects and correlates are studied. Individuals vary in the acculturation strategies they choose and these can in turn be related to acculturative stress. The role of acculturation in shaping behaviors and attitudes is so strong that fairly clear patterns can be identified despite the variety of ethnic groups studied and the methodological limitations of some studies in terms of the measurements used or the limited samples studied.

At the same time, it is important to keep in mind the admonition proposed by some authors (e.g., Hunt, Schneider, & Comer, 2004) that, at times, acculturation has been used to explain differences in behavior or attitudes that can best be explained in terms of socioeconomic status or of the difficulties encountered by individuals who have poor English language skills, suffer poverty, or face the problems associated with being a newly arrived individual in a foreign culture.

Research has shown that individuals exposed to a new culture undergo a process of change in their worldviews, their attitudes, their values, and their behaviors and that these changes show varying patterns across individuals as a function of their migration and generational history. As Berry (2003) notes, it is important to remember that many people have undergone and continue to experience the effects of acculturation and that most have survived and have been able to function in a productive way. Acculturation therefore does not imply either social or psychological pathology despite the significant emphasis that researchers, primarily psychologists, have placed on the negative aspects of acculturation. Except for some significant work on biculturalism (as mentioned above), a substantial number of studies have primarily searched for the negative consequences of the acculturation process (Chun et al., 2003).

Key Terms

Learning by Doing

- Answer the items of the Bidimensional Acculturation Scale found in Box 4.1 and score your responses by computing an average of your responses to items dealing with English and another average for the items dealing with Spanish. Analyze the differences in both averages based on your background and exposure to Latino culture. You can compute the average for your English-related questions by adding your responses to questions 1 through 3, 7 through 12, and 19 through 21 and then dividing by 12. Your average (or mean) for the Spanish-related questions can be computed by adding your responses to the other items and dividing by 12. The range of each mean score should be between 1 and 4.
- Interview five people of varying ethnic backgrounds and ask them to indicate what practices, attitudes, and beliefs characterize their ethnic group. You can ask, for example, about dating practices, who makes financial decisions at home, attitudes about women working outside the house, religious practices, the role of adults toward their aging parents, how involved are men in child rearing, and whether men cook. Find out if grandparents and parents held or hold the same beliefs and carried or carry out the same practices.
- Interview first and second generation immigrants and have them report on preferred language use in various settings and explore the role of external factors in shaping those preferences or practices. For example, ask which language they prefer at home, with their parents, with their children, at religious services, when watching television or movies.
- Imagine that you are about to move permanently to a new city where you do not speak the language. Make a list of the things you would need to do within the first five days in order to have a life that resembles your current conditions. Rate how stressful (on a scale of 1 to 10 with 10 being the highest level of stress) achieving each of those outcomes would be to you. Consider, for example, renting an apartment, getting a telephone line installed, registering for school, managing the public transport system, buying groceries when you cannot read the labels, opening a bank account, buying stamps, getting a driver's license, getting a government-issued identification card, learning what is appropriate to wear when going to school or looking for a job or when going to a party.

Suggested Further Readings

Berry, J. W. (2003). Conceptual approaches to acculturation. In K. M. Chun, P. Balls Organista, & G. Marín (Eds.), *Acculturation: Advances in theory, measurement, and applied research* (pp. 17–37). Washington, DC: American Psychological Association.

A comprehensive and updated overview of Berry's acculturation model and his perspectives on the model's implications.

Chun, K. M., Balls Organista, P., & Marín, G. (Eds.). (2003). *Acculturation: Advances in theory, measurement, and applied research*. Washington, DC: American Psychological Association.

This book presents comprehensive summaries and analyses of current perspectives on acculturation theories and their applications. The book includes contributions by some of the key contributors to our understanding of this complex process among ethnic minority groups in the United States.

Jacoby, T. (Ed.). (2004). *Reinventing the melting pot: The new immigrants and what it means to be American.* New York: Basic Books.

    An excellent and contemporary analysis of the processes and difficulties facing recent immigrants to the United States. The book analyzes various models of acculturation and social integration within the older perspectives of assimilation.

LaFromboise, T., Coleman, H. L. K., & Gerton, J. (1993). Psychological impact of biculturalism: Evidence and theory. *Psychological Bulletin, 114,* 395–412.

    A classic article on the effects of biculturalism that shows the positive results of learning more than one culture.

Padilla, A. M. (Ed.). (1980). *Acculturation: Theory, models, and some new findings.* Boulder, CO: Westview.

    This book presents a number of acculturation models and their implications for Latino families. A classic in the field.

Root, M. P. P. (1992). *Racially mixed people in America.* Newbury Park, CA: Sage.

    One of the first books to advocate for the need for social scientists to focus on the social and psychological characteristics of individuals of multiple ethnic backgrounds. The book presents a comprehensive overview of early research in the field.

Root, M. P. P. (1996). *The multiracial experience: Racial borders as the new frontier.* Thousand Oaks, CA: Sage.

    This book updates the previous book by the same author and identifies important areas of research as the nation becomes more multiracial and multiethnic.

Rumbaut, R. G., & Portes, A. (Eds.). (2001). *Ethnicities: Children of immigrants in America.* Berkeley: University of California Press.

    An important analysis of the experiences and characteristics of second generation individuals (the children of immigrants) primarily from sociological and anthropological perspectives. The book is based on the researcher's comprehensive studies of immigrants to the United States.

Sam, D. L., & Berry, J. W. (Eds.). (2006). *The Cambridge handbook of acculturation psychology.* Cambridge, UK: Cambridge University Press.

    An international collection of chapters analyzing research and theoretical perspectives on acculturation. The book benefits from the authors' experiences around the world in countries and among individuals who differ in their migration patterns and acculturational perspectives.

CHAPTER 5

INTERSECTING IDENTITIES

Racial, Ethnic, Gender, Sexual, and Class Dimensions

VIGNETTE

"Why do we have to label everyone?"

"Growing up in Odessa, Texas, in the early 1970s was an experience," remarked Damon, a 35-year-old African American male. As a child, he never really questioned why African American and European American neighborhoods in this town were divided by a railroad track. However, he remembered his mother speaking about how White people couldn't really be trusted and that he should be careful whenever he interacted with them. Again, Damon couldn't fully understand her strong emotions on this topic because he never really spent a lot of time with European Americans and he rarely thought about race. This changed, however, when he went to a rural college in the northeastern United States and noticed very few African Americans on campus and even fewer African Americans in the local community. When he went to local stores, he noticed that employees would single him out and follow him around to ensure that he wouldn't steal anything. European American customers, however, were left alone. In a stressful turn of events, his two European American male roommates began taunting him with racial slurs and at one point threatened his life although Damon didn't do anything to provoke them. Following these incidents, Damon began to wonder why people reacted so violently to the color of his skin. Damon was confronted with another layer of questions about his identity as he slowly came out and self-identified as a gay man. Upon moving to San Francisco, he found many new friends, but realized that the predominantly gay European American community was not entirely inviting or friendly. At gay social venues and events, he seemed mostly invisible to the European American clientele, and sometimes overheard them making racist remarks about African Americans and other ethnic minority groups. Looking toward other African American gay men for support, he discovered that some preferred to exclusively date and socialize with European American men because they didn't find ethnic minority men attractive. And in the heterosexual African American community, Damon found that some were homophobic and appeared uncomfortable speaking about gay issues. Damon commented, "In the gay community, I'm not totally accepted because I'm Black and in the Black community I'm not fully accepted because I'm gay. And growing up in Texas, people were also obsessed with racial categories. Why do we have to label everyone?"

Damon's experiences point to the multiple layers of individual and group identities and how they shape one's individual experience. Given the current system of social stratification in the United States, Damon's ethnic and sexual identities are possible targets for discrimination and prejudice. Moreover, his experiences as a gay African American man show that multiple facets of identity, particularly those linked to minority status, are often inextricably linked together, contributing to a unique set of life experiences and challenges. In Damon's case, it would be wrong to assume that his racial or sexual identity in isolation fully describe his life experiences because he doesn't experience these facets of his identity separately. In this chapter, we examine these and other facets of individual identity as studied by ethnic psychologists. Special attention is given to understanding racial, ethnic, gender, sexual, and class dimensions of identity, and how they interact, develop, and change over time. Finally, the relationship of these different dimensions of identity to an individual's well-being and psychosocial functioning is discussed.

WHAT IS IDENTITY? UNDERSTANDING THE MULTIPLE FACETS OF THE SELF

How do you define your personal identity? Is it even possible to categorize yourself in one particular way? Are certain facets of your identity, like your ethnicity and gender, more important to you than others, such as your social class or religious background? Or does this depend on the social context in which you find yourself, including whom you are with, what you are doing, and where you are at any given moment? Ethnic psychologists have examined these types of questions particularly in regard to racial, ethnic, gender, sexual, and class dimensions of identity. Although there is much debate about the definitions of racial, ethnic, gender, sexual, and class identities, many psychologists believe that they are social constructions, meaning that their definitions and categorizations are determined by prevailing sociopolitical attitudes and historical forces in society, rather than by biological or genetic factors. Conclusive evidence regarding the etiology of sexual identity or orientation has yet to be found, although some researchers believe that this construct emerges from a nature and nurture interaction (Garnets, 2002). Thus, ethnic psychologists and other health and social scientists still struggle to formulate operational definitions for these identity dimensions given their complex nature and the limited effectiveness of current self-report measures to accurately assess them. The following section offers some definitions of racial, ethnic, gender, sexual, and class identities from a psychological perspective.

DIMENSIONS OF IDENTITY IN A SOCIOCULTURAL CONTEXT

Racial Identity

Racial identity and ethnic identity are often erroneously treated as equivalent constructs in psychology research even though they are distinct, but overlapping, constructs that can affect psychological adjustment and mental health in different ways. Much of the confusion in distinguishing racial from ethnic identity stems from continuing uncertainty among psychologists about the actual meanings of culture, ethnicity, and race (Trimble, 2007). Furthermore, racial and ethnic identities share a few general characteristics that make it difficult to tell them apart. Both racial and ethnic identity (1) involve a sense of belonging to a group; (2) arise from a process of learning about one's group; (3) vary in importance and salience across time and context; (4) are associated with specific cultural behaviors and values, attitudes toward one's own group, and responses to discrimination (Phinney & Ong, 2007); and (5) are social constructions.

Still, it is important to recognize the differences between these two identity dimensions; **racial identity** refers to identification with a socially defined racial category or phenotype, which is influenced by racial stratification and historical oppression of racial minorities (Gillem, Cohn, & Throne, 2001; Helms & Cook, 1999). Thus, racial identity reflects an individual's awareness of and psychological responses to racial oppression formed through **racial socialization**—the process of learning about and ascribing meaning and value to socially constructed racial hierarchies and categories. In contrast, ethnic identity is primarily concerned with identification with one's culture of origin and its shared cultural traditions, history, and practices (Alvarez & Helms, 2001), formed through **cultural socialization** or the process of learning about and ascribing meaning and value to the cultural heritage and practices of socially constructed ethnic groupings or categories (Cokley, 2007; Helms, 2007). A more detailed definition of ethnic identity is presented below along with a description of its many different components.

Racial labels or categories should never be used by themselves to explain a person's behavior or psychological functioning because they lack conceptual meaning and often reflect a researcher's beliefs and biases about race rather than the actual behaviors and characteristics of research study participants (Helms, Jernigan, & Mascher, 2005). In this case, differences between racial groups on any given dependent variable (e.g., psychological distress, educational achievement) should not simply be attributed to "racial difference" because this doesn't really tell us anything—are these racial group differences due to economic disparity, parenting practices, racial socialization, school environments, or other factors? Researchers should instead focus their attention on identifying and studying the "latent constructs" or underlying reasons and processes that account for racial group differences rather than formulating conclusions based on some unspecified, or assumed racial attributes of psychological functioning, which perpetuates racial stereotypes (Helms et al., 2005).

Ethnic Identity

Ethnic identity refers to your subjective sense of membership and belonging to an ethnic group, which includes your attitudes, beliefs, knowledge, feelings, and behaviors associated with that particular ethnic group (Cokley, 2007; Ponterotto, Gretchen, Utsey, Stracuzzi, & Saya, 2003; Rotheram & Phinney, 1987). Jean Phinney, a leading investigator of ethnic identity, believes that ethnic identity is an aspect of one's social identity as studied in social psychology. In this case, ethnic identity can be viewed as part of your self-concept, which is based on your understanding of your membership in a particular social group (or groups) and the value and emotional significance that you attach to that membership (Phinney, 1990). Phinney and Ong (2007) have expanded this conceptualization of ethnic identity by outlining the many different components of this construct that have been studied in psychology research (for a summary, see Box 5.1).

Self-Categorization and Labeling refers to the types of labels and categories that people use to describe their membership in an ethnic group. Although this is the most basic component of ethnic identification, it can be tricky to measure using traditional paper-and-pencil measures because people might describe or label their ethnic heritage in multiple ways depending on their personal beliefs, acculturation levels, and social context. For instance, a person of Chinese descent might self-identify as Chinese, Asian, Chinese American, Asian American, or Asian Pacific Islander depending on whom they are with and how others might see them.

Commitment and Attachment is defined as individuals' sense of belonging and emotional ties to their ethnic group. This is another important component to consider because people might use a particular ethnic label to describe themselves, yet feel distant or detached from their ethnic group. If individuals feel a strong attachment or an emotional bond to their ethnic group and are personally invested in their ethnic group membership, then they show a *commitment* to their ethnic identity. However, commitment to an ethnic identity does not necessarily mean that a person has a stable and secure ethnic identity; commitment can be based on how one's parents or role models identify themselves without understanding what one's own commitment to an ethnic group actually means. This type of commitment to an ethnic identity without exploring and understanding its meaning is called "foreclosure."

Exploration involves seeking information and experiences about one's ethnic heritage through a wide range of activities that can include parti-cipating in cultural events and holidays, reading, and talking to family and ethnic community members to learn about one's ethnic heritage, practices, and traditions. Exploring one's ethnic heritage, which can be an ongoing experience in one's life, is essential to forming a secure and positive commitment to an ethnic identity, particularly during adolescence when identity formation becomes an important developmental task.

Ethnic Behaviors include any behaviors and practices that are associated with one's ethnic group including eating the ethnic group's food, speaking the ethnic group's language, practicing the religious rituals and traditions in one's ethnic group, and socializing with fellow ethnic group members.

Evaluation and In-Group Attitudes encompasses positive or negative attitudes about one's ethnic group, or the extent to which people feel comfortable with their ethnic group membership. This component of ethnic identity can operate independently from the others. For example, ethnic minorities who participate in their ethnic traditions and self-identify with their ethnic group can still have negative attitudes about their group and may want to be part of the dominant group, particularly if they have experienced racial discrimination and have internalized negative racial stereotypes about their ethnicity.

Values and Beliefs associated with one's ethnic group are another important component of ethnic identity. The extent to which individuals endorse and promote their ethnic group's belief system and values can reflect their closeness to their group. Measuring and analyzing this ethnic identity component poses some challenges because members of a particular ethnic group might not be able to reach agreement on what constitutes the values and beliefs of their group, and ethnic identity measures that assess the values and beliefs of a specific group cannot be used with other ethnic groups for comparative analyses.

Importance and Salience refers to the extent to which ethnicity is an important part of one's life. The importance and salience of ethnic identity can vary across different individuals and across time—ethnic identity is more important and salient for ethnic minorities compared to dominant group members due to experiences of racial stratification and discrimination. Also, individuals who exhibit a strong ethnic identity tend to report greater ethnic identity salience on a daily basis than those who have a weaker or low ethnic identity.

Ethnic Identity and National (or American) Identity. Phinney and Ong (2007) believe that ethnic identity is more fully understood when it is examined vis-à-vis national identity because both represent prominent, albeit independent group identities in many people's lives. In the United States, for instance, being an American and being a member of one's ethnic group are equally important and meaningful to many ethnic minorities. The relationship between ethnic and national identity varies across individuals, showing either positive or negative correlations or no correlation at all. Contrary to popular stereotypes, having pride in one's ethnic group membership and maintaining a strong ethnic identity do not weaken or compromise one's national identity or sense of being an American.

BOX 5.1

Components of Ethnic Identity

- Self-Categorization and Labeling—ethnic labels and categories that are used to describe oneself
- Commitment and Attachment—sense of belonging and emotional ties to one's ethnic group
- Exploration—seeking information and experiences related to one's ethnic heritage by participating in cultural activities
- Ethnic Behaviors—behaviors and practices associated with one's ethnic group
- Evaluation and In-Group Attitudes—positive or negative attitudes about one's ethnic group or level of comfort with one's ethnic group membership
- Values and Beliefs—endorsement and promotion of one's ethnic group's belief system and values
- Importance and Salience—extent to which ethnicity is an important part of one's life
- Ethnic Identity and National Identity—the relationship between one's identification with a particular ethnic group and with a particular nation or country

SOURCE: Phinney & Ong (2007).

When considering all of these components of ethnic identity, it becomes apparent that no single component can adequately capture a person's ethnic identity. Moreover, the ways in which people can experience and express their ethnic identities are innumerable when considering their unique experiences for each of these components. Thus, individuals who might use the same ethnic label to describe themselves might have altogether different attitudes, views, and feelings about their ethnic group, which can lead to diverse experiences and psychosocial issues around their ethnicity. In short, evaluating ethnic identity solely on the basis of someone's ethnic label is insufficient because it is akin to judging a book solely on the basis of its cover; thus, to fully understand the meaning and significance of ethnic identity, all of its cognitive, emotional, and behavioral components must be explored.

Gender Identity

Gender typing is the process by which children learn the behaviors, interests, and abilities that are associated with being masculine or feminine in their culture, whereas **gender identity** is an individual's fundamental sense of being male or female, shaped by gender typing yet potentially independent of social and cultural norms and rules for gender (Wade & Tavris, 2008). Culture plays an integral role in shaping societal assumptions and expectations about male and female responsibilities and abilities, or gender roles. For instance, in the Chinese culture, Confucian philosophical principles outline hierarchical family roles based on gender and age, requiring wives to assume a more nurturing family role, and husbands to assume more family leadership roles. Such gender roles and expectations are not based on actual biological sex differences or abilities, but are instead established by cultural beliefs and values and cultural and social structures and institutions (Pyke & Johnson, 2003). This is evidenced by the fact that the parameters of gender identity and gender roles vary across cultural and ethnic groups, and can transform and change across historical periods and with acculturation (Chun & Akutsu, 2003). Cultural notions of "two-spirited" or cross-gender individuals among American Indians and Alaska Natives speak to gender diversity across different cultural traditions. **Two-spirited individuals** are thought to be blessed with both a male and female spirit and historically many fulfilled spiritual, sacred, and ceremonial roles in their tribal communities (Balsam, Huang, Fieland, Simoni, & Walters, 2004; Garnets, 2002). Thus, two-spirited persons have historically been valued members in their tribes, considered to possess special spiritual gifts and powers, thereby challenging dominant Western models of gender identity that favor dichotomous gender categories and treat gender nonconformity as a sign of psychopathology.

Sexual Identity

Sexual identity or sexual orientation encompasses the broad range of sexual, emotional, and erotic attractions that exist among individuals (Wade & Tavris, 2008). According to Garnets (2002), new developments in the study of sexuality have contributed to more comprehensive conceptualizations of sexual identity in the following ways:

- Sexual identities are considered to be complex, multidimensional, and fluid, reflecting the fact that people of the same gender can be sexually, emotionally, and erotically attracted to one another in many different ways. This counters older, more simplistic views of sexual identity that were typically restricted to "heterosexual" and "homosexual" categorizations, and overlooked the broad continuum of sexuality existing within and between these categorizations.

- Sexual identity is experienced and expressed in many different ways; it encompasses erotic-emotional behaviors and fantasies, emotional attachments, self-identification, and current relationship status *in addition to* sexual behavior. In the past, sexual behavior was thought to be the defining feature of sexual identity; however, sexual behaviors and sexual fantasies can be independent from sexual identity.
- Sexual orientation can change across a person's lifetime and across different social and cultural contexts, whereas in the past it was thought to be fixed and unchanging.

Sexual identity formation and experiences among ethnic minorities can differ from those of European Americans. As reflected in Damon's experiences in the opening narrative of this chapter, forming an integrated sense of self and developing social bonds with different ethnic and sexual communities can be complicated by one's racial and sexual minority status. For lesbian and bisexual women of color, sexism can be an additional stressor that complicates their identity formation.

Class Identity

Class or socioeconomic status (SES) refers to one's financial and social standing. As noted in Chapter 2, different socioeconomic groups or classes have different degrees of access to society's wealth and resources, which can produce distinct life experiences and even different attitudes, values, and behaviors that are unique to their class groupings. SES can be examined on multiple levels, including neighborhood SES (e.g., educational levels and median household incomes of neighborhood residents), family SES (e.g., family income and family assets and savings), and individual SES (individual education levels, occupations, and incomes) (Chen & Paterson, 2006). It is important to consider these different levels of SES because each may have its own relationship or pathway to psychological adjustment and distinct implications for interventions. For instance, if neighborhood SES, rather than individual SES, is a stronger predictor of health and well-being, then community-level interventions that address neighborhood SES disparities might be more effective than interventions focused at the individual level.

Researchers have also found that a person's subjective sense of his or her economic status is an equally or even more powerful predictor of health and adjustment because it addresses their perceived ability to meet their daily needs, and consequent stress that they might be feeling from economic pressures. One study (Barrera, Caples, & Tein, 2001) identified a cross-culturally valid construct of subjective sense of economic hardship for African American, Mexican American (both English- and Spanish-speaking), and European American urban parents that included the following: (1) the inability to afford specific necessities for living, (2) a general sense that financial obligations outstrip the family's ability to meet them, (3) behavioral attempts to reduce expenses or generate more income to meet obligations, and (4) hopelessness that the future will bring a brighter financial outlook. By identifying these dimensions of subjective economic hardship, ethnic psychology researchers can more clearly understand how SES impacts ethnic minority health and psychosocial functioning.

HOW DO IDENTITIES INTERSECT? HETEROGENEITY AND HYBRIDITY IN A MULTICULTURAL WORLD

The ways in which people experience and express their identities rarely fit into "Black" or "White" or dichotomous categories and labels. Damon's experiences illuminate how his race and sexual orientation intersected to create his unique life experiences; thus, considering either of his identity dimensions in isolation overlooks their interrelationship and significance to his overall well-being and sense of self. Damon did not solely think of himself as an African American man because he believed that his ethnic group did not fully accept his sexual identity. Likewise, he didn't exclusively define himself by his sexual identity because he could not fully identify with a predominantly European American gay community. As such, Damon occupied a unique social position at the intersection of two minority identities. Social science scholars thus believe that there is tremendous "heterogeneity and hybridity," or diversity within and across various identity groupings. Indeed, when you reflect on the many groups that you identify with—whether they are groups tied to your ethnic, gender, or sexual identities—you will readily notice that not everyone in these groups thinks or acts alike. Instead, each group exhibits tremendous diversity along multiple, intersecting identity dimensions, which is a core feature of a multicultural world.

Ethnic psychology research provides compelling evidence for intersecting identities and their contribution to distinct life experiences. In statistical terms, this is often captured by "interaction effects" between different identity dimensions and background characteristics. For example, race and gender interaction effects for health disparities are well documented. In a study of European, African, Mexican, Puerto Rican, and Cuban American adults (Read & Gorman, 2006), women showed more functional health limitations than men across all ethnic groups. However, when race and gender interactions were examined, African American women were a special high-risk group exhibiting poorer health than European and African American men on all health measures (self-rated health, daily physical functioning, and being diagnosed with a life-threatening medical condition like heart disease, diabetes, or cancer) even after adjusting for the possible health effects of SES and other demographic factors.

The intersection between race and gender also produces variations in gender-related attitudes. African Americans in general show more critical understanding of the origins and extent of gender inequality than European Americans. However, when gender differences are also considered, African American women show the highest level of recognition and critical understanding of gender inequities while European American men are the least likely to perceive gender inequities and to understand their social origins (Kane, 2000). The distinct perspectives and life experiences of African American women, which are shaped by the intersection of gender, race, and class, spawned the "womanist" movement. Ethnic minority women and their allies initiated this movement as an alternative framework to feminism because it failed to recognize racism, ethnocentrism, and poverty as equivalent concerns to sexism (Lyons, Carlson, Thurm, Grant, & Gipson, 2006).

In sum, the complex and innumerable ways in which identity dimensions intersect speak to "multiplicity" and "hybridity" in the experiences and expressions of the self, even for individuals in single ethnic minority groups that are frequently mischaracterized as monolithic and homogeneous ethnic entities. By fully attending to the diversity and multiple realities that exist within and across ethnic groups, rigid racial, gender, sexual, and class stereotypes can be dismantled allowing for a more accurate and rich understanding of psychological phenomena in a multicultural context. In the following section, current research findings on the development and formation of different identity dimensions are outlined. Many of these conceptual models of identity development and formation do not always capture the dynamic interaction between multiple identity dimensions partly due to the practical constraints of current empirical research methods. Nonetheless, these models represent an important beginning to exploring the process and nature of the developing self.

MODELS OF IDENTITY DEVELOPMENT AND FORMATION

Racial Identity Development

Racial identity development models are informed by a social constructionist perspective of race that proposes that racial identity is a response to racial hierarchies and racial oppression in society (Helms, 1995). Research on racial identity development has mostly focused on the formation of Black racial identity among African Americans, an area of scholarship that was sparked by the critical examination of race and race relations between African and European Americans during the civil rights movement in the United States.

One of the first and most widely referenced models of Black racial identity development was established by a pioneering researcher in this area of study, William E. Cross, Jr. Cross's model of racial identity development was based on his "theory of nigrescence" (1971, 1995). *Nigrescence* is a French term for "turning Black" and Cross used this term to describe the process of accepting and affirming a Black identity in the context of American race relations (Vandiver, 2001). In Cross's original model (1971), he proposed that African Americans progress through a series of five racial identity stages that reflect different attitudes, feelings, and responses toward racism in their lives. He labeled these five sequential stages as Pre-Encounter, Encounter, Immersion-Emersion, Internalization, and Internalization-Commitment (see Box 5.2). In the Pre-Encounter stage, individuals adopt a pro-White identity by favoring dominant group attitudes and behaviors while denigrating and deemphasizing their Black identity, resulting in low self-esteem and internalized racism. Individuals in this first stage might say things like "I hate being Black" or "I can't stand my Black facial features." In the Encounter stage, individuals begin to recognize the importance of race and racial issues in American society, begin to question their previously held beliefs and attitudes about race, and reevaluate their racial identity following a personal event (e.g., witnessing or experiencing racism for the first time; meeting someone in their racial group who exhibits racial pride and defies negative racial stereotypes). The next stage, Immersion-Emersion, occurs when individuals fully *immerse* themselves in Black culture (e.g., by adopting an African name, favoring clothing and music that is associated with Black culture, exclusively socializing with other Blacks, and increasing their involvement in Black organizations and activities) and develop a strong pro-Black identity that idealizes or romanticizes Black culture. Strong anti-White racial attitudes also arise during this third stage, which can generate feelings of anger or hatred toward the White dominant group and ongoing acts of racial oppression. Emersion occurs when individuals gradually emerge from and relinquish their anti-White stance, achieve greater calm, and take a more rational approach to reevaluating the meaning of race and racial identity in their lives. This eventually leads to Internalization, when individuals accept their Black identity on an emotional and intellectual level. In this stage, a stable Black identity is established, but race and racial identity are no longer the central concerns in one's daily life. Instead, one's racial identity recedes to the background of one's daily activities and it is viewed in the same light as other aspects of the self. Finally, in Internalization-Commitment, individuals fully internalize a positive and secure Black identity, and commit themselves to promoting racial equality and civil rights through social activism.

BOX 5.2

Cross's Stages of Racial Identity Formation

1. Pre-Encounter—Pro-White racial identity and devaluation of own Black racial identity.

2. Encounter—Initial recognition of the importance of race and questioning of previously held racial beliefs.

3. Immersion-Emersion—Full immersion into Black culture; development of a pro-Black identity, which can lead to anger and hatred toward Whites. Emergence from these negative emotions to a point of greater understanding and rational evaluation of race.

4. Internalization—Acceptance of Black racial identity on an emotional and intellectual level. Race and racial identity are no longer central concerns in daily life.

5. Internalization-Commitment—Fully internalized positive Black racial identity and commitment to promoting racial equality, including supporting civil rights of other disenfranchised racial groups.

SOURCE: Cross (1971, 1995).

Evaluating Cross's Model of Racial Identity Development

Cross and other researchers studying Black racial identity have since recommended a number of revisions and updates to Cross's original model of nigrescence. Namely, there is growing recognition that Cross's proposed stages can be too rigid in how they portray racial identity development. Although people's responses to racism can change and grow, racial identity development may not necessarily occur in such a fixed and linear fashion— people from different age groups can show many different features of racial identity development simultaneously, and they might even regress toward earlier stages of development depending on social and life circumstances (Parham, White, & Ajamu, 2000). For instance, a person might move away from an anti-White stance as seen during Emersion, but then revert back to this stance and reenter Immersion when placed under duress when experiencing racism. Thus, the notion of a developmental hierarchy of racial attitudes, beliefs, and behaviors in Cross's model is problematic and not fully supported by current research (Quintana, 2007). Additionally, the proposed stages in Cross's original model are more complex and layered than originally assumed. Cross and his colleagues have acknowledged this point and have since identified additional racial identity dimensions or experiences in the Pre-Encounter, Immersion-Emersion, and Internalization stages in subsequent studies (Vandiver, 2001; Vandiver, Fhagen-Smith, Cokley, Cross, & Worrell, 2001). For instance, an expanded model of Cross's nigresence proposes three different pre-encounter identities, two separate immersion identities, and two internalization identities, underscoring the point that multiple attitudes, feelings, and responses to racism can occur within a single stage of racial identity development (Vandiver et al., 2001). Later, Cross (1995) also found few differences between the Internalization and Internalization-Commitment stages, and thus he combined both of these stages under Internalization.

Despite some of the conceptual limitations to Cross's model and the need for more comprehensive validation studies, research has found that exposure to racism can spark an exploration of one's racial identity and heighten sensitivity to racial discrimination as originally proposed (Quintana, 2007). Additionally, Cross's model has sparked much scholarship and debate on the nature of racial identity and how it unfolds in racially oppressive societies. Cross and his colleagues fully acknowledge that identifying the many possible ideologies and responses to race is an ongoing journey, often leading to more, unexpected findings that require further investigation (Vandiver, 2001). Although Cross's model of racial identity development requires additional exploration, it has influenced numerous models of identity development, including models of minority, ethnic, feminist, womanist, lesbian, and gay identity development, and it has led to the creation of a widely used self-report measure of nigresence that is still being analyzed and studied with Blacks today (Vandiver, 2001). The influence of Cross's model on psychological identity research is highlighted in the next section on ethnic identity development.

Ethnic Identity Development

Similar to racial identity development models, ethnic identity development models propose that individuals move progressively through a series of stages in their search for a stable and secure identity. Unlike racial identity development models, however, ethnic identity development models do not exclusively focus on individuals' responses to racism and racial oppression, but instead focus on individuals' ethnic group ties and membership. Another main distinction between ethnic and racial identity development models is the ethnic populations that are used to validate and study them. Research on ethnic identity development tends to focus on Latino and Asian American populations while studies of racial identity development tend to focus on African American populations (Phinney & Ong, 2007). Reasons for these ethnic differences in study samples are somewhat perplexing, but they might reflect biases among researchers about the life experiences and conditions of different ethnic minority groups. For example, African Americans have been racialized throughout history to such an extent that their race rather than their ethnic or cultural characteristics receives more attention in social science and health research (Landrine & Klonoff, 1996). Nonetheless, racial and ethnic identity development issues are pertinent to all ethnic minority groups given their shared historical experiences of racial oppression in the United States, and the significance of ethnic group affiliation to their overall psychosocial adjustment.

Jean Phinney (1992), a leading researcher of ethnic identity, developed an early-stage model of ethnic identity development based on ego identity development theory and her own findings on ethnic identity formation among ethnic minority adolescents. Phinney also attempted to integrate key ideas from earlier racial and ethnic identity formation frameworks into this model, including key ideas from Cross's model of racial identity development. In this model, Phinney proposes that individuals begin in a state of indifference, confusion, or minimal awareness about their ethnicity, and move toward more complex, flexible, and informed ways of thinking about their ethnic group membership and heightened appreciation of multiculturalism. Phinney outlined this process of ethnic identity development along three different sequential stages labeled as "Unexamined Ethnic Identity," "Moratorium," and "Achieved Ethnic Identity."

Stage 1: Unexamined Ethnic Identity

This beginning stage of ethnic identity formation is characterized by a state of either "diffusion" or "foreclosure." Individuals who are in a state of diffusion show little if any interest in ethnic and racial issues, have no commitment to any particular ethnic group, and have not explored the meaning of their ethnicity; in short, ethnicity is simply a nonissue for those in diffusion. For instance, in a study of ethnic identity development among adolescents (Phinney, 1989, 1992), an African American female who exhibited diffusion stated, "Why do I need to learn about who was the first Black woman to do this or that? I'm just not too interested." In the same study, a Mexican American adolescent male in this first stage likewise stated, "My parents tell me . . . about where they lived, but what do I care? I've never lived there." Individuals who experience diffusion may not have faced or been exposed to ethnic issues in their life (e.g., discrimination and prejudice based on ethnic group membership) and thus have few or no opinions or thoughts on this subject.

In such cases, there is minimal acknowledgment and awareness of ethnic group differences, and little understanding and knowledge of one's own ethnicity and of other ethnic groups. If asked about their ethnicity, people in diffusion might confound nationality with ethnicity by self-identifying as "American" without much thought or consideration of what this might actually mean. For instance, European Americans who grew up in predominantly European American neighborhoods and schools have never faced ethnic discrimination or considered the meaning of their ethnicity, and pay little attention to racial issues may be in a state of diffusion.

Foreclosure is another feature of this first stage that is distinct from diffusion. Unlike diffusion, individuals who exhibit foreclosure make a commitment to an ethnic identity, but they do not explore its meaning, and usually base it on the self-identification of parents and family. This was expressed by a Mexican American adolescent male who exhibited foreclosure: "I don't go looking for my culture. I just go by what my parents say and do, and what they tell me to do, the way they are" (Phinney, 1992). In this case, the ethnic label, cultural values, and attitudes of the parents and family are adopted without independently formulating an ethnic identity through questioning and exploration. This might include readily accepting both positive and negative views of one's ethnic group without question. Ethnic minorities in this early stage might show a preference to belong to the dominant group. An Asian American adolescent male who experienced foreclosure explained, "If I could have chosen, I would choose to be American White, because it's America and I would then be in my country" (Phinney, 1992). In some cases, ethnic minorities in foreclosure also prefer what they perceive to be dominant group physical characteristics and traits by altering their physical appearance. For instance, some in the Asian American community opt for cosmetic surgery to acquire an epicanthic fold or crease on their eyelids in an attempt to look White. Also, in the African American community, individuals might attempt to artificially lighten their skin tone. Some ethnic minorities also might internalize negative attitudes and stereotypes about their own ethnic group. This can be seen in ethnic minorities who criticize or put down their own ethnic group or only date European Americans believing that the physical features of their own ethnic group or of other ethnic minorities are less attractive.

Stage 2: Moratorium

This stage is characterized by active exploration of one's identity through inquiry and experimentation. Individuals begin showing an interest in their ethnic background by asking questions and learning about their ethnic practices and traditions with family members. Also, individuals may begin reading articles and books about their ethnic group, participating in their group's cultural activities or organizations, and gaining a heightened political consciousness. A Mexican American female teen who was in Moratorium discussed this process: "I want to know what to do and how our culture is different from others. Going to festivals and cultural events helps me to learn more about my own culture and about myself" (Phinney, 1992). Active exploration of one's ethnic identity during this stage can be precipitated by a shocking personal or social event that challenges beliefs and attitudes about race in the first stage. For ethnic minorities, this might entail experiencing racism for the first time, which challenges their indifferent racial attitudes and their beliefs in a color-blind world where skin color and race are irrelevant. Likewise, ethnic minorities who might have preferred dominant group membership over their own ethnic group membership will begin to realize that they will never be fully accepted or treated equally by dominant group members. They may thus gain a greater awareness of the negative effects of racism on their personal lives and realize that dominant group cultural values and beliefs may not be beneficial or relevant to them. Ethnic minorities also might enter this stage after acquiring new information that forces them to reevaluate their previously held negative views and stereotypes about their own ethnic group. For instance, Asian Americans who might believe that Asians are nonassertive might encounter a civic leader in their ethnic community who shatters this stereotype. Likewise, a Latino who feels ashamed of his cultural upbringing may meet another Latino who is proud of his cultural heritage. These types of new information or shocking experiences can raise the fundamental question of "What is the meaning of my ethnicity?" for the first time, which can lead to a crisis of identity as noted by a Japanese American male adolescent: "There are a lot of non-Japanese people around me and it gets pretty confusing to try and decide who I am" (Phinney, 1992). An identity crisis in Moratorium sparks a personal search for an ethnic identity that incorporates a new and growing appreciation of one's ethnic group and allows for unique self-expression of one's ethnic group membership.

Stage 3: Achieved Ethnic Identity

In this last stage, individuals finally develop an inner sense of security with their ethnic identity and can appreciate the unique features of their own culture and of other cultures. Ethnic diversity and multiculturalism are valued. Identity conflicts and problems from the previous stages are resolved and negative images and stereotypes of their ethnic group are replaced with feelings of positive self-worth and self-acceptance. There is a greater sense of control and flexibility in defining oneself; rigid and narrow ethnic categorizations are eschewed in favor of an ethnic identity that is congruent with their self-concept and allows them to feel comfortable in their own skin. A Mexican American female teen in this final stage of achieved ethnic identity explained, "People put me down because I'm a Mexican, but I don't care anymore. I can accept myself more." An African American girl in this final stage expressed similar sentiments: "I used to want to be White, because I wanted long flowing hair. And I wanted to be real light. I used to think being light was prettier, but now I think there are pretty dark-skinned girls and pretty light-skinned girls. I don't want to be White now. I'm happy being Black" (Phinney, 1992).

Evaluating Phinney's Model of Ethnic Identity Development

Cross-sectional and longitudinal research with ethnically diverse adolescent and young adult samples indicates that ethnic identity formation follows this developmental hierarchy of stages as proposed in Phinney's model (Phinney, 1989; Phinney & Chavira, 1992; Phinney & Rosenthal, 1992); adults are more likely to be in the Achieved Ethnic Identity stage and adolescents in the Moratorium stage although a small subset of youth show regression to earlier developmental stages (Ponterotto & Park-Taylor, 2007; Quintana, 2007).

Still, there are some caveats to this stage model. First, ethnic identity diffusion and foreclosure in the first stage may be difficult to distinguish from one another suggesting that they may not be entirely distinct experiences as originally proposed (Phinney, 1989). Additionally, the experience of one's ethnic self is not as static or fixed as suggested by these stages, but can instead vary on a daily basis depending on changing situational contexts. In a study of Chinese American adolescents, the extent to which they reported feeling "Chinese"—an experience called "ethnic salience"—changed depending on what they were doing, whom they were with, and what types of situations they encountered. As might be expected, they were more likely to feel Chinese when they were participating in ethnic behaviors (e.g., "speaking Chinese, eating Chinese food), and being in the presence of other Chinese people, including their family members (Yip & Fuligni, 2002). Ethnic identity development also shows important gender differences. African American girls show faster ethnic identity formation than African American boys possibly because they participate in cultural and ethnic customs to a greater extent than boys and are often seen as being the carriers of cultural values and traditions in the African American culture (Phinney & Rosenthal, 1992).

Thus, researchers have questioned the actual nature of Phinney's proposed ethnic identity stages and whether they accurately account for the dynamic and multidimensional properties of ethnic identity development. In response to these criticisms, Phinney and Ong (2007) proposed an alternative approach to studying ethnic identity development that focuses entirely on its *process*. Their rationale for this new process approach is that an active process of investigation, learning, and commitment lies at the core of ethnic identity development. These researchers believe that by measuring two fundamental processes—*exploration* of identity issues and *commitment* in relevant identity domains—a clearer picture of ethnic identity development and its relationship to psychosocial adjustment across different ethnic groups and contexts can be achieved. Phinney and Ong (2007) developed the Multigroup Ethnic Identity Measure-Revised (MEIM-R) to measure these two processes of ethnic identity exploration and commitment (see Table 5.1). Exploration and commitment can be assessed separately or together to examine four possible ethnic identity statuses that capture the basic propositions in Phinney's earlier model: (1) identity diffusion—individuals do not engage in either process, (2) identity foreclosure—individuals make a commitment to an ethnic identity without exploring it, (3) moratorium—individuals are in the process of exploring their ethnic identity without making a commitment, and (4) achieved identity—individuals have explored key identity issues and formed a commitment to an ethnic identity (see Table 5.2). Empirical evidence suggests that these two processes are highly related to each other, which supports the theory that exploration is unlikely without a certain degree of commitment, and that stronger commitment results from heightened exploration (Phinney & Ong, 2007). More research on the MEIM-R needs to be conducted to confirm whether it actually captures the process of ethnic identity development and can accurately predict psychological outcomes. Still, it presents new opportunities to explore how ethnic identity actually develops across diverse populations, and the significance of ethnic identity exploration and commitment to psychosocial functioning.

Table 5.1   Self-Report Items Assessing Exploration and Commitment on the Multigroup Ethnic Identity Measure-Revised (MEIM-R)

Exploration
I have spent time trying to find out more about my ethnic group, such as its history, traditions, and customs.
I have often done things that will help me understand my ethnic background better.
I have often talked to other people in order to learn more about my ethnic group.
Commitment
I have a strong sense of belonging to my own ethnic group.
I understand pretty well what my ethnic group membership means to me.
I feel a strong attachment toward my own ethnic group.

SOURCE: Phinney & Ong (2007).

Table 5.2 Four Possible Ethnic Identity Statuses Based on Ethnic Identity Exploration and Commitment

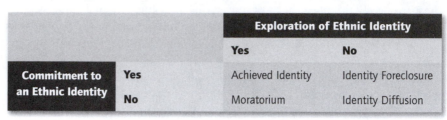

		Exploration of Ethnic Identity	
		Yes	**No**
Commitment to an Ethnic Identity	**Yes**	Achieved Identity	Identity Foreclosure
	No	Moratorium	Identity Diffusion

Factors Shaping Ethnic Identity Development

A burgeoning body of research shows that ethnic identity development is shaped by a dynamic interplay of individual, social, and environmental factors. In particular, studies have highlighted developmental, family, social, and acculturation factors that potentially elicit different experiences, expressions, and views of one's ethnicity.

Developmental Factors. Studies have shown that an individual's developmental stage and tasks can affect his or her ethnic and racial identity development. According to Eriksonian theory, the primary developmental task during adolescence is to form a secure and stable identity through exploration and questioning of one's group affiliations and personal beliefs, values, and goals (Erikson, 1950). Research shows that ethnic and racial identity formation follows this developmental trajectory such that individuals show heightened exploration and questioning of ethnicity and ethnic group membership during their adolescent years. During this developmental stage, adolescents begin to develop an ethnic group consciousness (Quintana, 1998) and begin to think about their group identity in more abstract ways (e.g., ethnic heritage, birthplace, ethnic beliefs, and values) that are perceived to be stable across different contexts and part of a unified sense of self (e.g., a bicultural Mexican American identity) (Phinney, 1993). This normative process of actively searching for an ethnic or racial identity during adolescence does not necessarily elicit an identity crisis involving heightened levels of stress and conflict as researchers had once assumed. Instead, exploration and questioning of one's ethnicity and race appears to be much more subtle and gradual beginning in early adolescence and lasting until late adolescence and possibly early adulthood (Phinney, 1992; Quintana, 2007).

Family Factors. In many respects, the family is where an individual's ethnic identity development first begins. Parents teach their children about the cultural beliefs, values, traditions, and expectations of their ethnic group, albeit to varying degrees, and in the process convey to them what it means to be a member of their ethnic group. Parents can also impart positive or negative views and attitudes about their own ethnic group and about others, which can further influence their offspring's ethnic self-identification. Studies have shown that children are more likely to develop strong ethnic identities if their parents possess strong ethnic identities themselves (Farver, Narang, & Bhadha, 2002), act as role models and provide guidance to their children for living in a multicultural community (Phinney & Rosenthal, 1992), and promote cultural maintenance in their families (Phinney, Romero, Nava, & Huang, 2001).

Social Factors. Minority status and community characteristics are key social factors that influence ethnic identity development. For minority youths, ethnicity is often the most important part of their identity due to the presence of racial stratification (Phinney, 1993). In this case, minority status can heighten "ethnic self-awareness" or the degree to which individuals are consciously aware of their ethnicity. Asian American college students in Boston, for instance, showed greater ethnic self-awareness than their European American counterparts when they were perceived to be the ethnic minority in a social situation (Kim-Ju & Liem, 2003). Interestingly, the Asian American students in this study also showed heightened ethnic self-awareness when they were the ethnic majority in a social situation largely because they were unaccustomed to being in this type of social setting.

Minority status can also contribute to internalized racism, which undermines development of a secure and stable ethnic identity. In a study of ethnically diverse 10th graders in Los Angeles, more Asian American students stated that they would prefer to be White if they could change their ethnic group membership compared to their African American and Hispanic peers. This finding might be related to restricted or limited access to positive Asian American images in the popular media or in politics. In support of this notion, these same Asian American students had difficulties naming leading Asian American personalities who could serve as role models (Phinney, 1989).

Community characteristics also play an important role in ethnic identity development. The ethnic density of one's neighborhood and the ethnic composition of family and social networks, and daily settings (e.g., schools and neighborhoods), potentially have more effects on ethnic identity formation and psychological adaptation than national policies on immigration and cultural diversity (Phinney, Horenczyk, Liebkind, & Vedder, 2001). Also, youth who possess strong ethnic identities are more likely to belong to ethnic communities that are structured and organized, cohesive, provide a sense of kinship, possess cultural institutions that are central in everyday life, and have community leaders who can act as role models (Phinney & Rosenthal, 1992).

Acculturation Factors. Acculturation effects on ethnic identity development have been reported for Asian American and Latino groups. Among Asian American and Latino college students, recent immigrants who came from families with low English proficiency and resided in ethnically similar immigrant neighborhoods showed the strongest ethnic identities throughout their college years compared to their more acculturated peers (Sears, Fu, Henry, & Bui, 2003). Studies have also reported an overall weakening of ethnic identity with acculturation although this seems to be an oversimplification; different components of ethnic identity may be stable and resilient to cultural shifts while others are more susceptible to change. For instance, cultural values, positive attitudes and feelings about one's ethnic group, and ethnic loyalty have been shown to be resilient to acculturation while knowledge and awareness of one's cultural heritage may diminish across generations (Phinney & Rosenthal, 1992).

Different acculturation modes also have variable effects on ethnic identity development. In one study, South Asian Indian adolescents who exhibited integration had stronger ethnic identities, exhibited greater exploration and understanding of their ethnic identity, and were more appreciative of other ethnic groups compared to those who exhibited marginalization or separation (Farver et al., 2002).

Multiracial Identity Development

I have been queried about my racial identity (or erroneously, my "nationality"). People, mostly White, have wondered why I do not choose to "pass" as White. Other people, mostly Black, have demanded to know why I say I am biracial instead of "just admitting" I am Black. I have been scrutinized and found to be "not Black enough" by some, whereas others have deemed me "too into racial issues." People have given me advice on how I should talk, think, act, and feel about myself racially. Repeatedly, people have tried to define my existence for me. . . . What this has done is forced me to examine myself. (C. B. Williams, 1999, p. 34)

This passage illustrates the distinct ethnic identity issues and challenges that multiracial individuals often encounter in their daily lives. These types of negative racial experiences contribute to **"otherness status,"** which is a form of social marginalization and social isolation on the basis of race, including societal pressures to "fit" into specified racial categorizations (Root, 1990). Otherness status is literally seen on demographic forms and questionnaires that require multiracial people to check the "other" box if they do not fit into specified racial categories. The meaning of this term "other" is not only vague and confusing, but it also overlooks the fact that multiracial individuals can have multiple ways of identifying themselves.

In a comprehensive review of the multiracial identity literature, Shih and Sanchez (2005) summarized key psychosocial issues that complicate multiracial identity development:

- *Conflict Between Private and Public Definitions.* Multiracial individuals often feel conflicted when their private definitions of their self do not match how the public or society defines them. In these situations, feelings of frustration and marginalization arise from social pressures to meet public expectations and views of their racial heritage.

- *Justifying Identity Choices.* Multiracial persons typically have to justify how they define themselves particularly when faced with ongoing questions about and challenges to their membership in different ethnic groups. This can lead to self-doubt and constant introspection and questioning about their identity selection.

- *Forced-Choice Dilemmas.* Multiracial individuals face social pressures to define themselves in one particular way, whether it's a single racial category, a mixed race identity, or some other identity that does not allow for more fluid and integrated experiences of one's multiracial self. Feelings of distress, guilt, and fragmentation can occur in these situations when multiracial individuals feel like they have to reject or deny a part of their racial heritage to fit into these limiting categories.

- *Lack of Role Models.* Multiracial individuals face the added challenge of finding positive multiracial role models in the community who can either help steward them through their identity search or show them possible ways to lead healthy and racially integrated lives. Multiracial public figures that might serve as role models are often rendered invisible in the popular media by casting them as monoracial individuals. For example, Tiger Woods, one of the most highly regarded athletes of his time, is often exclusively portrayed as an African American role model although his mother is Asian American.

- *Conflicting Messages.* Multiracial youth are often exposed to conflicting messages about race from their family and their community. In their interracial family, parents might directly or indirectly communicate to their multiracial children that race is not necessarily an issue and that different racial groups live in peaceful coexistence. Parents might also communicate to their multiracial children that people unconditionally accept their multiracial heritage. However, when multiracial children enter the community they are confronted with racial discrimination and prejudice and interracial conflict, which can leave them feeling confused, distressed, and unable to integrate their multiple racial identities.

- *Double Rejection.* Multiracial persons often face rejection by the dominant group and other ethnic minority groups, particularly if people do not associate their physical features with a particular racial group. This experience of double rejection results in isolation, psychological stress, and the lack of a stable and supportive reference group for their identity search.

Some researchers believe that these psychosocial issues associated with multiracial identity require a new and more complex understanding of identity development than what is currently offered in monoracial or monoethnic identity models (Root, 1990). One study of African and European American biracial teens, for instance, showed that their search for an identity is much more layered and complex than that of monoracial teens (Gillem, Cohn, & Throne, 2001). These biracial African and European American teens faced the challenge of integrating multiple racial identities, negotiating conflicting relationships with both dominant and ethnic minority groups, and gaining their acceptance. Although this is a potentially stressful experience, some of the biracial teens in this study emerged from it with a more sensitive and balanced understanding of dominant and ethnic minority group racial experiences, particularly if they had a positive and loving relationship with both of their monoracial parents. Other studies have likewise shown that biracial adolescents experience their ethnicity and race in distinct ways from their monoracial peers. In a study of ethnically diverse high school students from the southwestern United States (self-identified Black, White, Asian, Latino, Asian/White, Black/White, Latino/White, Asian/Black, Asian/Latino, and Black/Latino students), biracial adolescents reported stronger ethnic identities than their monoethnic White peers, but weaker ethnic identities than those reported by their monoethnic minority peers (Bracey, Bamaca, & Umana-Taylor, 2004). These findings suggest that biracial teens are more likely than monoracial White teens to explore their ethnic identities because they must cope with more complicated and pressing racial identity issues and concerns in their daily lives. However, these racial identity issues and concerns can lead to confusion and less commitment to an ethnic identity.

Current models of racial identity development do not fully capture these unique multiracial experiences because they are exclusively based on the experiences of monoracial persons. Poston (1990) outlined specific shortcomings to monoracial identity development models when considering these types of multiracial identity experiences:

- *Monoracial identity models do not allow for the integration of more than one group identity.* The process of integrating and negotiating different, and at times conflicting, group identities, as in the case of negotiating ethnic minority and dominant group identities, is often entirely overlooked by monoracial identity models.
- *Monoracial identity models imply that multiracial individuals must reject one or more of their ethnic affiliations.* Cross's model, for instance, proposes that Blacks who enter a state of Immersion may develop anti-White and pro-Black attitudes. This poses problems for biracial Black and White individuals, however, because they cannot necessarily reject a part of themselves, particularly if they have positive relationships with a parent or family members from the dominant group.
- *Monoracial identity models assume acceptance from the minority group of origin.* In Cross's Immersion-Emersion and Internalization stages, acceptance by the Black community is assumed and in many respects required for the formation of a stable and secure Black racial identity. However, biracial Black and White individuals may face discrimination and rejection in the Black community, especially if they have physical features that are perceived to be more similar to Whites.

Biracial identity development models have been developed to address these limitations to monoracial identity frameworks. Most of these identity development models propose that healthy identity development involves moving from a diffuse or unspecified racial identity to a monoracial identity imposed by society, typically eliciting feelings of ambivalence and struggle, until a distinct biracial identity is individually defined and established (Gillem, Cohn, & Throne, 2001).

Biracial Identity Resolution Strategies

One of the first models of biracial identity development was proposed by Maria Root, a pioneering researcher of biracial and multiracial identity experiences. Based on her clinical work with biracial adolescents, Root (1990) believed that biracial identity conflicts and issues, particularly pressures to compartmentalize different parts of one's ethnic heritage, are typically resolved in four different ways:

Accepting of the Identity Society Assigns. This resolution typically occurs in racially oppressive societies where biracial individuals do not have the freedom to choose their racial identity. In these societies, an ethnic minority group identity is typically imposed on a biracial individual if he or she has physical features that are associated with the minority group. This can be a positive resolution if the biracial individual feels a sense of belonging to the racial group to which he or she is assigned. For instance, a biracial Black and White individual who is assigned a Black identity by society may feel supported and fully accepted by his or her African American extended family, which can then become a stable and secure reference group.

Identification With Both Racial Groups. Individuals who follow this resolution are likely to self-identify in a biracial manner by describing their racial background as "part African American, part European American" or "mixed," for example. This can be a positive resolution strategy if their personality remains consistent across groups and they are fully accepted by both groups. Biracial individuals who exhibit this resolution tend to view their mixed race heritage as a positive marker of their uniqueness and individuality. Root believed that this may be the most idealistic identity resolution and may only occur in those regions of the country where there is greater tolerance and high numbers of mixed marriages and biracial children.

Identification With a Single Racial Group. Although this resolution looks like the first resolution, individuals who exhibit this resolution actively select their racial identity even if it is different from the identity that family members and society assign or possibly conflicts with their physical features. This resolution can be a positive experience if biracial individuals are not marginalized by their selected groups and they do not suppress their other race. Difficulties arise when their chosen group membership is contested or questioned by their reference group, requiring them to develop coping strategies to deal with this situation.

Identification as a New Racial Group. Feeling kinship with other biracial individuals more than with any other racial group is a main feature of this resolution strategy. Shared experiences with social marginalization that come with otherness status may encourage biracial individuals to bond with one another and form a new racial group. Root (1990) believes that this resolution strategy can be seen in the *hapa haole* community (half White, half Asian) in Hawai'i. Biracial individuals in this community often move fluidly between different racial groups without feeling constrained to identify with any particular racial label. They view themselves as being apart from specific racial groups, yet do not feel marginalized because they have formed a new and stable biracial reference group.

Stage Models of Biracial Identity Development

More recent models of biracial identity development have expanded upon some of Maria Root's key propositions. For example, Collins (2000) believed that biracial identity development transpires along a progressive stage-like sequence as depicted in stage models of ethnic and racial identity development. Like others who study the biracial experience, however, Collins emphasized that the different stages or phases of biracial identity encompass different identity questions and issues than those found in monoethnic and monoracial models. Based on interviews with biracial individuals of Japanese and European American descent, he outlined four different phases of development, which he labeled Phase I—Questioning and Confusion, Phase II—Refusal and Suppression, Phase III—Infusion and Exploration, and Phase IV—Resolution and Acceptance.

Phase I—Questioning and Confusion. This phase is characterized by constant feelings of differentness, confusion, and discomfort as one struggles to formulate a racial identity without a clear reference group. Ongoing questions by others about one's racial background (e.g., constantly facing the question, "What are you?") coupled with persistent discrimination and stigmatization contribute to feelings of alienation and isolation during this phase.

Phase II—Refusal and Suppression. After facing constant questions and challenges around one's racial background, individuals attempt to define themselves in this phase. This is a crucial phase of development because individuals strive to identify with a clear reference group or search for multiple reference groups. Individuals may choose one group over the other during this time and deny or suppress the identity that they have rejected. A positive identity can begin to develop if biracial individuals have the opportunity to socialize and interact with people from culturally diverse backgrounds, other biracial people, and role models in the community who affirm individual difference. Biracial individuals thus begin to formulate an identity based on their social interactions outside of the family during this stage.

Phase III—Infusion and Exploration. This stage is marked by confusion and guilt over choosing one identity over the other raising the question of, "What about my other half?" Biracial individuals may feel uncomfortable with the identity that they had selected and may attempt to integrate their other identity. During this time, overidentification with the identity that they had rejected can occur. For instance, biracial Japanese and European American individuals who have identified solely as a European American while rejecting or suppressing their Japanese heritage in Phase II may feel guilty about this and self-identify exclusively as a Japanese American in this phase.

Phase IV—Resolution and Acceptance. Biracial individuals enter this phase when they fully accept their biracial identity, marked by such statements as, "I am who I am." An integrated sense of self is established by treating both of their racial heritages as equally important aspects of the self. This experience of recognizing and valuing each side of one's identity is akin to blending individual colors from a color palette—when two distinct racial identities are fused together, they form an altogether new biracial identity that is appreciated and affirmed for its uniqueness.

Evaluating Models of Biracial Identity Development

The identity development models offered by Root and Collins highlight a number of important distinctions between biracial and monoracial identity development. In sum, biracial individuals face added questions and challenges to their identity early in their lives that can generate internal conflict, confusion, and even guilt over their racial group membership. A stable and secure racial identity can be achieved, however, if they can successfully navigate social and family pressures to define themselves in particular, often confining ways, and eventually develop a positive sense of self that matches how they feel and experience their mixed race heritage. Supportive family environments, multicultural communities, and biracial or multiracial social networks that affirm and value multiracial identity can facilitate this process and help to diffuse otherness status.

As with monoracial and monoethnic identity development models, more research is needed to support the basic principles and features of biracial identity development models. The notion that identity development follows distinct sequential stages or phases, as proposed in Collins's model, requires added investigation because researchers have questioned whether this actually occurs. Additionally, research that explores development of more than one racial or ethnic identity tends to exclusively focus on biracial groups, with little attention to the multiracial experience. It is plausible that people with more than two racial backgrounds (e.g., a person with African American, Asian American, and Latino heritages) may have qualitatively different identity experiences. The fundamental questions faced by biracial individuals—for example, "Who am I?" "Which racial groups do I belong to?" "How do I integrate my different races?"—can assume added complexity given that such individuals need to negotiate more racial reference groups and race relations. Resolving these and other questions concerning biracial and multiracial identity development pose a number of challenges to ethnic psychology researchers (Root, 1998). Finding and recruiting a diverse pool of biracial and multiracial study participants is particularly challenging. Typically, researchers look for specific racial or ethnic groups based on an individual's last name, but this method is unfeasible or nearly impossible to follow with biracial and multiracial populations because their mixed heritage cannot be detected in this way. Using convenience samples (e.g., targeting biracial student organizations on college campuses or biracial social organizations for study recruitment) may bias or skew research results in unexpected ways. Although these research issues are difficult to address, they warrant special consideration because biracial and multiracial persons are the fastest growing racial population in the United States as discussed in Chapter 1.

Gender Typing and Gender Identity Formation

A relatively new body of ethnic psychology research has begun to examine how cultural beliefs and values influence gender typing and gender identity development. An ethnic minority group may engage in gender typing by socializing its members at a very young age around culturally prescribed gender behaviors, or specific cultural beliefs about what it means to be a man or a woman. However, the gender identity of individual members may not necessarily conform to their group's cultural beliefs about gender. Gender can therefore be represented and expressed in multiple ways within any given ethnic group. Research with Asian Americans, African Americans, and Latinos/Latinas indicates that a broad array of cultural, social, and political factors shape how gender is represented and expressed in each of these ethnic communities.

Asian American Gender Identity Issues

Research on Asian American gender identity issues has linked Confucian philosophical principles with specific family and social roles for men and women. This philosophical tradition, which has its roots in sixth-century China (Solomon & Higgins, 1997), promotes patriarchal family and social structures giving men greater authority and privileges than women in their family and social roles (E. Lee, 1997). Men are expected to fulfill their roles as the head of their household and primary provider for their families while women are expected to fulfill a more nurturing and supportive family role, caring for their children and attending to daily household chores. These types of gender role expectations are associated with specific gender typing experiences—males are taught to sustain their family's status and reputation in the community, with explicit instructions to fulfill their parents' wishes and to meet familial obligations as standard bearers of their family name (Liu, 2002). These types of gender role expectations and gender typing experiences are particularly salient for the oldest sons in a family who are typically afforded the greatest family and social privileges, and, upon entering adulthood, are expected to assume a family leadership role. Asian American women who live in these types of patriarchal environments have altogether different gender typing experiences; Confucian principles instruct them to assume a secondary role to their husbands, and to subsume their individual needs and wishes to those of their husband, in-laws, and children. Researchers have noted that these types of gender typing experiences in patriarchal societies—which generally afford greater status and privilege to men—heighten the risk for domestic violence by condoning male power assertion and domination over women (I. J. Kim, Lau, & Chang, 2007).

Still, some researchers believe that these types of gender representations and images associated with Asian Americans are limiting, historically imposed by the dominant group, and based on negative stereotypes that overlook the heterogeneity in Asian American gender identities and gender roles. For instance, studies have found that Asian American men may not necessarily follow "traditional" Confucian family roles, but may instead share in domestic tasks and household responsibilities with their wives (Chua & Fujino, 1999). Additionally, Asian American women in patriarchal environments may appear to have a secondary supportive role to their husband, but this might be an artifact of public appearance—behind the doors of their family household, wives actually hold tremendous sway and influence in family decision making, but they practice their authority in a more discrete way that prevents their husbands from losing face in public where he is expected to be the head of his household (E. Lee, 1997). Finally, newer waves of Asian immigrant women are rapidly breaking away from traditional gender role expectations by joining the workforce in greater numbers and achieving greater earning power and financial independence (Kawahara & Fu, 2007). Thus, Asian American men and women construct their gender identities in multiple ways that defy one-dimensional and rigid gender stereotypes. If this is the case, then why do we see highly stereotyped gender images of Asian Americans in the media?

Television shows, movies, and the Internet abound with images of the passive and emasculated Asian American male, the emotionally detached and unaffectionate Asian American father and husband, the hypersexual or subservient Asian American female "geisha," and the hyperfeminine and fragile

Asian female "lotus blossom." Researchers believe that racial stratification and racial oppression lie at the heart of this matter (Espiritu, 1997). In a study of U.S.-born and foreign-born Korean and Vietnamese women (Pyke & Johnson, 2003), the nature and effects of "controlling images" on the social construction of Asian American gender identities were explored. **Controlling images** are stereotyped and negative racial and gender images that are intended to subordinate minority groups and to justify and affirm dominant group power and norms. For the Korean and Vietnamese women in this study, controlling images negatively affected how they constructed and enacted gender in their daily lives in several ways. First, the controlling image of Asian American men as domineering and patriarchal individuals led these women to believe that they could only achieve individual freedom and egalitarian relationships with White men, which discouraged some from even considering relationships with Asian American men. Second, the controlling image of Asian American women as subservient, passive, and quiet individuals caused some women to believe that they had to lose or reject their Asian heritage in order to become independent and assertive women. Likewise, these women reported that White men sometimes believed that they could find greater subservience from Asian women in a relationship. Lastly, these controlling images of Asian American men and women obscured or dismissed variations in their gender behaviors, including reversals in their expected gender roles or hierarchies. In short, controlling racial and gender images produce tension and conflict in the relationships between Asian American women and men, and they especially discourage Asian American women from seeking relationships with their Asian American male counterparts. At the same time, controlling images glorify the White dominant world as a place of absolute gender equity that can cause Asian American men and women to believe that their ethnic identity is incompatible or at odds with their desired gender identity; thus, they might believe that achieving a positive egalitarian or flexible gender identity can only be achieved if they denounce their ethnic heritage and assimilate into White culture.

African American Gender Identity Issues

African American gender identities have also been distorted and stereotyped by controlling images. Historically, African American men have been stereotyped as being deviant, irresponsible, and neglectful in their family and social roles. Popular media images of the angry and hypersexual Black man, the inveterate African American substance abuser, and the absent African American father have sustained these negative stereotypes. Similar to the experiences of other ethnic minority groups, these types of controlling images ignore diverse and positive constructions of gender, and they dehumanize African American men, complicating their attempts to achieve upward mobility in a racially stratified society. In a study of African American manhood, alternative representations of gender identity were presented to African American men from diverse socioeconomic backgrounds (Hammond & Mattis, 2005). This study attempted to uncover a broad range of views on African American manhood by presenting their African American male respondents with one open-ended question—"What does manhood mean to you?" Fifteen different dimensions of African American manhood emerged from the respondents' answers to this question; the most frequently occurring dimension—"responsibility-accountability"—was mentioned by almost half of all respondents. This dimension of African American manhood, which emphasized the importance of taking responsibility for the welfare of one's family and of others, and being accountable for one's personal actions, thoughts, and behaviors, directly contradicted prevailing negative stereotypes and controlling images of African American men. Additional analyses in this study highlighted four larger, interrelated categories of African American manhood. First, respondents described manhood in the context of relationships, believing that manhood included being connected to God, themselves, family, community, and others. Second, manhood was portrayed as a fluid and adaptive process in which positive male traits were believed to develop with time and life experience. Third, manhood was seen as a redemptive process—by becoming an active family and community member, past mistakes and behaviors could be corrected or rectified and one's humanity could be regained. Fourth, being proactive was considered to be a requirement of manhood, such that men were expected to be smart and independent thinkers, anticipate threats or barriers to healthy identity development, and initiate positive behaviors that nurtured their male identities. Thus, these findings illustrate that African American men experience and express their gender identity in multilayered ways that defy one-dimensional gender and racial stereotypes. Moreover, the respondents' frequent mention of the dimension of responsibility-accountability, and their shared view of manhood as involving social and spiritual interconnectedness, life experience, redemption, and proactive behaviors, reflects their overall concerns about dismantling these negative stereotypes, and presenting their own notions of manhood in a more humane fashion.

Recent studies have also begun to explore how African American women construct their gender identities. One study found that African American women report both distinct and common constructions of femininity in comparison to European American women (E. R. Cole & Zucker, 2007). In regard to common views, both African and European American women believed that femininity includes three primary components: (1) a *feminine appearance*, or wearing feminine clothes, grooming, and the presentation of one's home, was considered an important and public aspect of femininity; (2) *feminine traits or demeanor,* encompassing socially desirable traits for women, and (3) *traditional gender role ideology,* or a fundamental belief that women and men are best-suited to fulfill different roles and duties, with women being the best candidates for domestic roles and men being highly suited for work and leadership roles. Still, this shared view of femininity between the African and European American women in this study did not mean that they experienced its components in the same way. In this case, the African American women were more interested than European American women in maintaining a feminine appearance, yet were more likely to describe themselves as feminists. Furthermore, European American women who self-identified as feminists predictably rejected traditional gender role ideology although this was not the case for the African Americans who self-identified as feminists. Thus, African American women appeared to have culturally distinct notions of feminism that contradicted prevailing European American feminist beliefs. Although E. R. Cole and Zucker (2007) acknowledged that these findings might have stemmed from a lack of specificity in how they measured and defined feminism (study participants were simply asked to rate their agreement to the statement, "I am a feminist"), they noted that other studies have likewise found different interpretations and experiences of feminism for African American women. For instance, they note that studies have found that African American women who work outside of the home still believed that their husbands should maintain the traditional role of a family provider because it was essential to their husband's self-esteem and masculinity.

Latino/Latina Gender Identity Issues

Much of the scholarship on Latino and Latina gender identities has focused on the constructs of "machismo" and "marianismo," respectively. **Machismo** refers to a broad set of stereotyped hypermasculine Latino traits that include male dominance, aggression, fearlessness, bravery, authoritarianism, promiscuous behavior, virility, excessive alcohol use, stoicism, reserved or restricted emotions and aloofness, sexism, oppressive and controlling behaviors toward women and children, autonomy, strength, bravado, responsibility, honor, respect, and being a good provider and protector of women, children, and less fortunate members of society (J. B. Torres, Solberg, & Carlstrom, 2002). These stereotyped traits have contributed to narrow and rigid representations of

Latino gender identity manifested in a number of controlling images, including the overly possessive and emotionally volatile Latino husband, the emotionally distant and authoritarian Latino father, and the promiscuous Latin lover. Again, these types of controlling images discount or dismiss alternative manifestations of Latino masculinities and are often used by the dominant group to justify and sustain racial stratification.

The counterpart to machismo is **marianismo** (or the cult of Maria, the Virgin Mary, or the Madonna), which refers to a broad set of stereotyped feminine traits that idealize the moral virtues and personal character of Latinas. Marianismo is often used to elevate Latinas' gender identity by casting them as being morally and spiritually superior to Latinos, possessing an innate ability to endure hardship and suffering, and being self-sacrificing, humble, modest, reserved, and giving and generous. Some researchers believe that although these virtuous qualities are based on narrow gender stereotypes, they are not entirely detrimental because they offer positive Latina gender representations that express loyalty, compassion, and generosity. Still, there continues to be much debate over the meaning and significance of machismo and marianismo to Latino/Latina gender identity, gender typing, and overall psychosocial functioning. This debate has included new critical interpretations of these constructs that call attention to their multidimensional and complex characteristics. For instance, one study (J. B. Torres et al., 2002) found that traditional definitions of machismo (e.g., authoritarian, emotionally restrictive, controlling) were endorsed by only a minority of their diverse Latino sample (Mexican American, Puerto Rican, Cuban, Central and South American, and multiracial Latino men). Instead, Latino participants defined and expressed machismo in much more complicated ways, revealing five distinct dimensions to this construct:

- *Contemporary Masculinity*—flexible gender roles characterized by a preference for cooperation and harmony, less demand for family respect and obedience, and less traditional views of male and female gender roles. They also reported less conflict over their life roles.
- *Machismo*—respect for family remains an important concern, but it is expressed within a caring and emotionally expressive context without demands for control and dominance.
- *Traditional Machismo*—dominant and rigid male gender behaviors characterized by demands for family respect and obedience, holding traditional views of male and female gender roles, being highly conflicted with balancing life roles, emotionally reserved, and more controlling. Latinos who fell into this category seemed to embody many of the negative hypermasculine stereotypes of machismo.

- *Conflicted/Compassionate Machismo*—emphasizes maintaining tradition and defining masculinity through success and achievement. At the same time, there are attempts at being emotionally expressive and empathic in relationships. Men in this category struggle to balance various roles and relationships and they may experience gender identity conflicts as they attempt to meet different, and at times conflicting, cultural, relational, and societal gender expectations.
- *Contemporary Machismo*—values harmonious family relationships and attempts to achieve them by being aware of emotions and expressing them effectively. Although achievement and success is tied to masculinity, balance between work, family, and leisure is valued. Men in this category thus show a strong connection to their families and an "emerging machismo" that successfully integrates cultural tradition, relationships, and societal demands into a masculine identity.

These different dimensions of machismo underscore the need to move away from one-dimensional stereotypes of Latinos in order to fully understand the heterogeneous ways in which they experience and enact gender. Moving away from such stereotypes includes refuting the assumption that machismo is inextricably linked to Latino ethnic identity. One study, for instance, found that ethnic membership was not related to endorsement of traditional male gender roles for Latino adolescents (Abreu, Goodyear, Campos, & Newcomb, 2000). In fact, the European American adolescents in this study were more likely to endorse traditional male gender roles, which argues against the idea that characteristics of machismo are part and parcel of being Latino.

In summary, the cultural histories and traditions, social conditions, and minority status of ethnic minority groups intimately shape how they enact gender typing and develop gender identities. Historically, controlling gender and racial images have been imposed upon ethnic minorities in the popular media, ultimately limiting our understanding of their gender identity formation. New research on ethnic minority gender identity, however, is beginning to reveal the multidimensional and complex ways in which men and women of color construct and experience gender in their daily lives.

Sexual Identity Formation

Understanding how ethnic minorities construct their sexual identities still requires much exploration because most of the literature on sexual identity development has focused on the experiences of gay European American men. A few studies over the last decade indicate that ethnic minority gay and lesbian identity formation, often known as the "coming out" process, can be qualitatively different from that of European Americans due to minority and cultural factors. In regard to minority factors, gay and lesbian people of color must contend with stressors associated with double minority status based on their race and sexual orientation. Not only must they deal with homophobia in larger society, but they also encounter racial discrimination in a predominantly White gay and lesbian community. For ethnic minority lesbians, the added experience of sexism presents yet another set of challenges to their identity formation. In terms of cultural factors, cultural beliefs, and values pertaining to marriage and relationships, traditional gender roles, family role expectations, and the discussion of sex in the family and community present additional challenges to exploring and developing gay and lesbian identities. Moreover, ethnic minority groups that perceive the gay and lesbian community as being exclusively European American might equate gay and lesbian self-identification as a rejection of one's ethnic heritage. In these circumstances, ethnic minority gays and lesbians potentially face isolation, discrimination, and marginalization in dominant society and in their own families and ethnic communities. These types of life experiences require ethnic minority gays and lesbians to negotiate multiple, often competing, cultural and social demands, which can complicate their attempts to establish an integrated sexual identity.

In a study of African American, Latino, and European American youths who self-identified as gay, lesbian, or bisexual, ethnic differences were found for sexual identity integration, but not for identity formation (Rosario, Schrimshaw, & Hunter, 2004). **Identity formation** in this study was defined as a part of the coming out process in which individuals become aware of their sexual preferences and begin to explore their lesbian, gay, or bisexual identities, whereas **identity integration** comes later, when individuals learn to accept their sexual identities, overcome internalized homophobia by adopting positive attitudes about their sexuality, feel more comfortable about disclosing their sexual identity to others, and become more engaged in the lesbian, gay, and bisexual communities. All of the youth in this study showed the same developmental trajectory of identity formation by experiencing its milestones at the same point in their lives regardless of their ethnicity. However, when it came to identity integration, African American youth were less engaged with the gay, lesbian, and bisexual community, felt less comfortable with others knowing about their sexual identities, and had disclosed their sexual identities to fewer people compared to their European American peers. Interestingly, this changed with time—these same African American youth established a stronger integrated sexual identity than the European American youth over a one-year period, suggesting that once they overcame cultural pressures against self-identifying as gay, lesbian, or bisexual, they became even more committed to that identity. For the Latino youth, sexual identity formation and integration were sometimes similar to both African and European American youth. Specifically, the Latino youth were similar to European American youth in regard to their comfort level with others knowing about their sexuality, yet they were similar to African American youth in disclosing it to fewer people. The authors of this study hypothesized that these somewhat contradictory findings might reflect Latino cultural values of "familism," which promotes family support and cohesion, and *"respeto"* or respect for family elders and authority figures. In this case, Latino gay, lesbian, and bisexual youth may feel comfortable about their sexuality knowing that their families will always support and accept them, yet feel reluctant to disclose it to their families out of concern for potentially upsetting older family members.

Asian Americans also experience unique cultural issues in sexual identity formation. The model minority stereotype places pressure on Asian Americans to follow social conventions and norms, which can discourage them from claiming a sexual identity that is considered nonnormative or deviant by some in society. Chan (1995) outlined additional cultural factors that can complicate the coming out process for Asian Americans:

- *Distinct cultural conceptualizations of sexuality.* Asian Americans and other ethnic groups may not necessarily identify with fixed and rigid sexual categories like "homosexual" or "bisexual" as defined by the dominant group. Instead, they may experience and view their sexuality along a more fluid and broader continuum.
- *Lack of identification with the gay and bisexual community.* Asian Americans, like other ethnic minorities, may be reluctant to identify with the gay, lesbian, and bisexual communities because they are mostly European American. Furthermore, if they experience or witness racial discrimination by European American gays, lesbians, and bisexuals, they may find it especially difficult to integrate their ethnic and sexual identities.
- *Concerns that one's ethnic identity will be negated or overlooked by others.* Asian Americans may be hesitant to self-identify as gay or lesbian because others might then solely focus on their sexual orientation and completely disregard or ignore the significance of their ethnicity to the overall sense of self.
- *Distinctions between private and public selves.* For traditionally identified Asian Americans, sexuality and sexual behaviors are considered private rather than public matters (Chan, 1995). Thus, sexual identity

is considered part of the private self that is left to one's own discretion. The public self, however, conforms to behaviors that bring honor to one's family. Because coming out is a very public statement, it violates cultural norms for keeping sexual matters private, particularly when it is potentially stigmatizing or shameful to one's family. Keeping sexual matters private is even enforced for heterosexual Asian Americans. Asian American kids from traditionally identified families often report rarely seeing their parents kiss, hug, or hold hands with each other in public. Imagine, then, the conflict that many gay and lesbian Asian Americans experience as they come to terms with expressing their own sexuality that might be considered a cultural taboo. As such, Asian American gays and lesbians may be more likely to come out to people from other ethnic groups rather than in their own families or ethnic communities (Hom, 1996).

- *Familial obligation.* Similar to other collectivistic cultures, Asian Americans may hide their gay and lesbian sexual identities due to family expectations and obligations. The expression of sexuality among traditionally identified Asian Americans is mainly reserved for procreation and the continuation of the family name. This is especially the case for sons who are expected to produce heirs who will carry on the family name and family traditions.

Gender adds another important layer to sexual identity formation. Lesbians of color must simultaneously deal with the multiple minority stressors of sexism, heterosexism, and racism within the dominant culture and in their own ethnic groups, all of which can impact their sexual identification (Greene, 1997). A study of African American and Latina lesbians showed that their sexual identity development was more similar to each other than that of European American lesbians (Parks, Hughes, & Matthews, 2004). In general, women of color in this study were younger when they began to question their sexual orientation and spent more time deciding whether they were lesbian compared to European Americans. Additionally, lesbians of color reported significantly less disclosure to persons outside of their families than White lesbians. When age was considered, older women of color were somewhat more likely than their younger counterparts to have disclosed their sexual identity to family members, whereas older White women were far less likely than younger White women to have done so. Still, Parks et al. (2004) noted that lesbians from all ethnic backgrounds also share common experiences, particularly in regard to the lack of visible lesbian role models, facing silence or prejudicial attitudes about same-gender sexual orientation, dealing with the presumption of heterosexuality by others, and pervasive homophobia in society.

In sum, sexual identity development represents a complex balancing act for many ethnic minorities, in which competing concerns and demands associated with their sexual orientation, ethnicity, race, and gender must be negotiated and reconciled. Forming an integrated sense of self is complicated by living in socially stratified environments where being anything other than heterosexual is considered deviant or nonnormative, and serves as justification for social marginalization or even violence. Variations in the way ethnic minorities experience and express their sexuality are innumerable when considering that sexual identity, like other aspects of the self, occurs along a broad continuum that transcends fixed categories and classification schemes. No single factor can reliably predict one's sexual orientation whether it is heterosexual, homosexual, bisexual, or otherwise (Garnets, 2002). Likewise, there is no single pattern for sexual identity development. Researchers are beginning to acknowledge these points by moving away from older stage models of sexual identity development. Moreover, many are beginning to acknowledge that the construction of sexuality is in many respects an individual journey, and that notions of "sexual identity" are more accurately framed as "sexual identities" to reflect the tremendous diversity and heterogeneity that exists within ethnic minority communities.

RELATIONSHIP OF IDENTITIES TO PSYCHOSOCIAL ADJUSTMENT

Different dimensions of the self affect psychological functioning and overall mental health in variable and important ways. The following section highlights key research findings on the relationship of ethnic, racial, biracial and multiracial, gender, sexual, and class identities to multiple indices of individual health and well-being.

Racial Identity and Adjustment

Self-Esteem

Racial identity is linked with self-esteem through "racial identity schemas." **Racial identity schemas** are a set of beliefs and emotional responses related to race that individuals are socialized to during their development, influencing how race-related information is interpreted and internalized into overall individual identity (Alvarez & Helms, 2001). The types of racial identity schemas that people hold reflect their stage of racial identity development. For Asian Americans, more sophisticated racial identity schemas (i.e., Immersion-Emersion and Integrative Awareness) were positively related to collective self-esteem (the quality of a person's evaluation of himself or herself as a member of a racial group), while less sophisticated schemas (i.e., Conformity) were negatively associated with collective self-esteem. Recent studies also show that minority status and associated racial stigmatization does not always lead to poor self-esteem as one might expect, although this might be due to other factors (e.g., individualism, willingness to talk about oneself) that can affect how people respond to self-esteem questionnaires (Quintana, 2007).

Psychological Adjustment and Mental Health

African American children are at lower risk for depression and are protected against the negative effects of criminal victimization when they reside in neighborhoods characterized by strong racial identification and racial pride (Simons et al., 2002). The cultural values and traditions in these neighborhoods foster meaning, belonging, and optimism among African American youth in the face of stressful and violent living conditions.

Physical Health

Socially constructed racial categories and identities are intimately tied to health outcomes as noted in Chapter 8. One study found that African Americans and Hispanics were less likely than European Americans to receive smoking cessation advice from their health care providers (Houston, Scarinci, Person, & Greene, 2005). Reasons for these racial differences were not explored, but they might stem from racial discrimination and racial stereotyping in the health care system and, for Hispanics, language barriers. In this study, racial identity also interacted with other identity dimensions in affecting health care advice. For example, smoking counseling differences that were found between African Americans and Whites were greater among individuals who had lower incomes and lacked health insurance.

Perceptions of Racism

Stages of racial identity development are related to perceptions of racism. Among a national sample of African Americans, those who were least likely to report experiencing or witnessing racism against their family tended to show features of Cross's "Pre-Encounter" stage of racial identity development. As previously noted, this stage is characterized by weak identification with their

African American group, a preference for dominant group culture and assimilation, weak connection to their African American group, and a tendency to deny the existence of prejudice in the lives of African Americans (Hyers, 2001). Although those exhibiting Pre-Encounter features reported high life satisfaction, they possessed low self-esteem possibly because they tended to attribute experiences of racism to their own actions rather than to the presence of racial stratification.

Ethnic Identity and Adjustment

Self-Esteem

Phinney (1992) found that a strong ethnic identity (self-identification with one's ethnic group, participation in one's ethnic group traditions and cultural practices, feeling a sense of belonging and membership to one's ethnic group, and having a secure sense of one's ethnicity) was positively related to self-esteem for American high schoolers of Asian, African, Hispanic, White, and multiethnic descent. By college age, however, this relationship only held true for ethnic minorities indicating that ethnicity was more likely to remain an important part of their lives compared to their White peers (Phinney, 1992).

Studies also show that the relationship between ethnic identification and self-esteem can vary across ethnic minority groups depending on individuals' developmental stage and their ethnic group's experiences with racial stratification (Negy, Shreve, Jensen, & Uddin, 2003), the ethnic identity component that is being examined and the importance of ethnicity to different individuals (Phinney, 1990), and ultimately how individuals respond to and deal with their ethnicity in their daily lives (Phinney, Lochner, & Murphy, 1990). Ethnic composition of one's residency is another important factor that can moderate the relationship between ethnic identification and self-esteem. One study found that ethnic identity was related to self-esteem for Latinos only if they resided in areas where their specific Latino group was the largest Latino population (Umana-Taylor, Diversi, & Fine, 2002).

Psychological Adjustment and Mental Health

Ethnic minority adolescents who focus on the positive aspects of their ethnic group, feel strongly connected to their ethnic group, and exhibit ethnic pride are more likely to report positive adjustment, higher academic achievement, greater well-being, and less depression and less nonracial stress in their lives (Quintana, 2007). High ethnic identification is also related to an overall positive quality of life, marked by good physical health, positive psychological functioning, satisfaction with social relationships and social support, and satisfaction with one's physical environment (Utsey, Chae, Brown, & Kelly, 2002).

The positive effects of ethnic identification on psychological adjustment may be related to variable effects of ethnic identity components on coping skills and abilities. For instance, one study found that high affirmation and belonging, ethnic identity achievement, and high involvement in ethnic behaviors were significantly related to coping strategies. In general, for African American students, these three indicators of a strong ethnic identity were related to desirable coping behaviors (e.g., cognitive restructuring) and, for European American students, infrequent use of negative coping strategies (e.g., self-criticism, blaming others) (Zaff, Blount, Phillips, & Cohen, 2002). Along similar lines, a study of urban African American adolescents from low-SES families found that a strong and positive ethnic identity was associated with more active coping (active exploration and evaluation of a problem, developing effective problem solving strategies), less acceptance of aggression, and fewer aggressive behaviors (McMahon & Watts, 2002). Interestingly, this finding still held true even when self-worth and self-esteem were controlled suggesting that a strong ethnic identity had its own independent effects on psychological well-being. Thus, having a strong and positive ethnic identity was independently related to positive coping and less aggression for this sample of adolescents. Other studies have likewise shown that a strong ethnic identity is related to positive coping skills, a sense of mastery in meeting life's challenges, and optimism (Phinney & Rosenthal, 1992) and generally results in less loneliness and depression for African American, Mexican American, and European American middle school students (Roberts et al., 1999).

Still, the relationship between one's ethnic identification and psychological adjustment and mental health can vary according to the salience or centrality of ethnicity in an individual's daily life. Chinese American adolescents with strong ethnic identification reported less anxiety and depression and more positive well-being when their ethnicity was especially salient or central in their daily activities and social settings (Yip & Fuligni, 2002). Lastly, researchers have found that strong ethnic identification does not necessarily promote positive adjustment in some circumstances. One study found that strong ethnic identification among White and Hispanic college students was associated with ethnocentrism and negative attitudes toward different ethnic groups (Negy et al., 2003).

Protection Against Discrimination and Racism

Among Filipino Americans, ethnic pride, involvement in cultural practices, and a commitment to Filipino American culture buffered stress from perceived discrimination, and reduced risk for depression (Mossakowski, 2003). Also, Hispanic adolescents who have secure ethnic identities appear to be more resistant to negative information about their ethnic group than their peers who have insecure ethnic identities (Phinney, Chavira, & Tate, 1993). Among African American adolescents, a positive connection with their ethnic group buffered against the negative effects of discrimination on academic performance and classroom behavior (Wong, Eccles, & Sameroff, 2003). However, ethnic identification did not moderate the negative effects of discrimination for a sample of Asian American college students (R. M. Lee, 2003). The author of this study surmised that ethnic identification does not involve specific coping skills to deal with discrimination, but instead represents a psychological asset that contributes to overall well-being (R. M. Lee, 2003).

Research also indicates that the possible ways in which ethnic identification buffers against discrimination may not be entirely straightforward. Instead, the protective effects of ethnic identification may represent a complex interaction between levels of discrimination in one's environment and one's strength of ethnic identification. When faced with a high level of discrimination, Latino, Asian, and African American youth with weak ethnic identification have higher self-esteem than those youth who have strong ethnic identification. On the other hand, those who have strong ethnic identification tend to have higher self-esteem in environments with low levels of discrimination (Quintana, 2007).

Risk for Drug Use

In an ethnically diverse sample of seventh graders, a strong sense of ethnic affiliation, attachment, and pride was associated with stronger personal antidrug beliefs and greater concern over potential reactions from friends if they used drugs (Marsiglia, Kulis, Hecht, & Sills, 2004). Interestingly, this finding was particularly true for the European American students and less so for American Indians and Mexican Americans most likely due to differences in the salience or importance of ethnicity in their lives. The European American students in this study represented a numerical minority in their schools and neighborhoods; thus, their ethnic identity was perhaps more salient and closely attached to their daily functioning than for their ethnic minority peers.

Biracial/Multiracial Identities and Adjustment

Self-Esteem

In a study of biracial and monoracial adolescents, strong ethnic identification was positively related to higher self-esteem (Bracey et al., 2004). This finding suggests that ethnic identification serves as a protective factor against the negative effects of discrimination and racial stereotypes by offering adolescents expanded support from multiple racial groups when forming their identities.

Psychological Adjustment and Mental Health

Early theories of multiracial psychological adjustment suggested uniform and consistent patterns of identity conflicts, psychological distress, and poor psychological outcomes (Root, 1992). However, more recent research offers more positive portrayals of biracial youngsters as being self-confident, creative, and well adjusted when raised in a supportive family, neighborhood, and social network and in integrated schools (Gibbs & Hines, 1992). Again, this seems to be related to racial identity formation; research shows that a positive and stable biracial or multiracial identity is associated with greater life satisfaction and less depression (Suzuki-Crumly & Hyers, 2004). Given these new findings, researchers are beginning to critically reexamine widely held beliefs that multiracial individuals are doomed to experience chronic unhappiness, identity crises, a poor self-concept, and greater psychopathology. Shih and Sanchez (2005) arrived at the following conclusions after conducting a comprehensive review of research on multiracial identity and psychological adjustment:

- *There is evidence for both positive and negative psychological adjustment among multiracial individuals.* This contradicts traditional theories proposing uniform patterns of identity conflict and maladjustment. Thus, it appears that multiracial identity can provide important resources, like expanded support from multiple ethnic communities, which can contribute to personal resilience rather than to stress.
- *The direction of study findings is influenced by research strategies and methods.* In this case, findings vary by
  - *the types of populations that were studied.* Studies reporting negative psychological adjustment (e.g., higher levels of depression, problem behaviors, poor school performance, and low self-esteem

typically) focused on clinical samples while those reporting positive adjustment (e.g., happiness, high self-esteem) examined nonclinical samples.

o *the historical period when the study was conducted.* More negative outcomes (e.g., social rejection and isolation) were reported in studies that were conducted before the 1990s while more positive outcomes (e.g., social acceptance and improved peer relationships) are reported in more recent studies. This trend suggests that social attitudes toward interracial marriages and the multiracial community may be improving. Conversely, this trend may also reflect improvements in study methods and sample selection.

o *the psychological outcome under examination and the monoracial ethnicity of the comparison group.* When compared with monoracial European Americans, multiracial individuals appeared to have more negative outcomes (e.g., depression and behavioral problems). However, when multiracial individuals were compared with monoracial ethnic minorities, their psychological adjustment patterns varied according to the outcome that was studied (e.g., multiracials tended to show stronger academic performance but less racial pride than monoracial ethnic minorities).

In sum, the relationship between multiracial identity and psychological adjustment is much more complex than what was originally proposed in earlier psychological theories. These earlier theories characterized the multiracial experience as being fraught with chronic identity conflicts, high levels of psychological distress, and poor psychological outcomes. Generally speaking, however, more recent studies report more positive or variable outcomes that are tied to individual, group, and social factors, and the types of research methods and measures that are utilized.

BOX 5.3

How Does Family Environment Affect Multiracial Identity Development?

A study found that multiracial college students were more conflicted about their ethnic identity around their peers, and reported more adjustment difficulties at college if they came from families that did not support their mixed race heritage (Jourdan, 2006). Thus, a family environment that promotes positive

(Continued)

(Continued)

exploration and discussion of mixed race identity can reduce risk for identity conflicts and psychosocial problems. The importance of family environment on multiracial identity development was highlighted by the experiences of Kevin, a mixed race college student in this study:

Kevin's mother is Chinese, and his father is African American and Caucasian. He explained that his ethnic identity was a source of contention in his family. Throughout his life, Kevin received mixed messages from his family regarding his ethnic identity.... Kevin did not have a home environment that allowed him to share his thoughts and feelings regarding his ethnic identity; thus, he was unable to develop a secure ethnic identity, making him feel unconnected to all ethnic groups.... He asserted that his maternal grandmother did not accept his father because his father is African American and Caucasian. Kevin stated that this family experience led him to conclude that all Chinese people were racist. Furthermore, he explained that his father told him that all Chinese people were evil and that he should identify as African American. Therefore, he received conflicting messages from his grandmother and father regarding which ethnicity was desirable and acceptable. He has heard negative and confusing information about all facets of his ethnic background from different members of his family; thus, he does not feel connected to a particular ethnic group. He stated, "I decided my ethnicity is Kevin. I don't really think I have an ethnicity anyway. I feel very alienated from all groups—Blacks, Chinese, Whites, everyone. I find the most amount of exclusion from Chinese." ... He then described a feeling of being different every time he walked into a college classroom; he also reported that he wanted to escape whenever he was in a room of people who were White. In an attempt to form a connection with people in college, Kevin became involved with an African American group and a Chinese American group on campus. However, he did not feel connected to either of these groups. He explained, "I guess when I went to meet with the Chinese people, they didn't know what the hell I was. So how the hell could they feel like any bond with me? I would just meet with the Chinese people and they didn't even know what to make of me, you know, let alone feel any sense of camaraderie, you know, like they were all under the yoke of a common oppressor. And the same thing with Black people, they don't know what the f@*! I am, how the hell can they ever, you know, feel that way." Kevin went on to explain that people always viewed him as being different, thus creating a barrier in his interactions with others. As a result, he said that he constantly felt insecure and rejected.... Kevin described this constant feeling of insecurity in his interactions with others in college and the larger community. He stated that he had never formed a close connection with a particular ethnic group and instead felt rejected by all ethnic groups. (Jourdan, 2006, pp. 332–338)

What are the key psychosocial difficulties that Kevin is facing? How are these issues tied to his family's responses to race? Do Kevin's identity experiences reflect any features of Root's or Collins's models of biracial identity development? Which ones?

Gender Identity and Adjustment

Body Image

In a predominantly African American sample of urban elementary school children, higher feminine identification was unrelated to body image contrary to expectations (Lyons et al., 2006). This finding suggests that African American girls may have a broader notion of femininity as a result of racial socialization, which emphasizes women's competence, resourcefulness, and versatility, and resisting narrow gender role definitions imposed by the dominant group. In this same study, a masculine gender role was positively associated with body image suggesting that certain traditional masculine traits (e.g., instrumental behaviors or assertiveness) foster a positive self-concept, including positive thoughts about one's body and physical skills. For the boys in this sample, their interest and participation in sports may be an important moderator in this relationship, influencing their perceived competencies in physical activities and ultimately their body image.

Risk for Drug Use

In a study of predominantly Mexican American eighth grade students, gender identity proved to be a much more powerful predictor of drug use than a person's gender label (Kulis, Marsiglia, & Hurdle, 2003). Specifically, four different gender identity dimensions had differential relationships with drug use behaviors and attitudes. These four different gender dimensions included aggressive masculinity (dominance and control over others), assertive masculinity (confidence and assertiveness), affective femininity (nurturing and expressive aspects of femininity), and submissive femininity (dependence and inadequacy). In general, aggressive masculinity was consistently associated with undesirable outcomes while the other three gender identity dimensions were associated with more positive outcomes. Specifically, aggressive masculinity was tied to more drug use (alcohol, cigarettes, and marijuana), earlier drug initiation, and weaker antidrug attitudes. In contrast, assertive masculinity, affective femininity, and submissive femininity had selected protective effects: Assertive masculinity was associated with less lifetime alcohol and cigarette use and stronger antidrug attitudes, affective femininity was associated with lower lifetime use for all three drugs and stronger antidrug attitudes, and submissive femininity was associated with lower alcohol and marijuana use. Kulis and colleagues (2003) assert that these positive outcomes from these latter three identity dimensions may mirror positive and adaptive qualities of machismo and marianismo. Still, the relationship between these gender identity dimensions and drug outcomes often involved complex interactions with other personal characteristics. For example, the impact of gender identity dimensions on drug outcome was strongly mediated by acculturation. Submissive femininity was only a significant protector against marijuana use for more acculturated Mexican Americans while aggressive masculinity was related to greater use of all three drugs for more acculturated Mexican Americans, and more marijuana use for less acculturated Mexican Americans.

Sexual Identity and Adjustment

Psychological Adjustment and Mental Health

A study of Latino gay men showed that they experienced a unique set of stressors and resultant psychological stress that were linked to their inter-secting sexual, ethnic, and class identities (Diaz, Ayala, & Bein, 2004). The Latino gay men in this study reported multiple instances of verbal and physical abuse, rude mistreatment, and discrimination based on their sexual orientation and their ethnicity. Moreover, many reported feeling uncomfortable in gay venues because of racism and racially based sexual objectification in the gay community, mostly consisting of White middle-class men. Latino gay men reported, for instance, that White men often approached and viewed them as exotic sex objects because of their ethnicity. In addition to these racial and sexual identity stressors, these Latino men also reported financial stressors that included the inability to pay for basic necessities such as food and shelter. High levels of psychological distress were associated with exposure to these racial, sexual, and financial stressors, contributing to risky sex practices (engaging in sex while under the influence of drugs or alcohol, being with sex partners who resisted condom use) in an attempt to alleviate stress and anxiety. These findings thus illustrated that psychological distress from racism, financial hardship, and homophobia elevates risk for HIV infection for Latino gay men.

Other studies of ethnic minority LGBT (lesbian, gay, bisexual, and transsexual) individuals have likewise reported high levels of psychological distress. In a study of American Indian "two-spirits" (individuals who self-identify as lesbian, gay, bisexual, or unsure, and embody both feminine and masculine spirits), high rates of alcohol use were reported as a means to increase their sociability, decrease feelings of inferiority, manage their mood, and relieve tension (Balsam et al., 2004).

Still, other studies have shown that not all ethnic minority LGBTs are at increased risk for psychological difficulties. One study found that among same-sex-attracted middle and high school students, African Americans and Whites reported more suicidal thoughts than other-sex-attracted youth, but this was not the case for Latino or Asian/Pacific Islander same-sex-attracted youths (Consolacion, Russell, & Sue, 2004). Study results also showed higher levels of depression for Latino, African American, and White same-sex-attracted youth compared to other-sex-attracted youth, but this was not true for same-sex-attracted Asian/Pacific Islanders. Lastly, only African American and White same-sex-attracted youths reported lower self-esteem than other-sex-attracted youth. The authors of this study noted that these findings indicate that ethnic minority same-sex-attracted youth exhibit variable risk for psychological difficulties. They clearly stated, however, that the nonsignificant findings for some of the ethnic minority groups in this study, namely for Asian/Pacific Islanders, do not necessarily mean that they do not experience stressors as a result of their multiple minority status. Rather, it may be the case that some ethnic minority LGBTs can effectively adapt to discriminatory social situations by "readjusting" their identity and focusing on the identity dimension that is not disparaged or oppressed in that social situation.

Class Identity and Adjustment

Physical and Mental Health

As mentioned at the beginning of this chapter, socioeconomic status (SES) is an important indicator of class identity that is intertwined with racial identity. Health research continues to reveal significant health disparities between racial minorities and European Americans caused by the combined effects of economic hardship and racial stratification. SES, race, and health are linked together in the following ways:

- Racism and institutionalized discrimination prevent ethnic minorities from gaining upward social mobility that can improve health outcomes.
- Disproportionately more racial minorities conduct their daily lives in impoverished and stressful living and work environments that contribute to chronic and disabling physical health conditions.
- Low SES ethnic minorities face cumulative stressors and disadvantages throughout the course of their life leading to a "weathering" of their health as they age and a shortened life span.
- Ethnic minorities may somatize their stress from racial discrimination and poverty, which can negatively affect their perceptions of their overall health and well-being (Sudano & Baker, 2006).

Still, the ways in which SES affects health are not always clear; thus, researchers are beginning to examine the different facets or dimensions of SES to determine whether they have independent and complex pathways to health. For instance, a community study of low SES Mexican Americans found that **objective social status** (an individual's income, educational level, and occupation) had stronger associations with health outcomes when compared to those tied to **subjective social status** (an individual's perceived social position in society) (Franzini & Fernandez-Esquer, 2006). Studies have also found that "neighborhood SES" and "family SES" have independent relationships to health. In a study of European and African American adolescent health, neighborhood SES was a composite of neighborhood education levels, family employment status, median family income, and median value of owner-occupied homes, while family SES was based on household income and a family's liquid assets or savings. Findings showed that low neighborhood SES was positively related to adolescent obesity and exposure to discrimination. Thus, people living in low SES neighborhoods may experience greater stress from discrimination and consequent health problems. Low SES neighborhoods also tend to lack safe and clean civic spaces (e.g., public parks, hiking and walking paths) and healthy food options, preventing adolescents from engaging in outdoor physical activities and maintaining a healthy diet. This study found that family SES was also negatively related to adolescent obesity suggesting that poor families may not be able to afford healthy food options, organized physical activities for their children, and preventative health care (Chen & Paterson, 2006). A study of African, Hispanic, and European American youth likewise found that social disadvantage experienced on individual and neighborhood levels increased risk for developing unhealthy behaviors that contribute to cardiovascular disease such as poor dietary habits, low physical activity, and smoking (R. E. Lee & Cubbin, 2002).

Low SES and race have also been associated with health disparities in HIV treatment and survival rates. One study reported that HIV-infected ethnic minority adults with low SES backgrounds receive fewer health care services, including effective and expensive antiretroviral treatment (Cunningham et al., 2005). This same study also found that HIV-infected impoverished individuals of all ethnicities had an 89% greater risk of death than wealthier individuals, and those with less than a high school education had a 53% greater risk of death than those with more formal education.

Chapter Summary

In this chapter, we examined the interrelationship between different facets of individual and group identities. All of these facets—racial, ethnic, gender, sexual, and class identities—are complex in their development, interaction with one another, and expression in our daily lives. Over the past three decades, ethnic psychology researchers have primarily studied racial, ethnic, gender, and class identity dimensions, whereas sexual identities are currently garnering greater attention in the field. Additionally, the preponderance of identity research is based on African American, Asian American, and Hispanic/Latino study samples with relatively less attention afforded to American Indians. As such, much more research on these underrepresented topics and populations is needed to better understand the broad range of human experience associated with multiple and hybrid identities.

Key Terms

Controlling Images (page 165)

Cultural Socialization (page 138)

Ethnic Identity (page 139)

Gender Identity (page 142)

Gender Typing (page 141)

Identity Formation (page 170)

Identity Integration (page 170)

Machismo (page 167)

Marianismo (page 168)

Objective Social Status (page 184)

Otherness Status (page 156)

Racial Identity (page 138)

Racial Identity Schemas (page 173)

Racial Socialization (page 138)

Sexual Identity (page 142)

Subjective Social Status (page 184)

Two-Spirited Individuals (page 142)

Learning by Doing

Tracing Your Ethnic Identity Development

- Think about how you have experienced your ethnicity throughout the course of your life.
- What components of ethnic identity are most salient to your daily life?
- Has the way in which you identify yourself and how you feel about your ethnic group membership changed or remained the same? What do you think are some factors that have contributed to this?
- Consider Phinney's early model of ethnic identity development.
- What stage of ethnic identity development would you place yourself in? Why?
- If you are biracial or multiracial, what identity resolution strategy in Root's model captures your identity experiences?

- What contextual factors have influenced your ethnic identity development?
- Do you feel that these models of ethnic and biracial identity development capture your personal search for an ethnic identity?
- What do you think are the strengths and limitations of these models?
- How do other facets of your identity intersect with your ethnicity to form who you are today?

Suggested Further Readings

Chin, J. L. (Ed.). (2000). *Relationships among Asian American women*. Washington, DC: American Psychological Association.

An in-depth exploration of gender, ethnic, and racial issues for diverse Asian American women.

Eng, D., & Hom, A. (Eds.). (1998). *Q&A: Queer and Asian American*. Philadelphia, PA: Temple University Press.

An engaging interdisciplinary reader consisting of personal narratives, essays, fiction, and art that illustrate the multiplicities of queer Asian American identity.

Greene, B. (Ed.). (1997). *Ethnic and cultural diversity among lesbians and gay men* (Vol. 3, Psychological Perspectives on Lesbian and Gay Issues Series). Thousand Oaks, CA: Sage.

A pioneering overview of psychological issues for lesbian and gay people of color, covering key empirical, theoretical, and clinical topics.

Helms, J. E. (Ed.). (1993). *Black and White racial identity*. Westport, CT: Praeger.

Written by one of the leading researchers of racial identity in the country, this book presents key tenets of Black racial identity development and formation, measurement strategies, and racial identity research findings.

Philip, C. (2007). *Asian American identities: Racial and ethnic identity issues in the twenty-first century*. Amherst, NY: Cambria Press.

A comprehensive overview of the historical, psychological, and social issues surrounding the development of the Asian American identity.

Root, M. P. P. (Ed.). (1996). *The multiracial experience: Racial borders as the new frontier*. Thousand Oaks, CA: Sage.

A compendium of insightful commentaries, research findings, and analyses of multiracial identities, offering important insights into the meaning and experience of mixed race descent.

Singley, B. (Ed.). (2002). *When race becomes real: Black and White writers confront their personal histories*. Chicago, IL: Lawrence Hill.

Compilation of essays from a talented group of writers who expose the long and challenging legacy of race in the United States and the meanings of racial identity in their personal lives.

CHAPTER 6

FAMILY STRUCTURE, RELATIONS, AND SOCIALIZATION

VIGNETTE

"In my family, we never openly say, 'I love you.'"

Jon is a 39-year-old, first generation Chinese American, and the oldest son in his family. When Jon was a teenager, his parents decided to move the family from Hong Kong to the United States in search

(Continued)

(Continued)

of greater educational opportunities for their children. Although Jon describes his parents as being caring and kind, he often wishes that they were more verbally expressive and open with him. Whenever Jon visits his parents for dinner, he notices that they "never really talk about anything." To Jon's dismay, his parents rarely ask him about what is going on in his life and almost never inquire about his thoughts and feelings about personal matters. Instead, his parents typically ask him seemingly superficial questions—"Why do you look so thin? Have you been eating?" "Have you spoken to your sister or grandmother lately?" Once Jon answers these questions, he notices that they often just sit in silence for the remainder of the meal. Jon never thought twice about his interactions with his parents until he spent time with his friends' families. On one occasion, he had dinner with his fourth generation Chinese American friend, Chris, and his family. Jon was surprised to see that Chris and his family freely talked about how they were feeling and how they were doing in their lives. Jon was especially taken aback when Chris's mother told her son that she loved him and followed this with a hug. Afterwards, Jon told Chris, "In my family, we never openly say, 'I love you.'" Jon is becoming frustrated by this situation because he wants to share his feelings with his parents, particularly his concerns over his family responsibilities. As the oldest son in his family, Jon's parents expect him to support them and possibly to let them live with him during their retirement. Jon is conflicted about this; he doesn't want to be a "bad son," but he feels the need to "do his own thing" and be completely independent from his family at times. He feels guilty about this because his parents' sacrifices allowed him to graduate from a prestigious college and become financially successful. Also, Jon appreciates how his parents continue to deliver him home-cooked Chinese meals once a week, which he understands to be a cultural expression of their love. Consequently, Jon feels reluctant to discuss his concerns fearing that he may be disrespectful and insensitive to his parents. What should Jon do?

How would you describe your relationship with your family? Does your culture have specific rules and expectations about how you should behave with certain family members? For instance, are you expected to act differently when in the presence of older members than with those who are your age or younger than you? When you were growing up, did your parents encourage you to freely express your feelings and thoughts to them, or did they expect you to dutifully listen to them without question? These questions about the nature of your family relationships, family communication styles, and parenting can be answered from different angles depending on your cultural perspectives of family life. Your culture essentially provides you with a set of rules and expectations about how families should ideally function in the world. In our opening narrative, Jon's experiences highlight family communication styles and family role expectations seen in many first generation Asian American immigrant households.

Jon is trying to negotiate his family's collectivistic norms, which compel him to consider the needs and concerns of his parents over his own. Additionally, certain teachings from Confucian philosophy—namely, showing respect toward elders and fulfilling family obligations as the oldest son—influence what he considers to be appropriate versus inappropriate interactions with his parents. As Jon spends time with other families, like Chris's, who might be more acculturated, or with families who follow different cultural traditions, he may feel more at odds with his parents over their expected family roles and relationships. This chapter will explore these and other ethnic minority family issues by highlighting the broad influence of cultural norms, values, and beliefs on family life from an ecological perspective of family functioning.

AN ECOLOGICAL PERSPECTIVE OF FAMILY FUNCTIONING

According to an **ecological perspective** of family functioning, family well-being and development are shaped by different **"ecologies"** or social contexts and relationships that are part of each family member's life (Bronfenbrenner, 1986; Bronfenbrenner & Morris, 1998) (see Figure 6.1). The immediate home environment is perhaps the first thing that comes to mind when considering the effects of social context on family functioning. For instance, ethnic minority home environments that are bicultural, collectivistic, and include extended family arrangements, are associated with positive child-rearing goals that in turn contribute to healthy child development (Harrison, Wilson, Pine, Chan, & Buriel, 1990). Family ecologies can also include an extensive range of social settings and relationships outside of the home. Children spend a significant portion of their day at school, in their peer groups, and in recreational organizations. Parents' lives also unfold in multiple settings, most notably in their workplaces and adult social circles. All of these different social settings and relationships influence how family members grow, develop, and relate to one another. In the vignette above, Jon's social interactions with Chris's family shifted his own cultural attitudes on family communication, which in turn affected his relationship with his parents. Jon's peer circle thus plays an important role in shaping his behavior and family interactions at home as proposed by the ecological perspective of family functioning.

An ecological perspective also recognizes that ethnic minority families face distinct environmental challenges or stressors that can disrupt their overall functioning and well-being. In particular, two specific ecological challenges—**minority status** and **acculturation**—have been highlighted in the ethnic psychology literature (McLoyd, Cauce, Takeuchi, & Wilson, 2000;

Figure 6.1 Ethnic Minority Family Ecologies

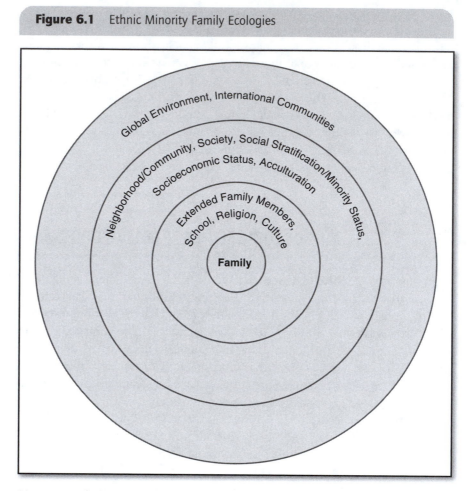

SOURCE: Bronfenbrenner (1986); Bronfenbrenner & Morris (1998).

B. W. K. Yee, Huang, & Lew, 1998). As outlined in Chapter 2, minority status results from social stratification and having restricted access to society's wealth and resources. Ethnic minority families face historical barriers to quality education, affordable health care, high-income jobs, safe neighborhoods, and even healthy living environments. In this chapter, we discuss how such barriers can lead to family stress and psychosocial problems. Immigrant and refugee families face the added ecological challenge of acculturation. As mentioned in Chapter 4, acculturation can be a stressful experience when individuals cannot meet the demands of new cultural environments, including meeting demands to learn a new language and new cultural norms and values. As we will see in this chapter, such instances of acculturative stress can strain family relationships when parents and their children adjust to a new culture at different rates.

Although an ecological perspective highlights environmental and social factors that impact family functioning, families are far from being passive entities. **Family agency,** or a family's capacity to actively promote and safeguard its own welfare and development, illustrates this point. Family agency is manifested in different ways, including when families transform or shape their social environments and institutions that they come into contact with. For instance, research shows that many immigrant Latino and Asian American families actively participate in civic life through their churches or religious organizations (Lorentzen, Chun, Gonzalez, & Do, in press). Religious activities—whether centered on political advocacy for immigrant rights or gang prevention activities for youth—can help immigrant families build certain strengths and skills that promote their growth and development. Family agency is also witnessed when families effectively respond to the demands of daily living (e.g., securing food and shelter, locating public transportation, enrolling children in school), fulfill normative developmental tasks (e.g., adjusting to the birth of a new infant, altering family roles and responsibilities), and cope with unexpected crises (e.g., medical emergencies, forced relocation to another country).

In sum, family functioning is shaped by the many different environments and social relationships that are part of the daily lives of family members. Families can likewise change or alter their environments to enhance their development and adaptation to new cultural settings. The ability of families of color to meet their daily needs and negotiate normative life transitions is complicated by the added stressors of discrimination and prejudice. Therefore, the diverse life experiences of ethnic minority families can only be fully appreciated by exploring the cultural, socioeconomic, and historical contexts in which they unfold.

HOW DO YOU DEFINE A FAMILY? FACTORS AFFECTING FAMILY STRUCTURES AND HOUSEHOLD ARRANGEMENTS

This appears to be a simple question until you consider all of the different family constellations that are seen in American society today. The "nuclear family"—a family consisting of a father, mother, and their children—was considered the standard unit of American family life in much social science research published in the last century. However, shifting sociopolitical attitudes toward gender roles and marriage, and significantly higher divorce rates in the United States, have pushed for broader definitions of the family since that time. Historical assumptions about nuclear family functioning have also been called into question. Research with families from across the world indicates that nuclear families do not necessarily function in isolation from extended kin and are not universally individualistic as once proposed (Georgas et al., 2001). Furthermore, the nuclear family unit does not fully capture how ethnic minority families organize and sustain themselves. In addition to nuclear family households, ethnic minority families maintain multigenerational households, single-parent households, and households that are headed by grandparents or other family relatives. In some ethnic minority communities, these types of households are more "normative" than the nuclear family household and form the foundation for healthy family functioning. There are numerous factors contributing to diverse family structures across ethnic minority groups.

Migration

Multigenerational or extended family households are formed when new immigrants to the United States join family members or relatives who have gained legal citizenship and can sponsor their immigration. The Asian American and Latino communities have the highest proportion of new immigrants to the United States and the highest percentage of multigenerational homes (Lugalia & Overturf, 2004). Often, this extended household arrangement serves as an important support network for new immigrants who face acculturation stressors like learning the English language, adjusting to American cultural norms, and maintaining one's cultural identity and traditions in a new country.

Socioeconomic Status (SES)

Ethnic minority family structures are also shaped by family income and economic resources. As noted in Chapter 1, a significant proportion of ethnic minority families fall below the federal poverty line, which is approximately $18,104 annual income for a family of four (Lugalia & Overturf, 2004). Low SES ethnic minority families must often pool their limited resources together in extended or multiple family households to meet their basic living needs. Multiple family households are those where families share a roof even though they are biologically unrelated. In addition to consolidating capital, extended or multiple family households can provide instrumental family support to its members in the form of shared child care and assistance with daily chores and household duties. The link between SES and family household composition is likewise found among the relatively fewer ethnic minority families who are financially affluent. High SES ethnic minority families sometimes maintain dual or multiple residences in different countries. For example, there is a unique living arrangement in which Asian nationals might have a primary residence in Asia while maintaining a secondary residence in the United States. This dual or transnational family residence is often established so that a family's youth can receive an American education. Youth in these secondary homes are called "parachute kids" because they land temporarily in the United States where they live alone or with siblings until they finish their schooling. Some researchers believe that this type of household arrangement can be stressful for immigrant youth given their isolation from their families, academic demands, and acculturation stressors.

Exposure to Stress and Trauma

Disrupted family systems can result from war and civil strife, natural disasters, and stress from racial and social stratification. In regard to war and civil strife, Southeast Asian refugee families endured tremendous loss of life and property, separation from family members, and treacherous migration and refugee camp experiences that threatened their survival and in many cases permanently altered the composition of their families (Abueg & Chun, 1996). In one of the first large-scale mental health needs assessment studies of Southeast Asian refugees, 55% of the entire sample reported separations from or deaths of family members, with 30% experiencing multiple separations or losses from the Vietnam War and civil strife in their home countries (Gong-Guy, 1987). For the Cambodian women in this study, more than one in five experienced the death of their husbands. Upon their arrival to the United States, many Southeast Asian refugees encountered acculturation stressors, which exacerbated their stress and increased their risk for family dysfunction. Complicating matters was the possibility of persecution and death if these families ever returned to their home countries to search for family members who were left behind or missing.

African Americans and American Indians have also experienced high levels of stress from the historical legacy of racial and social stratification in the United States. During the time of slavery, slave masters forcibly separated African family members from one another in an attempt to weaken or destroy their family bonds and ties to their homelands (Schaefer, 1996). For American Indians, removal from tribal homelands and enforced enrollment of their youth in American boarding schools, where they were isolated from their families and tribes and prohibited from practicing their culture, represented significant family stressors (D. W. Sue & Sue, 1999).

Social scientists have commented that institutionalized oppression and social marginalization continue to impact African American and American Indian family structures. Impoverished and dangerous living conditions, chronic exposure to racism and discrimination, and limited opportunities for educational and economic advancement increase family stress, which in turn heightens the risk for divorce or separation among couples, or death of a spouse or family member from stress-related illnesses. This can partly explain the high rate of single-parent households that are seen in African American and American Indian communities. Approximately 30% of African American and 20% of American Indian family households are headed by single women compared to 9% for European American households (Lugalia & Overturf, 2004). Children from disrupted family systems may also be placed in the homes of family members and relatives. These types of family arrangements are often stereotyped by dominant society as signs of family pathology or dysfunction because they do not conform to the nuclear family structure. However, these stereotypes erroneously equate family structure with family functioning (R. B. Hill, 1998). Furthermore, the diverse family structures of ethnic minority families can actually reflect family resilience and family agency or adaptation to chronically stressful life conditions. Finally, family structures like extended or single-parent households, contrary to negative stereotypes, can be nurturing family environments. It is not uncommon for African American children to be raised in large extended families consisting of "blood" and "nonblood" relatives who act as important role models and share in child-rearing or parenting responsibilities (Franklin, Boyd-Franklin, & Draper, 2002). Also, one-parent African American families exhibit flexible family roles and strong kinship bonds that foster greater family cohesiveness than many two-parent families (R. B. Hill, 1998).

Cultural Values and Beliefs

A family's cultural belief system and attitudes and values about family relations and responsibilities also shape their organization and structure. Generally speaking, Asian Americans, African Americans, Latinos, and American Indians historically share a collectivistic social orientation that promotes strong kin ties, close family living arrangements or extended family households, and a sense of family obligation or duty to the family. For Latinos, this is often witnessed by **familism** or **familialism,** which is defined as being strongly grounded in one's family, valuing family closeness and cohesion, believing that family responsibilities should take precedence over individual needs or goals (Parke, Coltrane, Borthwick-Duffy, Powers, & Adams, 2004), preferring to live in proximity to family, and relying on them for emotional and instrumental support (Gil, Wagner, & Vega, 2000). Findings on the nature and effects of familism and family obligation on ethnic minority family life tend to be mixed. Studies with Latinos show that familism can strengthen family cooperation, family contact, and extended family support (Parke et al., 2004), although familism tends to weaken with acculturation (Gil et al., 2000). Other studies, however, show that the weight of family obligation can cause distress and family conflict. For instance, Korean and Korean American caregivers who endorse familism report feeling burdened and distressed when trying to meet family expectations to care for elderly family members with dementia (Youn, Knight, Jeong, & Benton, 1999).

The intimate links between cultural values and family structure are also seen for Asian American families who follow Confucian principles on family relationships, roles, and duties. Confucian teachings support a **patrilineal** family structure that affords greater authority, privileges, and status to older males in the family (Ching, McDermott, Fukunaga, & Yanagida, 1995; Park & Cho, 1995). This type of family structure is thus hierarchical in nature—the father is the figurative head of the family who is responsible for providing for the family and for making family decisions. Also, the children in the family are expected to show **filial piety** or respect for the needs and concerns of the family over their own, especially when elderly family members are concerned. When the oldest son comes of age, he is expected to assume the mantle of leadership in his family by caring for his parents in their senior years and by providing instrumental support to other family members.

Two-way communication or negotiation between parents and children is disallowed in patrilineal families. Family conflict can arise in this situation as children become socialized to American culture and desire more open communication with their parents (as was the case for Jon in the vignette at the beginning of the chapter). Still, these Confucian prescriptions for family organization and relationships, as with familism, should not be over-generalized because they can produce stereotypical portraits of ethnic minority family life. Some Asian American families may only follow certain Confucian teachings or none at all. Also, Asian American families who adhere to patrilineal family structures are not necessarily experts in Confucian philosophy, but may simply follow certain practices because they learned them from previous generations. In short, ethnic minority families differ in regard to their understanding and practice of specific cultural beliefs and practices.

FAMILY FUNCTIONING, SOCIALIZATION, AND ADJUSTMENT

Do ethnic minority family members interact and support one another in culturally unique ways? How do ethnic minority parents equip their children with essential life skills and lessons? Does acculturation affect the gender roles and attitudes of married couples? What are the distinct challenges that ethnic minority families face and how do they cope with them? These types of questions point to the broad topics of ethnic minority family functioning, socialization, and adjustment. Much of the research on these topics is concentrated on parenting and parent-child relationships, academic achievement, couple relationships, and family stress and coping. The following sections highlight major research findings in these areas.

Parenting Styles

Developmental psychologists have spent much effort studying the ways in which parents socialize, nurture, and discipline their children, and the effects of their parenting practices on their children's adjustment and development. One widely referenced parenting model specifies three primary parenting methods or styles based on observations and interviews of mostly European American, middle-class parents with preschool-age children (Baumrind, 1971, 1980): **Authoritarian parenting** is characterized by highly controlling, demanding, and overly strict parenting. Parents falling under this category emphasize obedience and respect for authority and place high standards on their children. Children are not allowed to negotiate or openly disagree with their parents and if parents perceive any transgressions, they use punitive disciplinary measures. **Authoritative parenting** reflects more of a democratic or reciprocal relationship between parents and their children; parents set high standards and place demands on their children, but they allow their children to share their opinions and concerns without unduly imposing their parental authority or will. In regard to discipline, parents favor reasoning and explanation for their rules or decisions over physical punishment. Also, parents encourage their children to be independent and to reflect on their actions and behaviors. Parents who exhibit **permissive parenting** do not place high standards on their children, exercise little parental control, and can be neglectful of their parental responsibilities. They tend to believe that children should be allowed to follow their own impulses and desires without parental monitoring or interference. Permissive parents are thus less concerned with child discipline than authoritarian and authoritative parents, and may consult with their children on family policies or decisions (see Table 6.1).

Table 6.1 Parenting Styles: Baumrind's Classification

Authoritarian Parenting	
• Controlling	Example: "Do as I say; I'm the parent!"
• Demanding	
• Overly strict	
• No negotiation	
• Demands obedience	
• High standards	
Authoritative Parenting	
• Places limits; but tries to encourage independence	Example: "This isn't like you to do this. Let's talk about what's going on."
• Encourages communication between parent and child	
• High standards	
Permissive Parenting	
• Little control and involvement by parent	Example: "Whatever you want to do is fine with me."
• Lets the child do whatever he or she wants to do	

SOURCE: Baumrind (1971, 1980).

Past research with White non-Hispanic children indicates that authoritative parenting is the most effective parenting style and is related to better childhood adjustment outcomes compared to authoritarian or permissive parenting. Specifically, children who have authoritative parents tend to be more intellectually curious, self-controlled, self-reliant, and content compared to children from authoritarian or permissive households (Berns, 2004). Some ethnic psychology researchers have questioned the generalizability of these findings given the ethnic homogeneity of the study samples on which they are based. Furthermore, reported relationships between authoritarian, authoritative, and permissive parenting styles and childhood adjustment have not been consistently found for ethnic minority families. This is partly explained by cultural group differences in perceptions and beliefs about various parenting techniques or styles. African American observers who are asked to evaluate videos of African American mother-daughter interactions tend to see less parental restriction and less conflict compared to non-African Americans watching the same videos (McLoyd et al., 2000).

Mandara and Murray (2002) developed three new categories of parenting styles that overlap with the authoritarian, authoritative, and permissive categories, but also incorporate distinct cultural features of African American parenting (see Table 6.2).

Table 6.2 African American Parenting Styles

Conflict-Authoritarian	Outcomes
• Little concern or warmth • Overly strict • High standards but controlling	• High conflict • Distress • Moderate racial socialization
Cohesive-Authoritative	**Outcomes**
• Concerned and warm • Engaged • Provide structure and support • Encourage independence • High standards without being controlling	• High self-esteem in children • High proactive racial socialization • Low defensive racial socialization • High emotional stability in children
Defensive-Neglectful	**Outcomes**
• Neglectful • Little concern and emotional affection • Little importance placed on child's growth and achievement • Highly critical • Rigid family hierarchies • Punitive	• High family conflict • Chaotic family relationships • High defensive racial socialization • Low empowering racial socialization

SOURCE: Mandara & Murray (2002).

Conflict-Authoritarian

Similar to the authoritarian parenting style, parents in the **conflict-authoritarian** category show little concern and warmth toward their children, are overly strict and controlling toward their children, and disallow their children from expressing their feelings or questioning family rules. Although parents in this category also emphasize achievement like parents who are cohesive-authoritative, their drive for achievement is not necessarily focused on intellectual activities. Also, children may feel conflicted about meeting parental demands because their family environments and activities tend to be unstructured and their parents can be neglectful. Other features of this category include high levels of family conflict, distressed family relationships, and moderate levels of racial socialization. The demographic characteristics of the African American families in this study (Mandara & Murray, 2002) who were categorized as conflict-authoritarian were the following: (1) 63% were headed by married couples; (2) parents had moderate levels of formal education; (3) the average number of children in the household (2.7) was greater than cohesive-authoritative families, but fewer than defensive-neglectful families; (4) their average annual income was lower than cohesive-authoritative households, but higher than defensive-neglectful families; and (5) they attended church often and had a high regard for religion.

Cohesive-Authoritative

Parents in the **cohesive-authoritative** category express concern and warmth toward their children, engage them in intellectual activities, and provide a structured and supportive family environment. Similar to the authoritative parenting style, cohesive-authoritative parents emphasize the personal growth and independence of their children, encourage their children to express themselves openly, value achievement and high standards without being overly rigid or controlling, and tend to avoid punitive disciplinary measures. Some distinct cultural features of this parenting category include high **"proactive racial socialization"**—parents emphasize positive racial identity and pride in their racial group—and low **"defensive racial socialization"**—parents do not teach their children to dislike other racial groups nor do they imitate behaviors of White children. In this study sample (Mandara & Murray, 2002), African American families who were cohesive-authoritative possessed the following characteristics: (1) 58% were headed by married couples; (2) parents completed more formal education and had higher annual incomes (approximately $32,000) than those parents in the other two categories; (3) parents had an average of two children; (4) they attended church on a regular basis; and (5) they exhibited high overall family functioning.

Defensive-Neglectful

Proportionally fewer families in this study (Mandara & Murray, 2002) fell into the **defensive-neglectful** category. However, the relatively few who were classified as defensive-neglectful showed the greatest risk for poor family functioning as reflected by high family conflict and chaotic family relationships. Parents also exhibit neglectful parenting, show little concern and emotional affection toward their children, and place little importance on their child's personal growth and academic achievement. Similar to conflict-authoritarian parents, defensive-neglectful parents could be highly critical of their children and they used punitive discipline methods, and had rigid and hierarchical family structures. Other features of defensive-neglectful parents included high levels of "defensive racial socialization"—parents taught their children to dislike other racial groups while failing to promote racial pride—and low levels of "empowering racial socialization"—proactive racial socialization that promotes positive racial identification and a belief in overcoming life obstacles despite racial barriers. The demographic background of defensive-neglectful families in this study included the following: (1) parents had significantly lower educational levels and average annual incomes than families in the other two categories; (2) they had an average of three children; and (3) they attended church less frequently than families from the other two categories.

Finally, Mandara and Murray (2002) found that these three family types were related to African American adolescent self-esteem, ethnic identity, and adjustment. Adolescents who had cohesive-authoritative parents had the highest self-esteem, were more likely to participate in cultural activities and traditions, and valued African American culture to a greater extent than their peers from conflict-authoritarian and defensive-neglectful families. Lastly, adolescents from cohesive-authoritative families appeared to be more emotionally stable than their counterparts in the other two categories. These findings indicate that aspects of authoritative parenting are tied to positive family functioning and childhood adjustment for both African and White non-Hispanic families.

Other studies have similarly found important linkages between a supportive, nurturing, and consistent parenting style and positive childhood adjustment and family functioning. Among inner-city African American and Latino families, consistent parental discipline, parental involvement in their children's lives, open communication, and emotional support and closeness are associated with lower risk for violent delinquent behavior (robbery, assault, and sexual assault) for youth (Gorman-Smith, Tolan, Zelli, & Huesmann, 1996).

Studies also show that ethnic groups might view parenting and child discipline methods in culturally distinct ways. For instance, African and non-Hispanic Whites may have different viewpoints on spanking or corporal punishment as a disciplinary method. White parents tend to view spanking as a "parent-oriented" form of physical discipline or a method that promotes obedience to parents. However, African American parents tend to view spanking as both a parent-oriented and "child-oriented" form of physical discipline. In this latter case, African American parents also believe that spanking helps their children become self-respecting and responsible adults (Whaley, 2000). There also seem to be cultural differences in how children react to spanking. White children tend to exhibit disruptive behaviors when their parents use spanking while this is not necessarily so for African American children, suggesting that cultural differences exist for parental and child views and experiences of physical punishment (Whaley, 2000).

Asian American parents and their children also possess culturally distinct views of parenting and child discipline that can be overlooked or misinterpreted when using standard parenting measures. Past findings that characterize Chinese American parents as being authoritarian, restrictive, and controlling may not be entirely accurate because they do not fully account for certain cultural practices. In one study (Chao, 1994), Chinese American mothers of preschool-age children scored higher than their White counterparts on standard measures of authoritarian parenting and parental control. However, these same Chinese mothers, unlike the White mothers, were also more likely to endorse Chinese child-rearing practices related to child "training" even after controlling for mothers' scores on authoritarian and parental control measures. Although the Chinese concept of "training" overlaps with authoritarian features of parental authority, parental control, and high parental standards, it is a culturally distinct parenting concept because it also involves highly supportive and caring parenting. Furthermore, this Chinese notion of training involves different motives than those underlying authoritarian parenting; it aims to teach children culturally appropriate behaviors and skills that will help them achieve academic success, and meet societal and family expectations.

The differences mentioned above might partially explain why high parental control or parental monitoring does not consistently predict poor adjustment for Asian American youth and Asian American family functioning. Chinese American adolescents who felt that their parents closely monitored their behaviors (e.g., knowing their whereabouts, who they were with, and whether they complied with a set bedtime) were less likely to show depressive symptoms than their peers who reported less parental monitoring (S. Y. Kim & Ge, 2000). Likewise, Korean adolescents might associate parental control with parental warmth and attentiveness (Rohner & Pettengill, 1985). Lastly, immigrant Chinese parents who report feeling competent in their parenting and in control of their children report more positive relationships with their children (Ying, 1999).

Findings on ethnic minority parenting underscore the need to account for diverse worldviews and cultural parenting practices that are overlooked or, in the worst-case scenario, misrepresented by standard measures of parenting. Although established parenting categories or styles are helpful in understanding the significance of parental warmth, control, and involvement, they should not be treated as absolute or complete representations of ethnic minority parenting or family functioning. This is especially important to remember when considering widely referenced authoritarian, authoritative, and permissive parenting categories, which can be overgeneralized for ethnic minority parents. Narrow portrayals of African and Asian American parents as being highly authoritarian, punitive, and emotionally distant from their children prove this point.

Ethnic psychology research has shown that ethnic minority parents can show a wide variety of behaviors. African American parents can prefer nonphysical forms of discipline like discussing matters with their children (Bradley, 1998) and African American single parents who receive support from extended family are more likely to show features of authoritative parenting (R. D. Taylor, Casten, & Flickinger, 1993). Additionally, Chinese American parents may encourage their child to be independent, especially if they feel that it will improve their child's chances for academic success (Lin & Fu, 1990), and acculturated Japanese American parents might prefer that their children openly share their thoughts with them and participate in family decision making (McDermott et al., 1983).

Parent-Child Relationships

Research on ethnic minority parent-child relationships has examined the quality and tone of parent-child interaction, the types of issues that tend to elicit conflict, possible reasons for such conflict, and the psychological consequences of parent-child discord. Most of the research on parent-child conflict actually focuses on parents and their adolescent offspring due to a number of developmental changes that come with adolescence. The adolescent years are marked by a restructuring of family and social relationships during which teens can become more argumentative, rebellious, and experience greater mood fluctuations than in their earlier years (M. Cole, Cole, & Lightfoot, 2005). Ethnic psychology researchers are interested in understanding cultural issues that arise during parent-child conflict, including whether conflict issues are tied to specific cultural practices and beliefs and whether conflict is associated with acculturation differences between parents and children.

Research on conflict issues indicates that ethnic minority parents and their adolescent offspring tend to argue about mundane daily activities of family life such as chores, homework, academic achievement, and choice of activities. However, parent-adolescent disagreements can vary by generational status, age, ethnicity, gender, and family income. For instance, African American parents and their offspring report fewer disagreements about chores over time possibly due to a cultural emphasis on responsibility and collectivism (Smetana & Gaines, 1999).

Conflict issues can also involve disagreement about specific cultural values. For Asian American parents and their adolescents, this includes conflicts over autonomy, familial obligation or responsibility to the family, respect for elders, traditional gender role expectations, cultural expressions of affection, academic achievement, career choice, and dating (Chun & Akutsu, 2003). Disagreements over cultural values can also vary by gender and with acculturation. In a study of immigrant Vietnamese adolescents (Rosenthal, Ranieri, & Klimidis, 1996), endorsement of traditional family values (e.g., support of traditional gender roles, filial obligation, respect for elders, dating and marriage, and expression of feelings) decreased with acculturation while endorsement of autonomy and independence increased for all adolescents. However, this pattern was stronger for girls than boys. The girls valued traditional values less and were more likely than boys to report more conflict with their parents if they perceived a discrepancy in values between themselves and their parents. These findings suggest that Vietnamese immigrant girls experience more acculturation difficulties and potentially more conflict with their parents because of strict gender role expectations and perceived "double standards" in their families.

The above results are similar to findings in another study that showed that Vietnamese adolescent girls, unlike their adolescent male counterparts, reported more problems relating to their parents (Q. D. Tran & Richey, 1997). Some researchers believe that these instances of parent-adolescent conflict are not entirely related to acculturation or to specific features of a culture. Phinney and her colleagues (Phinney, Ong, & Madden, 2000) found that parents tend to endorse family obligation more so than their adolescent offspring regardless of their ethnic backgrounds. This finding suggests that parents are generally inclined to maintain existing norms and expectations while adolescents generally tend to question them regardless of whether they have an immigrant or nonimmigrant background. The effects of parent-adolescent disagreements over values might also be similar across ethnic groups. One study found that parent-adolescent disagreement on family obligation is associated with lower adolescent life satisfaction for both Vietnamese and European Americans (Phinney & Ong, 2002).

Parent-adolescent conflict can become even more complicated when there are language differences. Children who are more proficient in English than their immigrant parents may be placed in the role of "language brokers" for their families (Chao, 2006). This can be a stressful experience for youth who are expected to assume adult roles and responsibilities such as paying household bills, assisting siblings in the educational system, and serving as interpreters for their parents during medical exams. At the same time, these youth may be required to shift back into their role as a child in home settings. Past research shows that these role shifts and language brokering duties can lead to depression and anxiety for youth in immigrant households (Chun, 2006).

With the onset of adolescence, youth often desire greater **individuation** or separation from their parents and increased contacts outside of the home, which can weaken parent-adolescent closeness. These developmental changes can be even more pronounced for Asian American and Latino adolescents who prefer to speak another language than their immigrant parents. Adolescents who spoke with their parents in different languages (e.g., mother speaks in Spanish and her adolescent offspring replies in English) reported fewer conversations with them and more emotional distance compared to adolescents who speak the same language (V. Tseng & Fuligni, 2000). Such instances of "nonreciprocal language use" may result in miscommunication or misunderstandings especially when it comes to expressing emotions or difficult concerns (V. Tseng & Fuligni, 2000).

Acculturation also seems to influence reported communication difficulties. Chinese immigrant mothers who perceive a significant acculturation gap between themselves and their children are more likely to report communication problems with them (Buki, Ma, Strom, & Strom, 2003). In those ethnic minority families that have open and effective parent-adolescent communication, adolescent offspring tend to show better psychosocial adjustment. For African American and Latino families, open and receptive communication between mothers and adolescents about sex decreases the likelihood that adolescents will participate in sexual risk-taking behaviors (Kotchick, Dorsey, Miller, & Forehand, 1999).

Academic Achievement

Do you feel that the color of your skin affects how your teachers and fellow students interacted with you in the classroom? Did anyone in your family ever attend college and did this influence your selection of a university and major, your preparation for the ACT or the SAT, and your current study habits? When you study long hours in the library, do you see it as a means of getting ahead in life and possibly as a means of helping your entire family move ahead too? Or do you experience your studies simply as an intellectual exercise or perhaps sheer drudgery? These types of questions revolve around the key issues of race and immigrant effects on ethnic minority academic achievement.

In regard to racial effects, racial group membership often determines the challenges that families face in securing a quality education for their children and accessing educational resources. This is most apparent when considering the characteristics and resources of public schools in racially stratified neighborhoods and cities. Public schools in predominantly ethnic minority districts are typically located in unhealthy and stressful environments (near freeways or busy intersections, high density and high crime areas), have physical facilities that are in disrepair, lack up-to-date instructional materials and equipment (textbooks, computer labs, and Internet access), have little or no honors or advanced placement courses that are needed for admission to prestigious colleges, and lack essential support staff (e.g., college guidance counselors, health staff, academic tutors). Contrast this with the environments and resources of public schools in predominantly upper- to middle-class neighborhoods where mostly dominant group members reside. Often, it resembles a tale of two cities on all of these dimensions of school environment and instructional resources. Thus, the race toward educational success does not always begin on a level playing field for ethnic minority students, especially if their family members have little or no formal education as seen in many immigrant households.

Complicating matters is the issue of **racial tracking** in the educational system. Ethnic minority youth are more likely to be overlooked for placement in honors or advanced academic courses beginning in elementary school regardless of their academic abilities and potential. Unfortunately, talented ethnic minority students are "tracked" into remedial or regular courses that do not match their academic skills and intellect, preventing them from becoming competitive candidates for college admission. For example, African Americans are overplaced in special educational services (Losen & Orfield, 2002), and they are less likely to be identified for gifted and talented programs (D. Y. Ford, Harris, Tyson, & Frazier Trotman, 2002). In a longitudinal study that followed over 2,000 students from 9th to 12th grade, African American students were less likely than White non-Hispanic students to be moved into honors or advanced math courses (Hallinan, 1996).

Racial tracking is tied to teachers' and educational administrators' racial stereotypes of ethnic minority students. African American students are rated more negatively (less cognitive ability, less motivated, less verbal) than Asian or White students. Teachers' low expectations and negative views of African American youth negatively affect the youths' self-concepts, motivation, academic achievement, and future ambitions, and can thus become self-fulfilling prophecies (Franklin et al., 2002). Contrary to negative racial stereotypes of ethnic minority students, studies have found that poor African American and Latino families with elementary school children are enthusiastic about education, strive to provide supportive environments for academic achievement, and hold high expectations for academic success (Stevenson, Chen, & Uttal, 1990). Furthermore, Mexican American teens with formally educated, supportive, and involved parents possess high educational aspirations (Plunkett & Bamaca-Gomez, 2003).

Research on immigrant effects has examined whether the family environments, cultural beliefs, and individual attributes of new immigrant youth affect their academic performance. Much of this research attempts to explain why certain immigrant groups like Chinese, Japanese, and Korean Americans show high academic achievement despite facing economic hardship and having few educational resources at their disposal. Studies typically compare GPAs, achievement test scores, and college performance between foreign- and U.S.-born student populations. Additionally, family characteristics, including cultural beliefs about education, are compared for immigrant and nonimmigrant groups. Generally speaking, immigrant students perform as well as American-born students; however, differences in academic achievement arise when demographic factors are closely examined. In a study of 12th graders enrolled in public education (Fuligni & Witkow, 2004), both immigrant and American-born students basically showed the same academic progress into college even though the immigrant students assumed added responsibilities for making financial contributions to their households. Differences in academic achievement were revealed when students' ethnicity, family SES, and the educational backgrounds of their parents were analyzed. Latino and Filipino American students from low SES families, and those who had parents with little formal education, showed low achievement in some areas in college. However, high aspirations for educational achievement and familial obligation or a sense of duty to one's family promoted academic success. These findings suggest that family background, resources, and cultural values play an important role in the educational success of ethnic minority students.

Researchers have also stated that societal and historical conditions and perceived opportunities for upward mobility in a racially stratified society shape academic achievement. S. Sue and Okazaki (1990) hypothesized that educational success among Asian American groups can be explained by **relative functionalism.** According to this hypothesis, Asian Americans tend to view education as a means for upward mobility. S. Sue and Okazaki explain that certain occupations and career paths that do not necessarily require a formal education (e.g., those in the entertainment and sports industries and in organized labor) have been historically closed to Asian Americans due to institutional racism and discrimination. Evidence for this lies in the conspicuous absence of highly visible Asian Americans in film, television, and sports. However, careers that require a formal education (e.g., engineering, medicine, and law) have been less restrictive to Asian Americans and are viewed as viable means for getting ahead by this ethnic community. Consequently, those Asian American students who equate studying with social and economic upward mobility are more likely to focus on their studies and academic achievement. This idea has been supported by past studies showing that Asian American students are more likely to view and experience their studies as an effective and positive means to become successful in life (Alva, 1993; Asakawa & Csikszentmihalyi, 1998). Still, it is important to counter racial stereotypes that portray Asian American students as the model minority. This stereotype, which portrays all Asian American students as high-achieving academic whiz kids or the "model minority," is wholly inaccurate given the significant academic difficulties and high drop-out rates that are seen in certain segments of this population, such as among Southeast Asian refugees. Moreover, this stereotype has been historically used to reinforce stratification by pitting ethnic minority groups against one another, and by obscuring the real effects of racial and social stratification on educational performance.

Couple Relationships

Gender roles and attitudes, predictors of marital conflict and divorce, and cultural issues and risk factors for domestic violence are main topics of ethnic minority couple research. In regard to gender roles, investigators have examined how certain cultural beliefs or value systems inform the types of responsibilities and duties, communication patterns and styles, and interactions between men and women. Often, families socialize their children around cultural gender role expectations early in their development. In a study of Chinese American teens (Fuligni, Yip, & Tseng, 2002), girls showed more family involvement and family obligations than boys such as sharing a family meal, helping to clean the house, running errands, caring for siblings, or cooking meals. These same girls were also more likely than boys to experience daily conflicts with their parents over negotiating these family obligations with the time spent with friends and studying. These findings indicate that Chinese American girls are more likely than boys to struggle with gender role expectations to fulfill daily family and household duties.

Similar gender role expectations have been reported for Latino couples. Researchers have commented that Latino men are socialized to assume a dominant position in couple relationships, and to provide for and protect their wives and families (Grebler, Moore, & Guzman, 1973). Women in return are expected to follow their husbands, maintain the household, and perform daily child-rearing duties. These types of Latino/Latina gender role prescriptions, often characterized as "machismo" and "marianismo" for men and women, respectively, are defined and discussed at length in Chapter 5.

Suffice it to say, the cultural meaning and subtle nuances of Latino and Latina gender roles are often overlooked in research, which unfortunately perpetuates one-dimensional, racial stereotypes (J. B. Torres et al., 2002). As explained in Chapter 5, Latino/Latina gender behaviors and attitudes can vary with differences in individual backgrounds and life experiences. For instance, studies have reported that Latinos/Latinas who have more formal education and have lived in the United States longer are less likely to endorse traditional gender roles than newer Latino/Latina immigrants to the United States who have less formal education (Chun & Akutsu, 2003).

For African American men and women, past studies report more egalitarian gender roles, partly stemming from historical job discrimination that prevented African American men from becoming the sole breadwinner or primary family provider (S. A. Hill, 2001). African American women thus continue to make important economic contributions to their families by seeking gainful employment and sharing household duties with their husbands.

Research on marital conflict shows that ethnicity is not a reliable predictor of how frequently marital conflict occurs. This refutes racial stereotypes of African Americans as high-conflict couples, which stem from older studies that did not control for socioeconomic status, educational levels, family structure, and experiences of racial discrimination, all of which affect stress levels in couples (McLoyd, Harper, & Copeland, 2001). The negative effects of economic hardship on couple functioning were seen in a study of African American couples—those who were impoverished exhibited significantly higher rates of separation than those who possessed greater financial resources (Shaw, Winslow, & Flanagan, 1999).

Domestic violence can be difficult to study in ethnic minority populations because of cultural stigma and fear of retribution by family members if problems are discussed with persons outside of the family. This is especially the case for new immigrant women who must contend with a series of interrelated cultural, gender, and socioeconomic issues that make it dangerous and potentially life-threatening to report domestic violence. For instance, Asian American immigrant women who experience physical violence might be reluctant to seek help because of loss of face issues and traditional gender role attitudes. **Loss of face** is defined as a person's social integrity, which is tied to one's ability to meet the role responsibilities and expectations of a valued social group like one's family (Zane & Mak, 2003). Asian American women who are battered may be hesitant to report their husbands' violence because they fear that it will bring loss of face not only to themselves, but to their entire family as well. This is reinforced by patriarchal family structures that require women to assume a passive and obedient role to their husbands (Tang, Cheung, Chen, & Sun, 2002).

Certain cultural values like filial obligation and filial piety, which compel family members to subsume individual desires and needs to the interests and well-being of the entire family, further discourage Asian American women from leaving their abusive husbands (Bhandari Preisser, 1999; C. Tran & Des Jardins, 2000). In the Japanese culture, the concept of ***gaman*** is a valued cultural trait ascribing character and strength to those who endure and withstand hardship without complaint (Ho, 1990). Japanese women who endorse this concept might feel that their individual character depends on their ability to endure and remain in an abusive relationship in order to keep the family intact (Ho, 1990). Finally, immigrant women in general are often reluctant to seek help and relocate with their children due to English-language difficulties, economic hardship, and fear of deportation, all of which contribute to feelings of isolation and despair.

The causes of domestic violence against ethnic minority women represent an interaction between class, culture, gender, and immigration status (Bui & Morash, 1999). This means that a couple's risk for domestic violence varies depending on each partner's socioeconomic status, cultural beliefs and norms, beliefs about what it means to be a man or woman, and acculturation experiences. From a feminist perspective, domestic abuse is not simply an issue of violence, but one of control and the familial, social, and historical forces that promote male dominance and control. In a study of South Asian Indian women (Mehrotra, 1999), reported abuse included mental, verbal, emotional, and economic abuse in addition to physical abuse. Economic abuse entailed not being allowed to control economic resources and household finances. One South Asian Indian woman who had a high-paying job reported that her paychecks were directly deposited into her husband's bank account and she was restricted to a weekly allowance that he controlled. The women in this study also reported that their husbands tried to assert their dominance and control by isolating them from their family and friends. The relationship between violence against women and male dominance was found for Korean Americans as well. In one study, severe violence against Korean American wives was four times higher in male-dominant couples in which men held decision-making power, compared to that of egalitarian couples where men and women jointly made family decisions (J. Y. Kim & Sung, 2000).

Domestic violence in male-dominant households can also stem from **status inconsistency,** which is defined as a loss of socioeconomic status and occupational prestige following immigration to another country. Immigrant men who held high-paying and prestigious positions in their country of origin are often unable to gain equivalent positions in a new country due to language barriers, lack of similar occupations, difficulties transferring professional degrees and training, and discrimination. Status inconsistency can arise when these immigrant men are relegated to lower-paying or low-status jobs or become unemployed, which can damage their self-esteem and lead to frustration, anger, and depression. In one case study (Chun, Akutsu, & Abueg, 1994), a Vietnamese refugee who fled to the United States following the Vietnam War was forced to leave his position as a high-ranking South Vietnamese general and assume a new role as a social worker. For this individual, status inconsistency contributed to depressive symptoms, loss of face, and a feeling of shame. Immigrant men who experience status inconsistency, possess low self-esteem, and cannot effectively manage their anger and frustration are at risk for becoming perpetrators of domestic violence.

Some immigrant men might also become abusive when feeling threatened by shifting gender roles. Immigrant women who once assumed a secondary role to their husbands may be required to seek gainful employment and help make monetary contributions to the family household after relocating to the United States. Men who hold rigid gender role attitudes may react violently to this shift in responsibilities, especially if their wives become the primary or sole household provider and become more independent. In one study (I. J. Kim & Zane, 2004), Korean American male batterers showed greater anger and less anger control than White male batterers due to higher occupational and economic stress and possibly due to traditional gender role attitudes. Still, the link between traditional role attitudes and domestic violence may vary depending on an individual's educational level, age, and socioeconomic status. In a sample of highly educated, older, upper-middle-class Chinese Americans, there was no relationship between gender role attitudes and domestic violence (Yick, 2000).

Family Stress and Coping

Economic hardship and poverty continue to stress ethnic minority family functioning and relations. The negative impact of poverty on family life is most pronounced for households that are headed by single women. Poverty rates of children in these households are almost five times that of children in married-couple households (Lugalia & Overturf, 2004). When ethnic minority status is added into this picture, poverty rates increase substantially. Ethnic minority children who live in homes that are solely headed by their mothers show the highest rates of poverty—50% of American Indian and over 47% of African American and Latino children under

18 years of age in mother-only family groups live in poverty (Lugalia & Overturf, 2004).

There is a growing body of research that examines the effects of economic hardship on the well-being of ethnic minority youth. Much of this research points to a **family stress model,** which posits that the family environment mediates or is related to the relationship between economic disadvantage and youth adjustment (Hammack, LaVome Robinson, Crawford, & Li, 2004; McLoyd, 1990, 1998). In African American families, economic pressures (being unable to make ends meet or to afford daily living expenses including housing, food, clothing, and medical expenses) are associated with depression in parents and disrupted parenting practices, which in turn lead to child behavioral problems and childhood depression and anxiety (Conger et al., 2002).

Family dysfunction in poor ethnic minority families is often mis-attributed to a **culture of poverty,** characterized by inherently deviant cultural norms and values, particularly among the urban poor. However, this racial stereotype overlooks the fact that structural inequalities and concentrated poverty lead to social isolation of ethnic minority families, which ultimately compromises their overall functioning. In impoverished neighborhoods, important institutions like businesses, schools, social clubs, and community and voluntary organizations decline and often disappear leaving families without important resources to sustain their development (Rankin & Quane, 2000). Research clearly shows that greater access to capital and financial resources can improve ethnic minority family functioning. For example, when financial resources are perceived to be adequate, African American mothers are more likely to perceive themselves as being effective parents. Furthermore, African American mothers who view themselves as effective parents are more likely to create a structured and organized family life for their children (Seaton & Taylor, 2003), and are more likely to emphasize educational goals, respect for others in the community, and concern for others when raising their children (Brody, Flor, & Morgan Gibson, 1999).

Some researchers have noted that although poor ethnic minority families may lack financial capital, they may still have an abundance of **social capital,** which is defined as social support and resources that come from one's social relationships and connections within one's family and community (Fuligni & Yoshikawa, 2003). Social capital can include cultural resources or traditions in the family that promote mutual support and interdependence. For instance, extended kin support from grandparents is a form of social capital for many ethnic minority families. From a family resource management perspective, grandparents provide valuable human resources in terms of time, human energy, and skills that can help families meet life demands and accomplish their goals (Tam & Detzner, 1998). Grandparents or other relatives can also provide skilled child rearing and play a key role in the cultural socialization and ethnic identity development of the children.

Social capital is also derived from social networks in one's ethnic community such as those found in religious organizations and churches. Social capital from religious organizations can partly offset the stress of poverty by providing essential cultural, instrumental, and emotional support. A large-scale study of Asian American, Central American, and Mexican American immigrant communities in the San Francisco Bay Area found that religious organizations helped low-income immigrant families develop and thrive by (1) helping them to maintain important cultural traditions and transnational family and ethnic community support networks, (2) offsetting status inconsistency by providing leadership roles and opportunities, (3) helping family members cope with acculturation stressors and racial discrimination, and (4) providing culturally appropriate means to address existential and spiritual questions about life changes and hardships (Lorentzen et al., in press).

Racism and discrimination represent additional stressors that ethnic minority families must confront. One study found that African American children who reside in a highly discriminatory community are at greater risk for depression (Simons et al., 2002). Moreover, this finding was not restricted to those children who were targets of discrimination; simply witnessing incidents of discrimination against members in their ethnic or racial group also increased the children's risk for depression. However, living in a neighborhood that displayed ethnic identification and pride lowered the risk for childhood depression. Researchers report that chronic racial discrimination exacerbates the negative effects of ongoing life stressors in African American families. For African American mothers, racial discrimination exacerbated their cumulative life stressors, psychological distress, and the negative effects of their psychological distress on their parent-child and couple relationships (Murry, Brown, Brody, Cutrona, & Simons, 2001).

Ethnic minority families often deal with racism and discrimination by practicing different forms of racial socialization, as witnessed in the different African American parenting styles previously discussed. Additionally, one study of African American racial socialization practices found that parents were more likely to teach their children about their African American cultural history and heritage rather than teaching racial bias and discrimination or encouraging social distance and wariness toward dominant White culture (Hughes & Chen, 1997). Again, social capital from religious organizations can buffer the harmful effects of racism and discrimination on ethnic minority family functioning.

For African Americans, religious organizations offer an environment for positive self-evaluation through prayer along with instrumental and emotional support from fellow church members (Harrison-Hale, McLoyd, & Smedley, 2004). African American churches often act as an extended family to their members and as a social agency by providing homeless shelters, food programs, nursing home programs, counseling, GED preparation programs, and even physical fitness centers (Sanders, 2002).

The benefits of church attendance and church affiliation on African American family functioning are gradually being documented in ethnic psychology research. In African American two-parent families from the rural South, high parental religiosity (measured by church attendance and perceived importance of church) was associated with more cohesive family relationships, less marital conflict, and fewer behavioral and emotional problems in adolescents (Brody, Stoneman, & Flor, 1996). For African American families in the Midwest, regular church attendance by parents was related to fewer parental reports of oppositional behavior, peer conflict, depression, and immaturity in their children (Christian & Barbarin, 2001). African American youth who attended church or religious services on a regular basis were also less likely to engage in premarital intercourse and less likely to use alcohol, cigarettes, and marijuana (Steinman & Zimmerman, 2004).

Chapter Summary

In this chapter, we examined ethnic minority family functioning from an ecological perspective to illustrate how different social relationships, environments, and social institutions shape, and are themselves shaped by, the collective lives of family members. Diverse patterns of family functioning emerge across ethnic minority families based on their distinct structures and relationships, and the varied life demands, stressors, and resources in their respective ecologies. For families of color, the ecological challenges of acculturation and minority status can heighten their family stress and restrict their access to important coping resources, complicating their ability to navigate normative developmental changes and life transitions. Still, ethnic minority families should not be narrowly viewed from a deficits model of family functioning because doing so would completely overlook their many strengths and instances in which they successfully exercise their family agency. To this end, a growing number of ethnic psychologists are focusing their attention on the resiliency, positive characteristics, and cultural resources of ethnic minority families that promote and safeguard family development and well-being.

Key Terms

Acculturation (page 189)

Authoritarian Parenting (page 196)

Authoritative Parenting (page 196)

Cohesive-Authoritative Parenting (page 199)

Conflict-Authoritarian Parenting (page 198)

Culture of Poverty (page 211)

Defensive-Neglectful Parenting (page 199)

Defensive Racial Socialization (page 199)

Ecological Perspective (page 189)

Ecologies (page 189)

Familialism (page 194)

Familism (page 194)

Family Agency (page 191)

Family Stress Model (page 211)

Filial Piety (page 195)

Gaman (page 209)

Individuation (page 204)

Loss of Face (page 208)

Minority Status (page 189)

Patrilineal (page 195)

Permissive Parenting (page 196)

Proactive Racial Socialization (page 199)

Racial Tracking (page 205)

Relative Functionalism (page 206)

Social Capital (page 211)

Status Inconsistency (page 209)

What Is the Ecological Context of Your Family Life?

As noted at the beginning of this chapter, the many ways in which family members relate to one another, organize or structure their family roles, and fulfill their daily tasks are influenced by the diverse ecologies that each family member inhabits. Think of your own family for a moment.

- What are the different types of family ecologies that you and your family members inhabit in your daily lives?
- How do these family ecologies shape how your family functions? For example, how do your family members relate to one another, how are duties and tasks assigned to family members, and how does your family meet its daily needs as well as new life challenges?
- If you belong to an ethnic minority family, how have the ecological challenges of minority status and acculturation affected your family life? Have these ecological challenges brought your family members closer together or pulled them apart?
- Can you think of instances in which your family showed "family agency" during difficult or challenging times? How have these instances shaped how you view your family, including what you believe to be your family's strengths and limitations? Do these instances of family agency serve as a source of inspiration and guidance in your daily life? How so?

Suggested Further Readings

Berry, J. W. (2004). An ecocultural perspective on the development of competence. In R. J. Sternberg & E. L. Grigorenko (Eds.), *Culture and competence: Contexts of life success* (pp. 3–22). Washington, DC: American Psychological Association.

Written by one of the leading acculturation scholars, this book chapter examines how different cultural environments shape the acquisition and development of cultural competencies and skills.

Berry, J. W., Phinney, J. S., Sam, D. L., & Vedder, P. (Eds.). (2006). *Immigrant youth in cultural transition: Acculturation, identity, and adaptation across national contexts.* Mahwah, NJ: Lawrence Erlbaum.

An international team of scholars presents new research findings on ethnic identity formation, cultural adaptation, and development for youth across the globe.

Bornstein, M. H., & Cote, L. R. (Eds.). (2006). *Acculturation and parent-child relationships: Measurement and development.* Mahwah, NJ: Lawrence Erlbaum.

A seminal book in the field that presents pioneering research on the conceptualization and measurement of acculturation, and acculturation influences on family development and parent-child relations.

Contreras, J. M., Kerns, K. A., & Neal-Barnett, A. M. (Eds.). (2002). *Latino children and families in the United States: Current research and future directions.* Westport, CT: Praeger/Greenwood.

This publication presents state-of-the-art research on Latino parenting and child development, and offers culturally appropriate research and measurement strategies for Latino families.

Georgas, J., Berry, J. W., van de Vijver, F. J. R., Kagitçibasi, C., & Poortinga, Y. H. (Eds.). (2006). *Families across cultures: A 30-nation psychological study.* New York: Cambridge University Press.

Assembles some of the top cross-cultural researchers to examine the diversity of family environments, relations, and lives across different cultural contexts.

Lee, E., & Mok, M. R. (2005). Asian families: An overview. In M. McGoldrick, J. Giordano, & N. Garcia-Preto (Eds.), *Ethnicity and family therapy* (3rd ed., pp. 269–289). New York: Guilford.

A professional overview of clinical and therapy issues for Asian American families examining the many ways in which cultural values and norms, and minority and immigrant experiences influence Asian American family life.

McLoyd, V. C., Hill, N. E., & Dodge, K. A. (Eds.). (2005). *African American family life: Ecological and cultural diversity.* New York: Guilford.

This book illustrates the diversity of African American family lives, presenting recent research findings on African American family ecologies and family development.

Quintana, S. M., & McKown, C. (Eds.). (2008). *Handbook of race, racism, and the developing child.* Hoboken, NJ: John Wiley.

This handbook provides unique insights into the meaning and significance of race in children's lives from the perspectives of an international group of scholars.

Sutton, C. E. T., & Broken Nose, M. A. (2005). American Indian families: An overview. In M. McGoldrick, J. Giordano, & N. Garcia-Preto (Eds.), *Ethnicity and family therapy* (3rd ed., pp. 43–54). New York: Guilford.

An invaluable resource for clinicians that covers key cultural, social, and historical factors shaping American Indian family relations and functioning.

Yee, B. W. K., DeBaryshe, B. D., Yuen, S., Kim, S. Y., & McCubbin, H. I. (2007). Asian American and Pacific Islander families: Resiliency and life-span socialization in a cultural context. In F. T. L. Leong, A. G. Inman, A. Ebreo, L. H. Yang, L. Kinoshita, & M. Fu (Eds.), *Handbook of Asian American psychology* (2nd ed., pp. 69–86). Thousand Oaks, CA: Sage.

Presents key conceptual frameworks to understand Asian American family functioning, along with a comprehensive review of Asian American family research topics and findings.

CHAPTER **7**

SOCIAL BEHAVIOR IN AN ETHNICALLY DIVERSE SOCIETY

VIGNETTE

A True Story by One of the Authors (G.M.)

Having graduated from a Jesuit high school where students were challenged academically and shown respect and personal attention, I was looking forward to starting college and unprepared for becoming the victim of prejudice. Having just migrated to the United States, I was unaware of options available to college students and followed the suggestions of our neighbors and enrolled at a large community college. This was in the early 1970s in a southern state with a large Latino population. One of my courses was an introduction to my major. The course was required and a prerequisite for all other courses in the program. The first day of class, approximately 50 students filed into the classroom looking forward to starting a new year. Soon the professor, let's call him Dr. Jones, walked into the classroom, went through the class list, distributed the syllabus, and started to describe what the course was about. As Dr. Jones was describing the tests and projects expected of all students, he raised his voice for all of us to hear and clearly announced: "A word of caution to all of you. I don't like cheaters and people who plagiarize or copy homework assignments from other students." He then looked and pointed directly at the 10 or so of us who had a Spanish surname and said, "All of you Hispanics, pay attention. I know you all cheat, so the best grade you can get in this class is a C because I never know if the work is yours or if you just copied it from a friend." Some of us stayed enrolled in the course and indeed got no higher than a C as the final grade. We were too afraid to appeal to staff and faculty about the unfairness of the situation or even to talk about it to others. I then transferred to a Jesuit university in the Midwest and "the rest is history." I often wondered whatever happened to Dr. Jones. In a sense, he is responsible for motivating me to become a social psychologist and to try to understand why people feel and act that way toward those individuals who happen to be different.

The purpose of this chapter is to briefly review the psychological literature that deals with some of the effects of living in a diverse, multiethnic community. Obviously, the sheer magnitude of the topic makes it necessary to limit coverage to two components: first, the attitudinal and behavioral effects of being exposed to members of an ethnically diverse social environment and, second, the psychosocial effects of interacting with diverse others at school and at work. We start this chapter by talking about stereotypes as reactions to encountering diverse individuals and as basic components of the processes of prejudice and discrimination. We then review ways in which prejudice, discrimination, and racism can be changed or prevented. Finally, we review the benefits that are part of living in a social and ethnically diverse society—benefits that affect Whites as well as members of ethnic minority groups.

STEREOTYPES, PREJUDICE, AND DISCRIMINATION

Stereotypes, prejudice, and discrimination are of particular importance when we study the social and psychological effects of living in an ethnically diverse society. You may have already covered these concepts in your foundational courses in psychology, sociology, or ethnic studies classes and therefore we will only briefly describe them here.

There have been a large number of definitions that have been used by researchers and policymakers to better understand stereotypes. Those definitions tend to consider **stereotypes** as mental images that include personal, social, or ethical characteristics that we tend to assign to individuals who belong to members of specific human groups. We can, therefore, talk about **ethnic stereotypes** as the characteristics that we consider are common among members of specific ethnic groups.

Likewise, there are a number of definitions that can be found in the literature of the social sciences for prejudice and discrimination. The definitions found in Box 7.1 emphasize the cognitive nature of stereotypes (as generalized beliefs about people) that are associated with evaluative or affective reactions, and in the case of **prejudice,** those affective reactions are usually negative or unfavorable. Often, the existence of certain stereotypes and prejudices lead to differential treatment of members of certain groups **(discrimination)** on the part of those individuals who hold the stereotypes and prejudices **(interpersonal discrimination)** or as demanded by policies or even laws **(institutional discrimination).**

BOX 7.1

Basic Definitions

Stereotypes

- Beliefs and opinions about the characteristics, attributes, and behaviors of members of various groups (Whitley & Kite, 2006, p. 6)
- Generalized beliefs about groups and their members (APA, 2007, p. 475)

Prejudice

- Attitude directed toward people because they are members of a specific social group (Whitley & Kite, 2006, p. 7)
- Unfavorable affective reactions to or evaluation of groups and their members (APA, 2007, p. 475)

(Continued)

(Continued)

Discrimination

- Treating people differently from others based primarily on membership in a social group (Whitley & Kite, 2006, p. 8)
- Interpersonal discrimination is differential treatment by individuals toward some groups and their members relative to other groups and their members, and institutional discrimination involves policies and contexts that create, enact, reify, and maintain inequality (APA, 2007, p. 475)

In the vignette, Dr. Jones exemplified how these three concepts resided in one individual and affected the way he acted. The professor held the *stereotypes* that Latinos were untrustworthy because they "all" cheated and plagiarized in their school work. His negative feelings toward actions that compromise academic honesty had been generalized to all Latinos, and he held on to those *prejudicial attitudes* as characteristics of all Latinos. Furthermore, he felt justified in *discriminating* toward all Latinos by only awarding a grade no higher than a C, even to individuals who excelled in their class performance. So even though he had never met the new Latino students in his class or had any reason to believe that they would cheat on exams and papers, he overgeneralized his stereotypes and prejudices and declared them cheaters, dishonest and unreliable students.

As could be expected, all human groups can be the subject of stereotypes, prejudice, and discrimination. Indeed, stereotypes, prejudices, and discrimination can be measured or identified when we differentiate people in terms of their gender, national origin, religious beliefs, sexual preferences, health status, political opinions, socioeconomic status, or almost any other type of variable or characteristic. They are manifested in a variety of ways including jokes (e.g., "How many [insert group name] does it take to change a light bulb?"), statements (e.g., "I don't trust those people, they are always trying to get something for nothing"), attitudes (e.g., "I don't like nurses who are [insert group name]"), and of course actions (e.g., not serving people from a certain group at a restaurant or shop). As mentioned above, discrimination can at times be institutionalized as it was in the United States when African Americans were not allowed to go to the same schools as Whites, or marry Whites, or even drink from the same water fountains as Whites. Other examples of institutionalized discrimination include apartheid in South Africa or countries where the foreign born are not allowed the right of citizenship.

Recently, the American Psychological Association (APA, 2007) issued a resolution condemning discrimination of all types and urging psychologists to study ways to decrease the effects of discrimination. As mentioned in the APA resolution (parts of which appear in Box 7.2), not only is discrimination an abridgement or limitation of human rights, but together with stereotypes and prejudice it has a number of negative consequences for the individuals who are their target including distress, anxiety, lowered self-esteem, and psychosomatic disorders. Indeed, the Hispanic students that bore the negative effects of Dr. Jones's biases felt intimidated and powerless to change their situation. In addition, stereotypes, prejudice, and discrimination can create negative social environments including rejection of certain individuals, social disparities (e.g., in education, housing, income, health status) and intergroup hostility, conflict, crime, and even genocide.

BOX 7.2

Some Effects of Prejudice, Stereotypes, and Discrimination

- Negative cognitive, affective, motivational, and behavioral effects among members of stigmatized groups
  - Anger and anxiety
  - Depression
  - Lower aspirations

- Internalization of characteristics
  - Self-blame
  - Believing negative stereotypes
  - Poorer psychological well-being including lower self-esteem

- Negative intergroup relations including distrust
- Hostile environments
  - Feelings of rejection
  - Lack of self-confidence
  - Fright

- Violence, conflict, and genocide
- Unequal access to education, economic advancement, housing, security, health status, and services
- Damaging effects on perpetrators including their physical and mental health

SOURCE: APA (2007).

Stereotypes

As mentioned above, stereotypes are images or beliefs we hold of the characteristics typically associated with members of certain groups. A large number of stereotype studies have tried to identify the characteristics most frequently associated with members of specific groups as well as how stable or consistent those stereotypes are over time. Other researchers have been concerned about how those stereotypes are formed or changed. Unfortunately, much stereotype research has been conducted among college students, limiting the generalizability of the results to the whole population. Indeed, college students represent not only a small percentage of the population of the country but they also are unique in their level of education and in many cases in the levels of experiences with diverse individuals. Nevertheless, there are some studies that have used national samples of respondents and that allow us to understand stereotypes held by other women and men.

Surveys with large national samples have shown important differences in the ways ethnic minority groups are perceived in the United States. For example, an analysis of the 1990 General Social Survey, a large-scale survey with a representative sample of the nation's population, showed that Hispanic Americans in general were considered in less positive terms than Whites and than most of the other ethnic groups (Jews, Blacks, Asians, southern Whites) included in the survey (Smith, 1990). For example, Hispanics were considered to be poorer, less intelligent, and less patriotic than all other groups as well as lazier, more likely to be violence-prone, and to be living off welfare than all other ethnic groups except for African Americans. A later study also using the General Social Survey (Weaver, 2007) showed interesting differences between Latinos and Whites in the stereotypes they held of each other. White respondents held generally negative stereotypes of Latinos in terms of their wealth, work ethic, intelligence, and violent behavior. Furthermore, they perceived themselves in a more positive fashion than Latinos in each of those four areas. Latinos, on the other hand, had favorable images of Whites and in each of the four characteristics measured in the survey they perceived Whites more positively than Latinos in general.

How Are Stereotypes Developed?

Stereotypes are generalized perceptions we hold of people who belong to specific groups. In reality, they are overgeneralizations that lead us to ignore the individuality that is part of our humanity. As overgeneralizations, stereotypes can be formed by experiences we have with one or few individuals who are easily identifiable as members of an ethnic group that lead us to believe that all members share those characteristics (a phenomenon often called the **out-group homogeneity effect**). You may have had the experience of meeting an international student in your school from a country whose nationals you had never met (e.g., Kazakhstan). You enjoyed meeting the student—felt she was friendly, smart, intelligent, and open. Next time you talk about people from Kazakhstan, you may very well assign the same characteristics that you found in this student. Those characteristics have become initial stereotypes that you hold of people from that country.

Statements by others, particularly people personally important to you, can also be the source of stereotypes. As we grow up, we are often exposed to statements by relatives or teachers or coaches that help shape the stereotypes we hold of people who belong to certain groups. We may have heard, for example, our parents or teachers say that people from a certain group are intelligent and do well in school, or from coaches that members of an ethnic group are great ball players. Those statements can be the root for the stereotypes we hold, particularly when they become "confirmed" by personal experiences such as when you meet a member of the group who exhibits the characteristics you heard from your parents, teachers, or coaches.

Historical and political events also can influence the formation of stereotypes. Wars, for example, have seen the development of certain perceptions about the enemy that easily become part of a generalized stereotype of members of that group. We have seen that phenomenon in our country as the stereotypes of Germans and Japanese became fairly negative during World War II or in the case of the Vietnamese during the U.S.-Vietnam war of the 1960s and 1970s. Likewise, some stereotypes are formed by biased perceptions of national origin or loyalty based on skin color or national heritage. Indeed, research has shown that the definition of "American" is heavily related to Whiteness among Whites and even among some ethnic groups (Devos & Banaji, 2005) as well as to feelings of economic and social inclusion partly related to skin color.

But personal experiences and history and political events are not the only way in which stereotypes are formed. Mass media, whether electronic or printed, can also contribute to the formation of stereotypes and misperceptions (Peterson, Wingood, DiClemente, Harrington, & Davies, 2007) by, if nothing else, the frequency or absence with which members of an ethnic group are portrayed. For example, an analysis of television commercials shown in 1984 during prime time discovered that Latinos appeared in approximately 5% of commercials compared with 17% for African Americans; males from either ethnic group appeared at least 2.5 times more frequently than females (Wilkes & Valencia, 1989). These figures, of course, do not appropriately represent the actual number of African Americans and Latinos in the country at that time and further support a notion of an "invisible minority." The passing of time and the increase in the number of Latinos residing in the United States have not produced changes in these indicators, with Latino actors and models being basically absent from the media and from movies. When portrayed in movies or television programming, Latino males are often represented as violent individuals involved in criminal activities or both men and women as service personnel rather than as managers, teachers, politicians, or doctors (Nicolini, 1987).

Another source of ethnic minority stereotyping is advertising and mass marketing. Researchers and community leaders often have decried the negative images of African Americans, Asian Americans, and Latinos that some national advertising campaigns have promoted. A classic example is the case of the Frito Bandito animated character used to promote the sale of Fritos corn chips in the late 1960s. The Frito Bandito was portrayed as a mustachioed, sombrero-wearing, heavily accented, pistol toting Mexican thief who managed to cunningly trick people of their Fritos. Frito Lay, the distributor of Fritos, finally retired the Bandito in 1971 after mounting pressure from the National Mexican Anti-Defamation Committee and other groups (Don Markstein's Toonopedia, 2008).

While the use of negative images related to ethnic minority groups in advertising seems to have decreased significantly in the last decades, the potential for stereotype formation is still there. For instance, in 2002 Abercrombie & Fitch clothier dealt with controversy surrounding its sale of T-shirts featuring caricature faces wearing rice-paddy hats (reminiscent of early 1900s pop culture depictions of Chinese men) and carrying slogans such as "Wong Brothers Laundry Service—Two Wongs Can Make It White," "Wok-N-Bowl—Let the Good Times Roll—Chinese Food & Bowling," "Abercrombie and Fitch Buddha Bash—Get Your Buddha on the Floor" (Strasburg, 2002). There was an immediate outcry from many Asian Americans, especially in the San Francisco Bay Area, who viewed these images as demeaning and disrespectful. Representatives from Abercrombie & Fitch insisted that they were surprised by the negative reaction and had not intended to offend anyone—but instead had developed the product as a means of adding "humor" and "levity" to its clothing line (Glionna & Goldman, 2002). Hampton Carney, public relations representative, stated that the company had anticipated that "young Asian shoppers" as well as others would think the images were funny and would recognize this as just another product from a company known for its edginess and "making fun" of a broad range of subjects from "women to flight attendants to baggage handlers, to football coaches, to Irish Americans to snow skiers" (Strasburg,

2002, p. A1). However, within a couple of weeks, Abercrombie & Fitch pulled the line of T-shirts from its stores nationwide.

Also relevant is the use of images that portray ethnic minority groups in negative ways, such as sport team mascots or logos that use American Indian symbols or members of certain tribes or nations. A few years ago, the American Psychological Association (2005) issued a resolution calling for the termination of the use of all Indian mascots, symbols, images, and personalities used by schools and university athletic programs. The APA's position rested on growing research indicating that using these images produce negative effects on not only American Indians but all students by (1) conveying that it is acceptable to denigrate a culture through inaccurate presentations of American Indian culture; (2) establishing an unfriendly or even hostile learning environment for American Indian students by adopting representations that support negative stereotypes that are prevalent in the mainstream culture; (3) making it difficult for American Indian Nations to maintain a level of understanding and respect regarding their culture, spirituality, and traditions; and (4) engaging in a form of discrimination against American Indian Nations that can lead to negative interactions between groups and negative mental health consequences for American Indian and Alaska Native people.

Stereotype Characteristics and Effects

In general, one key characteristic of stereotypes is the fact that stereotypes seem to be rather rigid and difficult to change. Nevertheless, some studies have shown slow but certain changes in the content and intensity of stereotypes. For example, Weaver (2005), analyzing data from the large nationwide surveys mentioned above (the General Social Survey conducted in 1990 and in 2000), found that the stereotypes of Latinos held by Whites in terms of Latinos' industriousness, wealth, and intelligence had improved over the 10 years that passed between the surveys. At the same time, among African Americans, the perceptions they held of Latinos changed little in the decade except for stereotypes about their work ethic.

Another central characteristic of stereotypes is that they influence people's behavior not just in terms of supporting prejudice and discrimination (as discussed later in this chapter) but also in terms of how people act after internalizing the stereotypes that others have of them. Social psychologist Claude Steele (1997) identified what he terms **"stereotype threat"** to describe how situations where negative stereotypes are made apparent, even subtly, lead to diminished performance in minorities that is consistent with the stereotype. In addition, the threat of fulfilling the negative stereotype occurs in situations that are meaningful to the person's identity (e.g., academically oriented

African Americans or Latinos, or math-oriented women). For example, in one study (Steele & Aronson, 1995), the researchers gave both Black and White college students an academic performance test. In the control condition, respondents were asked to complete a questionnaire that asked general questions about their background (e.g., age, gender, major) prior to the test. In the second condition, participants completed a similar questionnaire that ended with a question asking about their race (the "race prime condition"). African American students in the race prime condition showed lower performance than both African American students in the control condition and White students in either condition.

Over the past two decades, stereotype threat consistent actions have been demonstrated in many studies with different groups including women, ethnic minorities, and the elderly—any group may potentially be vulnerable to stereotype threat in situations that matter to their personal identity (Steele, 1997). Shih, Pittinsky, and Trahan (2006), for example, showed that Asian American women performed better on a task that involved verbal activities when the researchers made them aware of their gender than when their ethnicity was made salient to them before performing the task. In another study, Asian American women performed better on a test of mathematics when their ethnicity was made salient when compared to an experimental condition where they were made particularly aware of their gender (Ambady, Shih, Kim, & Pittinsky, 2001). In these experiments, the research participants were acting according to the stereotype of women generally performing better in verbal than quantitative tasks and Asian Americans usually performing well in quantitative tasks.

According to Steele (1997), stereotype threat is not necessarily about internalizing the stereotype (truly believing, e.g., that you are inferior intellectually as a Black person); it is more about identifying with a particular situation (e.g., doing well in an academically challenging situation) and being stereotyped in it (e.g., believing that others will view your performance as evidence that Blacks do not perform as well as other ethnic groups in an academically challenging situation). The encouraging thing about these situations is that if they are truly situational, there is the possibility of reducing the threat through interventions at both individual and institutional levels that are geared to promote "identity safety," efforts to establish the value-added benefit of diverse social identities to environments. For instance, strategies can include school-based interventions to teach students about the expandability of intelligence—that intellectual achievement can continue to grow (e.g., Aronson, Fried, & Good, 2002) and that institutional practices can ensure an increase in fair and valid testing (e.g., Good, Aronson, & Harder, 2008).

The Effects of Ethnic Labels on Stereotypes

The label used to identify or talk about an ethnic group can be an important determinant of the stereotype we hold of the members of that group. Obviously, when individuals use negative or pejorative labels to talk about an ethnic group we can expect that they also hold negative stereotypes about its members. Unfortunately, our history is full of negative labels that people have used to refer to African Americans, Chinese Americans, Japanese Americans, Latinos, and many other groups. And often those labels have been associated with prejudicial attitudes about them as well as discriminatory behaviors.

Interestingly, researchers also have shown that stereotypes vary when groups are identified by labels that are not necessarily negative. In a study with undergraduate college students in Los Angeles (Fairchild & Cozens, 1981), the researchers found that a large proportion of the respondents considered Hispanics and Mexican Americans in a more positive way than individuals identified by the label "Chicanos". For example, Hispanics were considered to be talkative and tradition loving by large percentages of the respondents, while Mexican Americans were perceived as tradition loving and ignorant and Chicanos as ignorant and cruel. When White students from the same university were asked to freely produce traits they would assign to different Hispanic group labels, differential stereotypes were also obtained (Marín, 1984). For example, Hispanics were most frequently considered to be aggressive (19%), poor (16%), friendly (16%), and family oriented (13%), while Mexican Americans were most frequently considered to be poor (38%), aggressive (26%), lazy (19%), hardworking (16%), and family oriented (16%). As expected, Chicanos were considered to be different from Mexican Americans: aggressive (64%), family oriented (12%), hardworking (12%), and lazy (12%). This same study asked respondents to rate each of the ethnic groups and subgroups. The results showed that, in general, Mexican Americans were more positively evaluated than Chicanos although both labels share the same national heritage.

Prejudice and Discrimination

There is a vast literature in the social sciences, primarily in sociology and in social psychology that covers topics related to prejudice and discrimination toward ethnic minority groups. Much of this research has been summarized in excellent books (e.g., Oskamp, 2000; Whitley & Kite, 2006) that should be consulted in order to gain a more comprehensive perspective on a tremendously complex set of topics. This chapter has been designed to get you, the reader, interested in exploring further how prejudice and discrimination take place, their effects, and ways to reduce them, because the coverage of these issues here is by necessity limited.

As could be expected, there is a significant amount of research on prejudice and discrimination toward people who differ in terms of gender (e.g., research on sexism), sexual identity (including homophobic attitudes and behaviors), religious beliefs or practices (such as research on attitudes and behaviors toward Catholics, fundamentalists, Mormons, Muslims), political ideologies, physical characteristics and ability (e.g., discrimination toward persons with physical disabilities, obesity, learning disabilities), and other aspects that define human diversity. Nevertheless, it is ethnicity, and particularly race, that has received the largest amount of attention in the psychological literature on prejudice and discrimination.

Measuring Prejudice

A nationwide poll conducted in 2007 by Zogby International found that Americans hold strong biases against individuals who belong to certain ethnicities, or profess a particular religion, or have specific physical appearances or sexual orientation. For example, 67% of respondents to the survey said that they themselves would have no specific preference for being helped at a store by a White, Black, or Arab clerk. At the same time, 71% reported that "most Americans" would prefer a White clerk and that only 1% would prefer an African American clerk. In the same poll, 83% of the respondents said that Americans believe that Muslims are likely to be part of terrorism and 93% said that Americans believe men are most responsible for crime and extramarital affairs.

There is evidence that just living in an ethnically diverse society does not necessarily promote interactions or eliminate prejudice. For example, Weaver (2007) analyzed results of a national survey of adults and found that Latinos report interacting with Whites in higher proportions than the other way around. While 91% of Latinos reported personally knowing a White, only 75% of Whites reported such contact with Latinos. Significantly, approximately 70% of Latinos reported feeling close to a White person but only 48% of Whites reported such feelings regarding Latinos. Another study (Alba, Rumbaut, & Marotz, 2005) found that misperceptions about the ethnic composition of the country were related to negative attitudes toward immigration as well as prejudicial attitudes toward ethnic minority groups. Individuals who erroneously felt that Whites made up half or less of the population of the country were likely to express negative attitudes toward immigrants and toward members of ethnic minority groups. Changes in demography, therefore, are related to prejudicial attitudes unless strategies are devised to properly educate the population and to support the development of positive intergroup interactions as described later in this chapter.

Prejudice can also be measured by asking individuals to indicate the type of interpersonal contact or social interaction they feel comfortable engaging in across ethnic groups. This type of measure is usually called **social distance,** which was defined by the sociologist E. S. Bogardus (1959) as the level of social comfort and understanding that exists between individuals or groups. Typically, individuals are asked to indicate how likely they are to engage in a variety of activities with individuals or members of specific ethnic or social groups.

Social distance has been studied to measure prejudice across ethnic groups in the United States. In a recent study using a national sample of respondents, Weaver (2008) analyzed social distance in 1990 and 2000 toward various ethnic minority groups among African Americans, Asian Americans, Latinos, Jews, and Whites. Weaver measured social distance in two situations: (1) living in a neighborhood where half of the neighbors belonged to each of five specific ethnic groups (African Americans, Asian Americans, Jews, Latinos, or Whites), and (2) having a close relative marry an individual from each of the same five ethnic groups. The study showed that, in general, there was a tendency toward lower prejudice as measured by social distance between 1990 and 2000. The data from 2000 showed a tendency for respondents to be less accepting of ethnic minority group members marrying a close relative than having them as neighbors. Nevertheless, in general, all ethnic groups showed a preference for their own group and had little difficulty expressing preferences for specific ethnic groups. The data for this study are summarized in Table 7.1 and they show the general order or rank in which each ethnic group was preferred in both situations.

Whether racism and discrimination are treated as human processes or as the products of historical conditions (Gaines & Reed, 1995; Pike, 1992; Schuman, Steeh, & Bobo, 1985; Takaki, 1979), their effects have significant implications for the type of society in which we live. For example, an analysis (Pattnayak & Leonard, 1991) of positions usually assigned to African American and Hispanic baseball players has found that while White players tended to play central positions (e.g., pitcher and catcher), African Americans tended to be assigned the outfield and Latino ball players tended to play the infield (primarily shortstop and second base). These frequent assignments are perceived by the authors as limiting the possibilities of African Americans and of Latinos to move into leadership positions after they have stopped playing baseball. Further analyses of the types and frequency of discrimination suffered by ethnic minority individuals show that among other things,

Table 7.1   Social Distance Ratings

Acceptability as Neighbors

Ratings by African Americans	Ratings by Asian Americans	Ratings by Jews	Ratings by Latinos	Ratings by Whites
African Americans	Asian Americans	Jews	Whites	Whites
Whites	Whites	Whites	Latinos	Jews
Latinos	Jews	African Americans	Jews	Asian Americans
Jews	African Americans	Latinos	Asian Americans	Latinos
Asian Americans	Latinos	Asian Americans	African Americans	African Americans

Acceptability as In-Law Relatives

Ratings by African Americans	Ratings by Asian Americans	Ratings by Jews	Ratings by Latinos	Ratings by Whites
African Americans	Asian Americans	Jews	Latinos	Whites
Whites	Whites	Whites	Whites	Jews
Latinos	Latinos	Latinos	Asian Americans	Latinos
Asian Americans	African Americans	Asian Americans	Jews	Asian Americans
Jews	Jews	African Americans	African Americans	African Americans

SOURCE: Weaver (2008).

NOTE: Ratings are presented in order of preference and are not necessarily statistically significant within groups.

they often receive lower salaries than Whites (A. Torres, 1992) and have a lower number of housing possibilities (Yinger, 1988).

The Experience of Discrimination

Legally, discrimination is forbidden in our country. Nevertheless, there is ample evidence that members of ethnic minority groups continue to experience behaviors that are discriminatory in nature. For example, approximately 21% of Chinese Americans have reported being unfairly treated because of their ethnicity at the beginning of the 21st century (Goto, Gee, & Takeuchi, 2002) and 98% of African Americans reported experiencing discrimination during the 1990s (Landrine & Klonoff, 1996).

Among Latinos, a recent study (D. J. Pérez, Fortuna, & Alegría, 2008) found that approximately 30% reported having experienced discrimination and unfair treatment because of their ethnicity.

The frequency and nature of discrimination experiences differ in terms of a number of characteristics including national origin, gender, educational level, social class, and so on. For example, African Americans who trace their origin to the British Caribbean islands tend to report lower levels of discrimination than African Americans whose heritage is traced to Africa (Hunter, 2008). Cuban Americans and Latinos with high ethnic identity (who place great importance on their ethnicity) were less likely to report experiences with discrimination than other Latino groups or individuals who had lower ethnic identity (D. J. Pérez et al., 2008). Furthermore, ethnic minority women tend to experience "double discrimination" based on their gender and on their ethnicity and these effects are seen even in early childhood and in school experiences (Chavous, Rivas-Drake, Smalls, Griffin, & Cogburn, 2008).

Why Do People Discriminate?

A number of hypotheses have been proposed to explain why individuals hold prejudicial attitudes and discriminate against individuals who are different from themselves. One basic assumption, of course, is that holding negative stereotypes toward diverse others leads individuals to express prejudicial attitudes and enact discriminatory behaviors. Basically, people who are different and are believed to have negative characteristics are feared or disliked. Also relevant is the negative meaning associated in some societies to individuals with certain physical traits such as skin color, eye shape, body structure, hairiness, and so forth (R. E. Hall, 1994). Often, these beliefs about biological differences are supported by discriminatory social policies such as racial discrimination in the United States, apartheid in South Africa, or Nazi policies against Jews.

Misunderstandings and actual ignorance about cultural practices also play important roles in the development of prejudicial attitudes and discrimination. Traits valued in one culture (e.g., the personal significance of family members or the desire to allow individuals to save face) can be misinterpreted as "claniness" and exclusionary attitudes or negative personality traits. Indeed, lack of information or uncertainty about people's characteristics has been associated with a number of discriminatory behaviors and with differences in access to services (Balsa & McGuire, 2003).

For example, the Institute of Medicine (2002), in reviewing the literature on health care disparities between Whites and ethnic minority populations, concluded that "[i]ndirect evidence indicates that bias, stereotyping, prejudice and clinical uncertainty on the part of health care providers may be contributory factors to racial and ethnic disparities in health care" (p. 140). Much of these effects can be attributed to lack of knowledge and information about members of ethnic minority groups on the part of health care providers who are primarily White and usually uninformed about the cultures and traditions of the patients they treat (see Chapter 8 on physical health). Indeed, social psychologists (e.g., Fiske, 1998; Pettigrew, 1998) have long argued that lack of contact and poor information often produce stereotyping and assumptions of significant dissimilarity including stress and frustration. Nevertheless, contact by itself does not necessarily produce liking and in some cases it may create or reinforce stereotypes and prejudices.

Some recent psychological research (Mendes, 2007) has shown the role that uncertainty and unfamiliarity can have in producing certain prejudicial attitudes or behaviors. A study of people's reactions to working with an "unexpected other" (an Asian American speaking with a U.S. southern accent) showed that college students performed more poorly in an intellectual task when the partner did not conform to expectations in terms of physical appearance and speech patterns. When faced with the "surprising or unexpected other," individuals showed physical reactions related to stress and were less likely to smile. The researchers argued that those reactions may be related to the fact that uncertainty produces stress on the individual and lowers performance. Avoidance of individuals who are perceived as different can, therefore, make individuals feel less stress and lead to discriminatory behavior that decreases the likelihood of exposure to the different other.

Other researchers have argued that immigrant groups are feared because of the change they may bring about in the community (even though relatives or members of the receiving community may have been immigrants in the past) and that this fear of change may also support the development of prejudicial attitudes and discriminatory behavior (Alba et al., 2005). Also relevant is the fact that, often, ethnic minority groups exhibit demographic characteristics that support the development of prejudice on the part of members of other groups such as poverty and lower levels of educational achievement (APA Task Force on Socioeconomic Status, 2007).

The Role of Implicit Attitudes

A significant amount of research has recently been produced analyzing the role of explicit and implicit attitudes on prejudice and discrimination (Perugini, 2005). Implicit attitudes are usually perceived as affective reactions and associations held by individuals toward other people or toward behaviors that are subtle and not easily verbalized and therefore difficult to measure by surveys or attitude scales. These researchers argue that implicit attitudes are correlated with behaviors even if the individual is not completely conscious of the existence of the attitudes (Nosek, Greenwald, & Banaji, 2005; Shelton, Richeson, Salvatore, & Trawalter, 2005; Ziegert & Hanges, 2005). One approach to measuring implicit associations or attitudes has been to present individuals with visual stimuli that present two words or concepts (e.g., "Jewish" and "Good") and measure response latency or the amount of time it takes them to perform a task such as pushing a button when they feel the words or concepts are related or associated (the implicit association test or IAT). Other researchers have used level of activity of facial muscles (facial electromyography or EMG) to measure prejudicial attitudes toward people or toward some other stimuli (Vanman, Saltz, Nathan, & Warren, 2004).

While the details of the research methods are beyond this chapter, a recent study found that, indeed, people have different response time when they hold negative attitudes toward certain groups. For example, Christian students took longer to make associations of Muslim names with positive traits than to associate Christian names with positive characteristics, showing certain levels of implicit prejudice against Muslims (Rowatt, Franklin, & Cotton, 2005). That study also found that anti-Arab racism and authoritarianism and religious fundamentalism were associated with negative attitudes toward Muslims. As predicted by social identity theory (Tajfel, 1981), the evaluations of Christians toward their own group were more positive and favorable than toward the rejected group or "out-group" (Muslims) and this was true through self-report measures as well as through procedures designed to measure implicit, less external attitudes.

Prejudice and discrimination, of course, can manifest themselves in actions that at first may seem to be somewhat minor or innocuous. For example, what would you do if you received an e-mail message that was intended for another student? Do you reply indicating the mistake or simply hit the "delete" button? What if the message says that the student has received a highly competitive scholarship and must reply within 48 hours or lose the money? Finally, what do you think other students would do if the e-mail message was addressed to Hameed? A recent study (Bushman & Bonacci, 2004) analyzed the reactions of college students to receiving that e-mail message. Students had previously filled out an attitude scale that measured prejudice toward Arab Americans. The authors found that highly prejudiced students were less likely to return the message than those students with lower prejudice toward Arabs. In other conditions of the experiment, the e-mail was addressed to Brice (no difference in return rates by prejudiced and less-prejudiced students) or the content was changed to indicate that the student had not received the scholarship. In this latter condition, the prejudiced students were more likely to return the message than the less prejudiced. The study showed, therefore, that prejudice can also affect behavior even when individuals cannot be identified and can act surreptitiously to hurt those that they dislike (as done by the prejudiced students who failed to return the e-mail message).

RACISM

Prejudicial attitudes and discriminatory actions based on a person's or group's ethnic physical characteristics (often called phenotype) or race are central components of what is often labeled "racism." While racism is not totally different from discrimination based on ethnicity, much research has used the word "racism" to describe prejudice and discrimination toward ethnic minority groups particularly those ethnic minority groups or individuals that share a number of distinct body characteristics that differ from those of most Whites such as darker skin color, almond-shaped eyes, curlier hair, larger/broader nose or fuller lips, and so on.

As is true for many psychosocial phenomena, there are many definitions available in the literature to characterize racism. In an analysis of the psychosocial effects of racism, R. Clark and colleagues (R. Clark, Anderson, Clark, & Williams, 1999) define **racism** as "beliefs, attitudes, institutional arrangements, and acts that tend to denigrate individuals or groups because of phenotypic characteristics or ethnic group affiliation" (p. 805). An important aspect of the definition of racism proposed by Clark and his colleagues is that racism can occur across ethnic groups **(intergroup racism)** or within a given group **(intragroup racism).**

There is substantial evidence to show that racism, just like discrimination, has negative consequences for the individuals targeted by those attitudes and behaviors (R. Clark et al., 1999; K. R. King, 2005; Mossakowski, 2003). These consequences go beyond the loss of access to services and benefits (e.g., to education, jobs, housing, social advancement) to also limit personal and psychological growth. As a stressor, racism can be expected to produce psychological and physiological stress including anger, anxiety, depression, fear, aggression, poor job satisfaction, as well as a number of physiological reactions such as hypertension and damage to the immune system. Research has shown that racism produces these effects among Latinos (e.g., Finch, Kolody, & Vega, 2000), African Americans (e.g., Landrine & Klonoff, 1996), and Asian Americans (DeCastro, Gee, & Takeuchi, 2008; Mossakowski, 2003).

Results of a large-scale longitudinal study of people's health (Borrell, Kiefe, Williams, Diez-Roux, & Gordon-Larsen, 2006) showed that African Americans who reported experiencing high levels of racism (at school, while getting a job, at work, in public settings) also showed poorer self-reported physical and psychological health including depression and overall poorer sense of physical well-being. These findings were independent of the respondents' skin tone. A study with college students (K. R. King, 2005) also found that experiences of discrimination are stressful when they are perceived to be central to an individual's self-esteem or self-definition. Furthermore, a large-scale study of Asian Americans (DeCastro et al., 2008; G. C. Gee, Ro, Gavin, & Takeuchi, 2008; G. C. Gee, Spencer, Chen, & Takeuchi, 2007) has shown not only poorer health as the result of discrimination and racism but also engagement in risk behaviors such as cigarette smoking.

Racism has been studied by psychologists for a number of years and indeed studies such as those of K. B. Clark and Clark (1939) on children's racial preferences have been used in the landmark decision of the Supreme Court that made racial discrimination illegal. The Clarks' early study showed that African American children, when given a choice, would prefer a White doll to a doll that resembled them in skin color. The research suggested that the children had internalized a dislike for darker skin on individuals, preferring to play and to hold dolls that differed significantly from themselves in skin color. The findings of those early studies have been replicated with similar results even as late as the decade of the 1980s (Powell-Hopson & Hopson, 1988). Nevertheless, a later study by Burnett and Sisson (1995) showed that a large percentage of African American children (46%) showed no specific preference for the White or African American doll, with the next larger group showing a preference for the doll that resembled African Americans (37%). The authors argued that as children became older (after preschool years), they tended to prefer Black dolls more than younger children, who often chose White dolls. Overall, these studies have suggested that the racism present in our society has affected children to the point that they show a rejection of self or at least of others who look like them.

As members of a society that has lived painful examples of racism, we are likely to have learned the racial biases of our parents and grandparents and of society in general. Those perceptions affect our ability to work and study and live in an ethnically diverse environment and the prejudicial attitudes can become deterrents in acquiring the appropriate levels of cultural competence to function effectively in an ethnically diverse world (D. W. Sue et al., 2007).

Racial Microaggressions

In a very important article, the Asian American psychologist Derald Sue and his colleagues (2007) proposed that there are a number of relatively small and common behaviors that they called "racial microaggressions" that are racist in nature and that can have an impact in a variety of interpersonal relationships including therapy and instruction. D. W. Sue et al. (2007) define **racial microaggressions** as "brief and commonplace daily verbal, behavioral and environmental indignities, whether intentional or unintentional, that communicate hostile, derogatory, or negative racial slights and insults to the target person or group" (p. 273). Expanding on the definition proposed by Sue and his colleagues, we can define microaggressions as brief, subtle expressions or exchanges (verbal, nonverbal, or physical) that carry a negative connotation and are directed toward people who differ from the originating individual in terms of a variety of characteristics including gender, ethnicity, sexual orientation, religious beliefs, socioeconomic status, educational level, physical ability, nationality, and accent. Examples of microaggressions include avoiding someone's look, not shaking hands when meeting someone, moving to a different cashier line, ignoring someone's question or comment, and so on.

D. W. Sue and colleagues (2007) suggest the existence of three types of racial microaggressions: (1) micro-assaults, (2) micro-insults, and (3) micro-invalidations. Micro-assaults are explicit statements that constitute a verbal or nonverbal attack on an individual. Examples include name-calling, using racial/ethnic epithets, or using or displaying insulting symbols or behaviors (e.g., referring to someone as "Oriental" or "Spick," displaying a picture of a burning cross or of a "sleepy Mexican," or performing certain obscene or insulting hand gestures). Micro-insults are verbal or nonverbal communications that at a minimum are rude but often represent a derogatory reaction to a person's ethnicity or personal characteristics. Examples include questioning the role played by ability or skills in hiring or when a decision is made (e.g., asking, "Did we get the best qualified students regardless of race?" when analyzing the diversity of a student class) or ignoring someone's presence or contributions because of his or her ethnicity (such as when a supervisor ignores a question asked by a person of color or a salesperson ignores an ethnic minority individual waiting to be helped at a store). Micro-invalidations are defined by Sue and colleagues as "communications that exclude, negate, or nullify the psychological thoughts, feelings and experiential reality of a person of color" (p. 274). A poignant example mentioned by Sue et al. is when Asian Americans born in the United States are told how well they speak English. Additional examples of micro-invalidations are when an ethnic minority individual is told, "We don't do that here" or is asked, "Why do you people do that?" when dealing with certain cultural traditions and practices.

Box 7.3 presents some examples of racial microaggressions identified by D. W. Sue and his colleagues (2007). There are various different themes including the perceptions of individuals as foreigners in their own country, the assumption of criminality, beliefs on meritocracy, assuming pathology, and ascriptions of second-class status. These types of microaggressions are presented with examples of comments that a person could make as well as examples of the messages implied in the microaggression. An examination of the contents of this material is instructive in helping us become aware of how, at times unwittingly, we are able to offend individuals who differ from ourselves. Indeed, awareness of these microaggressions and ways to prevent them can be an important first step toward acquiring the level of cultural competence (or "openness to the other") that is a central component of a multicultural individual (Fowers & Davidov, 2006).

BOX 7.3

Types and Examples of Microaggressions

- Being perceived as a foreigner in your own country
  - Being asked, "Where were you born?"
  - Being told, "Your English is really good."

- Making judgments of a person's intelligence because of ethnicity
  - "You are a credit to your people."
  - "You are so smart and well spoken."

- Statements indicating that the person does not want to emphasize ethnicity
  - "When I look at you, I don't see your race or skin color."

- Assumption of criminality
  - Holding tight to a bag or a purse when in the presence of a person of color
  - Crossing the street when encountering a person of color
  - Following a person of color around a store

- Denial of racism
  - "I am not a racist; I have a lot of Spanish friends."
  - "Some of my best friends are Asian."

(Continued)

(Continued)

- Myth of meritocracy
  - "Only the best person should be hired."
  - "If you work hard, you can get ahead."

- Pathologizing values/behaviors
  - "Why do you people talk so loud?"
  - "Don't be so quiet."

- Assumption of second-class status
  - Person of color being mistaken for service personnel
  - Taxi driver who chooses not to stop for a person of color

SOURCE: Based on D. W. Sue et al. (2007).

THE EFFECTS OF PREJUDICE, DISCRIMINATION, AND RACISM

As mentioned above, in 2007, the American Psychological Association (APA) adopted a resolution on prejudice, stereotypes, and discrimination. The resolution summarized a number of areas in a person's life and in society that are affected by the experience of prejudice and discrimination. These effects range from poorer mental and physical health to difficulties in social relations. Box 7.2 highlights the areas that the APA felt were impacted by people's experiences of discrimination and prejudice based on research in psychology, public health, and other areas. As shown in the resolution by the APA, prejudice, discrimination, and racism have a variety of negative consequences for individuals who are subjected to them. This section highlights research on some of those negative results.

Employment

While illegal, discrimination and racism in employment can still be found in such subtle forms as the way in which job descriptions are drafted so that certain ethnic minority individuals cannot meet the requirements as well as in the behaviors of search committees or other individuals conducting the job interviews. The federal government as well as the states have established offices to investigate allegations or instances of discrimination and racism in employment. In addition, there are some subtle ways people are discriminated against based on minor characteristics or personal traits such as the frequent use of hand gestures, eye contact patterns, and accented speech.

Indeed, accented speech seems to be an important aspect of subtle racism. Research has shown that ethnic minority individuals who speak English with an accent tend to be treated differentially by members of other groups even if they speak grammatically perfect English. One of those studies (Davila, Bohara, & Saenz, 1993) analyzed data from a national sample of Mexican Americans and the study showed that independent of English-language proficiency, those speaking with an accent tended to earn lower wages than their peers who spoke with no accent and performed similar jobs.

Health

Research in psychology and in public health has shown that, generally, discrimination is associated with experiences of psychological stress and poorer mental and physical health (Harrell, Hall, & Taliaferro, 2003; Mays, Cochran, & Barnes, 2007; D. R. Williams, Neighbors, & Jackson, 2003). Indeed, an analysis of the literature conducted by D. R. Williams and his colleagues (2003) of large-scale studies showed that, generally, perceived discrimination was found to be associated with various mental health conditions (such as distress, anxiety, depression), changes in blood pressure, as well as consumption of alcoholic beverages and cigarette smoking.

Research with Chinese Americans showed that residential discrimination measured by housing segregation and redlining in mortgages (when lending institutions award limited or site-specific loans to members of minority groups) influences an individual's health status (G. C. Gee, 2002). In this study, the researcher used data from the Chinese American Psychiatric Epidemiological Study and from the home mortgage database and controlled for the possible effects of variables such as acculturation, age, social support, income, insurance, employment, poverty, and home value.

The effects of discrimination on people's health are discussed in greater detail in Chapter 8 of this book. Research on the health effects of prejudice, discrimination, and racism is important because it can point toward possible interventions to protect the health of ethnic minority individuals (Cain & Kington, 2003). Indeed, as Cain and Kington noted,

> Waiting for societal change, even change hastened through intervention, is not the only option for members of racial/ethnic groups who live within a discriminatory society. Research has pointed to possible

areas for intervention. . . . To the extent that racism/ethnic prejudice is a major source of stress, individuals can be taught stress-reduction techniques and to draw on the strength of their communities. Moreover, to the extent that research provides insight into the additional physical and economic pathways by which racism/ethnic prejudice harms health (e.g., via residential and occupational segregation), it will generate evidence necessary for informed action and policy change to reduce—and ultimately eliminate—racial/ethnic disparities in health. (p. 192)

Education

Data on educational performance among certain ethnic minority groups show troubling indicators. For example, close to 65% of African American fourth graders and more than 50% of American Indian fourth graders are not able to read at basic levels, and approximately 50% of Latino eighth graders cannot do mathematics at basic levels (The Education Trust, 2006). Nevertheless, research also shows that given the proper conditions, children from these ethnic groups can perform as well as White children.

Obviously, there are multiple reasons for these differences in performance and most of them are related to institutional or structural factors that make it difficult for many ethnic minority children to benefit from a proper education. An analysis of the educational conditions of large numbers of ethnic minority children shows that these gaps in educational achievement between White and many ethnic minority children are due to the fact that ethnic minority children tend to attend lower-quality schools with poorly prepared teachers or less experienced teachers that receive less state and local support monies than schools that educate primarily White children (The Education Trust, 2006).

The effects of poor-quality education for some ethnic minority children in the early years can be seen later in large high school drop-out rates and lower participation in college education (KewalRamani, Gilbertson, Fox, & Provasnik, 2007). For example, national data showed that in 2005 the percentage of high school dropouts was higher among Latinos than among other ethnic groups and that the percentage of African Americans and American Indians age 16–24 who were school dropouts was higher than among Whites and Asian Americans.

Environmental Racism

The last three or four decades have seen researchers and activists paying attention not only to the protection of the environment but also to the often unequal distribution of environmental hazards (Westra & Lawson, 2001). Analyses of environmental exposure to pollutants and other hazards have tended to show an uneven burden being placed on ethnic minority communities and the search for eliminating what some have called **"environmental racism"** or **"environmental inequity."** Indeed, the search for environmental justice where no group is forced to suffer a higher burden of exposure to environmental hazards or pollution is a central component of social justice. Included in this concern are analyses of the presence and distribution of physical, chemical, and biological pollution that can be found in the water, air, or ground as well as in the built environment (Northridge, Stover, Rosenthal, & Sherard, 2003; Westra & Lawson, 2001).

Related to the concerns for environmental justice is the fact that members of ethnic minority groups tend to perform behaviors or occupy jobs that disproportionately expose them to job-related dangers or come into contact with environments associated with illness and injury (Murray, 2003). Cigarette smoking, for example, produces poor health not just among smokers but also to those exposed to their smoke. Research on cigarette smoking among ethnic minority groups (Department of Health and Human Services [DHHS], 1998) has shown the existence of targeted marketing as well as high rates of cigarette smoking among certain ethnic minority groups.

Environmental racism is of relevance to psychologists because its prevention or solution often involves attitudes and behavior changes where psychological theories need to be applied. For example, preventing children from using contaminated fields for playing sports may require not just the setup of playgrounds in safe areas but convincing children to use the new play areas, which may be less familiar or less appealing. Attitude change theories can be an important aid in this effort. Likewise, helping smokers quit in order to lower exposure to environmental smoke (or secondhand smoke) affecting their children, relatives, and friends requires the use of a number of techniques based on the contributions made by psychologists (DHHS, 1998). (See Chapter 8 for a further discussion of environmental racism and physical health.)

REDUCING PREJUDICE, DISCRIMINATION, AND RACISM

A key concern of researchers and policymakers, of course, is to find ways to reduce the prejudice, discrimination, and racism that have been learned from early interactions at home, school, and playgrounds and later on while at work and in society in general (Oskamp, 2000; Sampson, 1999). This concern is relevant to ethnic groups that are demographically in the majority as well as to members of groups that are a statistical minority because of their ethnicity, body characteristics, religion, gender, and real or perceived power in society, among other things.

A number of approaches and strategies have been designed not only to expose individuals to diverse others but also to challenge and change prejudicial attitudes and expectations (Oskamp, 2000). These strategies include desegregating elementary and secondary schools, diversifying children's television programming, classes and workshops on diversity, involving individuals in personal sharing within a diverse context, diversifying universities and their curriculum, advertising campaigns, and many others (Adams, Biernat, Branscombe, Crandall, & Wrightsman, 2008; Dovidio, Glick, & Rudman, 2005; Oskamp, 2000).

While a number of theories and approaches have been proposed to understand the process of prejudice reduction (Oskamp, 2000), intergroup contact is probably one of the most frequently analyzed (Dixon, Durrheim, & Tredoux, 2005). Indeed, many theoretical approaches explain components of the intergroup contact process or are derivations of its propositions. This theoretical approach is the basis for building a diverse or multicultural society and it was originally proposed by Gordon Allport (1954).

The **contact hypothesis** maintains that prejudicial attitudes and emotions can be changed by bringing together diverse peoples. Indeed, major policy decisions such as the school desegregation ruling of the U.S. Supreme Court in 1954 (*Brown v. Board of Education*) as well as special techniques such as collaborative learning are based on significant psychological research (K. B. Clark, Chein, & Cook, 2004) and on the principles proposed by the intergroup contact hypothesis (Adams et al., 2008).

Intergroup Contact

Obviously, putting diverse people together in a group is not enough to change their prejudicial attitudes or discriminatory behavior. As a matter of fact, Allport (1954) initially argued that in order to be effective, **intergroup contact** needed to have four main characteristics: (1) group members needed to be perceived as having equal status at least within the group interaction; (2) the interaction would have institutional support and approval (by statements from people in authority or as supported by laws or customs); (3) cooperation across groups would be expected to produce a common goal; and (4) the interaction would allow individuals to get to know each other (often called "acquaintance potential").

More recently, Pettigrew (1998) suggested the importance of an additional characteristic: the possibility of becoming friends. These five conditions or characteristics of intergroup contact can exist in a variety of settings including universities as well as schools, the armed forces, voluntary associations, and work settings. For example, equal employment opportunities and affirmative action policies have made it possible for ethnic minority individuals to be part of workplaces where they can work alongside White colleagues on group projects. These settings will necessarily help reduce prejudicial attitudes held by all individuals involved as they share frustrations and successes and together move toward a common goal. The armed forces—which were desegregated by law before civil society was—are another place where the five conditions for effective intergroup contact can work quite well.

A large number of studies have analyzed the effectiveness of contact in bringing about a decrease of prejudice and discrimination (e.g., Chin, 2004; Dovidio et al., 2005; Weaver, 2007). A study with college students (Aberson, Shoemaker, & Tomolillo, 2004) showed that White students who had close friendships with African Americans or Latino students exhibited lower prejudicial attitudes toward either group than those who did not report such close friendships. Results from numerous studies tend to confirm results similar to these and support the effectiveness of the contact hypothesis.

Contact across ethnic groups under the conditions proposed by Allport (1954) and Pettigrew (1998) also produces important personal changes that go beyond eliminating prejudice and discrimination. A recent study with students at two California universities (Santos, Ortiz, Morales, & Rosales, 2007) investigated the effects of campus ethnic diversity on students' personal identity. Overall, a sense of inclusion, belonging, and acceptance was the most frequently mentioned result of being in an ethnically diverse campus environment although this result was more frequent among ethnic minority students than among Whites. A second result was related to how an ethnically diverse campus helped students develop multicultural competence, and this was equally important for White students and ethnic minority individuals. Among the negative effects identified, White students frequently mentioned a sense of discomfort with their own ethnic identity, a response that was less frequent among ethnic minority students. However, as the authors concluded, "for many students, experiencing an ethnically diverse campus community engendered a sense of belonging and inclusion within the institution, which was associated with a more positive and enriched sense of ethnic identity and adjustment to college" (Santos et al., p. 112).

School Desegregation

In 1954, the United States Supreme Court ruled (*Brown v. Board of Education*) that segregated education in schools violated the rights of ethnic minority children and ordered that schools should be desegregated.

This landmark decision promulgated the need for all children to receive education of equal quality. In addition, various researchers suggested in a brief filed with the Court that desegregation would have significant positive effects not just on children's learning but also on their social and psychological well-being (Adams et al., 2008; K. B. Clark et al., 2004). That long-term process has served as an important technique in tempering prejudice, discrimination, and racism among children of the last two or three generations and has allowed children of different ethnicities to grow and learn together.

Many studies have been conducted to analyze the positive effects of school desegregation where quality education has been made available to larger numbers of ethnic minority children (e.g., Pettigrew, 2004; Schofield & Hausmann, 2004). At the same time, other researchers have argued that while schools may not be formally segregated, they do not provide equal access and as a consequence produce significant performance gaps in children's learning across ethnic groups (e.g., Weinstein, Gregory, & Strambler, 2004). Although children of all ethnic backgrounds are no longer limited to segregated schools, school district regulations in many cases produce schools that are fairly homogeneous in the ethnicity of their students due to controls on school district borders and areas to be served by specific schools. These cases where schools are predominantly White or African American or Latino or Asian American exhibit the negative results of ethnically homogeneous schools where quality is not equivalent across schools and where prejudices may be created.

As a matter of fact, a recent study with elementary school children (McGlothlin & Killen, 2006) showed that ethnically homogeneous school environments can be related to prejudicial attitudes. When asked to interpret an ambiguous social situation, children in primarily White schools were more likely to attribute negative traits to African Americans than to Whites.

Without doubt, the Supreme Court ruling on school desegregation (often referred to as *Brown*) was an extremely important step in bringing about justice and a process where psychology played an important role. Nevertheless, much remains to be accomplished in this area (Adams et al., 2008). Recently, Fine (2004) summarized the impact of the decision by saying, "*Brown* was a bold move that harnessed social science to interrupt injustice. The *Brown* decision recast the normative as oppressive; the tolerated as intolerable. . . . But . . . the work of justice theorists and activists is two-fold: to interrupt oppression and then to sustain justice" (p. 509).

Other Promising Practices

In 1997, President Bill Clinton began a project to identify ways in which prejudice could be eliminated in the country. The President's Initiative on

Race, also called the One America Program, conducted a number of events across the country and produced reports and scientific analyses trying to better understand racism and prejudice while hoping to promote understanding across ethnic groups. As part of this process, social science researchers identified a number of strategies that have been used in order to promote dialogue, support education and understanding, build community, and solve race-related problems (Oskamp & Jones, 2000). This analysis of 59 high-profile programs dedicated to reduce prejudice and discrimination showed that the largest percentage of programs used primarily educational activities (47%) and interethnic dialogue (47%), followed by training of community leaders (41%), production of educational materials (39%), and public events such as conferences, lectures, and exhibitions (34%). Interestingly, only 29% of these programs were dedicated to promoting intergroup contact despite its effectiveness as demonstrated in psychological research.

THE BENEFITS OF AN ETHNICALLY DIVERSE SOCIETY

It is important to recognize that our experiences living in an ethnically diverse society like the United States imply being exposed to ethnically diverse individuals and to other individuals who differ because of who they are, what they believe, or how they act. These experiences with diversity can produce the negative by-products mentioned above including stereotyping, prejudice, and discrimination. At the same time, a diverse environment can also foment important and positive sociopsychological changes in individuals.

As mentioned in Chapter 4, one of the advantages of living in an ethnically diverse country is the ability of individuals to learn the values, norms, and expectancies of at least one other culture. This process of biculturation or of becoming bicultural or multicultural has a number of advantages including not only the ability to function appropriately and with ease in ethnically diverse environments but also the ability to think creatively, process multiple perspectives, and approach problems from multiple angles. As you may recall from the research mentioned in Chapter 4, bicultural individuals show significant cognitive flexibility by easily switching from one cultural framework to the other when exposed to culture-specific symbols or to cultural stimuli that are present in the social environment (Hong et al., 2000). Furthermore, bicultural individuals tend to show a strong sense of personal identity and positive attitudes toward diverse others (LaFromboise et al., 1993).

Another important benefit of living in an ethnically diverse country is the opportunity for students like you to attend universities and colleges where people from diverse backgrounds study and work together. These experiences are not only important for your personal and intellectual development but they also prepare you for the diverse work environment that you will find after graduation.

THE EFFECTS OF STUDYING AT A DIVERSE COLLEGE

Research on diversity within educational settings such as colleges or universities has shown a number of positive results that support the need not just for desegregating these environments but, more important, to make use of diversity to enhance the learning of all students. Researchers (e.g., Gurin et al., 2002; Hurtado, Carter, & Kardia, 1998) have argued that there are three types of diversity that affect a learning environment: (1) structural diversity, (2) classroom diversity, and (3) interactional diversity.

Structural diversity refers to the actual demographic composition of an institution or school. For example, a measure of the structural diversity of a university is the percentage of students that are people of color or the percentage that are women or the percentage of students that are non-Christians. Likewise, the number of faculty and staff that are women or persons of color is another measure of structural diversity.

Classroom diversity, on the other hand, is the level of curriculum diversification that has taken place in a learning environment. The key concern here is how much of the culture and experiences of diverse individuals have been incorporated into the curriculum. For example, we could ask universities if the curriculum includes a diversity graduation requirement or if students can pursue minors and majors in sexualities studies or ethnic studies or, more important, if diversity is woven into the curriculum so that physics students learn about the contributions made by ethnic minority physicists as well as by women and by researchers outside the United States.

Also important in measuring the diversity of colleges and universities is what Gurin and colleagues (2002) call **interactional diversity** to refer to the opportunities that students have to interact and exchange ideas with diverse students. Having conversations with individuals who think or act differently or who have varying cultural and historical traditions is one of the most important experiences provided by a diverse learning environment. These conversations challenge students' assumptions and force them to at least listen to different ways of perceiving the world. This last component is so important that it is included among the questions asked by the National Survey of Student Engagement (NSSE) that is used by a large number of universities to measure student involvement and engagement with their educational experiences.

Hurtado and colleagues (1998) argue that increasing the numerical presence of members of minority groups is the first step in creating a diverse learning environment that is beneficial to all students. Nevertheless, structural diversity is important because it makes possible the other types of diversity and it enhances the opportunities for interactions among diverse groups and across various settings (in the classroom, on campus, away from campus, and even online). High levels of structural diversity can be expected to help members of underrepresented groups to feel more comfortable at the institution and develop a greater sense of belonging and to achieve more (Gurin et al., 2002). Likewise, members of majority groups also benefit from being part of a diverse learning environment. For example, Bowen and Bok (1998) found that White graduates of a highly selective university who were involved in interactions with African Americans during their college years reported being effective workers in diverse environments after graduation.

Gurin and colleagues (2002) have argued that in order to obtain the benefits of a diverse learning environment, universities must go beyond structural diversity. This means providing opportunities for classroom diversity to occur where students learn about the culture, history, and social conditions of diverse groups. In addition, universities need to provide opportunities for interactional diversity to evolve whereby students of diverse backgrounds can freely and safely interact and exchange ideas and experiences. The basis for these recommendations is the findings from decades of research in the social psychology of intergroup contact as reviewed above (Allport, 1954; Pettigrew, 1998) as well as research conducted by social scientists at the University of Michigan. As summarized below, these studies showed that ethnically diverse students collaborating in common academic activities such as group projects, papers, presentations, field research, and performances can greatly benefit from a diverse learning environment.

The University of Michigan Studies

During the decade of the 1990s, the University of Michigan faced a lawsuit over its admission practices, which was ultimately decided by the Supreme Court. In preparing the university's response to the legal action, a number of research projects were conducted in order to show the benefits of an ethnically diverse learning environment. Patricia Gurin, a social psychologist at the University of Michigan, and her colleagues (1997; Gurin et al., 2002) conducted studies to identify the psychosocial benefits of studying in an ethnically diverse university. The project involved a number of research activities, including analyzing a large database of feedback previously provided by students at the university as well as in national surveys of university students. Dr. Gurin's guiding hypothesis was that students would be more involved in learning within a diverse environment demonstrating greater learning and complex thought processes than in ethnically homogeneous settings. In addition, she argued that diverse learning institutions are more likely to produce students who exhibit the motivation and skills to be part of diverse complex societies such as the United States.

After analyzing data from a national survey of students, Gurin (1997) found that structural diversity positively affected classroom diversity as well as interactional diversity. In general, when structural diversity was high, there was a greater likelihood of ethnic diversity being found in the curriculum as well as increased opportunities for students to meet and interact with other students who differed not just in terms of ethnicity but also in terms of values, beliefs, and opinions. Gurin and her colleagues also found that students who attended an ethnically diverse university were more likely to report having more ethnically diverse friends and coworkers (after graduating from college), discussing racial/ethnic issues, and enrolling in ethnic studies courses. It is important to note that White students who attended colleges with 25% or more ethnic minority students were more likely to show these results than those who attended colleges with a more homogeneously White student population.

Furthermore, the Michigan studies showed that students who were exposed to high classroom diversity and interactional diversity demonstrated active thinking, the improvement of academic skills, and increased motivation and engagement in the learning process. Once again, there was a direct relationship between the level of diversity experienced by White students and the positive cognitive and intellectual effects of being in a diverse learning environment.

Finally, those students who were exposed to high levels of classroom and interactional diversity at Michigan also showed higher levels of active citizenship and engagement with diverse people and with their communities. The results of these studies show quite clearly the importance of a diverse learning environment in enhancing the quality of education students receive as well as in promoting democratic values and skills. One key finding of the outcomes of the Michigan studies is that they show that the positive effects of studying at an ethnically diverse university accrue to minority students as well as to Whites. These results indeed show (to use a statement by the Supreme Court) the compelling need for diversity in higher education.

Chapter Summary

This chapter has examined the consequences of living in an ethnically diverse society such as the United States. Contact with individuals who differ in terms of their ethnicity produces positive and negative results as we learn how people differ in terms of their values, norms, beliefs, opinions, and behaviors. Becoming aware of these differences can produce a variety of results. Frequently, we form rigid images of the members of an ethnic group whereby we assign a select number of traits or characteristics to all members of the group (stereotypes). Sometimes, those characteristics are positive and, often, they are negative. Those stereotypes serve as the basis for creating prejudices toward members of the group based to a great extent on our evaluation of the traits we have assigned to the group. The behavioral correlates of those prejudices become discriminatory as we behave differentially toward various groups, favoring some and disliking others. Often, in our country, these discriminatory actions have been based on people's skin color and these racist actions have caused great pain to many individuals. But living in an ethnically diverse country does not have to produce negative results. Indeed, exposure to people who differ from who we are can lead to important gains in cognitive flexibility, problem-solving skills, and personal growth.

Key Terms

Classroom Diversity (page 246)

Contact Hypothesis (page 242)

Discrimination (page 219)

Environmental Inequity (page 241)

Environmental Racism (page 241)

Ethnic Stereotypes (page 219)

Institutional Discrimination (page 219)

Interactional Diversity (page 246)

Intergroup Contact (page 242)

Intergroup Racism (page 234)

Interpersonal Discrimination (page 219)

Intragroup Racism (page 234)

Out-group Homogeneity Effect (page 223)

Prejudice (page 219)

Racial Microaggressions (page 236)

Racism (page 234)

Social Distance (page 229)

Stereotypes (page 219)

Stereotype Threat (page 225)

Structural Diversity (page 246)

Learning by Doing

- Analyze how diversity has been incorporated into the curriculum of your university (most data should be available via your school's Web site) by listing characteristics such as (1) the percentage of majors and minors that are related to diverse populations in terms of gender, ethnicity, nationality, and religious faith; (2) the number of courses that are offered in your core curriculum or general education requirements that address all types of diversity (gender, ethnicity, socioeconomic status, sexualities, physical abilities, national origin, etc.); and (3) cocurricular offerings and research centers that support diversity. Then, analyze the Web site of another university that is similar to yours in terms of funding (public or private), size (number of students), and geographical location (urban or rural and area of the country).

- Watch about five prime-time television shows and two or three soap operas that attempt to show contemporary life in the United States and count how many non-White characters are part of the show. Do not analyze programs on ethnic networks such as BET, Telemundo, or Univision. Then, analyze the positions or roles of the ethnic minority characters and compare them to those of the White characters (e.g., how many are portrayed as rich or poor, or occupying positions of power such as doctors or judges, or working as maids, nannies, or lawn keepers?). Do the shows include people of color in percentages that reflect the population of the country? What do the differences in power or role significance say to you?

- Review 10 issues of mainstream lifestyle magazines (e.g., *People, Us*) and 10 issues of sports magazines (e.g., *Sports Illustrated)* and analyze, first, the percentage of individuals of each of the five major ethnic groups that are included (African Americans, American Indians, Asian Americans, Latinos, Whites). Then analyze the activities in which they are portrayed (e.g., playing sports, caring for children, dancing). How representative are those pictures of the ethnic composition of the country? How do the pictures contribute to the development or support of ethnic stereotypes? Repeat this analysis by using ethnic magazines such as *Ebony* and *Hispanic.*

Suggested Further Readings

Adams, G., Biernat, M., Branscombe, N. R., Crandall, C. S., & Wrightsman, L. S. (Eds.). (2008). *Commemorating* Brown: *The social psychology of racism and discrimination.* Washington, DC: American Psychological Association.
   A collection of essays reviewing the implications of the *Brown* decision by the Supreme Court from the perspective of social psychological theories and research.

Blaine, B. E. (2007). *Understanding the psychology of diversity.* Thousand Oaks, CA: Sage.
   This book includes an analysis of such psychological phenomena as categorization and stereotyping and their relationship to attitudes (prejudice) and behavior (discrimination). The book combines research addressing ethnic differences as well as other types of diversity (e.g., social class, sexuality).

Chin, J. L. (Ed.). (2004). *The psychology of prejudice and discrimination* (Vol. 2, Ethnicity and Multiracial Identity Series). Westport, CT: Praeger.
   This book includes a series of comprehensive reviews of research on various topics related to prejudice and discrimination. An excellent resource for researchers and students interested in gaining a more complete understanding of these complex social issues.

Dovidio, J. F., Glick, P., & Rudman, L. A. (2005). *On the nature of prejudice: Fifty years after Allport.* Malden, MA: Blackwell.
   A comprehensive resource that analyzes how our knowledge and understanding of prejudice has changed since the publication of Allport's important book on the topic. The book is an excellent resource for students wishing to gain a deeper understanding of this complex and important phenomenon and chronicles how far the field has developed.

Fouad, N. A., & Arredondo, P. (2007). *Becoming culturally oriented: Practical advice for psychologists and educators.* Washington, DC: American Psychological Association.

This book contains a number of practical suggestions on how psychologists can become more culturally appropriate and culturally sensitive. The authors have combined research findings with practical experiences into a useful handbook.

Oskamp, S. (Ed.). (2000). *Reducing prejudice and discrimination.* Mahwah, NJ: Lawrence Erlbaum.

A collection of essays on the theory and practice of reducing prejudice and discrimination by some of the best-known researchers in the field. The book includes comprehensive analyses of the research literature and of its practical implications.

Sampson, E. E. (1999). *Dealing with differences: An introduction to the social psychology of prejudice.* Fort Worth, TX: Harcourt Brace.

A comprehensive textbook on prejudice and discrimination of particular value because it combines sociological and psychological perspectives.

Sue, D. W. (2003). *Overcoming our racism: The journey to liberation.* San Francisco: Jossey-Bass.

An excellent and practical book on approaches that individuals, and particularly psychologists, can take in order to become not only more sensitive to cultural differences but also more respectful of racial/ethnic diversity.

Whitley, B. E., Jr., & Kite, M. E. (2006). *The psychology of prejudice and discrimination.* Belmont, CA: Thomson Wadsworth.

A recent analysis of the literature on prejudice and discrimination that is easy to read and comprehensive in its coverage.

Web Resources

American Psychological Association Resolution

http://www.apa.org/releases/ResAmIndianMascots.pdf

Provides access to the text of the resolution by the APA on the use of American Indian symbols as college mascots.

Anti-Defamation League

http://www.adl.org/main_Education/default.htm

This Web site includes a number of resources and training materials on combating prejudice and discrimination as well as anti-Semitism.

The Office of Ethnic Minority Affairs

http://www.apa.org/pi/oema/homepage.html

An official APA Web page with a large number of resources on the APA's activities as well as on important research dealing with ethnicity.

ReducingStereotypeThreat.org

http://www.reducingstereotypethreat.org

An excellent online resource for overviews of published research on stereotype threat.

Understanding Prejudice

http://www.understandingprejudice.org

A Web site that includes a large number of resources and activities to promote an understanding of all types of prejudice.

University of Michigan Admissions Lawsuits

http://www.vpcomm.umich.edu/admissions/legal/expert/toc.html

This Web site includes materials prepared for the lawsuit against the University of Michigan and although somewhat dated it includes excellent perspectives on the positive effects of a diverse learning environment.

CHAPTER **8**

PHYSICAL HEALTH

VIGNETTE

"Son, I've lost something."

Carmen is a 42-year-old woman of Mexican and Pima Indian ancestry. She is divorced with three children who range in age from 13 to 20 years old. Carmen grew up near Tucson, Arizona. She is one of five living children (her eldest brother, Joaquin, died two years ago from a massive heart attack). Her mother, Lucy, died just last year at the age of 63 from a severe stroke due to diabetes complications. Carmen was devastated by the loss of her mother, who had raised her and her siblings almost single-handedly (Carmen's father died from complications related to cirrhosis of the liver at the age of 35 when she was a small girl).

(Continued)

(Continued)

*Carmen vowed that she would not suffer the same fate as her mother and Joaquin. At 5' 2,"
and 170 pounds, Carmen is obese, and she is starting to breathe more heavily and experience joint
pain in her ankles, knees, and back. With the support of her sons, she decided to visit her community health center. The news the physician relayed to her, following a physical and laboratory work,
was disappointing. Similar to her mother and brother, Carmen's blood pressure is high, 160/110.
Moreover, the doctor issued the warning that she appears to be "pre-diabetic" with her blood sugar
level elevated high enough to warrant a significant change in diet and an exercise program to reduce
her weight.*

*Carmen met with a dietician who prescribed a daily meal plan that greatly differed from her
usual food preferences. "Remember, keep it low and small . . . LOW salt, LOW fat, LOW sugar, and
SMALL portions," the dietician stated. "You have trained your body to crave poor foods that will
slowly but surely lead to your premature death—but the good news is that you can recondition your
body to enjoy these 'healthy' foods."*

*"Am I killing myself? If this is true, I will stop this right now—but I don't know if I can eat the
types of food listed on this plan," Carmen thought. "Lots of fresh vegetables, fresh fruit, 'organic
recommended'—this stuff is expensive, and they don't sell this highfalutin food at my little grocery
store. And only a little oil—avoid animal fats, e.g., lard—What, no* manteca *[lard] for my fried bread;
no pork belly to season my stews?"*

*No sooner had she made it home, she desperately wanted a good "healthy" meal that would
stick to her ribs—meat, potatoes, bread, and of course, just a little something sweet to top it off. As
she bent over to pull out the fry pan and the oil to heat, she felt a sharp pain in her back and sore-
ness in her knees. She stopped herself, "Ay, this is a reminder. I have the body of a* vieja *[old woman].
I've got to stop the madness! OK, let's see, I have some carrots in the refrigerator, and maybe a little rice—I'll get some of that brown rice later (when I save up a little more cash—it's too expensive!).
I will add a little piece of chicken—boiled chicken for LOW fat. As she prepared the meal, she placed
the salt shaker out of reach to avoid temptation.*

*Her youngest son came home after school and asked what Carmen was making. "My new
'healthy' food," she replied. Carmen then took a bite and exclaimed, "Dios mio [My God]! Son, I've
lost something." "What did you lose, Mom?" "El sabor [flavor]," she moaned.*

As noted in this vignette, Carmen desperately wants a healthy life. She
knows that life can be short, having lost close family members to illness too
soon. Yet, her experiences illustrate the many challenges in achieving good
health, including differences in how we define "healthy" foods, economic
barriers to healthy choices, clashes between the cultural meanings of certain
foods with medically recommended diets, and lack of or inappropriate communication between health care providers and their patients.

This chapter will describe the apparent and persistent health disparities that exist among ethnic minority groups relative to non-Hispanic Whites in the United States. Factors that may play a protective or negative role in producing these differences will be reviewed, including demographic factors (e.g., sex, income, education), physiological/biological strengths and vulnerabilities, inaccessible and unaffordable health care, racism (social and environmental), and psychological characteristics (e.g., acculturation, stress, lifestyle behaviors). We conclude by examining characteristics of health interventions that demonstrate sensitivity to this large number of important biological, psychological, sociopolitical, and cultural variables.

INFLUENTIAL MODELS OF HEALTH

Biomedical Model

Some of our oldest views of health define it as an absence of disease or illness. Indeed, the popular **biomedical model** maintains that all illnesses can be explained on the basis of unusual physical processes, such as biochemical imbalances or structural abnormalities (S. Taylor, 2009). Attention is focused on a microlevel of analysis, where organisms (e.g., bacteria, viruses) or physical abnormalities lead to short-term or long-term illness. Hence, prominence is given to the disease process rather than to potentially interrelated psychological and/or social variables.

It is not difficult to recognize why the biomedical perspective has been so dominant in the field of medicine. Its roots are firmly embedded in Descartes' philosophy of **mind-body dualism,** the insistence that the mind is a distinct entity from the physical world, including the body (Deary, 2005). This focused ideology lends itself to research that identifies a single factor (biological malfunctioning) as responsible for the development of an illness. Furthermore, this model clearly emphasizes the need to detect the causes of physical pathology so that prevention methods or a cure might be found (Brannon & Feist, 2007). Many devastating illnesses such as polio and diphtheria are no longer of national concern because of the creation of effective vaccines that can prevent their development. Short-term, yet deadly, infectious **acute diseases** (e.g., tuberculosis, pneumonia) that attacked generations prior to the 20th century are not considered major threats to our longevity—at least in industrialized countries like the United States. Indeed, **chronic diseases** (e.g., cardiovascular or heart disease, cancer, diabetes) are currently the top killers in the United States (National Center for Health Statistics [NCHS], 2006). "Chronic" refers to the fact that generally these diseases persist for a longer period of time than acute diseases. In addition, while a number of factors may increase risks for the development of chronic diseases, typically significant determinants include people's lifestyle—behaviors that are highly related to illnesses such as smoking, overeating, and little or no exercise.

Biopsychosocial Model

Over the past few decades, many researchers have argued that a focus on physical/biological problems that lead to illness is shortsighted. Both health and illness are caused by more than the single factor of biological malfunctioning. Psychological and social factors can also determine whether one is healthy or sick. The model that best describes this view is the **biopsychosocial model** (Suls & Rothman, 2004). This model maintains that health and illness are caused by multiple factors that can potentially produce multiple effects related to health and disease (see Figure 8.1). According to this model, whether a particular treatment will cure a disease is dependent on psychological and social factors and cannot be explained by biological factors alone. For example, even with some knowledge of the pitfalls of eating certain foods, it is difficult for many to deny themselves the enjoyment of foods that they have eaten since childhood. Carmen's case illustrates that certain traditional foods of one's culture may not be necessarily healthy for the body but we need to consider the cultural and personal meanings of food. While food serves nutritional needs, food also serves a person's inner being or soul. To simply prescribe discontinuing certain foods without suggesting alternative foods or healthier recipes that may still nourish the person's soul will leave the individual feeling deprived and craving the forbidden foods more than ever.

An additional distinction of this model is the significance placed on the promotion of health. From this model's perspective, health becomes something that one achieves and manages by addressing biological, psychological, and sociological needs rather than something that is taken for granted or simply the by-product of the absence of illness (S. Taylor, 2009; World Health Organization, 1948).

CULTURE, ETHNICITY, AND HEALTH

Culture's and ethnicity's roles in determining health and illness are receiving increased attention from psychologists and other social scientists, as well as many health practitioners. Indeed, in a recent review of cultural and ethnic factors in health, Berry and Sam (2007) noted that our understanding of how

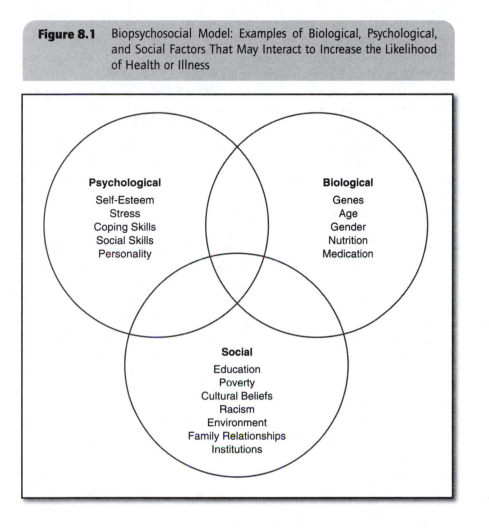

Figure 8.1 Biopsychosocial Model: Examples of Biological, Psychological, and Social Factors That May Interact to Increase the Likelihood of Health or Illness

Psychological
Self-Esteem
Stress
Coping Skills
Social Skills
Personality

Biological
Genes
Age
Gender
Nutrition
Medication

Social
Education
Poverty
Cultural Beliefs
Racism
Environment
Family Relationships
Institutions

these factors relate to health is heightened by the work conducted within a number of varied disciplines including medical anthropology, transcultural psychiatry, and cross-cultural health psychology. Research findings indicate that differences in health exist on both the individual/psychological and community/cultural levels in terms of cognitive conceptualizations, attitudes and normative values, behavioral responses to the body, and medical institutions and relationships (Berry & Sam, 2007). For example, knowledge about high blood pressure can be shaped by a community's norms about foods and behaviors that may impact hypertension—but these beliefs can vary from person to person via individual differences (e.g., demographics, comprehension), family practices, and social relationships within a cultural group (Berry & Sam, 2007).

Subgroup differences within ethnic minority populations can bear importance in anticipating health behavior. This is illustrated in a recent study by Shive and his colleagues (2007) in which they examined a nationally representative sample of Asian American subgroups (e.g., Chinese, Vietnamese, Koreans, Japanese, Filipino, Indian, Laotian) (N = 6,722). They assessed a number of differences in health behavior including sources of health information, ethnic/racial preference for physicians, and cancer screening among these groups. Several subgroup differences were noted. For instance, Indians from India were more likely to use the World Wide Web than Chinese, Koreans, and Filipinos. Koreans were significantly less likely to use printed materials than Filipinos and Japanese. Koreans were the most likely to prefer a physician similar to their own ethnicity and Indians indicated the least preference. Screening differences were also noted with Vietnamese, the least likely to have a complete physical exam, and Filipinos, the most likely. The percentage of women in the subgroups who did not get a Pap screening for cervical cancer ranged from 15.1% for Filipinos to 50% for Koreans. Given the variety of differences, Shive et al. (2007) noted the importance of considering the preferences and behaviors of specific groups when planning prevention or health care delivery.

Carmen's story highlights the need to consider culture from its most basic components discussed in Chapter 2, that is, attitudes, values, beliefs, and behavioral norms that are shared within her cultural group and across generations. Carmen is used to the foods of her culture. To explore how she might define "healthy" foods would likely lead to a response that illustrates that healthy food is food that is familiar in taste and satisfying. To ignore this value could lead to poor compliance on Carmen's part when changes in diet are required. Instead, some foodies, nutritionists, and chefs argue that traditional cultural foods can still be enjoyed and, with some adjustments, can be lower in calories, fat, and sodium than the original recipes of our elders (see Box 8.1). Moreover, you do not have to sacrifice the *"sabor"* for the health value of foods that are customarily preferred within cultures.

BOX 8.1

A New Taste of Soul Food

Lindsey Williams was overweight as a child. An admitted "food addict," Lindsey compulsively consumed calorie-, fat-, sugar-, and salt-laden foods. He was also a compulsive dieter—always hungry and starving in order to lose some pounds, but consistently rebounding with more weight. Moreover, he is the grandson of one of the most famous soul food chefs, Sylvia Woods, the "Queen of Soul Food." Her famous Sylvia's Restaurant in Harlem, New York, recently celebrated its 42nd anniversary.

Her food is enjoyed by locals, tourists, as well as music and movie celebrities, elite athletes, politicians, and other dignitaries. Cooking food is infused in the fiber of his family. While working in the music industry as an upper-level promoter and manager, the increased demands and stress took their toll and Lindsey became morbidly obese. Finally, at the depth of misery—after losing his job, marriage, house, and cars, he sought out help by joining a support group for food addicts. Building upon insights and social support gained through the group, Lindsey started a physical exercise regime to begin his journey of recovery and fitness. He also started a new career in catering. Although he had an educational upbringing in the family food business, he decided to take a new twist on traditional soul food. He was determined to change the concept of soul food from down-home comfort food that is flavorsome yet quite fattening into more sophisticated food that is still big on flavor and familiar in name yet made with more wholesome ingredients and designed with more flair. For example, collard greens can be sautéed in olive oil instead of cooked in pork fat; fresh vegetables can be lightly cooked with seasonings rather than using canned vegetables that contain a high level of sodium. Even staples of soul food, such as fried chicken, can be redesigned to be less caloric, but still good eating:

Oven-Fried Chicken*

Serves 6

    2 teaspoons dried thyme

    2 teaspoons dried oregano

    2 teaspoons dried basil

    2 teaspoons garlic powder

    2 teaspoons kosher salt

    2 teaspoons fresh pepper

    6 skinless, boneless chicken breasts

    2 cups plain nonfat yogurt

    2 cups Special K cereal, crushed with a rolling pin or in a food processor or coffee grinder

nonstick cooking spray

1. Preheat the oven to 375°.

2. In a large plastic bag, combine the thyme, oregano, basil, garlic powder, salt, and pepper. Shake well. Add two breasts at a time to the bag and shake to coat the chicken. Continue until all the breasts are coated.

3. Place the yogurt in a large bowl, and the cereal on a large plate. Dip each breast in the yogurt and then in the cereal. Place the chicken breasts on a baking sheet sprayed with nonstick cooking spray.

(Continued)

(Continued)

4. Bake for 35 to 45 minutes, until the chicken is brown and cooked through. Do not cover or turn the chicken during the baking process.

5. When the chicken is completely cooked, remove the baking sheet from the oven and let cool 10 minutes before serving.

Nutritional information per serving:

227 Calories, 32g Protein, 4g Fat, 194mg Sodium

At 5'5", Lindsey eventually reduced his weight from 400 pounds to 160 pounds. His catering business became highly successful and he now oversees Neo Soul Events and Catering. Soul food does not need to be equated with "bad" food. As Sylvia Woods states, "Soul food is just food cooked with a lot of love, and everyone should be able to eat it." Perhaps with continued creativity and lots of love, healthier soul food will increasingly become the new traditional food.

*"Oven-Fried Chicken" from *Neo Soul: Taking Soul Food to a Whole 'Nutha Level* by Lindsey Williams. Copyright © 2006 by Lindsey Williams. Used by permission of Avery Publishing, an imprint of Penguin Group (USA) Inc.

Given that the management and treatment of health problems may vary across cultures and even within subgroups of a particular culture, the need to develop more comprehensive and integrative models of human health exists. Perhaps a *biopsychosociocultural* model would best highlight the contributions of four major factors (biological, psychological, societal, and cultural) that are intricately interwoven in affecting people's health on both individual and group levels. Theorists, clinicians, and policymakers are compelled to examine these areas in order to offer the most comprehensive conceptualizations of health, illness, and intervention. Hence, multidimensional approaches offer the best promise of achieving parity in good health among various ethnic groups.

HEALTH DISPARITIES AMONG ETHNIC GROUPS

A large number of health surveys indicate that ethnic minorities are at higher risk for a number of illnesses relative to non-Hispanic Whites. Many of these findings have been produced by epidemiologists. **Epidemiology** is a special branch of biomedical research devoted to the study of the occurrence of disorders in populations or in special groups and the risk factors associated with these disorders (Tucker, Phillips, Murphy, & Raczynski, 2004). A subspecialty within epidemiology is **psychiatric epidemiology** that focuses on the study of the occurrence of psychiatric disorders and their associated risk factors in populations and in special groups (see Chapter 9 for a discussion of these disorders).

Of particular importance in epidemiology is the provision of information regarding the **prevalence** and the **incidence** of disorders. Prevalence is the *total number of cases* of a problem or disorder occurring in a population of a group at a given time (Tucker et al., 2004). Incidence is the *number of new cases* of a problem or disorder that occurs over a specific time period (Tucker et al., 2004). It is useful to compare the incidence and prevalence rates of disorders because these numbers can alert health authorities to the possibility of epidemics. For example, imagine that you have determined that the current prevalence of a disorder in a population is 10,000 cases. Then you determine that the incidence of that same disorder over the past 2 years is 5,000 cases. You now have reason to be alarmed as you recognize that roughly 50% of the cases have just been diagnosed in the past two years; the numbers have risen tremendously in a relatively short period of time. As an epidemiologist, you will want to identify factors that may account for these increasing numbers, including the characteristics or behaviors that appear in those who have the disorder (cases) compared to those who are not diagnosed with the disorder (controls). These characteristics/behaviors are what we call **risk factors** (Levy & Brink, 2005).

In identifying prevalence and incidence of diseases, we also can determine the **morbidity,** the proportion of illness or specific disease, in a population (S. Taylor, 2009). The morbidity of a population signals the general health of a group of people. We can also consider the rate of **mortality,** the frequency of death or death rate in a population (S. Taylor, 2009).

Defining Health Disparities

In 2000, a legal definition for **health disparities** was provided through United States Public Law 106–525, also known as the Minority Health and Health Disparities Research and Education Act:

> A population is a health disparity population if there is a significant disparity in the overall rate of disease incidence, prevalence, morbidity, mortality or survival rates in the population as compared to the health status of the general population.

These population groups may be characterized by gender, age, ethnicity, ancestry, education, income, social class, disability, geographic location, or sexual orientation. Hence, in order to demonstrate a disparity, it is necessary to make comparisons of prevalence rates of disorders among ethnic groups including European Americans or among various groups of interest. Within this text we have described the limitations of using a particular group (e.g., White European Americans) as the standard of comparison, but in the case of documenting characteristics that may place certain groups at high risk, large-scale, epidemiological studies offer our best glimpse into general trends in the larger population.

Although it is useful to make comparisons across groups in order to detect disparity, data are often not available for specific ethnic or ancestral groups. For example, we can list the incidence and prevalence rates of cardiovascular disease in Hispanics, but we do not consistently have information on the different subgroups that constitute this large category (Mexican Americans, Puerto Ricans, Cubans, etc.). The same is true for Asian Americans where we seldom have information for specific ancestries (Chinese Americans, Japanese Americans, Filipino Americans, etc.) and for American Indians (e.g., Hopi, Sioux, Black Foot, and hundreds of other tribes). This situation occurs because epidemiological researchers often group together (aggregate) individuals who share some cultural traits into one group. For example, health information for Japanese Americans is reported together with that of Chinese Americans and Laotians. Aggregation of data usually takes place because there are very few people in a given subgroup, and grouping them within a larger ethnic group may provide certain statistical power that is not available when the subgroups are considered individually. The problems inherent with aggregated data include the possibility that health difficulties may be masked by looking at the overall status of certain ethnic groups. For instance, Chinese Americans and Japanese Americans tend to generally exhibit healthier status than smaller Southeast Asian refugee groups such as the Hmong and the Mien—if all these groups are combined, one could easily conclude that most Asian Americans are fairly healthy (Zane, Takeuchi, & Young, 1994).

Statistics can also be reported in such a way as to diminish the severity of apparent differences in health problems in our country. We could attempt to concentrate on the "good news" (e.g., overall, Americans are living longer now than ever) and not address the persistent and worsening problems at hand (see Box 8.2). Acknowledging health disparities requires that we consider the possible causes that produced differences in health conditions across groups as well as our responsibility at all levels (e.g., individual, community, national, and political) to take action to diminish and eliminate these inequities.

BOX 8.2

Accentuate the Positive—Play Down the Negative? Taking a Hard Look at Health Disparities

On December 23, 2003, the U.S. Department of Health and Human Services (HHS) released an extensive report on racial disparities in health care. The *National Healthcare Disparities Report* was designed to provide an up-to-date, accurate overview of the inequalities in health care and reveal the causes for their persistence. Indeed, an earlier draft of the executive summary, prepared by HHS scientists and distributed in June 2003, indicated that problems were pervasive and race was a major determinant in quality and access to health care. However, major controversy ensued once it was revealed that the draft report had undergone significant revision after being reviewed by administrative officials. Critics charged that the version released in December played down the health disparities among groups and was less targeted at the lack of racial equality in health care.

An investigation conducted at the request of Rep. Henry A. Waxman and seven other members of Congress sought to identify why the HHS's conclusions differed from those of the Institute of Medicine, which documented overwhelming evidence of racial and ethnic disparities in health care and directed that strategies needed to be developed and implemented to alleviate or eliminate them (Smedley, Stith, & Nelson, 2003). The investigative report (U.S. House of Representatives, 2004) noted several differences between the June draft and the December version of the HHS report, namely:

- The December version of the *National Healthcare Disparities Report* greatly reduced the use of the word "disparity." The draft report defined the term and included it 30 times, but the final version failed to define it and referred to it only twice in the "key findings" section.
- The December version failed to conclude that health care disparities were national in scope. The scientists' draft had noted that racial, ethnic, and socioeconomic disparities are national problems that affect all aspects of care and medical conditions—in other words, that they are pervasive. In contrast, the final version stated that only some socioeconomic, racial, ethnic, and geographic differences are present.
- The December version replaced the findings on the social costs of disparities with a discussion of the "successes." For example, the executive summary noted that American Indians/Alaska Natives have a lower death rate from all cancers. However, the summary neglected to mention that this could be related to the fact that American Indians/Alaska Natives have a significantly shorter overall life expectancy as well as higher infant mortality compared to other American groups.
- The December version deleted important examples of health care disparities, including racial and ethnic minorities' higher risk of death related to HIV, being diagnosed with late-stage cancer, being placed in restraints in nursing homes, and receiving poor cardiac care following heart attacks. Instead, attention was given to less severe examples, such as Hispanics and American Indians/Alaska Natives having their cholesterol checked less often.

(Continued)

(Continued)

According to media reports, then–Secretary of Health and Human Services Tommy G. Thompson wanted to avoid a negative tone and message—and instead focus on highlighting successes rather than the disparities. "That's just the way Secretary Thompson wants to create change," said Karen Migdail, a spokeswoman at the Agency for Healthcare Research and Quality (AHRQ), the HHS unit that prepared the report. "The idea is not to say, 'We failed, we failed, we failed,' but to say, 'We improved, we improved, we improved'" (Milloy, 2004).

The U.S. House of Representatives Committee on Government Reform (2004) charged that the changes made by HHS in the disparities report serve as an example of the politicization of science. The alterations minimize the extent and severity of racial and ethnic disparities. Moreover, this reduction in attention undermines strategies and efforts to resolve these real problems.

In response to criticism, Secretary Thompson acknowledged that the HHS erred in revising certain scientific findings of report, stating, "There was a mistake made, and it's going to be rectified" ("Washington in brief," 2004). The AHRQ later released the version it had submitted to the Department for clearance. A copy of the report is available at http://www.ahrq.gov/qual/nhdr03/fullreport/index.html.

* * *

Reflect and discuss:

1. Beyond focusing on positive health outcomes, what could have been possible motivations for the omission of some of the serious health disparities and the changes in some conclusions from the executive summary report?

2. What are the consequences of focusing more on positive health outcomes than on emphasizing the significant and discrepant health problems experienced by certain groups? Conversely, what are the consequences of focusing more closely on health disparities than on the positive outcomes?

3. What would you suggest are some of the best ways to present a picture of the facts that will galvanize people (community residents, including politicians and other policymakers) to address the issue of health disparities with constructive and effective strategies?

Examples of Health Disparities

Epidemiological research among ethnic/racial groups shows important differences across and within ethnic groups. For some illnesses (e.g., cancer, heart disease), ethnic minority groups show morbidity rates that are very different from those of Whites or even some other ethnic groups. There has been a marked interest in the last few years to conduct research on why these disparities occur. As detailed later in the chapter, there are multiple possible reasons for these differences in morbidity and mortality, although the research is not conclusive. Before addressing the reasons for health disparities, we describe some of the most significant differences in health status across ethnic groups.

Mortality. While at times it is difficult to compare information from various studies because of methodological differences, it is possible to identify important disparities in mortality rates. The current estimate for life expectancy in the United States is 77.9 years (Centers for Disease Control and Prevention [CDC], 2006). To see if there are disparities, we can look at whether this average holds up across different groups, including women and men. We find that the current data indicate all-time-high life expectancies for males and females. The average life expectancy for women is 80.4 years; the average life expectancy for men is 75.2 years. This gender gap has narrowed over time; the 5.2-year difference is the smallest difference since 1946 (NCHS, 2006).

A reduction in differences among mortality figures across ethnic/racial groups also appears in recent data from the National Center for Health Statistics (see Figure 8.2). However, notable differences still exist among groups. For example, the difference between White and Black life expectancy

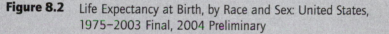

Figure 8.2 Life Expectancy at Birth, by Race and Sex: United States, 1975–2003 Final, 2004 Preliminary

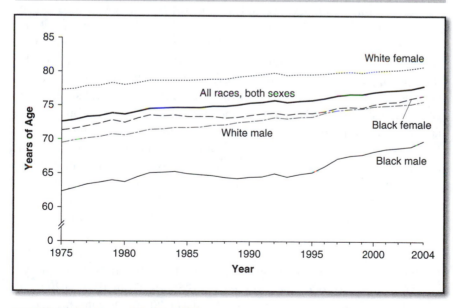

SOURCE: Miniño, Heron, & Smith (2006).

in 2004 was 5.0 years. Black males continue to have shorter life expectancy compared to White males. There is even more disparity between White females compared to Black males, with White females having a longer life expectancy.

Another aspect of mortality, infant mortality, is a particularly good index for detecting group differences because it is commonly used as a standard indicator of national and worldwide health status. Epidemiologic data reveal that infant mortality rates vary widely across racial/ethnic groups. For example, African Americans, American Indians and Alaska Natives, and Puerto Ricans all show infant death rates above the national mean of 6.86 deaths per 1,000 live births, whereas non-Hispanic Whites and Asian or Pacific Islanders average slightly below the mean with death rates of 5.76 and 5.53, respectively (MacDorman & Mathews, 2008). In particular, African Americans show the greatest disparity with an infant mortality rate of 13.63 deaths per 1,000 live births, roughly two times the national average (MacDorman & Mathews, 2008).

Examination of some of the leading causes of death in the United States also illustrates significant differences between groups. As an example, heart disease and cancer are the leading causes of death for African Americans, Hispanics, American Indians, Asian Americans, and non-Hispanic Whites (see Table 8.1; note for Asian Americans, cancer is the number one cause of death followed by heart disease). However, after these first two diseases, you will note that differences appear across the groups. For example, accidents have become the third leading cause of death for Hispanics and American Indians, whereas stroke is the third leading cause for Whites, African Americans, and Asian Americans. Disease related to the Human Immunodeficiency Virus (HIV) ranks as the ninth leading cause of death for African Americans, but does not appear in the top 10 leading causes of death for other groups across all ages. Chronic liver disease and cirrhosis rank as the fifth and sixth leading cause of death for American Indians and Hispanics, respectively, but does not appear in the top 10 for other groups. In addition, African Americans and Hispanics are more likely to die from homicide than other groups. Similarities and differences across groups lead to questions about whether there are specific vulnerabilities (physiological as well as behavioral) of certain ethnic groups to physical disorders and—equally as important— whether there are protective factors that serve to lower a group's susceptibility to certain diseases.

Coronary Heart Disease. Over the recent past, coronary heart disease (CHD) deaths have decreased in the United States. From 1993 to 2003, the mortality rate from CHD declined 30.2% (NCHS, 2006). Despite this pattern, heart disease continues to be the number one killer in the United States. Although CHD is the top cause of death for all racial and ethnic groups, the

Table 8.1   The Ten Leading Causes of Death in the United States (2003) Among the Total Population and Across Ethnic Groups: African Americans, Hispanics, Asian Americans, American Indians, and Whites (Non-Hispanic)

Total Population (both sexes, all ages)

1. Diseases of the heart
2. Malignant neoplasms (cancer)
3. Cerebrovascular diseases (e.g., stroke)
4. Chronic lower respiratory diseases
5. Accidents (unintentional injuries)
6. Diabetes mellitus (diabetes)
7. Influenza and pneumonia
8. Alzheimer's disease
9. Nephritis, nephrotic syndrome, and nephrosis (kidney disease)
10. Septicemia (blood poisoning)

African Americans (both sexes, all ages)

1. Diseases of the heart
2. Malignant neoplasms (cancer)
3. Cerebrovascular diseases (e.g., stroke)
4. Diabetes mellitus (diabetes)
5. Accidents (unintentional injuries)
6. Assault (homicide)
7. Nephritis, nephrotic syndrome, and nephrosis (kidney disease)
8. Chronic lower respiratory diseases
9. Human immunodeficiency virus (HIV) disease
10. Septicemia (blood poisoning)

Hispanics or Latinos (both sexes, all ages)

1. Diseases of the heart
2. Malignant neoplasms (cancer)

(Continued)

Table 8.1 (Continued)

3. Accidents (unintentional injuries)

4. Cerebrovascular diseases (e.g., stroke)

5. Diabetes mellitus (diabetes)

6. Chronic liver disease and cirrhosis

7. Assault (homicide)

8. Chronic lower respiratory diseases

9. Influenza and pneumonia

10. Certain conditions originating in the perinatal period

Asians or Pacific Islanders (both sexes, all ages)

1. Malignant neoplasms (cancer)

2. Diseases of the heart

3. Cerebrovascular diseases (e.g., stroke)

4. Accidents (unintentional injuries)

5. Diabetes mellitus (diabetes)

6. Influenza and pneumonia

7. Chronic lower respiratory diseases

8. Intentional self-harm (suicide)

9. Nephritis, nephrotic syndrome, and nephrosis (kidney disease)

10. Septicemia (blood poisoning)

American Indians or Alaska Natives (both sexes, all ages)

1. Diseases of the heart

2. Malignant neoplasms (cancer)

3. Accidents (unintentional injuries)

4. Diabetes mellitus (diabetes)

5. Chronic liver disease and cirrhosis

6. Cerebrovascular diseases (e.g., stroke)

7. Chronic lower respiratory diseases

8. Influenza and pneumonia

9. Intentional self-harm (suicide)

10. Nephritis, nephrotic syndrome, and nephrosis (kidney disease)

Whites (Non-Hispanics, both sexes, all ages)

1. Diseases of the heart

2. Malignant neoplasms (cancer)

3. Cerebrovascular diseases (e.g., stroke)

4. Chronic lower respiratory diseases

5. Accidents (unintentional injuries)

6. Alzheimer's disease

7. Influenza and pneumonia

8. Diabetes mellitus (diabetes)

9. Nephritis, nephrotic syndrome, and nephrosis (kidney disease)

10. Intentional self-harm (suicide)

SOURCE: NCHS (2005).

prevalence rates for CHD (which includes the diseases of arteriosclerosis—also known as "hardening of the arteries"—and atherosclerosis—the buildup of atheromas or plaques in the walls of the arteries), stroke, and hypertension (high blood pressure) vary considerably across groups (Myers & Rodriguez, 2003). For instance, in 2003, CHD death rates per 100,000 people were 241.1 for Black males and 209.2 for White males, compared to 160.3 for Black females and 125.1 for White females (NCHS, 2006).

Disparities also exist in the prevalence of risk factors associated with cardiovascular disease. Racial and ethnic minorities have higher rates of hypertension, tend to develop hypertension at an earlier age, and are less likely to undergo treatment to control their high blood pressure than White non-Hispanics. For example, from 1999 to 2002, the prevalence of hypertension in a sample of 7,000 U.S. adults was 40.5% among non-Hispanic Blacks, 27.4% among non-Hispanic Whites, and 25.1% among Mexican Americans over the age of 20 years (CDC, 2005b). Among those adults tested as having hypertension (defined as having an average systolic blood pressure equal to or greater than 140 mm Hg and diastolic blood pressure equal to or greater than 90 mm Hg or taking blood pressure medication), the proportion who were aware of having high blood pressure was 70.3% among Blacks, 62% among Whites, but only 49.8% among Mexican Americans (CDC, 2005b). During 1991–1999, almost 95% of U.S. adults had had a blood pressure screening within the previous two years; however, Hispanics had lower levels of blood pressure screenings than non-Hispanic Whites or non-Hispanic Blacks (CDC, 2002).

Being overweight and obese are important risks factors for heart disease where we can find disparities across groups.[1] In the United States, being an overweight adult is becoming more and more commonplace. According to a recent survey (NCHS, 2002), in 1999–2000, 64% of adults were overweight. This figure represents an increase when compared to the rate of 56% found among adults surveyed in 1988–1994. Similarly, 30% reported being obese in 1999–2000, whereas 23% reported this in the earlier survey. The risk of obesity is particularly significant for women who are African American, Hispanic (Mexican American), or who belong to certain American Indian/Alaska Native groups, as well as for Pacific Islander women (e.g., Native Hawaiʻians and Samoans). As a matter of fact, findings from the National Health and Nutrition Examination Survey (NHANES) indicate that the age-adjusted prevalence rates for obesity are higher for African American women (51% are obese and 78% overweight) and for Mexican American women (40% are obese and 72% overweight) than non-Hispanic White women (31% obese and 58% overweight) (NCHS, 2002).

Preventive actions such as regular cholesterol checkups also show disparities for certain racial and ethnic minorities. For instance, an analysis of the NHANES indicated that in 1999–2002 the proportion of Blacks and Mexican Americans screened for high blood cholesterol (defined as a total cholesterol level > 240 mg/dL or a participant reported taking cholesterol-lowering medication) during the preceding five years was lower than the proportion for Whites (CDC, 2005b). In addition, fewer Blacks and Mexican Americans with high blood cholesterol were told by a medical health professional of their diagnosed condition than were Whites with only 42% of Mexican Americans aware of their condition (CDC, 2005b). Unfortunately, data were not available for other ethnic minority groups; only non-Hispanic Blacks and Mexican Americans were oversampled for comparisons.

Cancer. Cancer represents over 100 diseases that all result from some malfunction in the cellular programming of our bodies (Kiberstis & Marx, 2002; S. Taylor, 2009). Although cancer is the second leading cause of death in the United States, recent data indicate that incidence and death rates from all cancers combined decreased since 1975 in men and women overall and in most racial and ethnic populations (Jemal et al., 2008). Nevertheless, the available epidemiological data indicate that ethnic minority groups suffer disproportionately from cancer. These populations are more likely to be diagnosed and die from preventable cancers than the overall U.S. population. They are also likely to be identified much later in the stage of the disease progression than through early screening. Consequently, some may receive little or no treatment, or even treatment that is not at the currently accepted standard of care, and this can lead to greater suffering and pain from terminal cancer.

Health disparities among ethnic groups are clearly illustrated by the higher overall cancer incidence and mortality rates of African Americans when compared to other groups. According to the National Cancer Institute (NCI, 2005), for men and women combined, Blacks have a cancer death rate higher than that of Whites (248.1 vs. 195.3 per 100,000). The death rate for cancer for Black men is notably higher than it is for White men (339.4 vs. 242.5 per 100,000). Death rates for specific types of cancers illustrate this disparity. The death rate for lung and bronchus cancer is higher for Black men than for White men (101.3 vs. 75.2 per 100,000). The prostate cancer mortality rate for Black men is roughly two and one-half times that of White men (68.1 vs. 27.7 per 100,000) (NCI, 2005).

Paralleling the death rate, certain racial/ethnic groups experience higher rates of specific cancers than other groups. Hispanic women continue to have the highest incidence rates for cervical cancer, but African American women have the highest death rate for cervical cancer—Hispanic women have the second highest death rate (NCI, 2005). African American men have more cancers of the lung, prostate, colon, and rectum than do non-Hispanic White men (American Cancer Society, 2005; NCI, 2005). African American women continue to have the highest rates of mortality from breast cancer (American Cancer Society, 2005; NCI, 2005).

While Asian/Pacific Islanders generally experience lower cancer rates overall compared with non-Hispanic Whites and other ethnic minority groups, this group and certain subgroups experience higher death and incidence rates for specific cancers. For example, Asian/Pacific Islanders experience the highest incidence rates of liver and stomach cancer (NCI, 2005). They also experience the highest death rates for liver and stomach cancer (NCI, 2005). Vietnamese women in the United States have a cervical cancer incidence rate significantly greater than White women (NCI, 2005). Alaska Native men and women suffer disproportionately higher rates of cancers of the colon and rectum than do Whites (NCI, 2005).

Diabetes. Diabetes is another comprehensive label that includes a set of diseases in which high blood sugar levels occur as the result of problems in the release or activity of insulin in the body. There are subtypes of diabetes. One is **type 1 diabetes**, also referred to as "juvenile-onset" diabetes or insulin-dependent diabetes mellitus, which is typically associated with biological, genetic, or environmental factors in its development. Even more common is **type 2 diabetes**, also known as "adult-onset" diabetes or non-insulin-dependent diabetes mellitus, which accounts for approximately 90 to 95% of all diagnosed cases of diabetes (National Center for Chronic Disease Prevention and Health Promotion [NCCDPHP], 2002). Older age, obesity, inactive lifestyle, family history of diabetes, or history of gestational (pregnancy-related) diabetes are typical risk factors. Although older age—"adult onset"—is traditionally associated with increasing risk of type 2 diabetes, many argue that the term "adult onset" is increasingly becoming a misnomer. Over the past 25 years, we have witnessed a larger number of youth diagnosed with this subtype, and the rising prevalence of obesity in youth is commonly associated with this increase (S. Taylor, 2009).

Although certain types of diabetes are more manageable than others, increasing attention has been placed on positive lifestyle changes that can prevent the serious complications that can result from these diseases such as blindness, amputation of limbs, cardiovascular disease and stroke, pain, and premature death. The prevalence and incidence of this disorder have increased sharply over the past 25 years. According to the American Diabetes Association, roughly 23.6 million children and adults (or 7.8% of the population) have diabetes in the United States (American Diabetes Association, 2006).

Ethnic disparities are also found in the case of diabetes. Compared to Whites (non-Hispanics), Hispanic/Latinos and African Americans are roughly twice as likely to suffer from type 2 diabetes. American Indians and Alaska Natives are 2.6 times more likely to be diagnosed with type 2 diabetes than Whites (NCCDPHP, 2002). Although Asian Americans and Pacific Islanders are typically overlooked in diabetes research due to the model minority stereotype and relatively lower obesity rates than other ethnic groups (Chesla & Chun, 2005), they likewise suffer from diabetes at twice the rate of European Americans (Joslin Diabetes Center, 2003; McNeely & Boyko, 2004). For Chinese Americans—the largest Asian American group—reported rates of type 2 diabetes have reached as high as three times that of European Americans (Wang, Abbott, Goodbody, Hui, & Rausch, 1999).

Taking a closer look within these ethnic groups, we also see diversity in risk. For example, within Hispanic/Latinos, Puerto Rican men and Mexican American women have some of the highest rates, while Cuban women have some of the lowest (Myers & Rodriguez, 2003). Pima and Papago Indians have the highest risks of diabetes—no wonder Carmen (a mixture of Mexican and

Pima Indian background) has a strong familial and now personal history of this disease (Myers & Rodriguez, 2003; NCCDPHP, 2002).

Complications associated with diabetes are also more prevalent in ethnic minority groups relative to Whites. For example, African Americans and American Indians experience more complications related to diabetes such as limb amputations and kidney disease than Whites (Myers & Rodriguez, 2003).

HIV and AIDS. For people between the ages of 25 and 44 years, HIV infection ranks as the fifth leading cause of death (NCHS, 2006). Currently, 40,000 new cases of HIV infection occur each year in the United States, and roughly 5 million cases occur annually worldwide (National Institute of Allergy and Infectious Diseases [NIAID], 2004). Over recent years, more attention has been given to the disparate number of ethnic minority populations affected by the HIV/AIDS pandemic, especially African Americans and Hispanics. According to reports from the Centers for Disease Control and Prevention, the increased risk among groups is striking: The rates of HIV/AIDS were 71.3 per 100,000 in the Black population, 27.8 per 100,000 in the Hispanic population, 10.4 per 100,000 in the American Indian population, 8.8 per 100,000 in the White population, and 7.4 per 100,000 in the Asian/Pacific Islander population (CDC, 2007b). Ethnic minorities also are disproportionately represented in pediatric AIDS cases. For example, although non-Hispanic Blacks are approximately 15% of the child population, they represent almost 60% of all pediatric AIDS cases (DHHS, 2006). Blacks in general constituted 49% of all HIV/AIDS cases diagnosed in 2005 (CDC, 2005a). Moreover, HIV infection is the number one cause of death for African American men ages 35–44. HIV/AIDS affects African Americans at a rate that is 10 times greater than that found in the U.S. White population (Karon, Fleming, Steketee, & DeCock, 2001). Since 1996, more AIDS cases have occurred among African Americans than any other U.S. racial/ethnic population (CDC, 2007b).

Although intravenous/injection drug users (IDUs) and gay men who engage in unprotected sex maintain the highest risk for HIV infection, alternative routes of transmission exist that increase the vulnerability of minority groups. Approximately 80% of HIV-infected women are minorities and most become infected through heterosexual transmission (CDC, 2007a). African American women are particularly vulnerable. In 2005, African American women's rate of AIDS diagnosis was approximately 4 times the rate for Hispanic women, and 23 times the rate for White women (CDC, 2005a). More attention is being given to "risky heterosexual sex" that might place women at a heightened vulnerability to contract HIV. (See Box 8.3 for a closer look at African Americans at risk for HIV/AIDS.)

BOX 8.3

African Americans at Risk for HIV/AIDS

Disparities in HIV infection and AIDS diagnoses are reported in increasing frequency for African Americans. African Americans at greatest risk include injection drug users (IDUs). The known risks associated with injection drug use are not new. Even during the earliest years of the HIV epidemic in the 1980s, the possible contamination of blood and associated infections that could occur while engaging in unsterilized needle sharing among drug users was well documented. However, what was not often discussed were the implications of how this disease could spread among groups—especially poor, minority groups at a faster pace because of their heightened risk of needle sharing due to limited access to clean needles and even the drug associated "brotherhood" of sharing needles. Exposure through injection drug use is the second leading risk category for African American women (McNair & Prather, 2004).

One of the highest risk groups for HIV infection is young African American men who have sex with men (MSM) (CDC, 2001). The proportion of African American MSM diagnosed with AIDS increased from 19% in 1990 to 34% in 1999 (Blair, Fleming, & Karon, 2002). Despite the introduction of highly active antiretroviral therapy (HAART) in the mid- to late 1990s, African American MSM had a higher number of diseases related to HIV infection and higher mortality rate following the diagnosis of AIDS compared to non-Hispanic Whites and Latino MSM (Blair et al., 2002). In a recent study, Hart and Peterson (2004) surveyed a large sample of young African American MSM age 18 to 25 years ($N = 758$) in Atlanta, Georgia. Respondents were recruited in popular venues (e.g., clubs, organizations, coffeehouses) frequented by African Americans. A significant number, 26.5% ($n = 201$), reported engaging in unprotected anal sex. Approximately 16.5% engaged in unprotected insertive anal intercourse; a larger number, 18.6%, engaged in the even more risky unprotected receptive anal intercourse. The risk of both unprotected receptive and insertive anal intercourse increased among respondents with a main partner as opposed to those who did not have a primary partner. Factors that predicted higher-risk behaviors were unsupportive peer norms regarding the use of condoms and not carrying condoms. Findings suggest that more attention must be given toward changing values and beliefs about condoms—in such a way that promotes more positive connotations about having them available and using them.

Men who have sex with men typically have been discussed in the context of gay men's sexuality. Yet, many argue that some men are not gay identified and engage in both unprotected sex with women and secret sex relations with other men. In recent years, these men are often referred to as **"men on the down low"** or "down low brothers" (J. L. King & Hunter, 2005). Cultural taboos and the stigma of homosexuality, failure of the monogamy ideal, confusion over one's sexual identity, or desire for sexual freedom and exploration are some of the possible reasons for nondisclosure.

An important consideration in the discussion of men on the down low is the reality that this phenomenon is *not* exclusive to African Americans. Secretly having sex with a person of one's own sex is a behavior that occurs within and across a wide variety of ethnic and racial groups.

As Boykin (2005b) argues, "The down low is just a Black version of 'the closet.'... [It] is just a new way of describing a very old thing." Furthermore, people decry the sensationalism of the down low as a means of further demonizing and pathologizing black men's sexual behavior—and black men in general (Boykin, 2005a).

Given the debate over the meaning and realities of the AIDS epidemic in Black communities, there is a need to consider other interpersonal factors and what has been termed **social-structural determinants** that are related to Black women's vulnerability, such as disproportionate incarceration rates of African American men, segregation of communities, and constraints on access to services for treatment and prevention of sexually transmitted diseases (Lane et al., 2004). Indeed, McNair and Prather (2004) note that the gender imbalance of the female-male sex ratio (more women and fewer available male partners) leads to fewer sex partner options for women and more options for men. Fewer viable male sex partners leads to an imbalance of interpersonal power for women and less room for women to negotiate safer sex precautions. Moreover, negative attitudes about condoms lead to lower levels of condom use. Women must also challenge myths they might hold that can increase their own risk—for example, the belief that as a Black woman she is not at risk (manifested by the belief that "it's mostly a gay White man's disease")—and the idea that if they are in a monogamous relationship, they are safe. An examination of these social-structural factors would necessitate interventions that are targeted on multiple levels: individual, institutional, and public policy (Boykin, 2005a).

Factors Associated With Health Disparities

In discussing health disparities among ethnic minorities, it is important to consider a number of factors that play a role in the physical health status of individuals. These factors can promote or hinder the well-being of a person or population. Although we can consider each protective or risk factor separately, it is important to note that many of these factors can share mutual influences on people's well-being. Furthermore, both risk and protective factors may coexist. While their presence can suggest the likelihood or probability of contracting a disease, they are not necessarily **causal factors**—that is, they may not *directly* lead to the onset of an illness. Being able to pinpoint the exact cause(s) for a disease is challenging and often impossible to prove through classic experimental studies. For example, we cannot design an experiment that definitively establishes that cigarette smoking leads to lung cancer because this would require that we randomly assign subjects (who have never smoked) to either an experimental smoking condition or a control no-smoking condition. We would then need to follow them for several years until the emergence of cancer would occur in some percentage of the participants. Both pragmatic and ethical constraints require that we rely on quasi-experimental studies to identify the co-occurrence of characteristics that appear in individuals with certain diseases versus those who are disease free. What follows is a summary of some of the primary factors that have emerged through epidemiological, correlational, and other quasi-experimental studies as possible explanations of health disparities.

Behavioral Lifestyle. A person's level of risk for illness is strongly related to her or his lifestyle. Nutritional choices, level of exercise, smoking, and other substance use or abuse are some of the lifestyle behaviors that have been clearly linked to many of the most prevalent health problems discussed in this chapter. Indeed, up until the past couple of decades, most of the illness prevention literature was focused on changing behavior patterns that may place individuals at higher risk for poor health. Yet, increased focus is currently being given to community and policy-level factors that also have a strong role to play in people's behavior and lifestyle choices. For a person like Carmen (in our opening vignette) to even begin to adhere to her recommended diet, she must be able to access healthy foods and be able to afford their cost. What are the types of restaurants in her immediate environment? Do they promote healthy eating—or will she be encouraged to eat high-fat, high-sodium, and high-caloric food (the exact opposite of her LOW prescribed ideal foods)? Poor areas generally have more restricted food options. These include both urban and remote rural areas where there are fewer supermarkets and a predominance of fast food outlets. Supermarkets in these areas are not well stocked in terms of fresh food options. If fresh produce is available, ironically, it may be quite expensive relative to some of the better markets in more affluent areas.

Developing behavioral health interventions for a particular ethnic community also requires comprehensive knowledge of their cultural health beliefs and practices. For instance, in the case of type 2 diabetes, recent Chinese immigrants to the United States may view and manage this illness in culturally distinct ways. One study found that Chinese immigrants attributed this disease to an imbalance of "hotness" and "coldness" in their bodies, and believed that specific foods or Chinese herbs possessed hot or cold properties that helped establish a healthy equilibrium in their body temperature (Chun & Chesla, 2004). Also, when managing this disease, Chinese immigrants monitored how much they told others about their diagnosis and dietary restrictions, ensured that their diet did not interrupt family meals, and demonstrated concern for family harmony despite feeling irritable and fatigued from this disease (Chesla & Chun, 2005). These types of accommodating diabetes management behaviors—reflecting the collectivistic social orientation and family centeredness of many first generation Chinese immigrants—are examples of cultural health practices that must be considered when formulating a culturally appropriate diabetes intervention.

Acculturation. Different possible health outcomes have been proposed to occur in the process of acculturation. It makes intuitive sense that the longer an immigrant group or individual lives within a new environment, the increased likelihood of the immigrant adopting the beliefs, values, and behaviors that are sanctioned in that country. But what has captured attention is a number of findings from epidemiology, sociology, and public health research that indicate immigrants (born in a foreign country) fare better than their U.S.-born counterparts on psychosocial and health indicators including education, criminal behaviors, and well-being (Nguyen, 2006). This is surprising given that many immigrants may experience a number of barriers that would place them at risk for maladjustment including low socioeconomic status (SES), poverty, exposure to crime and trauma, minority status, and difficulties accessing health care (Morales, Lara, Kington, Valdez, & Escarce, 2002; Nguyen, 2006). Together, these findings are termed the **immigrant health paradox** or "epidemiological paradox" (see Chapter 4) because these positive outcomes contradict well established evidence that suggests social and economic factors are important determinants of health and well-being (Morales et al., 2002; Nguyen, 2006). This paradox has been particularly apparent in Latinos, especially Mexican Americans (Morales et al., 2002).

At this time, the reasons for the health paradox are not quite clear. As discussed in Chapter 4, the **selective migration hypothesis** and **social stress hypothesis** describe two different predictions regarding the health outcome of immigrants as they transition and adapt to the United States. Briefly, the selective migration hypothesis or "healthy migrant effect" states that the strongest and healthiest choose to migrate. Thus, this select immigrant group would be more robust in terms of health issues than their family members born within the United States. The social stress hypothesis states that generations born within the United States may exhibit poorer health status than immigrants because of their increased exposure to stressors (e.g., discrimination, racism) and lower presence of protective traditions, behaviors, values, and beliefs that maintained health for earlier generations and are lost by the latter ones (Escobar, 1998). In addition, some theorists state that the health status of immigrants becomes more similar to the group to which they migrate toward (Berry, 1998; Lilienfeld, 1972).

Myers and Rodriguez (2003) reviewed a number of studies that investigated the role of acculturation in the co-occurrence of several major medical illnesses. Findings were mixed in terms of the consequences of acculturation on health status. For example, several studies have suggested that overall rates of cancer and diabetes become worse as acculturation level increases, and this risk is related to changes in knowledge, attitudes, and behaviors—especially lifestyle changes such as consuming more processed fatty foods and lack of exercise (e.g., G. Marks, Garcia, & Solis, 1990; Romero-Gwynn et al., 1993). Myers and Rodriguez (2003) reported that some researchers have theorized that as people become more upwardly mobile through the process of acculturation, they may become more motivated to live longer healthier lives and adopt ways of living that avoid negative health behaviors associated with risks for diabetes (Stern et al., 1991). Yet, other studies found little or no association between acculturation and certain illnesses, leaving the relationship less clear.

Accessible and Affordable Health Care. Clearly, one's health status will be influenced by the ability to access and obtain affordable and effective treatment. In many cases, ethnic minorities find it difficult if not impossible to obtain adequate health insurance coverage because of unemployment or the nature of their employment or to pay for services out of pocket. In a recent analysis of the 2005 Commonwealth Fund Biennial Health Insurance Survey, Doty and Holmgren (2006) reported that insurance coverage was not only inadequate for many ethnic minorities but that in many cases coverage was nonexistent. This situation is particularly problematic for the **"working poor,"** those who are working at minimum wage or slightly below and whose employer does not provide medical coverage. However, because they are employed, they may not meet the criteria for free or low-cost medical coverage. Roughly two thirds (62%) of working-age Hispanics and one third (33%) of African Americans were uninsured at one point during the year. This stands in contrast to 20% of working-age Whites. In addition, Hispanics were *less* likely to have a regular physician, to have been seen by a medical provider in the previous year, or to express confidence in their ability to obtain health care when needed. African Americans were most likely to receive nonurgent treatment through emergency room visits. In addition, low-income African Americans reported the highest number of chronic illnesses and other health problems. Although poverty is tied to one's ability to access and receive adequate medical care (Shi, 2001; see below), across all income levels, disparities in access and insurance coverage persisted for ethnic minorities compared to Whites.

Poverty. As mentioned in Chapter 1, non-Hispanic Whites have a poverty rate of 7.8% whereas the poverty rate for Blacks is 22.7%, Hispanics 21.4%, and Asian Americans 10.2% (U.S. Census Bureau, 2002). In addition to the disparity in poverty rates, the actual number of people at the lowest levels of poverty or **"extreme poverty"**—defined as living on less than half the income of the identified poverty line—is 15.3 million. This figure is the highest since the Census Bureau began collecting these data roughly 30 years ago ("Poverty Rate," 2004). Hence, the gap between the rich and the poor is wider than ever.

The relationship between poverty (and related characteristics such as unemployment or living within an economically depressed neighborhood) and health status has been examined in a number of studies over the past few decades. Health disparities have been consistently found for individuals that differ in SES, with the typical pattern being that those lower in SES are more at risk for negative health outcomes. The associated health risks of poverty include higher likelihood of low-birth-weight babies, premature death, unintentional injuries, and chronic illness (Aday, 1994; Adler et al., 1994; D. R. Williams & Collins, 1995).

In an important longitudinal study on the impact of sustained economic hardship, Lynch, Kaplan, and Shema (1997) examined data from over 1,000 individuals who were studied since 1965. Results showed a significant number of problems associated with people whose income was less than 200% of the poverty level. Those who were at this extreme level of poverty were more likely to have problems with managing daily activities (such as cooking, managing income, shopping, walking, eating, using the bathroom, and dressing) and exhibited symptoms of depression. The pattern of results indicated that economic hardship preceded the development of problems in living. Those who were young and healthy when the study began but experienced greater economic hardship over the next 25 years had the worst adjustment.

While it is well known that minority groups are disproportionately represented in low socioeconomic strata in the United States, less recognized is the fact that morbidity and mortality rates continue to be higher for certain ethnic minority groups even when group differences in income and social status are taken into account. For example, Y. Zhou, Dominici, and Louis (2006) studied the relationship between race, SES, and mortality risk in a sample of over 4 million Medicare members living in the northeastern United States. Findings showed that, overall, there was a statistically higher risk of death for Blacks compared to Whites. Whether risk was examined at an individual level or community level (based on zip code), Blacks fared more poorly in terms of mortality whether SES was or was not adjusted. Even though differences were lower when SES was adjusted at a community level, the fact that differences still existed led to the authors' conclusion that group differences in SES alone do not explain the association between race and mortality—at least for the Medicare population who are 65 years of age or older. It is, however, important to note that reducing SES differences between Blacks and Whites does help to reduce the disparity between their mortality risks.

Discrimination and Racism. The lingering aftermath effects of race and ethnicity after SES is controlled give us reason to focus on the consequential power of racism. Some have offered explanations for differences in health status that center on the stress produced by long-term exposure to adversity and the oppression of racism (D. R. Williams & Collins, 1995). According to a report from the Institute of Medicine (Smedley et al., 2003), several studies carefully document that ethnic minorities receive less intensive and poorer quality of health care than White patients, even when other significant factors (e.g., insurance status, level of income, health symptoms) are equal.

There are daily encounters with discrimination that accompany many of the factors associated with poor health including impoverished neighborhoods, exposure to violence, poor income, and unemployment (Browning & Cagney, 2003). The regularity of incidents such as being followed by security personnel in a department store for no apparent reason or being overlooked or treated badly by a hostess in a restaurant has been linked to hypertension and coronary heart disease (Lewis et al., 2006). Furthermore, ethnic minorities who perceive and relay incidences of discrimination and racism are more likely to engage in unhealthy behaviors (e.g., smoking) and report more physical and psychological distress than Whites or other ethnic minorities that do not perceive or report similar experiences (Barry & Grilo, 2003; Brondolo, Rieppi, Kelly, & Gerin, 2003; Klonoff & Landrine, 1999; Landrine, Klonoff, Corral, Fernandez, & Roesch, 2006).

Smedley (2008), one of the editors of the Institute of Medicine's 2003 report (Smedley et al., 2003), argues that while it is important to focus on health care and frontline strategies to reduce health disparities, the report stands as a testament to the critical response needed by our sociopolitical and economic systems. Disparities in health primarily mirror the social inequalities and injustices in the country and are primarily experienced by ethnic minorities and the poor. Inequalities within the broader political, social, and economic policies marginalize and disenfranchise these groups. Hence, Smedley (2008) issues a call to action on government policy reform:

> Eliminating health care inequality requires more than simply expanding insurance coverage among currently un- and underinsured populations. In particular, policymakers must attend to structural and community-level problems, such as the maldistribution of health care resources, the lack of effective mechanisms for underserved communities to participate in health care planning, and the presence of cultural and linguistic barriers in health care settings, to equalize access to high-quality health care. (p. 453)

A broader focus, designed to address the complex interaction of several systems of inequality, would require the identification of multiple targets and levels of intervention. These efforts would include attention to promoting equality on an environmental level (e.g., raising safety standards in the environment—see below and Box 8.4), in the educational sphere (e.g., by reducing disparities in school funding), at the employment level (e.g., adequate pay and benefits for work), as well as attending to direct service needs—services designed to address cultural needs, values, and behaviors of patients, a topic that is discussed later in this chapter.

Environmental Racism. Many argue that residents of ethnic minority communities have been wronged through their disproportionate exposure to environmental health risks. This has been labeled as **environmental racism,** which long-time civil rights activist Reverend Benjamin Chavis, Jr. defined:

> Environmental racism is racial discrimination in environmental policy-making. It is racial discrimination in the enforcement of regulations and laws. It is racial discrimination in the deliberate targeting of communities of color for toxic waste disposal and the siting of polluting industries. It is racial discrimination in the official sanctioning of the life-threatening presence of poisons and pollutants in communities of color. And, it is racial discrimination in the history of excluding people of color from the mainstream environmental groups, decision making boards, commissions, and regulatory bodies. (Chavis, 1993, p. 3)

Environmental racism, also sometimes referred to as **environmental injustice,** reflects the historical legacy of exploitation and oppression of various minority groups. Communities with predominantly African American, Hispanic/Latino, American Indian, or Asian American groups (often regardless of class) are more likely to be located near toxic municipal landfills, nuclear waste sites, energy plants, chemical warehouses, garbage incinerators, and other high-risk environmental facilities (Bullard, 1990; Bullard, Mohal, Saha, & Wright, 2007). The costs of such precarious placement are significant since living close to these types of facilities is linked to higher than normal levels of diseases including cancer, asthma and other respiratory disorders, skin diseases, low-weight births, blood poisoning, and high mortality rate. Environmental racism is also tied to property devaluation, increases in crime rates, poor quality of surrounding schools, and poor-quality housing. Because risky facilities are located close to neighborhoods, some residents may work at these sites, and thus expose themselves to high occupational hazards.

BOX 8.4

A Toxic Injustice

Chester, Pennsylvania, houses one of the largest collections of waste facilities in the country. It has the seventh-largest garbage-burning incinerator in the nation. In 1995, adjacent to the incinerator, the nation's largest infectious and chemotherapeutic medical waste autoclave operated for over a year. Before it was shut down, the plant brought in massive amounts of medical waste (three times more than produced in the state of Pennsylvania). During its operation, it was not unusual to find discarded waste lying in surrounding areas where children played. Several workers at the plant were accidentally stabbed by needles while handling the waste. Some had mysterious rashes and other medical problems that were difficult to diagnose. Close to the incinerator and plant is the sewage treatment facility that treats 90% of the sewage in Delaware County as well as sewage from local industries such as Conoco Phillips' oil refinery, Sunoco's oil refinery, Kimberly-Clark's paper mill, and various chemical companies. This toxic sewage sludge is burned in a sludge incinerator, releasing many toxic pollutants in the air, including mercury and arsenic. On average, one new company with toxic potential per year has proposed to build a plant in Chester. In early 2008, a newly formed multiracial, multigenerational, countywide student and community coalition organized and fought off a plan for the world's largest tire incinerator.

Chester has the highest infant mortality rate and highest percentage of low-weight births in Pennsylvania, and a mortality rate and lung cancer rate 60% higher than those of Delaware County. Sixty percent of children in Chester had significantly high levels of lead in their blood. Over 80% of Chester residents are people of color. The rate of poverty is 27%, which is more than twice the national average.

SOURCE: Data from Mike Ewall (2008), Energy Justice Network (www.energyjustice.net). For more information on the Chester struggle, see the DelCo Alliance for Environmental Justice Web site at www.ejnet.org/chester.

Attempts to rectify these dangers can be addressed through legal and legislative means. In response to public outcry, the Environmental Protection Agency established the Office of Environmental Justice in 1992 (Environmental Protection Agency [EPA], 2008a). In particular, the Environmental Justice Coordinators Council consists of front-line staff responsible for ensuring policy input, program development, and implementation of strategies through the agency (EPA, 2008b). However, cases of environmental racism can take several years of debate, bureaucracy, and legal maneuvering to clearly establish and receive adequate retribution (if any) for losses incurred. Of the few cases in which damages have been recognized, or plants and other toxic sites shut down, most of the initiative came from grassroots efforts by community residents, advocates, and other concerned citizens. Yet, policy must be transformed to realize a diligent commitment to basic human justice.

Spirituality and Religion. Dealing with health and other stressful difficulties through the use of spirituality or religion has long been cited as common-place across many cultural groups. Several reviews have highlighted the link between religiosity (e.g., attending church; adhering to the beliefs and practices of an organized religion) and spirituality (e.g., a search for meaning and values in life; connectedness with others, nature, or higher force) and positive physical and mental health status and longevity (Mueller, Plevak, & Rummans, 2001). Some consider religion and spirituality to be related though different constructs. *Religion* is often associated with one's group participation in an organized formal adherence to doctrine and denominational requirements of a social institution (P. C. Hill & Pargament, 2003; Simon, Crowther, & Higgerson, 2007). *Spirituality* is commonly used to refer to the personal, subjective meaning or relationship that one has with a higher power that may or may not be related to a religion (Armstrong & Crowther, 2002; P. C. Hill & Pargament, 2003). Although these distinctions may assist researchers in discovering the nuanced importance of various aspects of faith, some argue that there are inherent problems with drawing a line between religion and spirituality. Primarily, these concerns center on the varied social contexts and personal matters that are addressed in both religious and spiritual expression. Moreover, many people often experience and view their spiritual expression as one and the same with their religion or general sense of faith (P. C. Hill & Pargament, 2003).

Social science research on the relationship between religion and/or spirituality and health for ethnic minority populations has been limited and primarily focused on mainstream denominations of Protestant Christianity; less attention has been given to spirituality/religious issues of newer immigrant populations and ethnic minorities in the United States (Hufford, 2005). Yet, there have been some published accounts of cases that emphasize religious considerations in working with diverse cultural groups. As discussed later in this chapter, Anne Fadiman's popular *The Spirit Catches You and You Fall Down: A Hmong Child, Her American Doctors, and the Collision of Two Cultures* (1997) focuses on the tragic medical consequences that can occur in the midst of misunderstanding between an immigrant family's Hmong culture and religion and the doctors' biomedical orientation. Further, reviews and ethnographic studies that describe religious healing traditions such as the Afro-Cuban *santeria* and Mexican *curanderismo* have heightened awareness of the broad diversity of health beliefs and practices that may be utilized within heterogeneous ethnic communities (e.g., Applewhite, 1995; K. V. Holliday, 2008).

The growing research literature on U.S. ethnic minorities suggests a positive relationship between health status and religion/spirituality. For example, religion, prayer, and worship at church are considered dominant features in

African American culture (Chatters, Taylor, & Lincoln, 1999). To explore the role of spirituality and religion in assisting a sample of African American women (N = 18) manage breast cancer diagnosis, treatment, and posttreatment, Simon and her colleagues (2007) conducted a series of qualitative interviews. All the women self-identified as Christian, and, interestingly, each respondent mentioned spirituality/religiosity during the interview before questions were raised concerning this topic. The majority of women indicated that their spirituality and faith were important in supporting them throughout the breast cancer experience in terms of helping them in their reaction to and acceptance of the diagnosis, coping with negative treatment effects, finding meaning in life and desire to live, and finding a reason for their survival. Findings from this and other studies conducted with ethnic minorities suggest that a consideration by health professionals of ways in which they could explore how the patients' commitment toward their spirituality and religion might serve as a means of positive coping in their treatment and recovery from illness could be helpful and empowering to patients. Such an approach exemplifies what is called "culturally competent" health care.

CULTURALLY COMPETENT HEALTH CARE

Given the documented health disparities and multiple factors that can impede or facilitate meeting the health needs of ethnic minorities in the United States, we turn our attention toward **culturally competent health care.** "Cultural competence" in practice is often used interchangeably with related terms such as "cultural sensitivity," "cultural appropriateness," and "cultural awareness." According to J. R. Betancourt, Green, Carrillo, and Ananeh-Firempong II (2003), culturally competent health care is health care that acknowledges and incorporates—at all levels—the importance of culture, assessment of cross-cultural relations, vigilance toward the dynamics that result from cultural differences, expansion of cultural knowledge, and adaptation of services to meet culturally unique needs" (p. 293). Furthermore, this systematic approach to care recognizes that both social factors (e.g., socioeconomic status, education, risky environments, social stressors) and cultural factors are inextricably intertwined and can contribute to health disparities (J. R. Betancourt et al., 2003; Smedley, 2008). In order to approach a basic level of competent care for ethnic minorities, health services must be able to address these multiple factors.

In a comprehensive review that examined sociocultural barriers to health care and culturally competent practice, J. R. Betancourt and his colleagues (2003) identified three levels of health care (organizational, structural, and clinical) at which barriers occur that can lead to health disparities as well as possible targets of intervention.

Barriers to Health Care at the Organizational Level. The first level of barriers to health identified by J. R. Betancourt and his colleagues (2003) is at the level of the health care organization itself. Availability and acceptability of health care is influenced by whether the administrative leadership and the providers reflect the racial/ethnic minorities that they serve. For example, despite ethnic minorities representing roughly 28 to 30% of the population (U.S. Census Bureau, 2002), they represent less than 2% of individuals with senior leadership roles in health care management (R. M. Evans, 1999). Whether administrators design programs that are sensitive toward the needs of minority populations will be contingent on awareness gained through experience (e.g., having a shared cultural background and/or exposure to different ethnic groups) and education. However, if administrators lack experience and their education has been limited in terms of not having diversity of curriculum, training, and faculty mentors, there may be a cultural gap between the delivery of health services and the minorities they serve. Interventions designed to promote greater representation of medical professionals and health care managers (e.g., vigorous recruitment and retention of minority medical students, mentoring of minority candidates for upper-level administrative positions) are necessary.

Barriers to Health Care at the Structural Level. This second level of barriers to health proposed by J. R. Betancourt and colleagues (2003) refers to those conditions that are in place that may impede ethnic minority patients from receiving adequate and appropriate health care. Examples of structural barriers include little or no health insurance coverage, lack of prevention and early detection programs, lack of continuity of health care services, long wait times for clinic visits, difficulty in accessing transportation to and from clinics, lack of translated health assessment and educational materials for non-English-speaking/reading patients, and lack of interpreters to provide assistance in communication between the English-speaking providers and their patients who speak a different language.

Several studies document the importance of ensuring good communication to facilitate accurate understanding, diagnosis, and treatment. Members of diverse cultural groups may conceptualize health, illness, discomfort, and health care practices in different ways. These differences may lead to breakdowns in communication between people from different cultural backgrounds (Angelelli & Geist-Martin, 2005) (see Box 8.5).

Even for patients who have adequate mastery of English, the expression of disease symptoms may differ from majority individuals, which may lead to errors in diagnoses and treatment. Structural interventions are challenging because there are so many possible targets. However, basic to these interventions is a focus on *policy change*. Policy must be influenced on a number of levels including national, federal, and local. Electing officials truly committed to culturally competent health care through appropriate assessment, early detection, prevention, and treatment of ethnic minority populations is critical to transforming health care systemwide.

BOX 8.5

"The Spirit Catches You and You Fall Down"

In Anne Fadiman's (1997) study of a Hmong family, she vividly describes the culture clash that exists between Western medicine and the indigenous, spiritual beliefs of the immigrant family from Laos. This is a true story of the Lee family, who immigrated to Merced, California, in 1980. One year later, their daughter, Lia Lee, is born. Within her first 3 months of life, Lia suffers her first seizure. Initially, the parents consider treating her with a traditional herbal remedy, but the necessary herbs are not accessible in their new country. They also fear the doctors due to traumatic experiences related to their time spent in a refugee camp in Thailand. Finally, though, they end up seeking emergency treatment at the Merced Community Medical Center. Lia is diagnosed by her doctors as having epilepsy; however, her parents call it *quag dab peg* [the spirit catches you and you fall down].

Over the next few years, Lia visits the clinic several times. She is treated with a complex combination of drugs to manage the epileptic seizures. Lia's parents have difficulty following the complicated regimen, plus they believe that the medication is making her worse; consequently, they fail to comply with the doctor's instructions. From the medical point of view, the Lees are seen as negligent and therefore abusive. Eventually, Lia is placed in a foster home to ensure that she is properly treated. Her seizures do not stop. On November 25, 1986, Lia suffers a massive seizure that causes extensive brain damage. She is transported to a pediatric intensive care unit for stabilization. The doctors do not expect Lia to live more than a few days at the most, so they discharge her to her parents. The Lees believe that Lia's soul is lost. Their hope is to help her soul find its way back to her body. They enlist the help of a Hmong shaman to conduct a healing ceremony in their home, a traditional ceremony that involves the sacrifice of a live pig.

The story of Lia transcends a simple language barrier. In this case, the impasse illustrates how culture can shape contrasting worldviews concerning health. The biomedical culture is one that relates the seizure and its effects to the brain's function. Medication that alters physiology through changing brain chemistry will be seen as part of the solution. The Lees' view encompasses their cultural beliefs and spirituality; their understanding of health is tied to their religion that views illness as related to lost souls cured by sacrificial animal shamanism.

Fadiman (1997) makes the case that both the doctors and the parents care about the welfare of Lia, but neither is equipped to handle and understand the contrary nature of the other's culture and manner. Nevertheless, Fadiman acknowledges the importance of medical providers to at least explore the patient's beliefs and seek cultural interpretation (not just language translation) and guidance about how to best address the clash that will inevitably occur with differences.

Clinical Level of Competent Care. At its most intimate level, cultural competence begins with the practitioner's ability to relate to his or her patient in a culturally sensitive manner. Practitioners must be aware of their own attitudes and beliefs (including stereotypes and biases) regarding people of diverse backgrounds. Attitudes and beliefs are shaped by experiences, exposure to other cultures, and the norms of influential individuals and society in general. Culturally competent practitioners are aware that stressful social factors can be possible determinants of health. For example, attempts can be made to understand the patient's experiences dealing with racism and discrimination, poverty, or living in overcrowded or substandard conditions. Learning about patients' stressors as well as strengths and social supports can give a more complete picture of their current health status and potential resources that can assist in patients' recovery.

Additional education may take the form of learning more about culture-specific medical interventions. The term **complementary and alternative medicine (CAM)** is used to describe forms of medical intervention that are considered outside the mainstream of conventional Western medicine (see Box 8.6). Although both "complementary" and "alternative" are used to describe these interventions, the National Center for Complementary and Alternative Medicine (NCCAM) considers the forms of medicine different from each other (NCCAM, 2008). Complementary medicine is used *in combination with* conventional medicine; alternative medicine is used *in place of* conventional medicine (NCCAM, 2008). For example, meditation may be used as a complement with cardiovascular drugs to aid a patient's recovery following bypass surgery. A person may elect to use alternative detoxification procedures (to rid the body of toxic elements) to treat cancer instead of conventional surgery, radiation, or chemotherapy. Interventions considered CAM change over time, as they demonstrate efficacy, safety, and are included in conventional treatment or as new developments to health care emerge. Many therapies originally deemed "alternative" have grown in popularity and have demonstrated efficacy especially when combined with other forms of treatment (e.g., meditation, yoga, acupuncture, and some herbal therapies).

BOX 8.6

Complementary Medicine Modalities

Complementary and alternative medicine (CAM) includes an array of substances, practices, and modes of health care that can be classified into five categories:

1. **Alternative medicine systems** are modalities that have their own complete systems of theory and practice. Many of these systems were developed apart from and earlier than the conventional

(Continued)

(Continued)

medical approach of the United States. Some have developed in both non-Western and Western cultures. Examples:

- Acupuncture (ancient Chinese/Asian practice; non-Western)
- Traditional Chinese medicine
- Ayurveda (ancient Hindu system practiced primarily in India; non-Western)
- Homeopathic medicine (Western)
- Naturopathic medicine (Western)

2. **Mind-body therapies** include techniques designed to improve the mind's ability to affect physical functioning. These include techniques that were originally considered to be "alternative" and now are used quite frequently in conventional medical settings. Examples:

- Patient support groups (mainstream)
- Cognitive-behavioral therapy (mainstream)
- Meditation (CAM)
- Prayer (CAM)
- Yoga (CAM)
- Art, music, or dance (CAM)

3. **Biologically based practices** use substances found in nature, such as herbs, foods, and vitamins. Examples:

- Herbal remedies
- Dietary supplements (may include vitamins, minerals, herbs, enzymes, metabolites; under the Dietary Supplement Health and Education Act of 1994, these supplements are considered foods, not drugs)

4. **Manipulative and body-based practices** focus on manipulation and/or movement of a part or several parts of the body. Examples:

- Chiropractic movement
- Osteopathic movement
- Massage

5. **Energy medicine** includes those techniques that use energy fields thought to exist either around or within the body (e.g., qi gong, Reiki, Therapeutic Touch—"laying-on of hands") or through the use of electromagnetic fields (e.g., pulsed fields, magnetic fields) to maintain health or recover from illness.

SOURCE: Adapted from NCCAM (2008).

CAM use has become increasingly popular among the general population in the United States (Grzywacz et al., 2005). Recent studies reporting the demographic breakdown of "any use" of CAM find that middle-age adults (approximately 40–60 years of age) are the largest group of consumers (Institute of Medicine, 2005). In a large study that used data from the 2002 National Health Survey, Blacks and older adults reported the lowest use of CAM—if prayer is *not* considered; however, when prayer is included as CAM, they have the highest use (Barnes, Powell-Griner, McFann, & Nahin, 2004). In addition, Asian Americans report a higher use of CAM than Whites, but use of CAM is lower among Hispanics than among Whites (Barnes et al., 2004).

Depending on the culture and environmental context, traditional healers may be herbalists, shamans, *curanderos,* medicine men/women, or other types of religious/spiritual therapists. Some may practice in clinics or offices, but others may practice in homes or religious settings such as churches, temples, or sweat lodges. It is important to inquire and discuss patients' use of other medical interventions especially if they are taking supplements or engaging in activities that may be contraindicated with conventional medicine. For example, the use of certain popular herbal supplements such as ginkgo biloba, feverfew, and garlic can enhance circulation but should be avoided by people already taking medicines such as blood thinners (anticoagulants) or people before, during, or after surgery because they can increase bleeding (North American Spine Society, 2006).

Chapter Summary

This chapter provided an overview of some of the major health disparities that exist among ethnic minority groups compared to non-Hispanic Whites. We proposed that rather than focusing solely on biological vulnerabilities or other individual correlates of disease, it is critical to consider multiple determinants of positive or negative health status. Taking a multidimensional approach requires that we target individual factors such as lifestyle (diet, exercise, smoking, substance use), psychological characteristics (stress, social support), and structural factors (accessible and affordable health care, poverty, social and environmental injustices) as priorities for intervention. There must be a concerted level of commitment among medical theorists and providers, policymakers and politicians, as well as concerned individuals and groups to create change in order to achieve parity in health and culturally appropriate services for those in need.

Key Terms

Acute Diseases (page 255)

Biomedical Model (page 255)

Biopsychosocial Model (page 256)

Causal Factors (page 275)

Chronic Diseases (page 255)

Complementary and Alternative
   Medicine (CAM) (page 287)

Culturally Competent Health Care (page 284)

Environmental Injustice (page 281)

Environmental Racism (page 281)

Epidemiology (page 260)

Extreme Poverty (page 278)

Health Disparities (page 261)

Immigrant Health Paradox (page 277)

Incidence (page 261)

Men on the Down Low (page 274)

Mind-Body Dualism (page 255)

Morbidity (page 261)

Mortality (page 261)

Prevalence (page 261)

Psychiatric Epidemiology (page 261)

Risk Factors (page 261)

Selective Migration Hypothesis (page 277)

Social Stress Hypothesis (page 277)

Social-Structural Determinants (page 275)

Type 1 Diabetes (page 272)

Type 2 Diabetes (page 272)

Working Poor (page 278)

Learning by Doing

- Conduct a taste test with your friends of two types of foods that you like to eat—but can be high in calories, saturated fats, or sodium or treated with hormones, preservatives, or other chemicals. See if you can purchase a "healthy" alternative of the food (your local supermarket might offer some alternative/comparable items). You and your friends should taste the foods (regular vs. healthy alternatives) side by side. Note what you like and dislike about each product. Compare your answers with those of your friends. Do the advantages of the healthy alternative outweigh the disadvantages? What are some of the ways that you are defining a "healthy" alternative? Ask your friends how they define a healthy food.

Suggested Further Readings

Berry, J. W., & Sam, D. L. (2007). Cultural and ethnic factors in health. In S. Ayers, A. Baum, C. McManus, S. Newman, K. Wallston, J. Weinman, & R. West (Eds.), *Cambridge handbook of psychology, health, and medicine* (2nd ed., pp. 64–70). Cambridge, UK: Cambridge University Press.

Overview of studies from varied disciplines including cross-cultural health psychology, medical anthropology, and psychiatry that examines how culture informs our understanding of immigrants' and members of ethnic communities' health status and adjustment.

Kato, P. M., & Mann, T. (Eds.). (1996). *Handbook of diversity issues in health psychology.* New York: Plenum.

Health issues are examined across several groups including pediatric, adolescent, and elderly populations, men and women, varied sexual orientations, and African Americans, Asian Americans, Latinos, and Native Americans. Attention is also given to the impact of socioeconomic status and the health of ethnic minority populations.

Kazarian, S., & Evans, D. R. (Eds.). (2001). *Handbook of cultural health psychology.* San Diego: Academic Press.

Handbook takes a global perspective on major health issues affecting cultural groups including cardiovascular/heart disease, cancer, pain, HIV/AIDS, suicide, and health promotion.

LaVeist, T. A. (Ed.). (2002). *Race, ethnicity, and health: A public health reader.* San Francisco: Jossey-Bass.

Reader presents data on disparities in health outcomes and differential treatment provided in health care settings. Historical and political factors that relate to these differences are addressed.

Marmot, M., & Wilkinson, R. G. (Eds.). (2005). *Social determinants of health* (2nd ed.). New York: Oxford University Press.

Text examines social and economic factors that can lead to various health outcomes. It considers that health is dependent on not just individual behavior, but also structural factors (e.g., social, economic, institutional, and policy) and psychosocial environment (e.g., quality of neighborhood, stable workplace).

Note

1. Overweight and obesity are based on body mass index (BMI = weight in kilograms divided by the square of height in meters). For children and adolescents, overweight is defined as at or above the 95th percentile of the sex-specific BMI for age growth charts. For adults, obesity is defined as a BMI greater than 30 and extreme obesity is defined as a BMI greater than 40 (CDC, 2006).

CHAPTER **9**

PSYCHOLOGICAL DISTRESS AND TREATMENT ISSUES

VIGNETTE

"He's alright. He's just funny that way."

Jerome, a 25-year-old African American man, settles into his chair to watch the television. His day at work had not gone well. There were too many customers demanding his attention. Working at

(Continued)

(Continued)

Walmart is not good for the nerves, he concludes. He tries to follow the story line of a television drama, but keeps zoning out. At one point, he absentmindedly brushes his fingertips across his face. He is startled to look down at his wet hand. He brings his hand up to his cheek and notices that it is wet with tears from his eyes. He is crying and he can't figure out what is causing his level of distress.

Suddenly, there is an urgent knocking at his front door. Though he does not want company right now, he can hear his mother, Betty, yelling for him to open the door. Jerome pulls himself up from his seat. He feels heavy—his body feels large and out of shape. Further, a weight seems to press down on his shoulders. He steadies himself and breathes a long sigh. "I am carrying 'the weight of the world,'" he mutters.

"Where have you been?" his mother exclaims. "Huh?" Jerome is confused. "You were supposed to come over for dinner tonight—don't you remember?" Trying as hard as he can to remember, Jerome cannot recall making these plans. He states he had no memory of the dinner date, but his mother is not satisfied. "Something hasn't felt right for the longest time with you . . . you keep forgetting things, you don't seem interested in being around your people . . . you look messed up too . . . actually, you look tired and completely worn out!" Betty barely finishes her sentence when Jerome bursts into tears. He is sobbing uncontrollably. "Son, what's wrong?" For several minutes, Jerome cannot speak or look at Betty. Jerome struggles to understand the painful thoughts that clutter his mind and never seem to disappear—thoughts like: "Why does it seem so hard to get started?" "Maybe things would be better if I weren't around." "I feel so blue; life can't get harder than this." "I can't live like this!"

Finally, Jerome replies, "I'm just so tired and my head hurts." Betty moves closer to her son and makes an attempt to hug him, but Jerome quickly pulls away. "I don't feel good!" "Son, you've got to rest and get Jesus back in your life. Call me in the morning." Jerome mumbles, "Yeah, have a good night." He shuts the door and thinks, "I feel real bad, and my nerves are shot. I need a couple of drinks . . . or maybe more."

Outside of Jerome's apartment, Betty looks down and shakes her head. "He's alright . . . he's alright. He's just funny that way."

In this chapter, we discuss psychological distress as well as the variation in psychological adjustment within ethnic groups. Attention is focused on major, highly prevalent disorders such as depression, anxiety, and substance use problems, and the relationship of ethnicity and culture to their development and course. We also describe what are termed culture-bound syndromes or symptom constellations that are considered unique to particular cultural groups. Additional factors that precipitate or guard against psychological distress—for example, immigration and acculturation, social class, availability of social support, and so on—are examined. Recent guidelines and standards from professional psychological organizations support the perspective that culture influences the social behaviors and mental processes of individuals and the provision of mental health services (American Psychological Association [APA], 2002). This chapter concludes with a review of recommendations for those who are committed to improving their awareness of the relationship of ethnic and cultural issues in the provision of professional activities of assessment, intervention, and prevention.

MENTAL HEALTH AND PSYCHOLOGICAL DISTRESS

A Broader Perspective on Adjustment

Betty states that Jerome is "alright. He's just funny that way." What are the parameters that are used to define psychological distress? How do we distinguish between people who are simply unusual or "funny" and those who are pathologically maladjusted? What needs to be done when people (including family and friends) deny the gravity of symptoms and characteristics that may lead to the conclusion that an individual is mentally ill? The most popular diagnostic system in the United States, the *Diagnostic and Statistical Manual of Mental Disorders, Text Revision (DSM-IV-TR;* American Psychiatric Association, 2000), contains criteria for each specific disorder. Yet, agreement on what constitutes mental distress or illness has been a point of considerable debate, especially when discussed in the context of culture (Comer, 2007; S. R. Lopez & Guarnaccia, 2005; Maddux & Winstead, 2005).

Sensitivity to the influence of culture on adjustment would require the integration of multiple disciplines including anthropology, psychology, and psychiatry in order to appreciate the limits of traditional diagnosis of disorders such as depression, generalized anxiety, and schizophrenia (Kleinman, 1977). In addition, it would be important to recognize how culture can shape one's reaction and possible adaptation to and recovery from mental illness (Kleinman, 1977). As S. R. Lopez and Guarnaccia (2000) note, a cultural perspective requires the integration of the "social world" of the individual, an appreciation of social and environmental factors that can influence the adjustment of people on a daily basis. The incidence and prevalence of disorders will tell only part of the story of mental health in ethnic minority populations; we want to also consider variation in the expression of distress, factors that influence the development of illness, and prevention and intervention that facilitate adjustment.

PREVALENCE OF MAJOR PSYCHOLOGICAL DISORDERS

General Epidemiological Surveys

Psychiatric epidemiology is a specialized area within epidemiology (see Chapter 8). While epidemiological research serves to examine the patterns of medical diseases and disease risks among populations, psychiatric epidemiology is designed to examine patterns of mental illness and characteristics that may place particular groups of people at risk. There are a handful of widely cited national epidemiological studies of psychiatric disorders including the **Epidemiological Catchment Area Study (ECA**; Robins & Regier, 1991), the **National Comorbidity Survey (NCS**; Kessler et al., 1994), and the **NCS Replication Study (NCS-R**; Kessler, Chiu, Demler, & Walters, 2005; Kessler & Merikangas, 2004). The earlier studies were based on disorders and criteria identified in the *DSM-III-R* (e.g., Kessler et al., 1994; Robins & Regier, 1991), whereas the more recent ones used criteria based on the *DSM-IV* (e.g., Kessler et al., 2005). In the NCS and NCS-R, face-to-face interviews were conducted using the World Mental Health version of the Composite International Diagnostic Interview (CIDI), a structured clinical interview designed to assess several of the major mental health disorders (Kessler et al., 1994; Kessler et al., 2005).

Overall, the studies of the general U.S. population indicate that the prevalence of psychiatric disorders is high and the age of onset of these disorders tends to be young (e.g., Kessler et al., 2005). Roughly 30 to 50% of Americans are likely to be diagnosed with a *DSM-IV* disorder at some point in their life (Kessler et al., 2005). Furthermore, according to respondents' answers to questions about their early development, it appears that the first symptoms of these disorders are likely to occur during childhood or adolescence (Kessler et al., 2005).

Although it might seem like a large portion of the U.S. population is at risk, it should be noted that major mental illnesses are pervasive. For example, schizophrenia, bipolar disorder, depression, and panic disorder are found throughout the world among all racial and ethnic groups (Department of Health and Human Services [DHHS], 1999). Furthermore, a worldwide report of research on mental health and behavioral problems found that mental illness weighed heavily on the health, well-being, and abilities of peoples from different countries—especially low-income countries—even more so than some of the major acute (e.g., tuberculosis) or chronic (e.g., cardiovascular disease and cancer) diseases (Desjarlais, Eisenberg, Good, & Kleinman, 1996).

As noted in Chapter 8, large-scale epidemiological studies tend to compare the prevalence rates of illnesses for ethnic groups to those rates for White

European Americans. Despite the critical limitations of such an approach, these gross comparisons consistently yield findings that indicate ethnic minorities are generally overrepresented in the rates of diseases and high mortality. However, the diversity within and across minority groups, as illustrated by differences in educational attainment, income, social mobility, and other indicators of social status, can lead to mixed findings in regard to mental health status. For example, both earlier and more recent epidemiological studies indicate the prevalence of certain mental disorders for ethnic minorities living in the United States is similar to (or for some mental disorders lower than) that of European Americans (Breslau et al., 2005; DHHS, 1999; Kessler et al., 1994). However, most of these studies exclusively rely on data gathered from persons living within households—most fail to include those who are homeless or living in treatment centers, shelters, detention centers, jails, or hospitals (DHHS, 1999). Members of certain ethnic minority groups are more likely to be homeless, incarcerated, and have children placed in foster care (DHHS, 2001). The vulnerability of these "high-need" groups to psychological disorders is striking. The rate of psychological distress is significantly higher in these groups than in the general population (DHHS, 1999; Foulks, 2004a).

Hence, the rates of mental health disorders may be suppressed in community surveys that do not include members from these at-risk populations. Lastly, studies that report lower than expected lifetime prevalence rates of mental disorders among ethnic minorities have also found that the course of (or persistence of) their illnesses may be more severe among minorities than Whites (e.g., Breslau et al., 2005).

Surveys Specific to Ethnic Minority Communities

It is important to note that in the recent NCS-R, interviews were conducted with only English speakers (Kessler et al., 2005). The reason that this was done was that similar surveys were being coordinated with nationally representative samples of Latinos (with measures available in Spanish or English, depending upon the respondent's preference) and Asian Americans (with measures available in a number of Asian languages [Mandarin, Cantonese, Tagalog, and Vietnamese] or English, depending upon the respondent's preference) for the **National Latino and Asian American Study (NLAAS;** Pennell et al., 2004). In addition to the NLAAS and the NCS-R, the **National Survey of American Life (NSAL;** J. S. Jackson et al., 2004) is a national survey of household residents in the Black population and included 3,570 African Americans and 1,621 Blacks of Caribbean descent. Together, these three surveys are known as the **Collaborative Psychiatric Epidemiology Surveys (CPES;** Neighbors et al., 2007).

American Indians present significant challenges in terms of the traditional national surveys. Given the great cultural and linguistic diversity among the more than 300 federally recognized tribes plus 200 Alaska Native groups, assessing their mental health is difficult. Moreover, American Indians have not been included in sufficient numbers in many national surveys to allow strong estimates of prevalence and incidence of several disorders, yet several smaller-scale studies suggest high rates of disorders, especially alcohol-related and trauma-related disorders (Beals et al., 2005). The **American Indian Service Utilization, Psychiatric Epidemiology, Risk and Protective Factors Project (AI-SUPERPFP)** is a rare large-scale survey of 3,084 Southwest and Northern Plains Indians from two tribal groups living near or on home reservations. Tribal members between the ages of 15 and 54 years old were randomly sampled to determine the prevalence of common *DSM-IV* disorders and help-seeking patterns (Beals et al., 2005).

Data obtained through surveys that include a sizable representation of ethnic minorities represent some of our best knowledge regarding the current epidemiology of mental disorders among ethnic minorities in the United States. In addition, attention is given to disaggregate groups in terms of ethnicity and culture (e.g., Chinese, Filipino, Vietnamese; Puerto Rican, Mexican, Cuban; Northern Plains Indians and Southwest Indians; or African American and Black Caribbean). Immigration and other cultural variables are included in these studies such as **nativity** (U.S. born or foreign born), years of residence in the United States, language proficiency, age at the time of migration, and generational status. This information is invaluable in gaining insight into multiple variables that may influence the development and prevention of psychological distress and helping improve the cultural appropriateness of services. Findings from the ECA and NCS were critical in setting the national agenda regarding mental health care and planning, and it is the hope that these newer surveys of ethnic minority communities will help to highlight their pressing mental health needs.

Major Disorders in Ethnic Minority Populations

Although it is beyond the scope of this text to provide a comprehensive examination of the broad array of disorders that may exist within a given population, to get a general picture of psychological distress, we can look at a sample of common disorders (e.g., depression, anxiety, and substance use disorders) in terms of their impact on ethnic minorities.

Major Depression. Major depression has been examined in a number of epidemiological studies. According to the *DSM-IV-TR* (American Psychiatric Association, 2000), the primary symptoms of major depression include depressed mood, an inability to experience pleasure from activities that normally bring enjoyment for at least the past two weeks, plus at least four other psychological symptoms (e.g., feelings of hopelessness, worthlessness, guilt, or suicidal thoughts) and physiological symptoms (e.g., sleep disturbance, appetite changes, attention/concentration difficulties, fatigue). Generally, most experts concur that major depression is one of the most common, costly, and disabling of mental disorders on a global level (Compton, Conway, Stinson, & Grant, 2006; Grant et al., 2004). Major depressive disorder held the highest **lifetime prevalence** (i.e., the total number/percentage of individuals in a population who have experienced a particular disorder at some point in their life) of the specific disorders reported in the NCS-R (Kessler et al., 2005). Gender differences are documented for this disorder with lifetime prevalence of 15% for men compared to 35% for women (Kessler et al., 1994). Comparative analyses of data from two large cross-sectional studies indicated that prevalence rates of depression have increased over the past five decades (Compton et al., 2006). This increase was especially significant for Whites, Blacks, and Hispanics. Although a significant increase in prevalence was noted for Hispanics overall, Hispanic men and young Hispanic women (between the ages of 18 and 29) did not demonstrate a significant increase compared to other groups.

In a national sample of approximately 67,500 persons, among adults age 18 or older, the past-year prevalence of major depressive episode was highest among individuals reporting two or more races (10.1%), followed by American Indians or Alaska Natives (9.4%), Whites (7.6%), Hispanics (7.0%), Blacks (6.5%), and lowest for Asian Americans (3.6%) (Substance Abuse and Mental Health Services Administration, 2006) (see Figure 9.1). These findings support our earlier discussion in Chapter 5 on the complex relationship between individuals of multiple-race identity and adjustment. Further attention must be focused on multiracial individuals to deepen our understanding of the individual, group, and social factors that may be related to a greater percentage reporting major depression. Looking at the lower level of reported cases, one could initially conclude that the occurrence of major depression in Asian Americans is relatively low. However, in the National Survey on Drug Use and Health (as reported by the Substance Abuse and Mental Health Services Administration, 2006), Asian Americans are not disaggregated into different subgroups (e.g., Vietnamese, Chinese, Japanese Americans); thus, it is difficult to discern how rates of depression might vary between them. For the relatively few studies that actually do examine group-specific rates of depression, the findings can be quite surprising; Southeast Asian refugees, for instance, show rates of depression that are significantly higher than that of the general U.S. population (Abueg & Chun, 1996), underscoring the need for more sophisticated prevalence data on the mental health of Asian Americans.

Figure 9.1   Major Depressive Episode (MDE) in the Past Year Among Adults Age 18 or Older, by Race/Ethnicity, 2004–2005

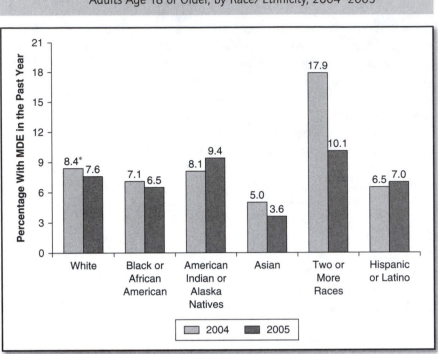

SOURCE: SAMHSA (2006).

NOTE: Due to low precision, estimates for Native Hawai'ians or Other Pacific Islanders are not shown.

*The difference between the 2004 estimate and the 2005 estimate is statistically significant at the .05 level.

In a recent study on racial and ethnic disparities in depression treatment (Alegría et al., 2008), the authors analyzed CPES data from a nationally representative sample of 8,762 persons. They found significant differences exist in the access to and quality of care for depression in ethnic and racial minority populations. Compared to non-Latino Whites, ethnic minority groups were less likely to receive access to any depression treatment even after controlling for the effects of socioeconomic variables such as poverty, insurance coverage, and education. Specifically, for individuals with depressive disorder, 40.2% of non-Latino Whites failed to access any mental health treatment, compared to 63.7% of Latinos, 68.7% of Asian Americans, and 58.8% of African Americans. Alegría and her colleagues (2008) proposed several factors as possible explanations for these access problems, including the significant under-detection of depression among less-acculturated patients and other minority groups (e.g., Rehm et al., 1999), concerns about loss of income that may occur while undergoing treatment, or the stigma that accompanies mental illness (e.g., Schraufnagel, Wagner, Miranda, Peter, & Roy-Byrne, 2006). In addition, Alegría et al. (2008) found that even when treatment was obtained, most people received inadequate care, especially African Americans and Asian Americans in the sample. Overall, Latinos, Asian Americans, and African Americans with depression were 9 to 23 percentage points less likely to receive care and adequate treatment for their depression compared to non-Latino Whites.

Anxiety Disorders. There are several different disorders that constitute the class of anxiety disorders in the *DSM-IV-TR.* These include panic disorder, agoraphobia, social phobia, specific phobia, obsessive-compulsive disorder, posttraumatic stress disorder (PTSD), and generalized anxiety disorder (American Psychiatric Association, 2000). Although the disorders have their own distinctive characteristics, most share in common the presence of excessive worrying, nervousness or fear, and persistent uncomfortable psychological and physical symptoms of stress or arousal. Moreover, these symptoms produce significant impairment in the person's life. Kessler and his colleagues (2005) reported that anxiety disorders were the most prevalent of all classes of disorders in their national survey with lifetime prevalence of 28.8% compared to 20.8% for mood disorders and 24.8% for substance use disorders.

Studies on anxiety disorders in Asian American and American Indian populations have been limited compared to those that have examined depression (e.g., C. B. Gee, 2004; Safren et al., 2000). However, some compelling findings have emerged when specific groups within these minority populations are evaluated. For instance, previous studies on Asian Americans have focused on acculturative stress associated with the experiences of recent immigrants and refugees (Iwamasa, 1997; J. Lee, Lei, & Sue, 2001). These individuals are particularly susceptible to increased anxiety as they adjust to a new cultural environment in the United States. Southeast Asian refugees are especially at risk for PTSD, in addition to depression, due to their experiences of multiple traumas and stressors spanning four different time periods (Abueg & Chun, 1996).

First, Southeast Asian refugees were exposed to "pre-migration traumas" or traumas in their home countries during the Vietnam War era. Such traumas centered around experiences of death and destruction from combat and civil discord, including witnessing the killings of close family members, being separated from their families, losing personal property, and facing political persecution by the government. For instance, former members of the South Vietnamese military were forcibly imprisoned in "reeducation camps" where they faced starvation, hard labor, and torture because of their wartime activities with American troops (Chun, Akutsu, & Abueg, 1994). Also, Cambodians faced mass genocide from 1975 to 1979, losing approximately a third of their entire national population under the oppressive rule of Pol Pot and the Khmer Rouge (Kinzie et al., 1990).

Upon fleeing their countries, Southeast Asian refugees then had to cope with "migration traumas" or traumas incurred during their exodus from their home countries. Such traumas included escaping while being shot at and pursued by the military, fleeing on crowded and unsafe boats, and enduring attacks by pirates who preyed on refugees in the open seas. The large wave of Vietnamese refugees who escaped war-torn Vietnam in the late 1970s and early 1980s, known as the Vietnamese "boat people" in the popular media, suffered greatly from migration-related traumas, with an estimated 200,000 dying at sea (E. Lee & Lu, 1989).

Next, Southeast Asian refugees endured "encampment traumas and stressors" or traumas and stressors associated with living in unsafe and unsanitary refugee camps scattered throughout Southeast and East Asia. Refugees applied for entry to countries around the globe while being detained in these camps, often waiting for several months before they knew their fate. Living conditions in the worst camps were highly stressful and dangerous with refugees being subjected to overcrowding, robbery, rape, and assault (Mollica, 1994).

Finally, Southeast Asian refugees faced "post-migration stressors" or stressors associated with adjusting to a new cultural environment. As noted throughout this text, these types of stressors are typically classified as "acculturative stressors" and can include pressures to learn a new language and new cultural norms, and any other difficulties in establishing a new life in an unfamiliar country.

As you might expect, the cumulative effects of these four types of traumas and stressors have contributed to some of the highest rates of anxiety disorders and other mental health problems observed for any ethnic minority group. For instance, reported percentages of Southeast Asian psychiatric patients who are diagnosed with PTSD are in excess of 80 to 90%, particularly for the most-traumatized refugee groups like the Hmong and Mien (Abueg & Chun, 1996).

Another Asian American group in which problems of anxiety have been noted is college students. J. Lee et al. (2001) highlighted a number of studies that span over two decades in which findings suggest heightened anxiety symptoms as well as loneliness, isolation, and social interaction difficulties among Asian American students compared to White American students.

In the AI-SUPERPFP (Beals et al., 2005), the most prevalent disorder for American Indian women was posttraumatic stress disorder while alcohol abuse and dependence were the most common disorders for men. For women in the Southwest tribe, anxiety disorders were more prevalent than either substance use disorders or depressive disorders. However, for Northern Plains women, rates of anxiety and substance use disorders were comparable, and rates of both types of disorders were higher than depressive disorders. The authors noted how the historical impact of disease and conflict coupled with the documented high rate of accidents and other frequent traumas within American Indian communities may lead to a greater vulnerability to a re-experiencing of painful and stressful life events through the expression of PTSD symptoms (Beals et al., 2005).

Recent attention has also been focused on greater risk of PTSD in Hispanic Americans (Pole, Best, Metzler, & Marmar, 2005). For instance, six months after exposure to Hurricane Andrew, Spanish-speaking Latinos had a significantly higher prevalence rate of PTSD than African Americans and Whites in a sample of South Florida residents (Perilla, Norris, & Lavizzo, 2002). Similarly, analyses of surveys conducted following the terrorist attacks of September 11, 2001, indicated that 14% of Hispanic American residents of New York developed PTSD, compared to 9% of African American and 7% of White residents (Galea et al., 2002). In addition to heightened risk of development of PTSD, greater severity of symptoms has been reported among Hispanics who are diagnosed with PTSD. For example, Hispanic veterans with PTSD reported, on average, more severe symptoms than veterans of other ethnic groups (Rosenheck & Fontana, 1996), and surveys revealed elevated PTSD symptoms among Hispanic police officers compared to non-Hispanic Whites and African American police officers (Pole et al., 2005).

Explanations for susceptibility to PTSD in Hispanics have included the possible higher presence of dissociative symptoms (i.e., symptoms of an altered state of conscious awareness) as an initial reaction to trauma in Latin American cultures—and dissociation is one of the strongest predictors for later onset of PTSD (Escobar, 1995; Ozer, Best, Lipsey, & Weiss, 2003; Pole et al., 2005). Another explanation offered is that Hispanics who maintain a closer adherence to their cultures of origin may tend to view trauma as an inevitable and unchangeable consequence of life (Perilla et al., 2002). Pole et al. (2005) suspected that such fatalistic beliefs could potentially impact posttraumatic coping, and this in turn would lead to less effective means of coping among less-acculturated Hispanics and heighten the group's sensitivity to PTSD.

As noted earlier, African Americans were found to have generally comparable rates of mental disorders to Whites in the large-scale ECA study when socioeconomic and other demographic factors are controlled (Robins & Regier, 1991). However, among individual anxiety disorders, Zhang and Snowden (1999) found that African Americans were more likely to suffer from phobic disorders than Whites. Others have reported higher rates of panic disorder (Neal & Turner, 1991) and somatization disorder (multiple physical symptoms with unknown physical causes that are felt to be related to stressors) in African American communities than in other communities (Robins & Regier, 1991; Zhang & Snowden, 1999). Furthermore, findings from descriptive studies have suggested the experience and expression of anxiety symptoms in African Americans are significantly influenced by culture and adaptation in highly stressed environments (Heurtin-Roberts, Snowden, & Miller, 1997).

Substance Use Disorders. The term "substance" is used in the *DSM-IV-TR* to refer to a variety of drugs that can alter our physical and mental functioning including prescribed or over-the-counter medications, illegal drugs, alcohol, tobacco, caffeine, nicotine, and inhalants (American Psychiatric Association, 2000). Substance use disorders primarily refer to two broad classes of disorders, those that are distinguished by substance abuse and those that are characterized by substance dependence. *Substance abuse* is considered a maladaptive pattern of behavior in which individuals rely on a drug excessively and persistently to the point that it negatively impacts their personal relationships, occupation, or welfare or the lives of others (Comer, 2007). *Substance dependence* (also known as *addiction*) is a more advanced pattern that includes the abuse of the drug as well as physical changes in the body's response to the drug. Two physical indicators of dependence are *tolerance* (where a person needs more and more of the substance to achieve the desired effect) and *withdrawal* (the experience of uncomfortable and even dangerous symptoms when the person tries to either completely discontinue the drug or reduce the amount of drug intake) (Comer, 2007).

In 2005, among individuals 12 years of age and older, the highest rate of substance abuse or substance dependence was among American Indians or Alaska Natives (21.0%) (Substance Abuse and Mental Health Services Administration, 2006). The lowest rate of dependence or abuse was among Asians (4.5%), whereas comparable rates were reported by Native Hawai'ians or Other Pacific Islanders (11.0%), individuals reporting two or more races (10.9%), Whites (9.4%), Hispanics (9.3%), and Blacks (8.5%) (Substance Abuse and Mental Health Services Administration, 2006). The elevated rate in American Indians/Alaska Natives relative to other groups is consistent with earlier studies that indicated high rates of substance use problems in American Indian communities—especially alcohol dependence in men (e.g., Kinzie et al., 1992; Kunitz et al., 1999).

Beals et al. (2005) examined sex differences in prevalence rates of substance use disorders in American Indians. Although substance use disorders were significantly more prevalent than either anxiety or depressive disorders in men, as noted above, anxiety disorders were either more prevalent or comparable to substance use disorders in women.

Dual Diagnosis. In order to deal with his painful feelings of distress, Jerome (in our opening vignette) states that he needs "a couple of drinks . . . or maybe more." If his drinking alcohol to cope with mental anguish becomes routine, excessive, and disruptive, one could question whether Jerome is actually dealing with the problems of abuse and addiction in combination with his poor mood state. When patients are determined to be suffering from more than one disorder, they are said to have **comorbid (co-occurring) disorders.** Comorbidity among psychiatric disorders appears to be high. For example, in the NCS, 56% of the respondents with a history of at least one disorder had two or more disorders (Kessler et al., 1994). In the NCS-R, 27.7% of respondents had two or more disorders in their lifetime and 17.3% had three or more (Kessler et al., 2005). In the fields of psychiatry and psychology, the term **dual diagnosis** is commonly used when describing a person who has a mental disorder and a substance-related disorder (as well as the term **"mentally ill and chemical abuser"** or **MICA**). This is because of the well-documented association between mental and substance use disorders. For example, in a national survey of adults, substance use disorders were significantly more common among individuals with mental health problems (e.g., depression, anxiety) than among individuals without these problems: Close to half of the respondents with a substance use disorder had mental health problems compared with approximately a quarter of all adults (K. M. Harris & Edlund, 2005). Moreover, serious mental illness was more than three times higher among adults who had a substance use disorder (K. M. Harris & Edlund, 2005).

It is estimated that 21.3% (5.2 million) of adults with serious psychological distress were dependent on or abused substances in 2005 (Substance Abuse and Mental Health Services Administration, 2006). These cases present as some of the most challenging and difficult cases to manage. Among the estimated cases, less than half (47.0%) received treatment for either their mental health disorder or substance use disorder while far fewer (8.5%) received assistance for both mental and substance use disorders. When treatment is provided, it is more than likely for mental health problems rather than substance use problems (Substance Abuse and Mental Health Services Administration, 2006).

Generally, dually diagnosed cases tend to have a poorer prognosis due to the multiplicative effects of symptoms from more than one disorder, as well as related psychosocial factors that can impair treatment effectiveness. Many of these factors are present in the high-risk groups discussed earlier in the chapter such as poverty, homelessness, acting-out behavior, likelihood of criminal history, and problems in social interactions (Bartels et al., 1993).

It is difficult to determine the actual number of ethnic minorities who have a dual diagnosis. It is often challenging to adequately tap into these cases in large-scale surveys. However, findings from the AI-SUPERPFP indicated significant levels of comorbidity among those American Indians with depressive and/or anxiety and substance use disorders (Beals et al., 2005). In clinical settings, it is not unusual for dually diagnosed persons to hide their drug abuse problem or for clinicians to fail to detect the symptoms and as a result under-diagnose this group. Patients may feel compelled to suppress their level of substance abuse due to pragmatic financial reasons in addition to the psychosocial ones. Many treatment agencies receive financial support to treat either mental disorders or substance abuse—only some are equipped and willing to treat both (Sciacca & Thompson, 1996). As such, it is not atypical for the MICA patient to be rejected as inappropriate for treatment in both substance abuse and mental health facilities—these are the people most likely to "fall through the cracks" and they deteriorate even further and lose whatever tenuous stability they might have had.

CULTURE-BOUND SYNDROMES—THEIR MANIFESTATIONS

Most of the studies reviewed in this chapter have primarily focused on Western expressions of psychological distress and symptoms of major disorders commonly recognized in the United States and in most parts of the world. Although it is necessary to have comparable descriptors of illness across groups in order to compare rates of disorder, there is the concern that we may underestimate rates of mental distress among members of ethnic groups who may express problems in culturally unique ways that are not commonly seen or fully understood by many psychologists and other mental health service providers who are trained in the United States.

The need for increased attention on culture's influence on psychopathology was recognized in the development of the *DSM-IV*. S. R. Lopez and Guarnaccia (2000) describe the efforts of a National Institute of Mental Health–funded task force charged with developing recommendations for how to incorporate a "cultural perspective" throughout the manual. Three primary contributions were published in the *DSM-IV*:

a. the inclusion of how cultural factors can influence the expression, assessment, and prevalence of specific disorders;

b. an outline of a cultural formulation of clinical diagnosis to complement the multiaxial assessment; and

c. a glossary of relevant cultural-bound syndromes from around the world. (S. R. Lopez & Guarnaccia, 2000, p. 576)

Although many felt that the *DSM-IV* made some advancement in its recognition of cultural influences on mental health compared to previous editions, some criticism was offered that additional task force recommendations were not addressed and that cultural issues continue to be peripheral in terms of their limited discussion throughout the text and the placement of a relatively brief formulation and list of culture-bound syndromes in an appendix (S. R. Lopez & Guarnaccia, 2000). Still, the inclusion of culture-bound syndromes has generated some research on these disorders and encouraged clinicians to consider the importance of acculturation and emic cultural expressions of psychological distress (Marín et al., 2003).

Culture-bound syndromes refer to recurrent patterns of unusual behavior and distressing experiences that are typically exhibited in certain areas of the world (American Psychiatric Association, 2000). Although a syndrome may be limited to a certain geographic location or cultural group, it is still considered to be problematic and may be known by a specific name by those who are likely to suffer from it. What is important to know about these disorders is that many consider their origin, manifestation, and response to social/therapeutic interventions to be heavily influenced by cultural factors within specific, localized societies or cultural groups—hence the term "culture bound" (American Psychiatric Association, 2000). The *DSM-IV-TR* includes several examples of culture-bound syndromes, but as noted above, these disorders are described within an appendix dedicated to cultural formulation of cases when using the manual (see Box 9.1 for examples).

BOX 9.1

Examples of Culture-Bound Syndromes

Ataque de nervios

An idiom of distress principally reported among Latinos from the Caribbean but recognized among many Latin American and Latin Mediterranean groups. Commonly reported symptoms include uncontrollable shouting, attacks of crying, trembling, heat in the chest rising into the head, and verbal or physical aggression. Dissociative experiences, seizure-like or fainting episodes, and suicidal gestures are prominent in some attacks but absent in others. A general feature of an *ataque de nervios* is a sense of being out of control.... (p. 899)

(Continued)

(Continued)

Falling-out or blacking out

These episodes occur primarily in southern United States and Caribbean groups. They are characterized by a sudden collapse, which sometimes occurs without warning but sometimes is preceded by feelings of dizziness or "swimming" in the head. The individual's eyes are usually open but the person claims an inability to see. The person usually hears and understands what is occurring around him or her but feels powerless to move. This may correspond to a diagnosis of Conversion Disorder or a Dissociative Disorder. (p. 900)

Ghost sickness

A preoccupation with death and the deceased (sometimes associated with witchcraft) frequently observed among members of many American Indian tribes. Various symptoms can be attributed to ghost sickness, including bad dreams, weakness, feelings of danger, loss of appetite, fainting, dizziness, fear, anxiety, hallucinations, loss of consciousness, confusion, feelings of futility, and a sense of suffocation. (p. 900)

Mal de ojo

A concept widely found in Mediterranean cultures and elsewhere in the world. *Mal de ojo* is a Spanish phrase translated into English as "evil eye." Children are especially at risk. Symptoms include fitful sleep, crying without apparent cause, diarrhea, vomiting, and fever in a child or infant. Sometimes adults (especially females) have the condition. (p. 901)

Qi-gong psychotic reaction

A term describing an acute, time-limited episode characterized by dissociative, paranoid, or other psychotic or nonpsychotic symptoms that may occur after participation in the Chinese folk health-enhancing practice of *qi-gong* [exercise of vital energy]. Especially vulnerable are individuals who become overly involved in the practice. This diagnosis is included in the *Chinese Classification of Mental Disorders,* Second Edition (CCMD-2). (p. 902)

Shin-byung

A Korean folk label for a syndrome in which initial phases are characterized by anxiety and somatic complaints (general weakness, dizziness, fear, anorexia, insomnia, gastrointestinal problems), with subsequent dissociation and possession by ancestral spirits. (p. 902)

Spell

A trance state in which individuals "communicate" with deceased relatives or with spirits. At times this state is associated with brief periods of personality change. This culture-specific syndrome is seen among African Americans and European Americans from the southern United States. Spells are not considered to be medical events in the folk tradition but may be misconstrued as psychotic episodes in clinical settings. (p. 903)

SOURCE: Excerpts from the *DSM-IV-TR* (American Psychiatric Association, 2000).

Scientific study on culture-bound syndromes has been limited. For many years, social scientists such as Yap (1974) and Guarnaccia and Rogler (1999) argued that limited research in this area is problematic given the significant number of immigrants who live in the United States. Clinicians are compelled to know what the latest research suggests in order to make accurate and appropriate diagnoses and to develop useful interventions for these disorders. Moreover, the *Diagnostic and Statistical Manual of Mental Disorders* has become increasingly popular internationally. Continuing efforts to increase our understanding of expressions of distress at a cross-cultural level will sustain the utility and significance of the *DSM* within the United States and abroad (Guarnaccia & Rogler, 1999).

An essential research question is: What is the relationship of culture-bound syndromes to the *DSM-IV* disorders? Guarnaccia and Rogler (1999) propose a systematic program of research that attempts to address the nature of a syndrome and its relationship to psychiatric disorders. The first step would require investigation of the nature of the phenomenon in terms of its distinguishing characteristics. Extensive review of the literature for studies of a particular syndrome is necessary. One should not assume, however, that if a disorder appears within the literature, this provides confirmation of its existence. It would be important to also tap into the familiarity and knowledge of a syndrome within a culture, that is, investigate whether members of a particular group recognize (or have experienced) a specific syndrome. This recognition is what is termed "salience of a phenomenon" (Guarnaccia & Rogler, 1999). Investigation through thorough descriptive studies conducted with members of the culture can further document the nature of the characteristics/symptoms or even subtypes that constitute the disorder.

As noted earlier, culture-bound syndromes are thought to reflect the social and cultural characteristics of the people most likely to be afflicted. As such, research should be designed to illuminate these social and cultural features so that clinicians may know who is at greatest risk (Guarnaccia & Rogler, 1999). The study of these cultural aspects of psychopathology should continue to inspire mental health professionals to go beyond merely describing "rare" and "exotic" cultural syndromes, and instead to seriously consider culture's profound influence on a broad range of disorders, including those that are well known, so that they can provide culturally competent care (W.-S. Tseng, 2006).

SERVICE UTILIZATION

Underutilization of services is a noted problem in the broad national surveys. Kessler and colleagues (1994), for example, reported that less than 40% of individuals with a reported disorder during their lifetime had ever received professional treatment, and only 20% with a recent disorder had received treatment during the past 12 months. While barriers may exist to some degree for many people living in the United States, there are added obstacles that are specific and more extreme in ethnic minority populations such as immigration and acculturation factors, limited economic resources, possible bias and mistrust of mental health professionals, communication barriers, and limited culturally acceptable (or appropriate) treatment interventions.

Selected Factors Influencing Effective Delivery of Mental Health Services

Immigration and Acculturation Factors. A methodological limitation of many of the national epidemiological studies is the reliance on proxy variables (e.g., nativity, increasing years of U.S. residency, language spoken, generation of respondent) to approximate acculturation status. Although not ideal for an in-depth understanding of acculturation as a complex multidimensional process (Marín et al., 2003), these variables do shed light on the importance of cultural and immigration factors in predicting utilization and satisfaction with help received.

Findings regarding utilization are complicated for certain groups. For example, early studies on Asian Americans indicated an underutilization of mental health services (Leong, 1986; Uba, 1994). Yet, in a recent study, Barreto and Segal (2005) concluded that Asian Americans' utilization is much more complex due to significant diversity among the different Asian American subgroups. Based on client and service records in the California Department of Mental Health, East Asians (Chinese, Japanese, and Koreans) used more services than Southeast Asians (Cambodians, Laotians, and Vietnamese), Filipinos, and other Asian groups (Asian Indians, Guamians, Hawai'ian Natives, Samoans, and others) (Barreto & Segal, 2005). In addition, the highest number of patients with a diagnosis of schizophrenia was in the East Asian group, which is consistent with other reports that indicate that Asian Americans may eventually use psychiatric services when their symptoms reach a certain point of significant severity (S. Sue et al., 1998). Nevertheless, the finding of greater utilization among East Asians was still significant even when diagnosis was taken into account (Barreto & Segal, 2005). Although Barreto and Segal (2005) did not directly assess the impact of acculturation on utilization, they noted that the Asian American subgroups that demonstrated the highest level of underutilization are members of populations that are historically more recent in their arrivals to the United States. Furthermore, they speculated that educational achievement is related to service utilization in that the groups with lower levels of attainment (e.g., Southeast Asians) are less likely to use mental health services than those higher in attainment (e.g., East Asians and Filipinos).

A similar pattern of findings was noted in the NLAAS (Abe-Kim et al., 2007), where use of mental health–related services was examined during a 12-month period. In a study of 2,095 Asian American adults (Chinese, Filipino, and Vietnamese participants were targeted, but the sample included individuals of other Asian ancestry), respondents were questioned about their service use and satisfaction with care. They were also assessed for the presence of any psychiatric disorder during the 12-month period according to the *DSM-IV* criteria. Abe-Kim and her colleagues (2007) reported that Asian Americans appeared to have lower rates of seeking service compared to the general population; 8.6% of Asian Americans sought service while 17.9% of the general population sought service according to data from the NCS-R (P. Wang, Lane, Olfson, Pincus, & Kessler, 2005). Differences in service utilization were noted between U.S.-born Asian Americans and immigrant individuals—those born in the United States used mental health services at a higher rate than those who emigrated from abroad (Abe-Kim et al., 2007). Furthermore, generational differences were noted with third generation respondents being more similar in their service use to the general population while second generation respondents were more similar to immigrants. Perception of helpfulness of care was also influenced by immigration status: Higher ratings were given by U.S.-born Asian Americans than by immigrants.

Alegría and colleagues (2007) studied the patterns of recent mental health service use among Latinos living in the United States, along with their perceptions of satisfaction with help received. Using data from the NLAAS, four Latino groups—Cuban, Puerto Rican, Mexican, and "other Latino"—were distinguished. Findings indicated overall mental health service use and specialty mental health services (e.g., professional mental health service providers seen in mental health clinics) were significantly higher in Puerto Ricans than all other Latino groups, with close to 1 in 5 Puerto Ricans (19.9%) reporting past-year services compared to 1 in 10 Mexicans (10.1%). Foreign-born Latinos and those who primarily spoke Spanish reported less use of specialty mental health services than U.S.-born Latinos and those who primarily spoke English, but there were no significant differences in the use of general medical services (e.g., general practitioners, family doctors, or nurses) for mental health problems. In addition, those who had lived in the United States for less than 10 years had significantly lower service use compared to those who had lived in the country for 21 years or more. Mexicans reported lower satisfaction with mental health services than those in the "other Latino" group. Immigrants who had lived in the United States for 5 years or less reported lower levels of satisfaction with services than those who had lived in the United States for more than 20 years. Overall, results indicated that cultural factors such as nativity, language, and years of residence in the United States related to mental health service utilization among Latinos. However, another factor—the presence of past-year psychiatric diagnoses—was also important in determining service. These findings only held up when respondents did not meet the criteria for any psychiatric disorders assessed. Puerto Ricans and U.S.-born Latinos still reported higher rates of mental health services than other Latino subgroups and foreign-born Latinos. Alegría et al. (2007) noted that cultural and immigration factors are especially important to consider for those Latinos who require preventative/screening services or who are symptomatic but do not yet fulfill criteria to warrant a psychiatric diagnosis.

Studies on the role of immigration status or nativity have typically examined Asian or Latino groups. However, as Miranda and her colleagues (Miranda, Siddique, Belin, & Kohn-Wood, 2004) noted, the Black population of the United States is becoming increasingly diverse. The percentage of foreign-born Blacks in the overall Black population increased from 1.3 to 7.8% between 1970 and 2000 with most of the immigrants coming from countries in the Caribbean and Africa (Population Reference Bureau, 2002). Miranda et al. (2004) compared the prevalence rates of depression, somatization (physical complaints/ailments), alcohol use, and drug use in a large sample of low-income women who were born in the United States, the Caribbean, or Africa. Results of analyses from data gathered in screening interviews indicated that U.S.-born Black women were 2.94 times more likely to experience depression than the African-born women and 2.49 times more likely than the Caribbean-born women. Rates of somatization were comparable across all three groups of women. Reported alcohol and drug problems were very low among all groups, with only 1% of the women reporting drug or alcohol problems. Similarly, data from the NSAL indicated that increasing years of U.S. residency was associated with increased risk for psychiatric disorders: Black Caribbean immigrants had lower rates of mental disorders than U.S.-born Black Caribbeans, and Caribbean Black women had lower 12-month and lifetime prevalence rates for anxiety and substance disorders than African American women (D. R. Williams et al., 2007). Even among Caribbean Blacks, first generation Blacks had lower rates of psychiatric disorders compared to U.S.-born Caribbean Blacks. Further, higher-generational status was significantly associated with increased risk for disorder. Overall, these results are consistent with studies that compare other U.S.-born ethnic groups (e.g., Mexican Americans, Asian Americans) with their foreign-born counterparts (e.g., Mexican immigrants, Asian immigrants)—the longer one lives in the United States may relate to an increased need for mental health services.

Despite this risk, further analyses of the NSAL data do not confirm that utilization matches need. Jackson and colleagues (2007) reported that African Americans and Caribbean Blacks used formal mental health care services at relatively low rates. In addition, other researchers have noted the tendency of ethnic minorities (e.g., Blacks and Asian Americans) to access mental health services when symptoms become so severe that they warrant urgent or crisis intervention (S. Sue et al., 1998). Because symptoms of mental illness may occur early in one's life, the ability to access preventative care as well as therapeutic care is critical to long-term prognosis.

Limited Economic Resources. Financial costs of mental health services can serve as a major deterrent to health care. Similar to physical health access barriers discussed in Chapter 8, ethnic minorities are often plagued by being uninsured—especially the working poor who may not qualify for public assistance but do not earn adequate mental health coverage through benefits. In 2001, the report from the Surgeon General stated that Hispanic Americans are the least likely group to have health insurance (public or private) with a rate of uninsurance at 37%, a rate twice that for Whites (DHHS, 2001).

Lack of adequate health insurance is related to lack of treatment for the major disorders reviewed earlier including depression (Harman, Edlund, & Fortney, 2004). However, Snowden and Thomas (2000) suggested that the relationship between poverty and mental health treatment, especially in mental health specialty clinics, is not as clear-cut as assumed. They noted that many poor individuals are able to access care through Medicaid, which provides significant financial support to poor individuals in need of mental health care. In their study, data from a representative sample indicated no significant differences in likelihood of receiving outpatient treatment between African Americans on Medicaid and Whites, but insured African Americans were significantly less likely to receive care (Snowden & Thomas, 2000). This finding suggests that those in the lowest income bracket may be prompted (most likely by serious illnesses) to obtain treatment within public service institutions that must provide treatment to underserved populations (although there is still the question of quality treatment afforded to those who are poor). Yet, those who are just outside eligibility for services (e.g., the "working poor") may end up with very poor service utilization. Complicating matters, logistical or practical barriers associated with poverty, such as working extended hours and lack of child care and transportation, further prevent many impoverished ethnic minority families from utilizing essential mental health services (Chun & Akutsu, 1999).

Clinician Bias and Client Mistrust. Clinician bias plays a significant role in patient diagnosis and treatment. If a person is misdiagnosed, then treatment will likely fail and the patient may be at risk for problems becoming worse as a result of delayed or inappropriate treatment. A number of studies have consistently found evidence that certain groups are less likely to receive appropriate diagnoses. For example, African Americans are more likely to receive diagnoses that are more severe, in terms of level and duration of illness (e.g., schizophrenia), than diagnoses that may be less severe or episodic in nature (e.g., mood disorder) (S. R. López, 1989; Snowden & Cheung, 1990). In one study, African American inpatients were approximately 1.5 times as likely as Whites to be diagnosed with schizophrenia compared to being only 0.60 times as likely to be diagnosed with a mood disorder; for outpatients, the racial discrepancy was less pronounced for patients with mood disorders but was greater for those with schizophrenia (Lawson, Hepler, Holladay, & Cuffel, 1994).

Other studies have found that European Americans and Asians are more likely to receive a mood disorder diagnosis than African Americans or Hispanics and that Asians and African Americans receive psychotic disorder diagnoses more frequently than European Americans (Foulks, 2004b). In a recent study on diagnosis and race, Schwartz and Feisthamel (in press; cited in Feisthamel & Schwartz, 2006) reported that counselors were more likely to diagnose schizophrenia and childhood disorders (e.g., attention deficit hyperactivity disorder, conduct disorder) in African Americans than European Americans.

Whaley (2004) proposed two distinct categories of diagnostic bias: (1) **clinician bias,** defined as the failure to adhere to the diagnostic criteria during psychiatric evaluations, and (2) **cultural bias,** defined as actual ethnic/racial differences in the expression of symptoms being unnoticed or misconstrued by diagnosticians. The achievement of a valid diagnosis requires that both biases be addressed—that is, adherence to diagnostic criteria is necessary, but attention must also be given to the cultural context in which ethnic minority behavior and emotions are expressed. Cultural bias has been offered, in part, as an explanation to the disproportionate diagnosis of certain disorders in particular ethnic groups (Feisthamel & Schwartz, 2006). Moreover, cultural bias may influence patients' perceptions of the quality of general medical care received and cultural competence of their providers (Johnson, Saha, Arbelaez, Beach, & Cooper, 2004) and raise suspicion and lack of trust toward their clinicians (Whaley, 2004).

Language Barriers. It is estimated that close to 47 million people—approximately 18% of the U.S. population—speak a language other than English at home, and in some states with a large immigrant/migrant population, that percentage increases (e.g., 40% in California, 31% in Texas, and more than 23% in Arizona, Hawai'i, Nevada, New Jersey, and New York) (data from the National Law Program as cited by Sturgeon, 2005). Although less than 11 million speak English "not well" or "not at all," many experts predict that there will be a growing number of U.S. individuals that will be significantly limited in their English proficiency (or limited English proficiency [LEP] persons) (Sturgeon, 2005).

The ability of mental health and general health care providers to communicate with and effectively treat these patients is challenging on both legal and professional grounds. In accordance with **Title VI of the 1964 Civil Rights Act,** providers receiving federal financial assistance are required to ensure the availability of appropriate and meaningful access to services even if patients have limited proficiency in English (DHHS, 2000).

Nonetheless, many LEP or non-English speakers have restricted access to either ethnically or linguistically similar providers (DHHS, 2001; Snowden, Masland, & Guerrero, 2007). These individuals typically struggle to enter, continue, and demonstrate gains in treatment (Snowden et al., 2007). In addition, they tend to require culturally adapted treatment procedures more so than clients who speak English more fluently and are higher in acculturation (S. Sue, Fujino, Hu, Takeuchi, & Zane, 1991).

Although efforts are made to hire bilingual and bicultural providers, treatment facilities will often rely on interpreters to assist in assessment and aspects of intervention. At best, formal interpreters can offer ready and critical assistance to achieve good and sound service to an increasingly diverse patient population. However, there are difficulties inherent with this strategy. Given the diversity of languages and limited number of bilingual staff, some agencies may resort to using informal interpreters (e.g., family members, nonclinical personnel) to provide translation on the spot. Iwamasa and Pai (2003) note how the use of the client's child or grandchild as translator can be in direct opposition to cultural roles assigned to family members and may even violate roles (e.g., a child placed in the position of questioning an elder may be perceived as challenging the elder's ascribed wisdom, respect, and authority). Even using formal interpreters may reduce the exposure and weaken the therapeutic bond between providers and clients, decrease patient confidentiality, lead to misunderstandings due to selective editing of translation, and increase inaccuracy in the *meaning* of what is being said (even if the actual words are accurate) (Sturgeon, 2005). Despite these challenges, research suggests that in order to provide a minimum level of culturally appropriate intervention, the ability of the therapist/provider to communicate with clients is essential (S. Sue, Zane, Hall, & Berger, 2009).

Cultural Acceptability Barriers. Acceptability barriers focus on cultural ways that individuals and groups cope with various stressors or are encouraged or discouraged from using mental health services. There are several ways in which culture can influence the awareness of mental distress and reactions toward formal mental health care. For example, certain groups such as Asian Americans and Latinos are more likely to express psychiatric distress through somatic or physical symptoms or **cultural idioms of distress,** cultural patterns that typically characterize maladjustment to stressors. For example, *ataque de nervios* is a cultural idiom of distress for Latino immigrants (Cortes, 2003). These types of culturally distinct expressions are intimately tied to a culture's views and beliefs about the causes of different psychological disorders. Ying (1990) found that first generation Chinese immigrant women might believe that depression is caused by both somatic and psychological factors, which might explain why some Chinese Americans express their distress through bodily symptoms. It might also explain why some Chinese Americans may be more inclined to initially seek medical assistance from a physician rather than a mental health professional to resolve their distress. Second, as noted in Chapter 6, problems may be viewed as more appropriately handled within the confines of the family rather than by outsiders. Only when symptoms become severe or acute—or the family is clearly overburdened by the stress and upheaval created by the mental disturbance—will an individual be referred into professional care (Pescosolido, Gardner, & Lubell, 1998). Third, some ethnic minorities may feel less inclined to seek services due to mistrust of health care professionals and lack of confidence that providers will be culturally sensitive to their concerns and experiences (Echeverry, 1997; Sanders Thompson, Bazile, & Akbar, 2004; Whaley, 2001).

Cultural influence is also expressed through attitudes like social stigma toward mental illness that many feel continue to be prominent in the United States. Threats to a person's ability to maintain his or her job, privacy, and social standing can be heightened when faced with the possibility of being ostracized for mental distress. Research indicates that Asian Americans may be reluctant to pursue mental health services because it can lead to a "loss of face," or feelings of shame and guilt if they are perceived as being unable to perform important social roles and responsibilities (Zane & Mak, 2003).

There is a tremendous need for more empirical investigation of cultural stigma surrounding mental illness because of its potential effects on acknowledging illness, help seeking, and medication adherence (Corrigan, 2004).

In a recent study by Anglin, Link, and Phelan (2006), a nationally representative sample of African Americans and Caucasian adults responded to telephone interviews that included vignettes focused on a hypothetical person with a mental illness. Respondents were questioned about their attitudes, beliefs, and opinions about the person. Findings indicated that African Americans were more likely than Caucasians to believe that mentally ill persons were likely to be violent, but they were also more likely to believe that the mentally ill should be given more leniencies in regard to punishment related to violence. We can also consider gender factors that highlight potential ways in which men are socialized to believe that "illness" is akin to being weak as opposed to the idealization of being strong. Some researchers suggest for certain groups there is an expectation that "life is hard," so feeling blue, hopeless, or anxious at times is natural given one's life circumstances (e.g., Sanders Thompson et al., 2004).

Another factor that influences acceptability is whether the person is aware that help is needed or necessary. For instance, Anglin and her colleagues (Anglin, Alberti, Link, & Phelan, 2008) examined different reactions to mental health care between a nationally representative sample of White and African American participants. Respondents were given a vignette centered on people living with mental illness. They were then questioned about whether professional mental health providers could provide assistance that would be helpful. They were also asked whether mental health assistance was necessary. Results suggested that although African Americans were more likely than Whites to believe that mental health professionals could treat individuals with disorders such as schizophrenia and major depression, African Americans were also more likely to believe that mental health problems could heal on their own. According to these authors, a positive belief in treatment effectiveness may not be sufficient to increase service utilization among groups (e.g., African Americans) who may not believe that treatment is necessary (Anglin et al., 2008).

PRACTICAL AND ETHICAL GUIDELINES FOR CULTURALLY SENSITIVE PRACTICE

As noted throughout this textbook, when addressing psychological problems (whether they are well-known psychiatric disorders or culture-bound syndromes), it will be important to approach culture beyond a simple focus on ethnoracial matters to include, for example, age, gender, sexual orientation, language, social class, religion, and disability issues. Given the changing demographics of the U.S. population, psychologists and other mental health professionals are increasingly expected to be aware of and relate to inherent cultural differences that may exist among diverse recipients of their services.

S. Sue et al. (2009) state that there are three levels in which cultural competence can be analyzed: (1) the service provider and treatment level, (2) the agency or institutional level (e.g., the planned delivery of services of a clinic, the hiring of diverse personnel, the availability of effective programs for diverse clientele), and (3) the system level (e.g., the broader institutions of care that are available in a community such as proximate health care clinics and organizations and related community agencies, schools, churches). Most attention has been given to this first level of analysis, examining the provider or clinician and the appropriateness and effectiveness of the treatment employed.

There are several models and definitions of culturally sensitive practice (Hall, Iwamasa, & Smith, 2003). Many include characteristics of culturally competent practitioners and basic components of effective care that promote cultural awareness. Some of the more recent definitions of culturally competent care describe it as a "system" that values the importance of culture in psychotherapy and includes assessment methods and interventions that are designed to address the unique dynamics that occur in the process of cross-cultural therapy and the needs of diverse clients (Whaley & Davis, 2007).

One of the most popular descriptions of culturally sensitive practice is presented in the American Psychological Association's *Guidelines on Multicultural Education, Training, Research, Practice, and Organizational Change for Psychologists* (2003). Emphasis is placed on the ideal characteristics mental health providers should aspire to possess in order to demonstrate cultural competence in the delivery of services. Drawing upon the framework initially presented by D. W. Sue, Ivey, and Pedersen (1996), the guidelines delineate three general areas in the conceptual scheme for cultural competence: cultural awareness and beliefs, cultural knowledge, and cultural skills.

1. *Being culturally aware of personal attitudes, values, and biases.* Cultural awareness involves mental health professionals' awareness of their attitudes and beliefs that can influence personal perceptions of clients who are different from themselves. These beliefs include stereotyping members of diverse cultural groups. Values and biases can also impact the provider's identification and conceptualization of the client's problem and the therapeutic relationship. Awareness of biases, both positive and negative, must be acknowledged and examined (APA, 2003; S. Sue et al., 2009).

2. *Seek cultural knowledge.* Mental health professionals are encouraged to seek education regarding different cultural groups (APA, 2003). Psychologists may increase contact with members of different cultural groups and participate in culturally varied activities in order to build trust in and appreciation for diversity. Interpersonal learning through contact with cultural groups may also illuminate cultural differences that exist among groups as well as the rich diversity within groups. The guidelines also note the need for institutions that effectively and broadly infuse multiculturalism into training curricula, services, and program evaluation.

3. *Develop culturally competent skills.* The third component of culturally competent care highlights that this process involves the acquisition of skills. Becoming proficient in these skills requires proper educational training, supervision, consultation, and experience (Whaley & Davis, 2007). These skills include the professional activities of assessment and intervention specifically geared toward a culturally diverse practice.

Pre-assessment and Pre-therapy Intervention. Considering the lower rates of therapy and high premature drop-out treatment rates for ethnic minorities, some psychologists have recommended instituting orientations for clients unfamiliar with the psychotherapeutic intervention (e.g., Acosta, Yamamoto, & Evans, 1982; S. Sue, 2006). Orientations need not be long; what is important is that the orientation be intentional in its purpose to demystify therapy and the client's and practitioner's roles in the process of treatment. At the beginning of therapy, clients can be nervous about the nature of therapy and what it means about them to be obtaining therapy. Therapists can explain what is expected of the client and what the client can expect of the therapist throughout the course of treatment. Encouraging the client to be active and engaged in treatment is important. The first few sessions should help clients prepare for the more active components of therapy. Preparation sessions tend to focus on developing rapport between therapist and client, educating the client about common symptoms of distress, and conducting a thorough assessment of the client's symptoms. Because individuals from culturally different populations may be less familiar with psychological testing than those from the mainstream, an explanation of assessment procedures may be necessary to reduce clients' discomfort regarding testing.

Assessment. Psychological assessment is conducted in a manner that is sensitive to the client's culture. S. Sue (2006) notes that cultural competency that requires certain personal characteristics can enhance this process. One of these characteristics is **scientific mindedness** (the ability to formulate hypotheses rather than hasty conclusions about the nature of the client and his or her problems). Assessment requires this sort of thoughtfulness, to consider alternative ideas and test assumptions based on sound measures and data in order to reach reliable and valid conclusions. In addition, S. Sue (2006) notes that culture-specific expertise regarding different ethnic groups (e.g., knowledge regarding their history of oppression, immigration experience, general belief systems and values) will complement specific strategies and skills.

As highlighted in Box 9.2, assessment is multidimensional in its targets of inquiry through **A**wareness of cultural similarities and differences, **E**xploration of psychosocial stressors, **I**nformation gathering, **O**bservation, and **U**tilization of culturally appropriate measures (AEIOU). A primary aspect of assessment is the *awareness* of the commonalities and the considerable diversity that exist within ethnic populations. Searching for commonalities and/or generalities can often lead to concerns about potentially stereotyping individuals on the basis of their membership in a certain group. S. Sue (2006) refers to a characteristic called **dynamic sizing** in which competent providers have an ability to know when to generalize regarding certain groups and when to individualize their knowledge. Dynamic sizing requires flexibility on the part of the clinician to value the determinants of culture without stereotyping or being overly inclusive of individuals. For example, knowing that Asian Americans may tend to be more collectivistic than individualistic in orientation compared to Whites can be a culturally sound description or it can run the risk of being an overgeneralization or stereotype. According to S. Sue (2006), those skilled in dynamic sizing avoid stereotyping individuals while still appreciating the cultural values, beliefs, or practices of a group. The provider needs to consider multiple individual factors (e.g., acculturation, gender, socioeconomic level) that can facilitate general knowledge regarding these groups.

BOX 9.2

Assessment From a Cultural Context Perspective (AEIOU)

Awareness of within-group differences

- o Consideration of acculturative influences
- o Consideration of SES differences

Exploration of sociocultural stresses

- o Acculturative stress
- o Experiences with discrimination/racism (note relationship to current psychological distress)

Information gathered includes

- o Personal and familial immigration and/or migration history
- o Language ability
- o Social supports
- o Community resources
- o Employment skills and job history
- o Cultural identity(ies)

Observation targets

- o Examination of engagement with the client
- o Awareness and interpretation of nonverbal cues

Utilization of culturally sensitive assessment strategies

- o Provision of bilingual services
- o Use of assessment instruments with demonstrated reliability and validity with specific ethnic populations
- o Explanation of assessment procedures for individuals less familiar with psychological testing
- o Translation of measures including documents of informed consent.

  Note: Language should be at a level that is understood by the client.

Assessment also entails the *exploration* of sociocultural stressors that can lead to poor adjustment in minority populations. In particular, the psychological and physical consequences of acculturative stress have been documented for various groups. For example, Louis Anderson (1991) noted that sources of stress that play a role in the vulnerability of Black Americans are often acculturative in nature. These sources include threats to African-centered or Afrocentric values of present-time orientation, spirituality, group centeredness, and oral expression. These acculturative stressors can require positive adaptation and adequate problem solving or else they produce stressful outcomes in the form of physical disorders and mental distress.

The collection of *information* in order to understand the client's current circumstances, history, and cultural influences is central to the assessment process. Data gathered can include information regarding the client's personal and familial immigration and/or migration history, language ability, social supports, community resources, employment skills and job history, and cultural identity(ies) (APA, 2003; S. Sue, 2006).

A basic aspect of assessment is *observation*. In face-to-face situations, observation is one of the first things that occurs in our engagement with each other and it can be conducted within several different settings. The opportunity to evaluate the client in the home, school, or work setting can be advantageous to capture a more naturalistic picture of the client's life. As a method of assessment, the provider will be examining the appearance and behavior of the client, and the ease or difficulty of establishing rapport. Especially in cross-cultural situations, nonverbal cues require sensitivity and interpretation on the provider's part.

In assessing clinical or research populations, professionals are encouraged to *utilize* assessment instruments whose validity and reliability have been established for members of the population tested (APA, 2002). If validity or reliability has not been established for a particular population, psychologists may use instruments and describe the strengths and limitations of test results, interpretation, and generalizability. In addition, certain established measures may be adapted for use with specific ethnic groups. Strategies utilized in the AI-SUPERPFP serve as examples of how measures can be modified to provide culturally competent assessment. Because the study was part of a larger collaborative research survey program (CPES), researchers were required to use the NCS's University of Michigan Composite International Diagnostic Interview (CIDI), but it was tailored for use in American Indian communities (Beals et al., 2002). Focus group interviews were conducted with tribal community members and service providers to help inform the adaptation of the CIDI to the study sample. This led to the elimination of certain items that required more in-depth questioning than a survey interview would permit. For example, concerns were voiced about possible confusion distinguishing between psychotic hallucinations and visions that may be encouraged and sanctioned by certain American Indian cultures, so certain standard questions about psychotic symptoms were dropped. In addition, questions about help-seeking extended beyond mainstream services to include traditional healers that might be utilized by members of the reservation communities such as medicine men and spiritual leaders (Beals et al., 2005).

Nontraditional Interventions. The historical roots of many popular well-established psychotherapies are embedded in European theories (e.g., psychodynamic) and early- to mid-20th century North American theories (e.g., behavioral and cognitive-behavioral) that were not necessarily developed with ethnic minority persons in mind. The possibility of modifying interventions to include more attention to multiculturally sensitive strategies is warranted given this past. Although clinicians may appropriately want to go the route of employing nontraditional interventions, care must be taken to receive appropriate consultation before doing so because such interventions could possibly lead to negative legal consequences, for example, being accused of facilitating unlicensed practice (California Psychological Association, 2004).

Several modified, culturally adapted interventions have appeared in the research literature over the past two decades. Examples include interventions centered on African American girls (Belgrave, 2002) and adults (Longshore & Grills, 2000), American Indians and Alaska Natives (De Coteau, Anderson, & Hope, 2006), Asian American youth and families (Zane, Aoki, Ho, Huang, & Jang, 1998), and Hispanic families (Santisteban, Suarez-Morales, Robbins, & Szapocznik, 2006). Culturally adapted interventions can involve the integration of rituals (e.g., sweat lodges, unity circles), prayer, cultural folklore or sayings, traditional values, and traditional foods (see S. Sue et al., 2009, for a review of culturally adapted intervention studies).

Humility in Practice. As a learning process, cultural awareness requires adherence to sound principles that guide practice, but also ongoing education and discoveries of the importance of culture in human behavior across a broad array of groups and individuals. Recognizing the limits of one's competence and obtaining appropriate training, study (e.g., reading of theoretical and applied culture-centered literature), consultation, and supervision are needed to enrich knowledge, skills, and sensitivity to cultural issues.

Evidence-Based Treatment. The need for efficacious treatment leads to another recommendation that has become increasingly popular. This is the idea of **evidence-based treatment,** care that adheres to guidelines that have been tested through rigorous empirical investigation. Indeed, in a supplemental report of the Surgeon General (DHHS, 1999) providers were strongly encouraged to implement effective treatment based on evidence-based guidelines to improve overall quality of care for minorities. In a recent review, Miranda and colleagues (2005) noted that outcome studies of interventions are evaluated in terms of efficacy and effectiveness. Efficacy studies are typically *randomized controlled trials,* designed to determine which particular components of treatment are critical to either predicted positive or negative outcomes. These are rigorous studies that require strict controls over the different treatment groups and conditions so that researchers can be confident in their interpretation of findings. Effectiveness studies may occur in actual community settings (e.g., homes, schools, churches) and may not have the rigor or control of efficacy research studies, but findings can usually be generalized to a broader array of groups or populations (Miranda et al., 2005; S. Sue et al., 2009). To date, there have been only a few published evidence-based treatment studies that have examined the efficacy of treatment for ethnic minority populations. However, recent findings have suggested that evidence-based treatments are promising in terms of their effectiveness with ethnic minority children and adults for a wide array of problems including major mental disorders and family problems (Miranda et al., 2005). It is hoped that further attention will be given to this type of intervention research, to determine the best practices for a diversity of people and issues.

Chapter Summary

This chapter presented a broad overview of psychological distress among the four major ethnic groups. We are only just beginning to get a clearer picture of the prevalence and incidence of mental disorders for groups that have often been under-researched in general population epidemiological studies. These data are invaluable for illuminating the vulnerabilities (risk factors) and strengths (protective factors) of ethnic minority groups and their relation to the development and prevention of mental illness. Further documentation and research of culture-bound syndromes will assist in defining and identifying the various expressions of distress and highlight the role of culture in the manifestation of disorders, including the major mental disorders. Finally, with continued attention to empirical outcome studies devoted to the integration of cultural factors and overall culturally competent care, we will begin to guide and shape treatment that is truly effective and worthwhile in producing healthy adjustment in individuals.

Key Terms

American Indian Service Utilization, Psychiatric Epidemiology, Risk and Protective Factors Project (AI-SUPERPFP) (page 298)

Clinician Bias (page 314)

Collaborative Psychiatric Epidemiology Surveys (CPES) (page 297)

Comorbid (Co-occurring) Disorders (page 305)

Cultural Bias (page 314)

Cultural Idioms of Distress (page 316)

Culture-Bound Syndromes (page 307)

Dual Diagnosis (page 305)

Dynamic Sizing (page 320)

Epidemiological Catchment Area Study (ECA) (page 296)

Evidence-Based Treatment (page 323)

Lifetime Prevalence (page 299)

Mentally Ill and Chemical Abuser (MICA) (page 305)

National Comorbidity Survey (NCS) (page 296)

National Latino and Asian American Study (NLAAS) (page 297)

National Survey of American Life (NSAL) (page 297)

Nativity (page 298)

NCS Replication Study (NCS-R) (page 296)

Psychiatric Epidemiology (page 296)

Scientific Mindedness (page 319)

Title VI of the 1964 Civil Rights Act (page 315)

Learning by Doing

- Generate a list of what you believe are popular yet distinct ways for expressing psychological distress within your culture. Ask at least two friends from different cultural backgrounds than your own to also develop lists of the common ways of expressing distress in their respective cultures. Compare the lists. Identify similarities and differences. How does culture shape the expressions of distress that differ among the lists? Does culture still exert an influence on the similar expressions? If yes, what role does it play in these expressions?

Suggested Further Readings

American Psychological Association. (2003). Guidelines on multicultural education, training, research, practice, and organizational change for psychologists. *American Psychologist, 58*(5), 377–402.

Provides guidelines adopted by the American Psychological Association to assist in improving cultural competence in multicultural education, training, research, and clinical and organizational settings of psychologists and related mental health professionals.

Sue, S., & Zane, N. (2006). Ethnic minority populations have been neglected by evidence-based practices. In J. C. Norcross, L. E. Beutler, & R. F. Levant (Eds.), *Evidence-based practices in mental health: Debate and dialogue on the fundamental questions* (pp. 338–345). Washington, DC: American Psychological Association.

Presents the challenges in applying evidence-based practices with ethnic minority populations.

Sue, S., Zane, N., Hall, G. C. N., & Berger, L. K. (2009). The case for cultural competence in psychotherapeutic interventions. *Annual Review of Psychology, 60,* 525–548.

Presents a review of different conceptualizations of cultural competency, arguments for and against cultural competency, examples of cultural competence in practice, and current guidelines for its use. Also includes discussion of empirical research that examines the efficacy of cultural competence interventions and newer evidence-based research studies.

Trinh, N. H., Rho, Y., Lu, F., & Sanders, K. M. (Eds.). (2009). *Handbook of mental health and acculturation in Asian American families*. Totowa, NJ: Humana Press.

The acculturation process and the mental health needs of Asian American individuals and their families are examined. Attention is given to the identification of common psychosocial stressors and strengths and resiliency of families. Recommendations for fostering adept clinical insights, assessment strategies, and interventions are provided.

Tseng, W.-S. (2006). From peculiar psychiatric disorders through culture-bound syndromes to culture-related syndromes. *Transcultural Psychiatry, 43*(4), 554–576.

Article provides a comprehensive historical overview of the development of concepts about exotic psychiatric disorders to more recent developments in the identification and classification of culture-bound syndromes. Argument is presented for including unique culture-related syndromes in the established psychiatric classification system and promoting the impact of culture on virtually every psychiatric disorder.

CHAPTER 10

AN EPILOGUE ON THE FUTURE OF ETHNIC PSYCHOLOGY

At this point, you have reached the final passages of this book and have learned a series of important facts about the psychology of ethnic minority groups in the United States. We hope you have gained an appreciation for the development and contributions of this field of study and the challenges that still remain in understanding the influence of culture and ethnicity and other identity dimensions on psychological functioning. Before we conclude, we would like to take this opportunity to highlight three select areas that deserve further attention on the part of researchers and practitioners, and issues that you might choose to address as part of your future studies or work in the field of ethnic psychology. The first area involves a burgeoning area of research commonly called **community-based participatory research (CBPR)** or **participatory action research (PAR).** CBPR is *an approach* to conducting research. In this type of research, scientists work in collaboration with community partners (e.g., community agency staff, residents and leaders, medical or mental health patients, homeless shelter residents—those people affected by the research question[s] and findings) (Israel, Eng, Schultz, & Parker, 2005; McIntyre, 2008) to promote the health and well-being of a community. The second area is a more recent trend that focuses on individuals' strengths and potential to overcome problems and/or reach positive outcomes such as love, happiness, and achievement. Termed **positive psychology** by its proponents, this is an area that is well suited for further investigation among minority populations, especially when one considers the topic of resilience— the ability to overcome seemingly insurmountable obstacles and in some cases even flourish. Finally, we conclude by addressing the political context within which ethnic psychology exists. What are the political implications as psychologists and other social scientists become increasingly adept at identifying and addressing the needs of a multiethnic, global society?

COMMUNITY-BASED PARTICIPATORY RESEARCH (CBPR)

One of the hallmarks of CBPR is the collaboration between researchers and community partners throughout all stages of a study—the identification of the study question, formulation of the research design, the implementation of methods and data collection, data analysis, and dissemination of findings. Hence, for the researcher, the focus is not on conducting research *on* community members, but instead the focus is on conducting research *with* them (Israel et al., 2005; McIntyre, 2008). The importance of this basic CBPR tenet becomes all the more apparent when considering that ethnic minority communities are often wary of research given their historical experiences of discrimination and prejudice in society, past negative experiences with research, or unfamiliarity with empirical investigations. Much of their fear and trepidation about research, however, can be allayed by including them as equal partners in a shared CBPR endeavor with the explicit aim of serving their community. Other key principles of CBPR also have special significance for ethnic minority psychology research. According to Israel et al. (2005), CBPR

- *builds on existing community strengths and resources.* A CBPR study can identify and expand cultural support networks and resources to enhance an ethnic minority community's ability to safeguard and promote the health of its members. For instance, CBPR investigators may help different community organizations and agencies (e.g., neighborhood churches and temples, community health clinics, schools, social service agencies) strengthen or expand their collaborative relationships, particularly if they share common goals and overlapping interests in certain community health issues.

- *integrates knowledge and intervention for the mutual benefit of all partners.* CBPR research is not only concerned with making contributions to our general body of knowledge or scholarship for health and social issues; it is also committed to ensuring that study findings are translated and made meaningful to those in the community for their benefit. CBPR researchers are thus expected to work with all partners to best determine how study findings can inform public policy and culturally appropriate interventions that benefit the community-at-large.

- *promotes a cooperative process of mutual learning and empowerment that addresses social inequalities or disparities.* Both researchers and community partners learn from each other and share their knowledge with one another in an egalitarian working relationship. Researchers learn about the cultural beliefs, norms, worldviews, or "local theories" of an ethnic community from their community partners, while community partners learn more about scientific inquiry from researchers. This mutual learning process helps to "ground" the study methods and findings in the cultural beliefs and life perspectives of an ethnic community, and it allows community members to develop new research skills and knowledge—all of which can help to address a community's health and social concerns.

- *disseminates findings and knowledge to all partners.* Researchers are expected to discuss the study data with community partners and to solicit their feedback prior to publishing or presenting study findings. In addition, community partners are duly acknowledged on all study publications and, in some instances, are enlisted as coauthors. The entire CBPR team also makes a concerted effort to publicize their study findings in the ethnic languages and media of the community to ensure that it reaches their target audience. A key idea behind this principle is "joint ownership" of the study data by all research partners.

- *focuses on long-term commitments and sustainable relationships among partners.* Many CBPR interventions striving to promote health and well-being in a community require sustained and joint efforts over extended periods of time before their benefits or anticipated effects can be fully realized. Therefore, CBPR is based on the understanding that researchers will not simply leave the community once they have gathered their data, but will remain a supportive and committed partner with the community until their mutually established goals are fulfilled. This requires all partners to develop permanent and stable relationships and communication channels for sustained collaboration and support once research funding has ended.

All three of the authors of this textbook have conducted CBPR with ethnic minority communities to develop culturally appropriate health interventions. For instance, Kevin Chun and his University of California at San Francisco colleague Catherine Chesla received a four-year CBPR grant from the National Institutes of Health for their Chinese Family Diabetes Project. A major aim of this project is to develop the first empirically supported type 2 diabetes management intervention for Chinese American immigrants. These researchers and their university research staff are working closely with two community partners in San Francisco's Chinatown, Cameron House and Northeast Medical Services, both of which are highly respected in the Chinese American immigrant community with long-standing records of community service. Together, these researchers and community partners are striving to integrate local theories or knowledge from Chinese American immigrants in adapting and testing a cognitive-behavioral intervention for type 2 diabetes management. Specifically, community agency staff share their insights and expertise on Chinese cultural norms, beliefs, and values, which informs the content and application of this intervention protocol. In addition, the university researchers help community agency staff develop new research skills, general diabetes knowledge, and cognitive-behavioral intervention techniques that can be used well beyond the duration of this study. To further ensure that the study is grounded in the cultural worldviews and daily lives of Chinese American immigrants, this CBPR study also enlists local Chinese American community leaders, health professionals, and immigrant community members to serve on a community advisory board, which provides important guidance and feedback on research methods. All partners in this CBPR project are jointly developing culturally appropriate strategies to promote the study in the local Chinese American immigrant community, and to disseminate the study findings once they have been established. Current strategies for promotion and dissemination include working with local Chinese-language media, including Cantonese and Mandarin television and radio outlets and newspapers that reach a wide audience of monolingual Chinese-language immigrant households. Through this partnership between academia and the community, the CBPR team hopes to strengthen their collaborative relationships and, most important, to improve the health and well-being of this traditionally underserved Asian American population.

POSITIVE PSYCHOLOGY AND THE ROLE OF RESILIENCE

As a field within psychology, ethnic psychology is committed to the study of various ethnic groups within the larger framework of understanding human behavior and adjustment. However, psychology is a field that has undergone its own transformations since its earliest beginnings. As Seligman and Csikszentmihalyi (2000) noted, prior to World War II, psychologists and analysts such as Terman, Watson, and Jung studied mental illness, but they also focused on the importance of humans' potential to lead satisfying and productive lives and noted the need to identify individual talents, skills, and assets. However, a significant shift occurred after 1945 in terms of psychology's emphasis on diagnosis and treatment of pathology and the growing demand for assessment. Hence, more attention was given to the medical/disease model in the field. The embrace of diagnostic systems (e.g., the *DSM*) and mental measurements (e.g., intelligence tests, personality tests) became the hallmark of mental health professionals. In the past three-plus decades, proponents of positive psychology argue that such a dominant focus on mental illness fails to consider a broad range of dynamics and traits related to human adjustment such as satisfaction, courage, interpersonal skills, hope, happiness, love, determination, perseverance, spirituality, and creativity (Seligman & Csikszentmihalyi, 2000).

The trend toward positive psychology retains much of psychology's commitment to empirical methods to discern what best helps people move through the challenges faced in life and flourish in their growth and development over time. The importance of documenting and facilitating the inherent strengths and capabilities in populations that are often considered "at risk" or "vulnerable" to psychosocial challenges cannot be overstated. If we can distinguish the protective factors that help individuals and groups stay intact, more sound input can be given to preventative interventions as well as treatment interventions for those in need. In particular, one construct is often presented in the positive psychology literature—**resilience,** defined as the ability to maintain one's stability through protective factors that lead to positive outcomes and healthy personality characteristics in children and adults faced with negative or aversive life experiences (Bonanno, 2004). To date, very few studies have been published that address the specific strengths and resilience of ethnic minorities, but they are growing in number. Two examples of research in this area follow.

Resilience in Elderly, Chronically Ill African Americans

As noted in Chapter 8, one of the greatest challenges in aging is facing one's mortality. As life expectancy increases, so are the odds of coping with at least one chronic illness. The resilience of elderly people as they face the wear and tear on their bodies is often not addressed in the research literature. Indeed, most studies have tended to include primarily European American participants. However, in a recent 10-year prospective study with 38 African American respondents between the ages of 65 and 91, Becker and Newson (2005) explored how philosophies about racism related to the management of chronic illnesses. In addition, cultural themes centered on survival in the face of death, religion as a source of power, and living through adversity were examined. All respondents were interviewed multiple times throughout the span of the study. Interviews were semistructured and contained many open-ended questions. Results of qualitative analyses showed that there was a remarkable resilience displayed in dealing with life-threatening illnesses. Despite initially feeling overwhelmed by the nature of the diseases, over the course of the study, respondents conveyed a sense of determination, perseverance, and moxie (a blend of courage and inventiveness) to withstand being consumed by negativity. Most seemed acutely aware of the barriers to health articulated in this book (e.g., culturally insensitive treatment, institutional detriments such as poor health, welfare, and insurance systems). Nevertheless, these African Americans consistently noted their right to equality, better services and treatment, resolve to remain independent, and faith in God to see them through adversity. Findings suggested the ability of ethnic minorities to develop culturally specific philosophies about resilience may be essential to their ability to manage and even thrive while dealing with the negative effects of physical illness and other stressors. Further study into identifying characteristics of resilience in different cultural elderly groups can contribute to our understanding of healthy aging processes within our increasingly diverse elderly population (Becker & Newson, 2005).

Latina Girls' Strengths

A recent book edited by Denner and Guzman (2006) highlights the potential of young Latina girls in the United States through both a theoretical and empirical lens. The editors note that although Latinos represent one of the fastest-growing ethnic minority groups, there are relatively sparse data on their development. In addition, the majority of studies address risky behaviors and pathology such as delinquency, teenage pregnancy, and depression. Nevertheless, the authors chose to highlight research that is committed to explicating positive growth in Latinas through exploration of cultural variables. For example, in one chapter, Romo, Kouyoumdjian, Nadeem, and Sigman (2006) analyzed conversations between Latino adolescents and their mothers. Conversations centered on dating, sexuality, and interpersonal conflicts. A primary question of the study was whether or not the topic of education and its value would spontaneously enter these dialogues. The researchers found, contrary to prior literature, Latina girls were not encouraged to marry and bear children at the expense of their education. Rather, the girls received clear messages to avoid or defer pregnancy until they had achieved their educational goals. Although there was no explicit directive, close to 70% of the mothers and their adolescents spontaneously discussed at least one educational theme. The importance of academic excellence was discussed regardless of the mother's educational level, income status, or immigrant status. Other positive messages conveyed to daughters included avoiding negative influences that were bound to emerge living within some of the disadvantaged neighborhoods and the importance of being *"bien educado"* or *"educación"* that recognizes the importance of moral and social development that should go hand in hand with scholarly achievement. Moreover, certain messages were related to positive outcomes in Latina girls—for example, discussions about avoiding negative influences were related to high GPAs. Overall, the findings supported the benefits of close parent-adolescent communication and cultural values of *familismo* (familialism) and *educación* that enhance resiliency among adolescents.

The studies by Becker and Newson (2005) and Romo and colleagues (2006) illustrate the potential of ethnic psychology to examine the strengths of ethnic minorities on various dimensions of adaptation (e.g., individual, family, group, and community) across the life span. In addition, supporting a strengths perspective provides empirical evidence for dismantling pathological stereotypes and misunderstandings between groups.

THE SOCIOPOLITICAL CONTEXT OF ETHNIC PSYCHOLOGY WITHIN THE UNITED STATES

As we have mentioned throughout the book, much has changed in the United States in the last few decades. Of particular importance is the fact that ethnic minority populations have grown not just in size but also in their role in society. Also of significance is the fact that large percentages of our country's cities are now populated by ethnic minorities, many of them having migrated from other countries but also from rural areas or from smaller towns in the United States. As such, it is not unusual to find in Chicago or New York or Los Angeles, or in almost any other city, a large number of ethnic minorities, some born in other countries but a large number being second and third generation citizens. Furthermore, these ethnic minority individuals are no longer living exclusively in low-income neighborhoods and often they are occupying positions of social and political importance. These phenomena have brought out a number of problems and opportunities that ethnic psychologists need to explore and contribute to solutions and positive changes together with other social and behavioral scientists.

The rapid urbanization of ethnic minority populations has made possible not just increases in income and education and employment status of a large number of ethnic minorities but also the magnification of problems associated with poor-quality housing, school dropouts, unemployment, discrimination, homelessness, household conflicts, and so on. In this context, psychologists must contribute to the definition and identification of the problems experienced by ethnic minorities in this century and also open the way for more and better research in areas often ignored by psychologists. We highlight some of these issues below.

Immigration

The total population of the United States is rapidly growing and is expected to continue increasing for the next few decades. For example, between 1966 and 2006, the total population grew by 100 million people. This increase is the product of improved health among the population, births, and immigration (Pew Hispanic Center, 2006). Latinos accounted for approximately 36% of this increase, followed by Whites (34%), African Americans (16%), and Asian Americans (13%). Of these increases, approximately 55% of the change was due to migration and to the births in the United States of children of immigrants.

Setting aside the political and economic issues related to immigration and migration policies, there are a number of psychological and social issues that are of concern to social scientists. One, of course, is the process of acculturation of immigrants, which was discussed in previous chapters of this book. A second, somewhat related issue involves the process of civic involvement or incorporation of immigrants within the United States. Research on Latino immigrants (Waldinger, 2007) shows, for example, that less than half of all Latino immigrants maintain close ties to their country of origin as measured by sending money to relatives (usually referred to as remittances), traveling back and forth, and making weekly telephone calls to relatives and friends left behind. These behaviors change as time passes and become even less frequent. Importantly, the sense of attachment and commitment to the United States among immigrants is high and increases as their length of residence in the country also increases.

Berry (2001) argued that a "psychology of immigration" is needed to integrate two central concerns of ethnic psychology: acculturation (see Chapter 4) and intergroup relations (see Chapter 7). These two areas were perceived by Berry as creating a psychological setting for analyzing how individuals develop their in-group characteristics and with whom and how they relate while adapting to a new culture.

Urban Psychology

While sociologists and other social scientists have paid attention to the phenomenon of the country's rapid urbanization and its impact on people's beliefs and actions, psychologists only recently began to pay attention to the process and its implications for mental health. Well over 10 years ago, psychologists began to emphasize the fact that some urban environments can be detrimental to people's well-being while others can be supportive and personally enhancing (Wandersman & Nation, 1998). Nevertheless, there is still much research needed to properly understand these associations.

Related to the effects of environmental stressors often associated with urban environments (e.g., noise pollution because of traffic and mass transit services, personal insecurity) are the attitudes and stereotypes linked with social phenomena such as poverty and the unequal distribution of services and resources. These aspects of urban environments not only have an effect on people's physical and mental health but also seem to support the development and maintenance of certain beliefs and stereotypes. As such, social conditions such as homelessness and poverty are often associated with stereotyped perceptions of their assumed reasons and the related worthiness of the individual.

A recent undated report of the APA Task Force on Urban Psychology (n.d.) suggested that psychologists needed to study three areas of particular importance. First, similar to the emphasis of positive psychology, is the analysis of the strengths of urban communities and not just of the deficits and problems associated with urban environments. As such, the task force suggested the need to focus research on identifying how personal coping, self-identity, health, and well-being were affected with urban conditions. A second area was the need to develop a renewed emphasis on the role of the physical environment in shaping human behavior and how the built world interacted with the ethnic characteristics of its inhabitants. The third area was related to the need to study how cities affect people's physical and psychological status.

Socioeconomic Status and Poverty

The study of the relationship between socioeconomic status and human behavior is fairly new in psychology. A recent report from the APA Task Force on Socioeconomic Status (2007) indicated that "socioeconomic status and social class are fundamental determinants of human functioning across the life span, including development, well-being, and physical and mental health" (p. 1). Despite this statement, we still lack a sufficiently large amount of research on how socioeconomic status affects human behavior and health.

As suggested by Bullock (2006), causal attributions for poverty tend to fall into one of three categories: One emphasizes character flaws (e.g., laziness, alcoholism, drug abuse), a second is centered on societal conditions (e.g., poor schooling, low salaries), while a third category emphasizes fatalism (e.g., bad luck). These assumptions about the reason or reasons for a person's status obviously affect how we react toward him or her and how worthy we feel he or she is of receiving personal or government aid (Greenwald, O'Keefe, & DiCamillo, 2005). All of these assumptions and attributions have important psychological implications that we are just beginning to study.

The involvement of psychologists in studying the impact of such social conditions as poverty is of particular importance not only because poverty levels are increasing in the United States but because they have been shown to affect behaviors as diverse as academic achievement and school performance (Orr, 2003) and chronic illnesses such as diabetes and hypertension (Kingston & Smith, 1997). Indeed, the APA Task Force (2007) suggested that social class influenced individuals in a number of ways including the type of health-promoting or damaging behaviors (e.g., alcohol use, cigarette smoking, nutrition), differential exposure levels to stress, exposure to classism and its related stereotypes, interpersonal behaviors (e.g., anger), parenting patterns, and environmental degradation, among others.

Chapter Summary

There is no doubt that psychology has evolved rapidly in the last few decades. The growth of ethnic psychology is a good example of how a field basically unknown just a few years ago has now blossomed and developed into a sophisticated and complex area of psychology. This growth reflects our respectful appreciation for diversity and exemplifies the maturity of the science and profession of psychology that is now ready to accept that there is much to learn from individuals who have traditionally been ignored in our research and in our writings. Recently, Arnett (2008) argued for the need to bring an international perspective into the study of psychological phenomena. The same is true of the need to analyze the effects of ethnicity on human behavior. As Mahatma Gandhi said, "I do not want my house to be walled in on all sides and my windows to be stuffed. I want the cultures of all lands to be blown about my house as freely as possible." We hope this book has helped you build that house that Gandhi spoke about and that you will contribute to its growth.

Key Terms

Community-Based Participatory Research (CBPR) (page 328)

Participatory Action Research (PAR) (page 328)

Positive Psychology (page 328)

Resilience (page 331)

REFERENCES

Abe-Kim, J., Takeuchi, D. T., Hong, S., Zane, N., Sue, S., Spencer, M. S., et al. (2007). Use of mental health-related services among immigrant and US-born Asian Americans: Results from the National Latino and Asian American Study. *American Journal of Public Health, 97*(1), 91–98.

Aberson, C. L., Shoemaker, C., & Tomolillo, C. (2004). Implicit bias and contact: The role of interethnic friendships. *The Journal of Social Psychology, 144,* 335–347.

Abreu, J. M., Goodyear, R. K., Campos, A., & Newcomb, M. D. (2000). Ethnic belonging and traditional masculinity ideology among African Americans, European Americans, and Latinos. *Psychology of Men & Masculinity, 1*(2), 75–86.

Abueg, F., & Chun, K. M. (1996). Traumatization stress among Asians and Asian Americans. In A. Marsella, M. Friedman, E. Gerrity, & R. Scurfield (Eds.), *Ethnocultural approaches to understanding post-traumatic stress disorder: Issues, research, and clinical applications* (pp. 285–299). Washington, DC: American Psychological Association.

Acosta, F. X., Yamamoto, J., & Evans, L. A. (1982). *Effective psychotherapy for low income and minority patients.* New York: Plenum.

Adams, G., Biernat, M., Branscombe, N. R., Crandall, C. S., & Wrightsman, L. S. (Eds.). (2008). *Commemorating* Brown: *The social psychology of racism and discrimination.* Washington, DC: American Psychological Association.

Aday, L. A. (1994). Health status of vulnerable populations. *Annual Review of Public Health, 15,* 487–509.

Adler, N. E., Boyce, T., Chesney, M. A., Cohen, S., Folkman, S., Kahn, R. L., et al. (1994). Socioeconomic status and health: The challenge of the gradient. *American Psychologist, 49,* 15–24.

Ainsworth, M. D. (1967). *Infancy in Uganda: Infant care and the growth of love.* Baltimore: Johns Hopkins University Press.

Ainsworth, M. D. (1989). Attachments beyond infancy. *American Psychologist, 44*(4), 709–716.

Alba, R., & Nee, V. (1999). Rethinking assimilation theory for a new era of immigration. In C. Hirschman, P. Kasinitz, & J. DeWind (Eds.), *The handbook of international migration: The American experience* (pp. 137–160). New York: Russell Sage Foundation.

Alba, R., Rumbaut, R. G., & Marotz, K. (2005). A distorted nation: Perceptions of racial/ethnic group sizes and attitudes toward immigrants and other minorities. *Social Forces, 84*(2), 901–919.

Alcalay, R., Sabogal, F., Marín, G., Pérez-Stable, E. J., Marín, B. V., & Otero-Sabogal, R. (1987–1988). Patterns of mass media use among Hispanic smokers: Implications for community interventions. *International Quarterly of Community Health Education, 8,* 341–350.

Alegría, M., Chatterji, P., Wells, K., Cao, Z., Chen, C., Takeuchi, D., et al. (2008). Disparity in depression treatment among racial and ethnic minority populations in the United States. *Psychiatric Services, 59,* 1264–1272.

Alegría, M., Mulvaney-Day, N., Woo, M., Torres, M., Gao, S., & Oddo, V. (2007). Correlates of past-year mental service use among Latinos: Results from the National Latino and Asian American Study. *American Journal of Public Health, 97*(1), 76–83.

Al-Issa, I. (1997). Ethnicity, immigration, and psychopathology. In I. Al-Issa & M. Tousignant (Eds.), *Ethnicity, immigration, and psychopathology* (pp. 3–15). New York: Plenum.

Allen, C. (1997). Spies like us: When sociologists deceive their subjects. *Lingua Franca, 7,* 31–39.

Allen, V. L. (Ed.). (1970). *Psychological factors in poverty.* Chicago, IL: Markham Publishing.

Allport, G. W. (1954). *The nature of prejudice.* Cambridge, MA: Addison-Wesley.

Alva, S. A. (1993). Differential patterns of achievement among Asian-American adolescents. *Journal of Youth and Adolescence, 22,* 407–423.

Alvarez, A. N., & Helms, J. E. (2001). Racial identity and reflected appraisals as influences on Asian Americans' racial adjustment. *Cultural Diversity & Ethnic Minority Psychology, 7*(3), 217–231.

Alvidrez, J., Azocar, F., & Miranda, J. (1996). Demystifying the concept of ethnicity for psychotherapy researchers. *Journal of Consulting and Clinical Psychology, 64,* 903–908.

Ambady, N., Shih, M., Kim, A., & Pittinsky, T. L. (2001). Stereotype susceptibility in children: Effects of identity activation on quantitative performance. *Psychological Science, 12,* 385–390.

American Cancer Society. (2005). *Cancer facts & figures 2005.* Available at http://www.cancer.org/docroot/STT/stt_0.asp

American Diabetes Association. (2006). *All about diabetes.* Retrieved November 15, 2008, from http://www.diabetes.org/about-diabetes.jsp

American Psychiatric Association. (2000). *Diagnostic and statistical manual of mental disorders* (4th ed., Text Revision). Washington, DC: Author.

American Psychological Association. (2002). Ethical principles and code of conduct. *American Psychologist, 57,* 1060–1073.

American Psychological Association. (2003). Guidelines on multicultural education, training, research, practice, and organizational change for psychologists. *American Psychologist, 58*(5), 377–402.

American Psychological Association. (2005). *APA resolution recommending the immediate retirement of American Indian mascots, symbols, images, and personalities by schools, colleges, universities, athletic teams, and organizations.* Available at http://www.apa.org/pi/oema/resolution_american_indian_mascots.pdf.

American Psychological Association. (2007). Resolution on prejudice, stereotypes, and discrimination. *American Psychologist, 62,* 475–481.

American Psychological Association Task Force on Socioeconomic Status. (2007). *Report of the APA Task Force on Socioeconomic Status.* Washington, DC: Author.

American Psychological Association Task Force on Urban Psychology. (n.d.). *Toward an urban psychology: Research, action, and policy.* Washington, DC: Author. Available at http://www.apa.org/pi/wpo/tf_report_urban_psychology.pdf

Anderson, J., Moeschberger, M., Chen, J. M., Kunn, P., Wewers, M., & Guthrie, R. (1993). An acculturation scale for Southeast Asians. *Social Psychiatry and Psychiatric Epidemiology, 28,* 134–141.

Anderson, L. P. (1991). Acculturative stress: A theory of relevance to Black Americans. *Clinical Psychology Review, 11,* 685–702.

Angel, R., & Tienda, M. (1982). Determinants of extended household structure: Cultural pattern or economic need? *American Journal of Sociology, 6,* 1360–1383.

Angelelli, A., & Geist-Martin, P. (2005). Enhancing culturally competent health communication: Constructing understanding between providers and culturally diverse patients. In E. Berlin Ray (Ed.), *Health communication in practice: A case study* (pp. 271–284). Mahwah, NJ: Lawrence Erlbaum.

Anglin, D. M., Alberti, P. M., Link, B. G., & Phelan, J. P. (2008). Racial differences in beliefs about the effectiveness and necessity of mental health treatment. *American Journal of Community Psychology. 42*(1–2), 17–24.

Anglin, D. M., Link, B. G., & Phelan, J. C. (2006). Racial differences in stigmatizing attitudes toward people with mental illness. *Psychiatric Services, 57,* 857–862.

Antonio, A. L. (2004). The influence of friendship groups on intellectual self-confidence and educational aspirations in college. *The Journal of Higher Education, 75,* 446–471.

Applewhite, S. L. (1995). Curanderismo: Demystifying the health beliefs and practices of elderly Mexican Americans. *Health & Social Work, 20*(4), 247–253.

Armstrong, T., & Crowther, M. (2002). Spirituality among older African Americans. *Journal of Adult Development, 9,* 3–12.

Arnett, J. J. (2008). The neglected 95%: Why American psychology needs to become less American. *American Psychologist, 63,* 602–614.

Aronson, J., Fried, C. B., & Good, C. (2002). Reducing the effects of stereotype threat on African American college students by shaping theories of intelligence. *Journal of Experimental Social Psychology, 38,* 113–125.

Asakawa, K., & Csikszentmihalyi, M. (1998). The quality of experience of Asian American adolescents in academic activities: An exploration of educational achievement. *Journal of Research on Adolescence, 8*(2), 241–262.

Baca Zinn, M. (1979). Field research in minority communities: Ethical, methodological, and political observations by an outsider. *Social Problems, 27,* 209–219.

Bahrick, H. P., Hall, L. K., Goggin, J. P., Bahrick, L. E., & Berger, S. A. (1994). Fifty years of language maintenance and language dominance in bilingual Hispanic immigrants. *Journal of Experimental Psychology General, 123,* 264–283.

Balls Organista, P., Chun, K. M., & Marín, G. (Eds.). (1998). *Readings in ethnic psychology.* New York: Routledge.

Balls Organista, P., Organista, K. C., & Kurasaki, K. (2003). The relationship between acculturation and ethnic minority mental health. In K. M. Chun, P. Balls Organista, & G. Marín (Eds.), *Acculturation: Advances in theory, measurement, and applied research* (pp. 139–161). Washington, DC: American Psychological Association.

Balsa, A. I., & McGuire, T. G. (2003). Prejudice, clinical uncertainty and stereotyping as sources of health disparities. *Journal of Health Economics, 22,* 89–116.

Balsam, K. F., Huang, B., Fieland, K. C., Simoni, J. M., & Walters, K. L. (2004). Culture, trauma, and wellness: A comparison of heterosexual and lesbian, gay, bisexual, and two-spirit Native Americans. *Cultural Diversity & Ethnic Minority Psychology, 10*(3), 287–301.

Baluja, K. F., Park, J., & Myers, D. (2003). Inclusion of immigrant status in smoking prevalence statistics. *American Journal of Public Health, 93,* 642–646.

Barnes, A. M., Powell-Griner, E., McFann, K., & Nahin, R. L. (2004). Complementary and alternative medicine use among adults: United States, 2002. *Advance Data from Vital and Health Statistics* (No. 343). Retrieved July 25, 2005, from http://nccam.nih.gov/news/report.pdf

Barrera, M., Jr., Caples, H., & Tein, J.-Y. (2001). The psychological sense of economic hardship: Measurement models, validity, and cross-ethnic equivalence for urban families. *American Journal of Community Psychology, 29*(3), 493–517.

Barreto, R. M., & Segal, S. P. (2005). Use of mental health services by Asian Americans. *Psychiatric Services, 56*(6), 746–748.

Barry, D. T. (2001). Assessing culture via the Internet: Methods and techniques for psychological research. *CyberPsychology & Behavior, 4,* 17–21.

Barry, D. T., & Grilo, C. M. (2003). Cultural self-esteem, and demographic correlates of perception of personal and group discrimination among East Asian immigrants. *American Journal of Orthopsychiatry, 73,* 223–229.

Bartels, S., Teague, G., Drake, R., Clark, R., Bush, P., & Noordsy, D. (1993). Substance abuse in schizophrenia: Service utilization and costs. *The Journal of Nervous and Mental Disease, 181*(4), 227–232.

Bastida, E. (2001). Kinship ties of Mexican migrant women on the United States/Mexico border. *Journal of Comparative Family Studies, 32*(4), 549–572.

Bauman, K. J., & Graf, N. L. (2003). *Educational attainment: 2000* (Census 2000 Brief C2KBR-24). Washington, DC: U.S. Census Bureau.

Baumrind, D. (1971). Current patterns of parental authority. *Developmental Psychology, 4*(1, Part 2), 1–103.

Baumrind, D. (1980). New directions in socialization research. *American Psychologist, 35,* 639–652.

Beals, J., Manson, S. M., Shore, J. H., Friedman, N., Ashcraft, M., Fairbank, J. A., et al. (2002). The prevalence of posttraumatic stress disorder among American Indian Vietnam veterans: Disparities and context. *Journal of Traumatic Stress, 15,* 89–97.

Beals, J., Manson, S. M., Whitesell, N. R., Spicer, P., Novins, D. K., & Mitchell, C. M. (2005). Prevalence of DSM-IV disorders and attendant help-seeking in 2 American Indian reservation populations. *Archives of General Psychiatry, 62,* 99–108.

Becker, G., & Newson, E. (2005). Resilience in the face of serious illness among chronically ill African Americans in later life. *Journal of Gerontology, 60B*(4), S214–S223.

Belgrave, F. Z. (2002). Relational theory and cultural enhancement interventions for African American adolescent girls. *Public Health Reports, 117*(1), 76–81.

Bernal, G., & Scharrón Del Rio, M. R. (2001). Are empirically supported treatments valid for ethnic minorities? Toward an alternative approach for treatment research. *Cultural Diversity & Ethnic Minority Psychology, 7,* 328–342.

Bernal, G., Trimble, J. E., Burlew, A. K., & Leong, F. T. L. (Eds.). (2003). *Handbook of racial & ethnic minority psychology.* Thousand Oaks, CA: Sage.

Berns, R. M. (2004). *Child, family, school, community: Socialization and support* (6th ed.). Belmont, CA: Thomson Wadsworth.

Berrol, S. C. (1995). *Growing up American: Immigrant children in America, then and now.* New York: Twayne.

Berry, J. W. (1980). Acculturation as a variety of adaptation. In A. M. Padilla (Ed.), *Acculturation: Theory, models and some new findings* (pp. 9–25). Boulder, CO: Westview.

Berry, J. W. (1998). Acculturative stress. In P. Balls Organista, K. M. Chun, & G. Marín (Eds.), *Readings in ethnic psychology* (pp. 113–117). New York: Routledge.

Berry, J. W. (2001). A psychology of immigration. *Journal of Social Issues, 57,* 615–631.

Berry, J. W. (2003). Conceptual approaches to acculturation. In K. M. Chun, P. Balls Organista, & G. Marín (Eds.), *Acculturation: Advances in theory, measurement, and applied research* (pp. 17–37). Washington, DC: American Psychological Association.

Berry, J. W., & Sam, D. L. (2007). Cultural and ethnic factors in health. In S. Ayers, A. Baum, C. McManus, S. Newman, K. Wallston, J. Weinman, et al. (Eds.), *Cambridge handbook of psychology, health, & medicine* (2nd ed., pp. 64–70). Cambridge, UK: Cambridge University Press.

Betancourt, H., & Lopez, S. (1993). The study of culture, ethnicity, and race in American psychology. *American Psychologist, 43,* 629–638.

Betancourt, J. R., Green, A. R., Carrillo, J. E., & Ananeh-Firempong, O., II. (2003). Defining cultural competence: A practical framework for addressing racial/ethnic disparities in health and health care. *Public Health Reports, 118*(4), 293–302.

Bhandari Preisser, A. (1999). Domestic violence in South Asian communities in America. *Violence Against Women, 5*(6), 684–699.

Bhopal, R. (2003). Glossary of terms relating to ethnicity and race: For reflection and debate. *Journal of Epidemiology and Community Health, 58,* 441–445.

Birman, D. (1998). Biculturalism and perceived competence of Latino immigrant adolescents. *American Journal of Community Psychology, 26,* 335–354.

Birman, D., Trickett, E., & Buchanan, R. M. (2005). A tale of two cities: Replication of a study on the acculturation and adaptation of immigrant adolescents from the former Soviet Union in a different community context. *American Journal of Community Psychology, 35,* 83–101.

Birman, D., & Trickett, E. J. (2001). Cultural transitions in first-generation immigrants: Acculturation of Soviet Jewish refugee adolescents and parents. *Journal of Cross-Cultural Psychology, 32,* 456–477.

Blair, J. M., Fleming, P. L., & Karon, J. M. (2002). Trends in AIDS incidence and survival among racial/ethnic minority men who have sex with men, United States, 1990–1999. *Journal of Acquired Immune Deficiency Syndrome, 31,* 339–347.

Blatt, S. J. (2004). *Experiences of depression: Theoretical, clinical, and research perspectives.* Washington, DC: American Psychological Association.

Blauner, R., & Wellman, D. (1973). Toward the decolonization of social research. In J. A. Ladner (Ed.), *The death of white sociology: Essays on race and culture* (pp. 310–330). New York: Vintage.

Bogardus, E. S. (1959). Race reactions by sexes. *Sociology and Social Research, 43,* 439–441.

Bolaffi, G., Bracalenti, R., Braham, P., & Gindro, S. (Eds.). (2003). *Dictionary of race, ethnicity & culture.* London: Sage.

Bonanno, G. A. (2004). Loss, trauma, and human resilience: Have we underestimated the human capacity to thrive after extremely aversive events? *American Psychology, 59*(1), 20–28.

Borrell, L. N., Kiefe, C. I., Williams, D. R., Diez-Roux, A. V., & Gordon-Larsen, P. (2006). Self-reported health, perceived racial discrimination, and skin color in African Americans in the CARDIA study. *Social Science & Medicine, 63,* 1415–1427.

Bowen, W. G., & Bok, D. (1998). *The shape of the river: Long-term consequences of considering race in college and university admissions.* Princeton, NJ: Princeton University Press.

Bowlby, J. (1969). *Attachment and loss: Vol. 1. Attachment.* New York: Basic Books.

Bowleg, L., Huang, J., Brooks, K., Black, A., & Burkholder, G. (2003). Triple jeopardy and beyond: Multiple minority stress and resilience among Black lesbians. *Journal of Lesbian Studies, 7*(4), 67–108.

Boykin, K. (2005a). *Beyond the down low debate: Sex, lies, and denial in Black America.* New York: Carrol and Graf.

Boykin, K. (2005b, February 3). 10 things you should know about the DL. *Sexuality.* Available at http://www.keithboykin.com/arch/2005/02/03/10_things_you_s

Bracey, J. R., Bamaca, M. Y., & Umana-Taylor, A. J. (2004). Examining ethnic identity and self-esteem among biracial and monoracial adolescents. *Journal of Youth and Adolescence, 33*(2), 123–132.

Bradley, C. R. (1998). Child rearing in African American families: A study of the disciplinary practices of African American parents. *Journal of Multicultural Counseling and Development, 26*(4), 273–281.

Brannon, L., & Feist, J. (2007). *Health psychology: An introduction to behavior and health* (6th ed.). Belmont, CA: Thomson Wadsworth.

Breslau, J., Kendler, K. S., Su, M., Aguilar-Gaxiola, S., & Kessler, R. C. (2005). Lifetime prevalence and persistence of psychiatric disorders across ethnic groups in the USA. *Psychological Medicine, 35,* 317–327.

Brewer, M. B., & Campbell, D. T. (1976). *Ethnocentrism and intergroup attitudes.* New York: John Wiley.

Brislin, R. W. (1980). Translation and content analysis of oral and written materials. In H. C. Triandis & J. W. Berry (Eds.), *Handbook of cross-cultural psychology* (pp. 389–444). Boston: Allyn & Bacon.

Brislin, R. W., Lonner, W. J., & Thorndike, E. M. (1973). *Cross-cultural research methods.* New York: John Wiley.

Brittingham, A., & de la Cruz, P. (2004). *Ancestry: 2000* (Census 2000 Brief C2KBR-35). Washington, DC: U.S. Census Bureau.

Brody, G. H., Flor, D. L., & Morgan Gibson, N. (1999). Linking maternal efficacy beliefs, developmental goals, parenting practices, and child competence in rural single-parent African American families. *Child Development, 70*(5), 1197–1208.

Brody, G. H., Stoneman, Z., & Flor, D. (1996). Parental religiosity, family processes, and youth competence in rural, two-parent African American families. *Developmental Psychology, 32*(4), 696–706.

Brondolo, E., Rieppi, R., Kelly, K. P., & Gerin, W. (2003). Perceived racism and blood pressure: A review of the literature and conceptual and methodological critique. *Annuals of Behavioral Medicine, 25,* 55–65.

Bronfenbrenner, U. (1986). Ecology of the family as a context for human development: Research perspectives. *Developmental Psychology, 22*(6), 723–742.

Bronfenbrenner, U., & Morris, P. A. (1998). The ecology of developmental process. In W. Damon (Editor-in-Chief) & R. M. Lerner (Vol. Ed.), *Handbook of child psychology: Vol. 1. Theoretical models of human development* (5th ed., pp. 993–1028). New York: John Wiley.

Brooks, T. R. (1992). Pitfalls in communication with Hispanic and African-American patients: Do translators help or harm? *Journal of the National Medical Association, 84,* 941–947.

Brown, D. R., Fouad, M. N., Basen-Engquist, K., & Tortolero-Luna, G. (2000). Recruitment and retention of minority women in cancer screening, prevention, and treatment trials. *Annals of Epidemiology, 10,* S13–S21.

Browning, C. R., & Cagney, K. A. (2003). Moving beyond poverty: Neighborhood structure, social processes, and health. *Journal of Health and Social Behavior, 44,* 552–571.

Bui, H., & Morash, M. (1999). Domestic violence in the Vietnamese immigrant community. *Violence Against Women, 5*(7), 769–795.

Buki, L. P., Ma, T. C., Strom, R. D., & Strom, S. K. (2003). Chinese immigrant mothers of adolescents: Self-perceptions of acculturation effects on parenting. *Cultural Diversity & Ethnic Minority Psychology, 9*(2), 127–140.

Bullard, R. D. (1990). *Dumping in Dixie: Race, class, and environmental quality.* Boulder, CO: Westview.

Bullard, R. D., Mohal, P., Saha, R., & Wright, B. (2007, March). *Toxic wastes and race at twenty, 1987–2007* (Report prepared for the United Church of Christ Justice and Witness Ministries). Available at http://www.ejrc.cau.edu/TWART-light.pdf

Bullock, H. (2006, June). *Justifying inequality: A social psychological analysis of beliefs about poverty and the poor.* Retrieved December 1, 2008, from the National Poverty Center at http://www.npc.umich.edu/publications/working_papers/

Buriel, R. (1984). Integration with traditional Mexican American culture and sociocultural adjustment. In J. L. Martinez & R. Mendoza (Eds.), *Chicano psychology* (2nd ed., pp. 95–130). New York: Academic Press.

Buriel, R., & Saenz, E. (1980). Psychocultural characteristics of college-bound and noncollege-bound Chicanas. *Journal of Social Psychology, 110,* 245–251.

Burnam, M. A., Hough, R. L., Karno, M., Escobar, J. I., & Telles, C. A. (1987). Acculturation and lifetime prevalence of psychiatric disorders among Mexican Americans in Los Angeles. *Journal of Health and Social Behavior, 28,* 89–102.

Burnett, M. N., & Sisson, K. (1995). Doll studies revisited: A question of validity. *Journal of Black Psychology, 21,* 19–29.

Bushman, B. J., & Bonacci, A. M. (2004). You've got mail: Using e-mail to examine the effect of prejudiced attitudes on discrimination against Arabs. *Journal of Experimental Social Psychology, 40,* 753–759.

Cabassa, L. J. (2003). Measuring acculturation: Where we are and where we need to go. *Hispanic Journal of Behavioral Sciences, 25,* 127–146.

Cain, V. S., & Kington, R. S. (2003). Investigating the role of racial/ethnic bias in health outcomes. *American Journal of Public Health, 93,* 191–192.

California Psychological Association. (2004). *Expertise series* (Division I: Clinical and Professional Practice). Available at http://www.cpapsych.org/displaycommon.cfm?an=16.

Centers for Disease Control and Prevention. (2001). HIV incidence among young men who have sex with men—seven U.S. cities, 1994–2000. *Morbidity and Mortality Weekly Report, 50*(21), 440–444.

Centers for Disease Control and Prevention. (2002). State-specific trends in self-reported blood pressure screening and high blood pressure—United States, 1991–1999. *Morbidity and Mortality Weekly Report, 51*(21), 456–460.

Centers for Disease Control and Prevention. (2005a). *HIV/AIDS surveillance report* (Vol. 17). Atlanta, GA: Author. Retrieved October 21, 2007, from http://www.cdc.gov/hiv/topics/surveillance/resources/reports/.

Centers for Disease Control and Prevention. (2005b). Racial/ethnic disparities in prevalence, treatment, and control of hypertension—United States, 1999–2002. *Morbidity and Mortality Weekly Report, 54*(01), 7–9.

Centers for Disease Control and Prevention. (2006). Deaths: Final data for 2003. *National Vital Statistics Reports, 54*(13). Retrieved January 15, 2007, from http://www.cdc.gov/nchs/data/nvsr/nvsr54/nvsr54_13.pdf.

Centers for Disease Control and Prevention. (2007a). *HIV/AIDS among women.* Retrieved March 7, 2008, from http://www.cdc.gov/hiv/topics/women/resources/factsheets/women.htm.

Centers for Disease Control and Prevention. (2007b). *HIV/AIDS surveillance report* (Vol. 19). Available at http://www.cdc.gov/hiv/topics/surveillance/resources/reports/.

Champagne, D. (1994). *Native America: Portrait of the peoples.* Detroit, MI: Visible Ink.

Chan, C. S. (1995). Issues of sexual identity in an ethnic minority: The case of Chinese American lesbians, gay men, and bisexual people. In A. R. D'Augelli & C. J. Patterson (Eds.), *Lesbian, gay, and bisexual identities over the lifespan: Psychological perspectives* (pp. 87–101). New York: Oxford University Press.

Chao, R. K. (1994). Beyond parental control and authoritarian parenting style: Understanding Chinese parenting through the cultural notion of training. *Child Development, 65,* 1111–1119.

Chao, R. K. (2006). The prevalence and consequences of adolescents' language brokering for their immigrant parents. In M. H. Bornstein & L. R. Cote (Eds.), *Acculturation and parent-child relationships: Measurement and development* (pp. 271–296). Mahwah, NJ: Lawrence Erlbaum.

Chatters, L. M., Taylor, R. J., & Lincoln, K. D. (1999). African American religious participation: A multi-sample comparison. *Journal for the Scientific Study of Religion, 38*(1), 132–145.

Chaudhary, N. (2004). Researching communities: Travails of working in the Indian subcontinent. *Cross-Cultural Psychology Bulletin, 38*(4), 5–13.

Chavis, B. (1993). Foreword. In R. D. Bullard (Ed.), *Confronting environmental racism: Voices from the grassroots* (pp. 3–5). Boston, MA: South End Press.

Chavous, T. M., Rivas-Drake, D., Smalls, C., Griffin, T., & Cogburn, C. (2008). Gender matters, too: The influences of school racial discrimination and racial identity on academic engagement outcomes among African American adolescents. *Developmental Psychology, 44,* 637–654.

Chen, E., & Paterson, L. Q. (2006). Neighborhood, family, and subjective socioeconomic status: How do they relate to adolescent health? *Health Psychology, 25*(6), 704–714.

Chesla, C., & Chun, K. M. (2005). Accommodating type 2 diabetes in the Chinese American family. *Qualitative Health Research, 15*(2), 240–255.

Chia, R. C., Allred, L., Cheng, B., & Chuang, C. J. (1999). Social interaction differences between Chinese and Americans. *Psychological Beiträge, 41,* 84–90.

Chin, J. L. (Ed.). (2004). *The psychology of prejudice and discrimination* (Vol. 2, Ethnicity and Multiracial Identity Series). Westport, CT: Praeger.

Ching, J. W. J., McDermott, J. F., Fukunaga, C., & Yanagida, E. (1995). Perceptions of family values and roles among Japanese Americans: Clinical considerations. *American Journal of Orthopsychiatry, 65*(2), 216–224.

Chiriboga, D. A. (2004). Some thoughts on the measurement of acculturation among Mexican American elders. *Hispanic Journal of Behavioral Sciences, 26*(3), 274–292.

Christian, M. D., & Barbarin, O. A. (2001). Cultural resources and psychological adjustment of African American children: Effects of spirituality and racial attribution. *Journal of Black Psychology, 27*(1), 43–63.

Chua, P., & Fujino, D. C. (1999). Negotiating new Asian-American masculinities: Attitudes and gender expectations. *The Journal of Men's Studies, 7*(3), 391–413.

Chun, K. M. (2006). Conceptual and measurement issues in family acculturation research. In M. H. Bornstein & L. R. Cote (Eds.), *Acculturation and parent-child relationships: Measurement and development* (pp. 63–78). Mahwah, NJ: Lawrence Erlbaum.

Chun, K. M., & Akutsu, P. D. (1999). Utilization of mental health services: Cultural and gender considerations for immigrant and refugee women. In L. Kramer, S. Ivey, & Y. Ying (Eds.), *Immigrant women and the U.S. health care delivery system: From policy to program* (pp. 54–64). San Francisco: Jossey-Bass.

Chun, K. M., & Akutsu, P. D. (2003). Acculturation among ethnic minority families. In K. M. Chun, P. Balls Organista, & G. Marín (Eds.), *Acculturation: Advances in theory, measurement, and applied research* (pp. 95–119). Washington, DC: American Psychological Association.

Chun, K. M., Akutsu, P. D., & Abueg, F. (1994). *A study of Southeast Asian veterans of the Vietnam War.* Paper presented at the 28th annual convention of the Association for Advancement of Behavior Therapy, San Diego, CA.

Chun, K. M., Balls Organista, P., & Marín, G. (Eds.). (2003). *Acculturation: Advances in theory, measurement, and applied research.* Washington, DC: American Psychological Association.

Chun, K. M., & Chesla, C. A. (2004). Cultural issues in disease management for Chinese Americans with type 2 diabetes. *Psychology and Health, 19*(6), 767–785.

Chun, K. M., Morera, O. F., Andal, J. D., & Skewes, M. C. (2008). Conducting research with diverse Asian American groups. In F. T. L. Leong, A. G. Inman, A. Ebreo, L. H. Yang, L. Kinoshita, & M. Fu (Eds.), *Handbook of Asian American psychology* (2nd ed., pp. 47–65). Thousand Oaks, CA: Sage.

Chung, R. H., Kim, B. S., & Abreu, J. M. (2004). Asian American multidimensional acculturation scale: Development, factor, analysis, reliability, and validity. *Cultural Diversity & Ethnic Minority Psychology, 10,* 66–80.

Clark, K. B., Chein, I., & Cook, S. W. (2004). The effects of segregation and consequences of desegregation. *American Psychologist, 59,* 495–501.

Clark, K. B., & Clark, M. K. (1939). Segregation as a factor in the racial identification of Negro pre-school children. *Journal of Experimental Education, 8,* 161–163.

Clark, R., Anderson, N. B., Clark, V. R., & Williams, D. R. (1999). Racism as a stressor for African Americans. *American Psychologist, 53,* 805–816.

Cokley, K. (2007). Critical issues in the measurement of ethnic and racial identity: A referendum on the state of the field. *Journal of Counseling Psychology, 54*(3), 224–234.

Cole, E. R., & Zucker, A. N. (2007). Black and white women's perspectives on femininity. *Cultural Diversity & Ethnic Minority Psychology, 13*(1), 1–9.

Cole, M., Cole, S. R., & Lightfoot, C. (2005). *The development of children* (5th ed.). New York: Worth Publishers.

Collins, J. F. (2000). Biracial Japanese American identity: An evolving process. *Cultural Diversity & Ethnic Minority Psychology, 6*(2), 115–133.

Comaroff, J. (1987). Of totemism and ethnicity: Consciousness, practice, and the signs of inequality. *Ethnos, 52*(3–4), 301–323.

Comer, R. J. (2007). *Abnormal psychology* (6th ed.). New York: Worth Publishers.

Compton, W. M., Conway, K. P., Stinson, F. S., & Grant, B. F. (2006). Changes in the prevalence of major depression and comorbid substance use disorders in the United States between 1991–1992 and 2001–2002. *American Journal of Psychiatry, 163,* 2141–2147.

Conger, R. D., Ebert Wallace, L., Sun, Y., Simons, R. L., McLoyd, V., & Brody, G. H. (2002). Economic pressure in African American families: A replication and extension of the family stress model. *Developmental Psychology, 38*(2), 179–193.

Consolacion, T. B., Russell, S. T., & Sue, S. (2004). Sex, race/ethnicity, and romantic attractions: Multiple minority status adolescents and mental health. *Cultural Diversity & Ethnic Minority Psychology, 10*(3), 200–214.

Constantine, M. G., Gainor, K. A., Ahluwalia, M. K., & Berkel, L. A. (2003). Independent and interdependent self-construals, individualism, collectivism, and harmony control in African Americans. *Journal of Black Psychology, 229,* 87–101.

Corrigan, P. (2004). How stigma interferes with mental health care. *American Psychologist, 59,* 614–625.

Cortes, D. E. (2003). Idioms of distress, acculturation, and depression: The Puerto Rican experience. In K. M. Chun, P. Balls Organista, & G. Marín, *Acculturation: Advances in theory, measurement, and applied research* (pp. 207–222). Washington, DC: American Psychological Association.

Crosby, F. J., Iyer, A., Clayton, S., & Downing, R. A. (2003). Affirmative action: Psychological data and the policy debates. *American Psychologist, 58,* 93–115.

Cross, W. E., Jr. (1971). Negro-to-Black conversion experience: Toward a psychology of Black liberation. *Black World, 20,* 13–27.

Cross, W. E., Jr. (1995). The psychology of nigrescence: Revising the cross model. In J. G. Ponterotto, J. M. Casas, L. A. Suzuki, & C. M. Alexander (Eds.), *Handbook of multicultural counseling* (pp. 181–198). Thousand Oaks, CA: Sage.

Cuellar, I., Arnold, B., & Gonzalez, G. (1995). Cognitive referents of acculturation: Assessment of cultural constructs in Mexican Americans. *Journal of Community Psychology, 23,* 339–356.

Cuellar, I., Harris, L. C., & Jasso, R. (1980). An acculturation scale for Mexican American normal and clinical populations. *Hispanic Journal of Behavioral Sciences, 2,* 199–217.

Cunningham, W. E., Hays, R. D., Duan, N., Andersen, R., Nakazono, T. T., Bozzette, S. A., et al. (2005). The effect of socioeconomic status on the survival of people receiving care for HIV infection in the United States. *Journal of Health Care for the Poor and Underserved, 6,* 655–676.

Damron-Rodriguez, J., Wallace, S., & Kington, R. (1994). Service utilization and minority elderly: Appropriateness, accessibility and acceptability. *Gerontology & Geriatrics Education, 15*(1), 45–63.

Davila, A., Bohara, A. K., & Saenz, R. (1993). Accent penalties and the earnings of Mexican Americans. *Social Science Quarterly, 74,* 902–916.

Deary, V. (2005). Explaining the unexplained? Overcoming the distortions of a dualist understanding of medically unexplained illness. *Journal of Mental Health, 14*(3), 213–221.

Deaux, K. (1999). An overview of research on gender: Four themes from 3 decades. In W. B. Swann, Jr., J. H. Langlois, & L. A. Gilbert (Eds.), *Sexism and stereotypes in modern society: The gender science of Janet Taylor Spence* (pp. 11–33). Washington, DC: American Psychological Association.

DeCastro, A. B., Gee, G. C., & Takeuchi, D. T. (2008). Workplace discrimination and health among Filipinos in the United States. *American Journal of Public Health, 98,* 520–526.

De Coteau, T., Anderson, J., & Hope, D. (2006). Adapting manualized treatments: Treating anxiety disorders among Native Americans. *Cognitive and Behavioral Practice, 13*(4), 304–309.

Del Pilar, J. A., & Udasco, J. O. (2004). Deculturation: Its lack of validity. *Cultural Diversity & Ethnic Minority Psychology, 10*(2), 169–176.

Denner, J., & Guzman, B. L. (Eds.). (2006). *Latina girls: Voices of adolescent strength in the United States.* New York: New York University Press.

Department of Health and Human Services. (1998). *Mental health: A report of the Surgeon General.* Rockville, MD: Author.

Department of Health and Human Services. (1999). *Mental health: A report of the Surgeon General.* Rockville, MD: Author.

Department of Health and Human Services. (2000). *Policy guidance on the Title VI prohibition against national origin discrimination as it affects persons with limited English proficiency.* Rockville, MD: Author.

Department of Health and Human Services. (2001). *Mental health: Culture, race, and ethnicity* [A supplement to *Mental Health: A Report of the Surgeon General—Executive Summary*]. Rockville, MD: Author.

Department of Health and Human Services. (2006). *Child health USA 2006.* Rockville, MD: Author.

Desjarlais, R., Eisenberg, L., Good, B., & Kleinman, A. (1996). *World mental health: Problems and priorities in low-income countries.* Oxford, UK: Oxford University Press.

Devos, T., & Banaji, M. R. (2005). American = White? *Journal of Personality and Social Psychology, 88,* 447–466.

Diaz, R. M., Ayala, G., & Bein, E. (2004). Sexual risk as an outcome of social oppression: Data from a probability sample of Latino gay men in three U.S. cities. *Cultural Diversity & Ethnic Minority Psychology, 10*(3), 255–267.

Dixon, J., Durrheim, K., & Tredoux, C. (2005). Beyond the optimal contact strategy: A reality check for the contact hypothesis. *American Psychologist, 60*(7), 697–711.

Don Markstein's Toonopedia. (2008). *The Frito Bandito.* Retrieved August 8, 2008, from http://www.Toonopedia.com/frito.htm.

Dor, J. (2001). *Introduction to the reading of Lacan: The unconscious structured like a language.* New York: Other Press.

Doty, M. M., & Holmgren, A. L. (2006, August). *Health care disconnect: Gaps in coverage and care for minority adults.* New York: The Commonwealth Fund.

Dovidio, J. F., Glick, P., & Rudman, L. A. (2005). *On the nature of prejudice: Fifty years after Allport.* Malden, MA: Blackwell.

Downey, G., & Coyne, J. (1990). Children of depressed parents: An integrative review. *Psychological Bulletin, 108,* 50–76.

Duncan, G. J., Brooks-Gunn, J., & Klebanov, P. K. (1994). Economic deprivation and early childhood development. *Child Development, 65,* 296–318.

Echeverry, J. J. (1997). Treatment barriers: Accessing and accepting professional help. In J. G. Garcia & M. C. Zea (Eds.), *Psychological interventions and research with Latino populations* (pp. 94–107). Boston: Allyn & Bacon.

The Education Trust. (2006). *Education watch: The nation. Key education facts and figures. Achievement, attainment and opportunity from elementary school through college.* Washington, DC: Author. Available at http://www2.edtrust.org/edtrust/summaries2006/USA.pdf.

Emde, R., & Buchsbaum, H. (1990). Didn't you hear my mommy? Autonomy with connectedness in moral self-emergence. In D. Cicchetti & M. Beeghly (Eds.), *The self in transition* (pp. 35–60). Chicago: University of Chicago Press.

Environmental Protection Agency. (2008a). *Environmental justice: Basic information, background.* Retrieved November 20, 2008, from http://www.epa.gov/compliance/basics/ejbackground.html.

Environmental Protection Agency. (2008b). *Environmental justice: Frequently asked questions.* Retrieved November 20, 2008, from http://www.epa.gov/compliance/resources/faqs/ej/#faq12.

Erikson, E. H. (1950). *Childhood and society.* New York: Norton.

Erkut, S., Alarcon, O., Coll, C. G., Tropp, L. R., & Garcia, H. A. (1999). The dual-focus approach to creating bilingual measures. *Journal of Cross-Cultural Psychology, 30,* 206–218.

Escobar, J. I. (1995). Transcultural aspects of dissociative and somatoform disorders. *Psychiatric Clinics of North America, 18*(3), 555–569.

Escobar, J. I. (1998). Immigration and mental health: Why are immigrants better off? *Archives of General Psychiatry, 55*(9), 781–782.

Espiritu, Y. L. (1997). *Asian American women and men: Labor, laws, and love.* Thousand Oaks, CA: Sage.

Evans, G. W. (2004). The environment of childhood poverty. *American Psychologist, 59,* 77–92.

Evans, R. M. (1999). Increasing minority representation in health care management. *Health Forum Journal, 42,* 22.

Ewall, M. (1999). *Environmental racism in Chester.* Available at http://www.ejnet.org/chester/ewall_article.html.

Fadiman, A. (1997). *The spirit catches you and you fall down: A Hmong child, her American doctors, and the collision of two cultures.* New York: Farrar, Straus and Giroux.

Fairchild, H. H., & Cozens, J. A. (1981). Chicano, Hispanic, or Mexican American: What's in a name? *Hispanic Journal of Behavioral Sciences, 3*(2), 191–198.

Faragallah, M. H., Schumm, W. R., & Webb, F. J. (1997). Acculturation of Arab-American immigrants: An exploratory study. *Journal of Comparative Family Studies, 28,* 182–203.

Farley, R. (2002). Racial identities in 2000: The response to the multiple-race response option. In J. Perlmann & M. C. Waters (Eds.), *The new race question: How the census counts multiracial individuals* (pp. 33–61). New York: Russell Sage Foundation.

Farver, J. A. M., Narang, S. K., & Bhadha, B. R. (2002). East meets West: Ethnic identity, acculturation, and conflict in Asian Indian families. *Journal of Family Psychology, 16*(3), 338–350.

Feisthamel, K. P., & Schwartz, R. C. (2006). Racial bias in diagnosis: Practical implications for psychotherapists. *Annals of the American Psychotherapy Association, 9,* 10–14.

Finch, B. K., Kolody, B., & Vega, W. A. (2000). Perceived discrimination and depression among Mexican-origin adults in California. *Journal of Health and Social Behavior, 41,* 295–313.

Fine, M. (2004). The power of the *Brown v. Board of Education* decision: Theorizing threats to sustainability. *American Psychologist, 59*(6), 502–510.

Fishman, J. A. (2000). Who speaks what language to whom and when. In W. Li (Ed.), *The bilingualism reader* (pp. 89–106). London: Routledge. (Reprinted from *La Linguistique,* 1965, *2,* 65–88)

Fiske, S. T. (1998). Stereotyping, prejudice, and discrimination. In D. T. Gilbert, S. T. Fiske, & G. Lindzey (Eds.), *The handbook of social psychology* (pp. 357–411). New York: McGraw-Hill.

Foner, N. (1999). The immigrant family: Cultural legacies and cultural changes. In C. Hirschman, P. Kasinitz, & J. DeWind (Eds.), *The handbook of international migration: The American experience* (pp. 257–274). New York: Russell Sage Foundation.

Ford, D. Y., Harris, J. J., III, Tyson, C. A., & Frazier Trotman, M. (2002). Beyond deficit thinking: Providing access for gifted American students. *Roeper Review, 24*(2), 52–58.

Ford, K., & Norris, A. E. (1991). Methodological considerations for survey research on sexual behavior: Urban African American and Hispanic youth. *Journal of Sex Research, 28,* 539–555.

Foulks, E. F. (2004a). Commentary: Racial bias in diagnosis and medication of mentally ill minorities in prisons and communities. *Journal of the American Academy of Psychiatry and the Law, 32*(1), 46.

Foulks, E. F. (2004b). Cultural variables in psychiatry. *Psychiatric Times, 24*(4), 28–30.

Fowers, B. J., & Davidov, B. J. (2006). The virtue of multiculturalism: Personal transformation, character, and openness to the other. *American Psychologist, 61*(6), 581–594.

Franklin, A. J., Boyd-Franklin, N., & Draper, C. V. (2002). A psychological and educational perspective on Black parenting. In H. P. McAdoo (Ed.), *Black children: Social, educational, and parental environments* (2nd ed., pp. 119–140). Thousand Oaks, CA: Sage.

Franzini, L., & Fernandez-Esquer, M. E. (2006). The association of subjective social status and health in low-income Mexican-origin individuals in Texas. *Social Science & Medicine, 63,* 788–804.

Fuligni, A. J., & Witkow, M. (2004). The postsecondary educational progress of youth from immigrant families. *Journal of Research on Adolescence, 14*(2), 159–183.

Fuligni, A. J., Yip, T., & Tseng, V. (2002). The impact of family obligation on the daily activities and psychological well-being of Chinese American adolescents. *Child Development, 73*(1), 302–314.

Fuligni, A. J., & Yoshikawa, H. (2003). Socioeconomic resources, parenting, and child development among immigrant families. In M. H. Bornstein & R. H. Bradley

(Eds.), *Socioeconomic status, parenting, and child development* (pp. 107–124). Mahwah, NJ: Lawrence Erlbaum.

Gaines, S. O., & Reed, E. S. (1995). Prejudice: From Allport to Dubois. *American Psychologist, 50,* 96–103.

Galea, S., Ahern, J., Resnick, H., Kilpatrick, D., Bucuvalas, M., Gold, J., et al. (2002). Psychological sequelae of the September 11 terrorist attacks in New York City. *New England Journal of Medicine, 13,* 982–987.

Gans, H. J. (1999). Toward a reconciliation of "assimilation" and "pluralism": The interplay of acculturation and ethnic retention. In C. Hirschman, P. Kasinitz, & J. DeWind (Eds.), *The handbook of international migration: The American experience* (pp. 161–171). New York: Russell Sage Foundation.

Garcia, R. L., & Diaz, C. F. (1992). The status and use of Spanish and English among Hispanic youth in Dade County (Miami), Florida: A sociolinguistic study, 1989–1991. *Language and Education, 6*(1), 13–32.

Gardiner, H. W. (2001). Culture, context, and development. In D. Matsumoto (Ed.), *The handbook of culture and psychology* (pp. 101–117). New York: Oxford University Press.

Garnets, L. D. (2002). Sexual orientations in perspective. *Cultural Diversity & Ethnic Minority Psychology, 8*(2), 115–129.

Garrett, M. T., & Pichette, E. F. (2000). Red as an apple: Native American acculturation and counseling with or without reservation. *Journal of Counseling & Development, 78,* 3–13.

Gee, C. B. (2004). Assessment of anxiety and depression in Asian American youth. *Journal of Clinical Child and Adolescent Psychology, 33*(2), 269–271.

Gee, G. C. (2002). A multilevel analysis of the relationship between institutional and individual racial discrimination and health status. *American Journal of Public Health, 92,* 615–631.

Gee, G. C., Ro, A., Gavin, A., & Takeuchi, D. T. (2008). Disentangling the effects of racial and weight discrimination on body mass index and obesity among Asian Americans. *American Journal of Public Health, 98,* 493–500.

Gee, G. C., Spencer, M. S., Chen, J., & Takeuchi, D. T. (2007). A nationwide study of discrimination and chronic health conditions among Asian Americans. *American Journal of Public Health, 97,* 1275–1282.

Georgas, J., Mylonas, K., Bafiti, T., Poortinga, Y. H., Christakopoulou, S., Kagitcibasi, C., et al. (2001). Functional relationships in the nuclear and extended family: A 16-culture study. *International Journal of Psychology, 36*(5), 289–300.

Gerth, H., & Mills, C. W. (Eds.). (1946). *From Max Weber: Essays in sociology.* New York: Oxford University Press.

Gibbs, J. T., & Hines, A. M. (1992). Negotiating ethnic identity: Issues for Black-White adolescents. In M. P. P. Root (Ed.), *Racially mixed people in America* (pp. 223–238). Thousand Oaks, CA: Sage.

Gibson, M. A. (1989). *Accommodation without assimilation: Sikh immigrants in an American high school.* Ithaca, NY: Cornell University Press.

Gil, A. G., & Vega, W. A. (1996). Two different worlds: Acculturation stress and adaptation among Cuban and Nicaraguan families. *Journal of Social and Personal Relationships, 13,* 435–456.

Gil, A. G., Wagner, E. F., & Vega, W. A. (2000). Acculturation, familism, and alcohol use among Latino adolescent males: Longitudinal relations. *Journal of Community Psychology, 28*(4), 443–458.

Gillem, A. R., Cohn, L. R., & Throne, C. (2001). Black identity in biracial Black/White people: A comparison of Jacqueline who refuses to be exclusively Black and Adolphus who wishes he were. *Cultural Diversity & Ethnic Minority Psychology, 7*(2), 182–196.

Glazer, N., & Moynihan, D. P. (1963). *Beyond the melting pot.* Cambridge, MA: MIT Press.

Glionna, J. M., & Goldman, A. (2002, April 19). Answering protests, retailer to pull line of T-shirts that mock Asians. *Los Angeles Times,* p. B1.

Goering, J. M. (1971). The emergence of ethnic interests: A case of serendipity. *Social Forces, 48,* 379–384.

Golding, J. M., & Aneshensel, C. S. (1989). Factor structure of the Center for Epidemiologic Studies Depression Scale among Mexican Americans and non-Hispanic Whites. *Journal of Consulting and Clinical Psychology, 1,* 163–168.

Golding, J. M., Aneshensel, C. S., & Hough, R. L. (1991). Responses to depression scale items among Mexican-Americans and non-Hispanic Whites. *Journal of Clinical Psychology, 47,* 61–74.

Golding, J. M., Burnam, M. A., Benjamin, B., & Wells, K. B. (1992). Risk factors of secondary depression among Mexican Americans and non-Hispanic Whites. *Journal of Nervous and Mental Disease, 181,* 166–175.

Gong-Guy, E. (1987). *The California Southeast Asian Mental Health Needs Assessment* (No. 85–76282A-2). Sacramento, CA: California State Department of Mental Health, Asian Community Mental Health Services.

Good, C., Aronson, J., & Harder, J. A. (2008). Problems in the pipeline: Stereotype threat and women's achievement in high-level math courses. *Journal of Applied Developmental Psychology, 29,* 17–28.

Gordon, M. (1964). *Assimilation in American life: The role of race, religion, and national origins.* New York: Oxford University Press.

Gorman-Smith, D., Tolan, P., Zelli, A., & Huesmann, L. R. (1996). The relation of family functioning to violence among inner-city minority youths. *Journal of Family Psychology, 10*(2), 115–129.

Goto, S. G., Gee, G. C., & Takeuchi, D. T. (2002). Strangers still? The experience of discrimination among Chinese Americans. *Journal of Community Psychology, 30,* 211–224.

Gouveia, V. V., Clemente, M., & Espinosa, B. (2003). The horizontal and vertical attributes of individualism and collectivism in a Spanish population. *The Journal of Social Psychology, 14,* 43–63.

Grant, B. F., Stinson, F. S., Dawson, D. A., Chou, S. P., Dufour, M. C., Compton, W., et al. (2004). Prevalence and co-occurrence of substance use disorders and independent mood and anxiety disorders: Results from the National Epidemiologic Survey on Alcohol and Related Conditions. *Archives of General Psychiatry, 61,* 807–816.

Gray, F. D. (1998). *The Tuskegee syphilis study.* Montgomery, AL: Black Belt Press.

Grebler, L., Moore, J. W., & Guzman, R. C. (1973). The family: Variations in time and space. In L. I. Duran & H. R. Bernard (Eds.), *Introduction to Chicano studies* (pp. 309–331). New York: Macmillan.

Greene, B. (1997). Ethnic minority lesbians and gay men. In B. Greene (Ed.), *Ethnic and cultural diversity among lesbians and gay men* (pp. 216–239). Thousand Oaks, CA: Sage.

Greenwald, H. P., O'Keefe, S., & DiCamillo, M. (2005). Why employed Latinos lack health insurance: A study in California. *Hispanic Journal of Behavioral Sciences, 27,* 517–532.

Grieco, E. M., & Cassidy, R. C. (2001). *Overview of race and Hispanic origin: 2000* (Census 2000 Brief C2KBR/01-1). Washington, DC: U.S. Census Bureau.

Grotevant, H. (1998). Adolescent development in family contexts. In W. Damon (Editor-in-Chief) & N. Eisenberg (Vol. Ed.), *Handbook of child psychology: Vol. 3. Social, emotional, and personality development* (5th ed., pp. 1097–1149). New York: John Wiley.

Grzywacz, J. G., Lang, W., Suerken, C., Quandt, S. A., Bell, R. A., & Arcury, T. A. (2005). Age, race, and ethnicity in the use of complementary and alternative medicine for health self-management: Evidence from the 2002 National Health Interview Survey. *Journal of Aging and Health, 17,* 547–572.

Guarnaccia, P. J., Angel, R., & Worobey, J. L. (1989). The factor structure of the CES-D in the Hispanic Health and Nutrition Examination Survey: The influences of ethnicity, gender, and language. *Social Science & Medicine, 29,* 85–94.

Guarnaccia, P. J., & Rogler, L. H. (1999). Research on culture-bound syndromes. *American Journal of Psychiatry, 156*(9), 13322–13327.

Guendelman, S., & English, P. B. (1995). Effects of United States residence on birth outcomes among Mexican immigrants: An exploratory study. *American Journal of Epidemiology, 142,* S30–S38.

Guendelman, S., Gould, J. B., Hudes, M., & Eskenazi, B. (1990). Generational differences in perinatal health among the Mexican American population: Findings from HHANES 1982–84. *American Journal of Public Health, 80,* S61–S65.

Guisenger, S., & Blatt, S. J. (1994). Individuality and relatedness: Evolution of a fundamental dialectic. *American Psychologist, 49,* 104–111.

Gupta, R., & Yick, A. G. (2001). Preliminary validation of the acculturation scale on Chinese Americans. *Journal of Social Work Research & Evaluation, 2,* 43–56.

Gurin, P. (1997). *Expert report.* Ann Arbor: University of Michigan. Available at http://www.vpcomm.umich.edu/admissions/legal/expert/gurintoc.html.

Gurin, P., Dey, E. L., Hurtado, S., & Gurin, G. (2002). Diversity and higher education: Theory and impact on educational outcomes. *Harvard Educational Review, 72,* 330–366.

Guthrie, R. V. (1998). *Even the rat was white: A historical view of psychology*. Boston: Allyn & Bacon.

Guthrie, R. V. (2004). *Even the rat was white: A historical view of psychology* (2nd ed.). Upper Saddle River, NJ: Pearson Education.

Hall, G. C. N., Iwamasa, G. Y., & Smith, J. N. (2003). Ethical principles of the psychology profession and ethnic minority issues. In W. O'Donohue & K. E. Ferguson (Eds.), *Handbook of professional ethics for psychologists: Issues, questions, and controversies* (pp. 301–318). Thousand Oaks, CA: Sage.

Hall, R. E. (1994). The "bleaching syndrome": Implications of light skin for Hispanic American assimilation. *Hispanic Journal of Behavioral Sciences, 16,* 307–314.

Hallinan, M. T. (1996). Race effects on students' track mobility in high school. *Social Psychology of Education, 1*(1), 1–24.

Hammack, P. L., LaVome Robinson, W., Crawford, I., & Li, S. T. (2004). Poverty and depressed mood among urban African-American adolescents: A family stress perspective. *Journal of Child and Family Studies, 13*(3), 309–323.

Hammond, W. P., & Mattis, J. S. (2005). Being a man about it: Manhood meaning among African American men. *Psychology of Men & Masculinity, 6*(2), 114–126.

Hansen, M. L. (1952). The third generation in America. *Commentary, 14,* 493–500.

Harman, J. S., Edlund, M. J., & Fortney, J. C. (2004). Disparities in the adequacy of depression treatment in the United States. *Psychiatric Services, 55,* 1379–1385.

Harrell, J. P., Hall, S., & Taliaferro, J. (2003). Physiological responses to racism and discrimination: An assessment of the evidence. *American Journal of Public Health, 93,* 243–248.

Harris, A. C., & Verven, R. (1996). The Greek-American acculturation scale: Development and validity. *Psychological Reports, 78,* 599–610.

Harris, A. C., & Verven, R. (1998). Acculturation as a determinant of Greek-American family values. *Psychological Reports, 83,* 1163–1172.

Harris, K. M., & Edlund, M. J. (2005). Use of mental health care and substance abuse treatment among adults with co-occurring disorders. *Psychiatric Services, 56,* 954–959.

Harrison, A., Wilson, M., Pine, C., Chan, S., & Buriel, R. (1990). Family ecologies of ethnic minority children. *Child Development, 61,* 347–362.

Harrison-Hale, A. O., McLoyd, V. C., & Smedley, B. (2004). Racial and ethnic status: Risk and protective processes among African American families. In K. I. Maton, C. J. Schellenbach, B. J. Leadbeater, & A. L. Solarz (Eds.), *Investing in children, youth, families, and communities* (pp. 269–283). Washington, DC: American Psychological Association.

Hart, T., & Peterson, J. L. (2004). Predictors of risky sexual behavior among young African American men who have sex with men. *American Journal of Public Health, 94,* 1122–1123.

Hattam, V. C. (2001). Whiteness: Theorizing race, eliding ethnicity. *International Labor and Working-Class History, 60,* 61–68.

Hays, D. G., & Chang, C. Y. (2003). White privilege, oppression, and racial identity development: Implications for supervision. *Counselor Education and Supervision, 43,* 134–145.

Helfand, J., & Lippin, L. (2002). *Understanding Whiteness/Unraveling racism: Tools for the journey.* New York: Thomson Learning.

Helms, J. E. (1990). *Black and White racial identity development.* Westport, CT: Greenwood.

Helms, J. E. (1995). An update of Helms' White and people of color racial identity models. In J. G. Ponterotto & J. M. Casas (Eds.), *Handbook of multicultural counseling* (pp. 181–198). Thousand Oaks, CA: Sage.

Helms, J. E. (2006). Fairness is not a validity or cultural bias in racial-group assessment: A quantitative perspective. *American Psychologist, 61,* 845–859.

Helms, J. E. (2007). Some better practices for measuring racial and ethnic identity constructs. *Journal of Counseling Psychology, 54*(3), 235–246.

Helms, J. E., & Cook, D. A. (1999). *Using race and culture in counseling and psychotherapy: Theory and process.* Needham Heights, MA: Allyn & Bacon.

Helms, J. E., Jernigan, M., & Mascher, J. (2005). The meaning of race in psychology and how to change it: A methodological perspective. *American Psychologist, 60*(1), 27–36.

Henry, J. M., & Bankston, C. L. (1999). Louisiana Cajun ethnicity: Symbolic or structural? *Sociological Spectrum, 19,* 223–248.

Herrnstein, R. J., & Murray, C. A. (1994). *The bell curve: Intelligence and class structure in American life.* New York: Free Press.

Heurtin-Roberts, S., Snowden, L. R., & Miller, L. (1997). Expressions of anxiety in African Americans: Ethnography and the ECA studies. *Culture, Medicine, and Psychiatry, 21,* 337–363.

Hill, P. C., & Pargament, K. I. (2003). Advances in the conceptualization and measurement of religion and spirituality: Implications for physical and mental health research. *American Psychologist, 58*(1), 64–74.

Hill, R. B. (1998). Understanding Black family functioning: A holistic perspective. *Journal of Comparative Family Studies, 29*(1), 15–25.

Hill, S. A. (2001). Class, race, and gender dimensions of child rearing in African American families. *Journal of Black Studies, 31*(4), 494–508.

Hirsch, H. (1973). Political scientists and other camaradas: Academic myth making and racial stereotypes. In R. O. de la Garza, Z. A. Kruswski, & T. A. Arcinego (Eds.), *Chicanos and Native Americans.* Englewood Cliffs, NJ: Prentice Hall.

Ho, C. (1990). An analysis of domestic violence in Asian American communities: A multicultural approach to counseling. *Women and Therapy, 9*(12), 129–150.

Hofstede, G. (1980). *Culture's consequences: International differences in work-related values.* Newbury Park, CA: Sage.

Holleran, L. K. (2003). Mexican American youth of the Southwest borderlands: Perceptions of ethnicity, acculturation, and race. *Hispanic Journal of Behavioral Sciences, 25,* 352–369.

Holliday, B. G., & Holmes, A. L. (2003). A tale of challenge and change: A history and chronology of ethnic minorities in psychology in the United States. In G. Bernal, J. E. Trimble, A. K. Burlew, & F. T. L. Leong (Eds.), *Handbook of racial & ethnic minority psychology* (pp. 15–64). Thousand Oaks, CA: Sage.

Holliday, K. V. (2008). Religious healing and biomedicine in comparative context. In B. W. McNeill & J. M. Cervantes (Eds.), *Latina/o healing practices: Mestizo and indigenous perspectives* (pp. 249–270). New York: Routledge/Taylor.

Hom, A. Y. (1996). Stories from the homefront: Perspectives of Asian American parents with lesbian daughters and gay sons. In R. Leong (Ed.), *Asian American sexualities: Dimensions of the gay and lesbian experience.* New York: Routledge.

Hong, Y.-y., Morris, M. W., Chiu, C.-y., & Benet-Martinez, V. (2000). Multicultural minds: A dynamic constructivist approach to culture and cognition. *American Psychologist, 55,* 709–720.

Houston, T. K., Scarinci, I. C., Person, S. D., & Greene, P. G. (2005). Patient smoking cessation advice by health care providers: The role of ethnicity, socioeconomic status, and health. *American Journal of Public Health, 95*(6), 1056–1061.

Hufford, D. J. (2005). *An analysis of the field of spirituality, religion and health (s/rh).* Retrieved July 5, 2008, from http://www.templetonadvancedresearch program.com/pdf/TARP-Hufford.pdf.

Hughes, D., & Chen, L. (1997). When and what parents tell children about race: An examination of race-related socialization among African American families. *Applied Developmental Science, 1*(4), 200–214.

Hui, C. H., & Triandis, H. C. (1986). Individualism-collectivism: A study of cross-cultural researchers. *Journal of Cross-Cultural Psychology, 17,* 229–244.

Hunt, L. M., Schneider, S., & Comer, B. (2004). Should "acculturation" be a variable in health research? A critical review of research on US Hispanics. *Social Science & Medicine, 59,* 973–986.

Hunter, C. D. (2008). Individualistic and collectivistic worldviews: Implications for understanding perceptions of racial discrimination in African Americans and British Caribbean Americans. *Journal of Counseling Psychology, 55,* 321–332.

Hurtado, S., Carter, D. F., & Kardia, D. (1998). The climate for diversity: Key issues for institutional self-study. *New Directions for Institutional Research, 25*(2), 53–63.

Hyers, L. L. (2001). African American ethnic identity orientation in two national samples: A secondary survey analysis study. *Journal of Black Psychology, 27,* 139–171.

Icard, L. D., Zamora-Hernandez, C. E., Spencer, M. S., & Catalano, R. (1996). Designing and evaluating strategies to recruit African Americans for AIDS/HIV interventions: Targeting the African-American family. *Ethnicity & Disease, 6*(3–4), 301–310.

Institute of Medicine. (2002). *Unequal treatment: Confronting racial and ethnic disparities in health care*. Washington, DC: National Academy of Science.

Institute of Medicine. (2005). *Complementary and alternative medicine in the United States.* Washington, DC: National Academy of Science.

Israel, B. A., Eng, E., Schultz, A. J., & Parker, E. A. (Eds.). (2005). *Methods in community-based participatory research for health.* San Francisco: Jossey-Bass.

Iwamasa, G. Y. (1997). Asian Americans. In S. Friedman (Ed.), *Cultural issues in the treatment of anxiety* (pp. 99–129). New York: Guilford.

Iwamasa, G. Y., & Pai, S. M. (2003). Anxiety disorders among ethnic minority groups. In G. Bernal, J. E. Trimble, A. K. Burlew, & F. T. L. Leong (Eds.), *Handbook of racial & ethnic minority psychology* (pp. 429–447). Thousand Oaks, CA: Sage.

Jackson, F. L. (1992). Race and ethnicity as biological constructs. *Ethnicity & Disease, 2,* 120–125.

Jackson, J. S., Neighbors, H. W., Torres, M., Martin, L. A., Williams, D. R., & Baser, R. (2007). Use of mental health services and subjective satisfaction with treatment among Black Caribbean immigrants: Results from the National Survey of American Life. *American Journal of Public Health, 97,* 60–67.

Jackson, J. S., Torres, M., Caldwell, C. H., Neighbors, H. W., Nesse, R. M., Taylor, R. J., et al. (2004). The National Survey of American Life: A study of racial, ethnic, and cultural influences on mental disorders and mental health. *International Journal of Methods in Psychiatric Research, 13*(4), 196–207.

Jahoda, G. (1988). J'accuse. In M. H. Bond (Ed.), *The cross-cultural challenge to social psychology* (pp. 86–95). Thousand Oaks, CA: Sage.

Jemal, A., Thun, M. J., Ries, L. A. G., Howe, H. L., Weir, H. K., Center, M. M., et al. (2008). Annual report to the nation on the status of cancer, 1975–2005, featuring trends in lung cancer, tobacco use, and tobacco control. *Journal of the National Cancer Institute, 100*(23). Available at http://seer.cancer.gov/report_to_nation/.

Johnson, R. L., Saha, S., Arbelaez, J. J., Beach, M. C., & Cooper, L. A. (2004). Racial and ethnic differences in patient perceptions of bias and cultural competence in health care. *Journal of General Internal Medicine, 19,* 101–110.

Jones, E. (1953). *The life and work of Sigmund Freud* (Vol. 1). New York: Basic Books.

Jones, J. M. (1992). Understanding the mental health consequences of race: Contributions of basic social psychological processes. In D. N. Ruble, P. R. Costanze, & M. E. Oliveri (Eds.), *The social psychology of mental health: Basic mechanism and applications* (pp. 199–240). New York: Guilford.

Jones, J. M. (2003). TRIOS: A psychological theory of the African legacy in American culture. *Journal of Social Issues, 59*(1), 217–242.

Jones, N. A., & Smith, A. S. (2003). A statistical portrait of children of two or more races in Census 2000. In M. P. P. Root & M. Kelley (Eds.), *Multiracial child resource book: Living complex identities* (pp. 3–12). Seattle, WA: Mavin Foundation.

Joslin Diabetes Center. (2003). *Growing diabetes in Asians.* Available at http://joslin .org/news/diabetes_growing_asians.shtml.

Jourdan, A. (2006). The impact of the family environment on the ethnic identity development of multiethnic college students. *Journal of Counseling & Development, 84,* 328–340.

Jung, C. (1967). *Collected works.* Princeton, NJ: Princeton University Press.

Kane, E. W. (2000). Racial and ethnic variations in gender-related attitudes. *Annual Review of Sociology, 26,* 419–439.

Karon, J. M., Fleming, P. L., Steketee, R. W., & DeCock, K. M. (2001). HIV in the United States at the turn of the century. *American Journal of Public Health, 91,* 1060–1068.

Kawahara, D. M., & Fu, M. (2007). The psychology and mental health of Asian American women. In F. T. L. Leong, A. G. Inman, A. Ebreo, L. H. Yang, L. Kinoshita, & M. Fu (Eds.), *Handbook of Asian American psychology* (2nd ed., pp. 181–196). Thousand Oaks, CA: Sage.

Kessler, R. C., Chiu, W. T., Demler, O., & Walters, E. E. (2005). Prevalence, severity, and comorbidity of twelve-month DSM-IV disorders in the National Comorbidity Survey Replication. *Archives of General Psychiatry, 62*(6), 617–627.

Kessler, R. C., McGonagle, K. A., Zhao, S., Nelson, C. B., Hughes, M., Eshleman, S., et al. (1994). Lifetime and 12-month prevalence of DSM-III-R psychiatric disorders in the US: Results from the National Comorbidity Survey. *Archives of General Psychiatry, 51,* 8–19.

Kessler, R. C., & Merikangas, K. R. (2004). The National Comorbidity Survey Replication (NCS-R). *International Journal of Methods in Psychiatric Research, 13,* 60–68.

KewalRamani, A., Gilbertson, L., Fox, M. A., & Provasnik, S. (2007). *Status and trends in the education of racial and ethnic minorities* (NCES 2007–039). Washington, DC: National Center for Education Statistics.

Kiberstis, P. A., & Marx, J. (2002, July 26). The unstable path to cancer. *Science, 297,* 543–569.

Kibria, N. (1993). *Family tightrope: The changing lives of Vietnamese Americans.* Princeton, NJ: Princeton University Press.

Kim, B. S., Li, L. C., & Ng, G. F. (2005). The Asian American values scale—multidimensional: Development, reliability, and validity. *Cultural Diversity & Ethnic Minority, 11,* 187–201.

Kim, I. J., Lau, A. S., & Chang, D. F. (2007). Family violence among Asian Americans. In F. T. L. Leong, A. G. Inman, A. Ebreo, L. H. Yang, L. Kinoshita, & M. Fu (Eds.), *Handbook of Asian American psychology* (2nd ed., pp. 363–378). Thousand Oaks, CA: Sage.

Kim, I. J., & Zane, N. W. (2004). Ethnic and cultural variations in anger regulation and attachment patterns among Korean American and European American male batterers. *Cultural Diversity & Ethnic Minority Psychology, 10*(2), 151–168.

Kim, J. Y., & Sung, K. (2000). Conjugal violence in Korean American families: A residue of the cultural tradition. *Journal of Family Violence, 15*(4), 331–345.

Kim, S. Y., & Ge, X. (2000). Parenting practices and adolescent depressive symptoms in Chinese American families. *Journal of Family Psychology, 14*(3), 420–435.

Kim, U. (2001). Culture, science and indigenous psychologies: An integrated analysis. In D. Matsumoto (Ed.), *Handbook of culture and psychology* (pp. 51–76). Oxford, UK: Oxford University Press.

Kim, U., & Berry, J. W. (1993). *Indigenous psychologies: Research and experience in cultural context.* Thousand Oaks, CA: Sage.

Kim-Ju, G. M., & Liem, R. (2003). Ethnic self-awareness as a function of ethnic group status, group composition, and ethnic identity orientation. *Cultural Diversity & Ethnic Minority Psychology, 9*(3), 289–302.

King, J. L., & Hunter, K. (2005). *On the down low: A journey into the lives of "straight" Black men who sleep with men.* New York: Random House.

King, K. R. (2005). Why is discrimination stressful? The mediating role of cognitive appraisal. *Cultural Diversity & Ethnic Minority Psychology, 11,* 202–212.

King, M. L., Jr. (1963). *I have a dream* [Speech]. Delivered at the Lincoln Memorial, Washington, DC.

Kington, R. S., & Smith, J. P. (1997). Socioeconomic status and racial and ethnic differences in functional status associated with chronic diseases. *American Journal of Public Health, 87,* 805–810.

Kinzie, J. D., Boehnlein, J. K., Leung, P. K., Moore, L. J., Riley, C., & Smith, D. (1990). The prevalence of posttraumatic stress disorder and its clinical significance among Southeast Asian refugees. *American Journal of Psychiatry, 147,* 913–917.

Kinzie, J. D., Leung, P. K., Boehnlein, J., Matsunaga, D., Johnston, R., & Manson, S. M. (1992). Psychiatry epidemiology of an Indian village: A 19-year replication study. *Journal of Nervous and Mental Disease, 180,* 33–39.

Kirkman-Liff, B., & Mondragón, D. (1991). Language of interview: Relevance for research of Southwest Hispanics. *American Journal of Public Health, 81,* 1399–1407.

Kleinman, A. M. (1977). Depression, somatization, and the "new cross-cultural psychiatry." *Social Science Medicine, 11,* 3–10.

Kleinman, J. C., Fingerhut, L. A., & Prager, K. (1991). Differences in infant mortality by race, nativity status, and other maternal characteristics. *American Journal of Disease in Children, 145,* 194–199.

Klonoff, E. A., & Landrine, H. (1999). Cross-validation of the schedule of racist events. *Journal of Black Psychology, 25,* 231–254.

Kluckhohn, C. (1961). The study of values. In D. N. Barrett (Ed.), *Values in America.* Notre Dame, IN: Notre Dame University Press.

Kluckhohn, C., & Strodtbeck, F. L. (1961). *Variations in value orientation.* New York: Harper & Row.

Kotchick, B. A., Dorsey, S., Miller, K. S., & Forehand, R. (1999). Adolescent sexual risk-taking behavior in single-parent ethnic minority families. *Journal of Family Psychology, 13*(1), 93–102.

Kulis, S., Marsiglia, F. F., & Hurdle, D. (2003). Gender identity, ethnicity, acculturation, and drug use: Exploring differences among adolescents in the Southwest. *Journal of Community Psychology, 31*(2), 167–188.

Kunitz, S. J., Gabriel, K. R., Levy, J. E., Henderson, E., Lampert, K., McCloskey, J., et al. (1999). Alcohol dependence and conduct disorder among Navajo Indians. *Journal of Studies in Alcohol, 60,* 159–167.

LaFromboise, T., Coleman, H. L. K., & Gerton, J. (1993). Psychological impact of biculturalism: Evidence and theory. *Psychological Bulletin, 114,* 395–412.

Landrine, H., & Klonoff, E. A. (1994). *African-American acculturation: Deconstructing "race" and reviving culture.* Thousand Oaks, CA; Sage.

Landrine, H., & Klonoff, E. A. (1995). The African American Acculturation Scale II: Cross-validation and short form. *Journal of Black Psychology, 21,* 124–152.

Landrine, H., & Klonoff, E. A. (1996). Cultural diversity and methodology in feminist psychology. *Journal of Black Psychology, 22,* 144–168.

Landrine, H., Klonoff, E. A., Corral, I., Fernandez, S., & Roesch, S. (2006). Conceptualizing and measuring ethnic discrimination in health research. *Journal of Behavioral Medicine, 29,* 79–94.

Lane, S. D., Rubenstein, R. A., Keefe, R. H., Webster, N., Cibula, D. A., Rosenthal, A., et al. (2004). Structural violence and racial disparity in HIV transmission. *Journal of Health Care for the Poor and Underserved, 15,* 319–335.

Lawson, W. B., Hepler, N., Holladay, J., & Cuffel, B. (1994). Race as a factor in inpatient and outpatient admissions and diagnosis. *Hospital and Community Psychiatry, 45,* 72–74.

Lee, E. (Ed.). (1997). *Working with Asian Americans: A guide for clinicians.* New York: Guilford.

Lee, E., & Lu, F. (1989). Assessment and treatment of Asian-American survivors of mass violence. *Journal of Traumatic Stress, 2,* 93–120.

Lee, J., Lei, A., & Sue, S. (2001). The current state of mental health research on Asian Americans. *Journal of Human Behavior in the Social Environment, 3*(3/4), 159–178.

Lee, R. E., & Cubbin, C. (2002). Neighborhood context and youth cardiovascular health behaviors. *American Journal of Public Health, 92*(3), 428–436.

Lee, R. M. (2003). Do ethnic identity and other-group orientation protect against discrimination for Asian Americans? *Journal of Counseling Psychology, 50*(2), 133–141.

Lee, S.-K., Sobal, J., & Frongillo, E. A. (2003). Comparison of models of acculturation: The case of Korean Americans. *Journal of Cross-Cultural Psychology, 34,* 282–296.

Lenski, G. E. (1966). *Power and privilege: A theory of social stratification.* New York: McGraw-Hill.

Leong, F. T. L. (1986). Counseling and psychotherapy with Asian Americans: A review of the literature. *Journal of Counseling Psychology, 33,* 192–206.

Lerner, M. (1980). *Belief in a just world: A fundamental delusion.* New York: Plenum.

Lévi-Strauss, C. (1966). *Pensée savage [The savage mind].* Chicago: University of Chicago Press.

Levy, D., & Brink, S. (2005). *A change of heart: How the people of Framingham, Massachusetts, helped unravel the mysteries of cardiovascular disease.* New York: Knopf.

Lewis, T. T., Everson-Rose, S. A., Powell, L. H., Matthews, K. A., Brown, C., Karavolos, K., et al. (2006). Chronic exposure to everyday discrimination and coronary artery calcification in African American women: The SWAN Heart Study. *Psychosomatic Medicine, 68,* 362–368.

Lilienfeld, A. M. (1972). *Cancer in the United States.* Cambridge, MA: Harvard University Press.

Lim, K. V., Heiby, E., Brislin, R., & Griffin, B. (2002). The development of the Khmer acculturation scale. *International Journal of Intercultural Relations, 26,* 653–678.

Lin, C. Y., & Fu, V. (1990). A comparison of child-rearing practices among Chinese, immigrant Chinese, and Caucasian-American parents. *Child Development, 61,* 429–433.

Lindsay, B. (1979). Minority women in America: Black American, Native American, Chicana, and Asian American women. In E. C. Synder (Ed.), *The study of women enlarging perspectives of social reality.* New York: Harper & Row.

Liu, W. M. (2002). Exploring the lives of Asian American men: Racial identity, male role norms, gender role conflict, and prejudicial attitudes. *Psychology of Men & Masculinity, 3*(2), 107–118.

Longshore, D., & Grills, C. (2000). Motivating illegal drug use recovery: Evidence for a culturally congruent intervention. *Journal of Black Psychology, 26*(3), 288–301.

Lopez, G. E. (2004). Interethnic contact, curriculum, and attitudes in the first year of college. *Journal of Social Issues, 60*(1), 75–94.

Lopez, S. R. (1989). Patient variable biases in clinical judgment: Conceptual overview and methodological considerations. *Psychological Bulletin, 106,* 184–203.

Lopez, S. R., & Guarnaccia, P. J. (2005). Cultural dimensions of psychopathology: The social world's impact on mental illness. In J. E. Maddux & B. A. Winstead (Eds.), *Psychopathology: Foundations for a contemporary understanding* (pp. 19–38). Mahwah, NJ: Lawrence Erlbaum.

Lopez, S. R., & Guarnaccia, P. J. J. (2000). Cultural psychopathology: Uncovering the social world of mental illness. *Annual Review of Psychology, 51,* 571–598.

Lorentzen, L., Chun, K. M., Gonzalez, J., & Do, H. (Eds.). (in press). *On the corner of bliss and nirvana: The religious lives of new immigrants in San Francisco.* Durham, NC: Duke University Press.

Losen, D. J., & Orfield, G. (2002). *Racial inequality in special education.* Cambridge, MA: Harvard Education Press.

Lucal, B. (1996). Oppression and privilege: Towards a relational conceptualization of race. *Teaching Sociology, 24*(3), 245–255.

Lugalia, T., & Overturf, J. (2004). *Children and the households they live in: 2000* (Census 2000 Special Report). Washington, DC: U.S. Census Bureau.

Lynch, J. W., Kaplan, G. A., & Shema, S. J. (1997). Cumulative impact of sustained economic hardship on physical, cognitive, psychological, and social functioning. *The New England Journal of Medicine, 337*(26), 1889–1895.

Lyons, A. L., Carlson, G. A., Thurm, A. E., Grant, K. E., & Gipson, P. Y. (2006). Gender differences in early risk factors for adolescent depression among low-income urban children. *Cultural Diversity & Ethnic Minority Psychology, 12*(4), 644–657.

MacDorman, M. F., & Mathews, T. J. (2008). *Recent trends in infant mortality in the United States* (NCHS Data Brief No. 9). Hyattsville, MD: National Center for Health Statistics.

Macklin, R. (2000). Informed consent for research: International perspectives. *Journal of the American Medical Women's Association, 55,* 290–293.

Maddux, J. E., & Winstead, B. A. (Eds.). (2005). *Psychopathology: Foundations for a contemporary understanding.* Mahwah, NJ: Lawrence Erlbaum.

Mandara, J., & Murray, C. B. (2002). Development of an empirical typology of African American family functioning. *Journal of Family Psychology, 16*(3), 318–337.

Mantsios, G. (2004). Media magic: Making class invisible. In P. S. Rothenberg (Ed.), *Race, class, and gender in the United States: An integrated study* (6th ed., pp. 560–568). New York: St. Martin's.

Marger, M. N. (2000). Ethnic stratification: Power and inequality. In M. N. Marger (Ed.), *Race and ethnic relations: American and global perspectives* (5th ed., pp. 36–68). Belmont, CA: Wadsworth.

Marín, G. (1984). Stereotyping Hispanics: The differential effect of research method, label, and degree of contact. *International Journal of Intercultural Relations, 8,* 17–27.

Marín, G. (1992). Issues in the measurement of acculturation among Hispanics. In K. Geisinger (Ed.), *Psychological testing of Hispanics.* Washington, DC: American Psychological Association.

Marín, G. (1993). Defining culturally appropriate community interventions: Hispanics as a case study. *Journal of Community Psychology, 20,* 375–391.

Marín, G., Balls Organista, P., & Chun, K. M. (2003). Acculturation research: Current issues and findings. In G. Bernal, J. E. Trimble, A. K. Burlew, & F. T. L. Leong (Eds.), *Handbook of racial & ethnic minority psychology* (pp. 208–219). Thousand Oaks, CA: Sage.

Marín, G., & Gamba, R. J. (1996). A new measurement of acculturation for Hispanics: The Bidimensional Acculturation Scale for Hispanics. *Hispanic Journal of Behavioral Sciences, 18,* 297–316.

Marín, G., Pérez-Stable, E. J., & Marín, B. V. (1989). Cigarette smoking among San Francisco Hispanics: The role of acculturation and gender. *American Journal of Public Health, 79,* 196–198.

Marín, G., Sabogal, F., Marín, B. V., Otero-Sabogal, R., & Pérez-Stable, E. J. (1987). Development of a short acculturation scale for Hispanics. *Hispanic Journal of Behavioral Sciences, 9,* 183–205.

Marín, G., Triandis, H. C., Betancourt, H., & Kashima, Y. (1983). Ethnic affirmation versus social desirability: Explaining discrepancies in bilinguals' responses to a questionnaire. *Journal of Cross-Cultural Psychology, 14,* 173–186.

Marín, G., & VanOss Marín, B. (1991). *Research with Hispanic populations* (Vol. 23, Applied Social Research Methods Series). Newbury Park, CA: Sage.

Markides, K. S., Coreil, J., & Ray, L. A. (1987). Smoking among Mexican Americans: A three-generation study. *American Journal of Public Health, 77,* 708–711.

Marks, G., Garcia, M., & Solis, J. M. (1990). Health risk behaviors of Hispanics in the United States: Findings from HHANES, 1982–84. *American Journal of Public Health, 80* (Suppl.), 20–26.

Marks, J. (1995). *Human biodiversity: Genes, race, and history.* New York: Walter de Gruyter.

Markus, H., & Kitayama, S. (1991). Culture and the self. *Psychological Review, 98,* 224–253.

Marsella, A. J. (1998). Toward a "global-community psychology": Meeting the needs of a changing world. *American Psychologist, 53,* 1282–1291.

Marsiglia, F. F., Kulis, S., Hecht, M. L., & Sills, S. (2004). Ethnicity and ethnic identity as predictors of drug norms and drug use among preadolescents in the US Southwest. *Substance Use & Misuse, 39*(7), 1061–1094.

Matsumoto, D., & Juang, L. (2004). *Culture and psychology* (3rd ed.). Belmont, CA: Thomson Wadsworth.

Mays, V. M., Cochran, S. D., & Barnes, N. W. (2007). Race, race-based discrimination, and health outcomes among African Americans. *Annual Review of Psychology, 58,* 201–225.

Mays, V. M., Flora, J. A., Schooler, C., & Cochran, S. D. (1992). Magic Johnson's credibility among African-American men. *American Journal of Public Health , 82,* 1692–1693.

McDermott, J. F., Char, W. F., Robillard, A. B., Hsu, J., Tseng, W.-S., & Ashton, G. C. (1983). Cultural variations in family attitudes and their implications for therapy. *Journal of the American Academy of Child Psychiatry, 22,* 454–458.

McGlothlin, H., & Killen, M. (2006). Intergroup attitudes of European American children attending ethnically homogeneous schools. *Child Development, 77,* 1375–1386.

McIntosh, P. (2004). White privilege: Unpacking the invisible knapsack. In P. S. Rothenberg (Ed.), *Race, class, and gender in the United States: An integrated study* (6th ed., pp. 188–192). New York: Worth.

McIntyre, A. (2008). *Participatory action research.* Thousand Oaks, CA: Sage.

McLoyd, V. C. (1990). The impact of economic hardship on Black families and children: Psychological distress, parenting, and socioemotional development. *Child Development, 61,* 311–346.

McLoyd, V. C. (1998). Socioeconomic disadvantage and child development. *American Psychologist, 53,* 185–204.

McLoyd, V. C., Cauce, A. M., Takeuchi, D., & Wilson, L. (2000). Marital processes and parental socialization in families of color: A decade review of research. *Journal of Marriage and the Family, 62*(4), 1070–1093.

McLoyd, V. C., Harper, C. I., & Copeland, N. L. (2001). Ethnic minority status, interparental conflict, and child adjustment. In J. H. Grych & F. Fincham (Eds.), *Interparental conflict and child development: Theory, research, and applications.* Cambridge, UK: Cambridge University Press.

McMahon, S. D., & Watts, R. J. (2002). Ethnic identity in urban African American youth: Exploring links with self-worth, aggression, and other psychosocial variables. *Journal of Community Psychology, 30*(4), 411–432.

McNair, L. D., & Prather, C. M. (2004). African American women and AIDS: Factors influencing risk and reduction to HIV disease. *Journal of Black Psychology, 30*(1), 106–123.

McNeely, M. J., & Boyko, E. J. (2004). Type 2 diabetes prevalence in Asian Americans: Results of a national health survey. *Diabetes Care, 27*(1), 66–69.

Mehrotra, M. (1999). The social construction of wife abuse. *Violence Against Women, 5*(6), 619–640.

Mena, F. J., Padilla, A. M., & Maldonado, M. (1987). Acculturative stress and specific coping strategies among immigrant and later generation college students. *Hispanic Journal of Behavioral Sciences, 9,* 207–225.

Mendes, W. B. (2007). Stereotype-busting people can spur stress, reduce cognitive performance. *Journal of Personality and Social Psychology, 92,* 11.

Meredith, L. S., Wenger, N., Liu, H., Harada, N., & Kahn, K. (2000). Development of a brief scale to measure acculturation among Japanese Americans. *Journal of Community Psychology, 28,* 103–113.

Milloy, C. (2004, January 21). How to slap a happy face on misery. *The Washington Post,* p. B01.

Miniño, A. M., Heron, M. P., & Smith, B. L. (2006). *Death: Preliminary data for 2004.* Hyattsville, MD: National Center for Health Statistics.

Minority Health and Health Disparities Research and Education Act. (2000). Pub. L. No. 106-525. Available at http://purl.access.gpo.gov/GPO/LPS10757.

Miranda, A. O., & Matheny, K. B. (2000). Socio-psychological predictors of acculturative stress among Latino adults. *Journal of Mental Health Counseling, 22,* 306–317.

Miranda, A. O., & Umhoefer, D. L. (1998). Depression and social interest differences between Latinos in dissimilar acculturation stages. *Journal of Mental Health, 20,* 159–171.

Miranda, J., Bernal, G., Lau, A., Kohn, L., Hwang, W., & LaFromboise, T. (2005). State of the science on psychosocial interventions for ethnic minorities. *Annual Review of Clinical Psychology, 1,* 113–142.

Miranda, J., Siddique, J., Belin, T. R., & Kohn-Wood, L. P. (2004). Depression prevalence in disadvantaged young Black women: African and Caribbean immigrants compared to U.S.-born African Americans. *Social Psychiatry and Psychiatric Epidemiology, 40,* 253–258.

Mishel, L., Bernstein, J., & Boushey, H. (2003). *The state of working America 2002–2003.* Ithaca, NY: Cornell University Press.

Mollica, R. (1994). Southeast Asian refugees: Migration history and mental health issues. In A. J. Marsella, T. Bornemann, S. Ekblad, & J. Orley (Eds.), *Amidst peril and pain: The mental health and well-being of the world's refugees* (pp. 83–100). Washington, DC: American Psychological Association.

Moore, J. W. (1973). Social constraints on sociological knowledge: Academics and research concerning minorities. *Social Problems, 21,* 65–77.

Morales, L., Lara, M., Kington, R. S., Valdez, R. O., & Escarce, J. J. (2002). Socioeconomic, cultural, and behavioral factors affecting Hispanic health outcomes. *Journal of Health Care for the Poor and Underserved, 13,* 477–503.

Morling, B., & Fiske, S. T. (1999). Defining and measuring harmony control. *Journal of Research in Personality, 33,* 379–414.

Mossakowski, K. N. (2003). Coping with perceived discrimination: Does ethnic identity protect mental health? *Journal of Health and Social Behavior, 44*(3), 318–331.

Mueller, P. S., Plevak, D. J., & Rummans, T. A. (2001). Religious involvement, spirituality, and medicine: Implications for clinical practice. *Mayo Clinic Proceedings, 76,* 1225–1235.

Murray, L. R. (2003). Sick and tired of being sick and tired: Scientific evidence, methods, and research implications for racial and ethnic disparities in occupational health. *American Journal of Public Health, 93,* 221–226.

Murry, V. M., Brown, P. A., Brody, G. H., Cutrona, C. E., & Simons, R. L. (2001). Racial discrimination as a moderator of the links among stress, maternal psychological functioning, and family relationships. *Journal of Marriage and Family, 63,* 915–926.

Myers, H. F., & Rodriguez, N. (2003). Acculturation and physical health in racial and ethnic minorities. In K. M. Chun, P. Balls Organista, & G. Marín (Eds.), *Acculturation: Advances in theory, measurement, and applied research* (pp. 163–185). Washington, DC: American Psychological Association.

National Cancer Institute. (2005). *SEER cancer statistics review.* Retrieved July 3, 2005, from http://seer.cancer.gov/csr/1975_2002/results_merged/topic_race_ethnicity.pdf.

National Center for Chronic Disease Prevention and Health Promotion. (2002). *Diabetes: Disabling, deadly, and on the rise.* Washington, DC: U.S. Government Printing Office.

National Center for Complementary and Alternative Medicine. (2008). *What is CAM?* Retrieved July 22, 2008, from http://nccam.nih.gov/health/whatiscam/.

National Center for Health Statistics. (2002). *National Health and Nutrition Examination Survey.* Available at http://www.cdc.gov/nchs/about/major/nhanes/nhanes01-02.htm.

National Center for Health Statistics. (2005). *Health, United States, 2004: With chartbook on trends in the health of Americans.* Hyattsville, MD: Author.

National Center for Health Statistics. (2006). *Health, United States, 2005: With chartbook on trends in the health of Americans.* Hyattsville, MD: Author.

National Institute of Allergy and Infectious Diseases. (2004). *Factsheet: How HIV causes AIDS.* Retrieved August 8, 2007, from http://www.niaid.nih.gov/factsheets/howhiv.htm.

Neal, A. M., & Turner, S. M. (1991). Anxiety disorders research with African Americans: Current status. *Psychological Bulletin, 109,* 400–410.

Neff, K. (2003). Understanding how universal goals of independence and interdependence are manifested within particular cultural contexts. *Human Development, 46,* 312–318.

Neff, K. D. (2001). Judgments of personal autonomy and interpersonal responsibility in the context of Indian spousal relationships: An examination of young people's reasoning in Mysore, India. *British Journal of Developmental Psychology, 19,* 233–257.

Neff, K. D., & Harter, S. (2002a). The authenticity of conflict resolutions among adult couples: Does women's other-oriented behavior reflect their true selves? *Sex Roles, 47,* 403–417.

Neff, K. D., & Harter, S. (2002b). The role of power and authenticity in relationship styles emphasizing autonomy, connectedness, or mutuality among adult couples. *Journal of Social and Personal Relationships, 19,* 827–849.

Neff, K. D., & Harter, S. (2003). Relationship styles of self-focused autonomy, other-focused connectedness, and mutuality across multiple relationship contexts. *Journal of Social and Personal Relationships, 20,* 81–99.

Negy, C., Shreve, T. L., Jensen, B. J., & Uddin, N. (2003). Ethnic identity, self-esteem, and ethnocentrism: A study of social identity versus multicultural theory of development. *Cultural Diversity & Ethnic Minority Psychology, 9*(4), 333–344.

Neighbors, H. W., Caldwell, C., Williams, D. R., Neese, R., Taylor, R. J., Bullard, K. M., et al. (2007). Race, ethnicity, and the use of services for mental disorders: Results from the National Survey of American Life. *Archives of General Psychiatry, 64*(4), 485–494.

Nguyen, H. H. (2006). Acculturation in the United States. In D. L. Sam, & J. W. Berry (Eds.), *The Cambridge handbook of acculturation psychology* (pp. 311–330). Cambridge, MA: Cambridge University Press.

Nguyen, H. H., & von Eye, A. (2002). The Acculturation Scale for Vietnamese Adolescents (ASVA): A bidimensional perspective. *International Journal of Behavioral Development , 26,* 202–213.

Nicolini, P. (1987). Puerto Rican leaders' views of English-language media. *Journalism Quarterly, 64*(2–3), 597–601.

Nisbett, R. E., Peng, K., Choi, I., & Norenzayan, A. (2001). Culture and systems of thought: Holistic versus analytic cognition. *Psychological Review, 108,* 291–310.

North American Spine Society. (2006). *Herbal supplements: "Natural" doesn't always mean safe.* Retrieved August 22, 2007, from http://www.spine.org/Documents/herbalsupplements_2006.pdf.

Northridge, M. E., Stover, G. N., Rosenthal, J. E., & Sherard, D. (2003). Environmental equity and health: Understanding complexity and moving forward. *American Journal of Public Health, 93,* 214.

Nosek, B. A., Greenwald, A. G., & Banaji, M. R. (2005). Understanding and using the implicit association test: II. Method variables and construct validity. *Personality and Social Psychology Bulletin, 31,* 166–180.

Nwadiora, E., & McAdoo, H. (1996). Acculturative stress among Amerasian refugees: Gender and racial differences. *Adolescence, 31,* 477–487.

Ogbu, J. (1978). *Minority education and caste.* New York: Academic Press.

Okagaki, L., & Sternberg, R. J. (1993). Parental beliefs and children's school performance. *Child Development, 64,* 36–56.

Okazaki, S., & Sue, S. (1995). Methodological issues in assessment research with ethnic minorities. *Psychological Assessment, 7,* 367–375.

Okazaki, S., & Sue, S. (1998). Methodological issues in assessment research with ethnic minorities. In P. Balls Organista, K. M. Chun, & G. Marín (Eds.), *Readings in ethnic psychology* (pp. 26–40). New York: Routledge.

Organista, K. C. (2007). *Solving Latino psychosocial and health problems: Theory, practice and populations.* New York: John Wiley.

Orr, A. J. (2003). Black-White differences in achievement: The importance of wealth. *Sociology of Education, 76,* 281–304.

Oskamp, S. (Ed.). (2000). *Reducing prejudice and discrimination.* Mahwah, NJ: Lawrence Erlbaum.

Oskamp, S., & Jones, J. M. (2000). Promising practices in reducing prejudice: A report from the President's Initiative on Race. In S. Oskamp (Ed.), *Reducing prejudice and discrimination* (pp. 319–334). Mahwah, NJ: Lawrence Erlbaum.

Ozer, E. J., Best, S. R., Lipsey, T. L., & Weiss, D. S. (2003). Prediction of posttraumatic stress disorder and symptoms in adults: A meta-analysis. *Psychological Bulletin, 129*(1), 52–73.

Padilla, A. M. (2001). Issues in culturally appropriate assessment. In L. A. Suzuki, J. G. Ponterotto, & P. J. Meller (Eds.), *Handbook of multicultural assessment: Clinical, psychological, and educational applications* (pp. 5–27). San Francisco: Jossey-Bass.

Padilla, A. M., & Perez, W. (2003). Acculturation, social identity, and social cognition: A new perspective. *Hispanic Journal of Behavioral Sciences, 25,* 35–55.

Parham, T. A., White, J. L., & Ajamu, A. (2000). *The psychology of Blacks: An African centered perspective* (3rd ed.). Upper Saddle River, NJ: Prentice Hall.

Park, I. H., & Cho, L. J. (1995). Confucianism and the Korean family. *Journal of Comparative Family Studies, 26*(1), 117–134.

Parke, R. D., Coltrane, S., Borthwick-Duffy, S., Powers, J., & Adams, M. (2004). Assessing father involvement in Mexican-American families. In R. D. Day & M. E. Lamb (Eds.), *Conceptualizing and measuring father involvement* (pp. 17–38). Mahwah, NJ: Lawrence Erlbaum.

Parks, C. A., Hughes, T. L., & Matthews, A. K. (2004). Race/ethnicity and sexual orientation: Intersecting identities. *Cultural Diversity & Ethnic Minority Psychology, 10*(3), 241–254.

Pattnayak, S. R., & Leonard, J. (1991). Racial segregation in major league baseball. *Sociology and Social Research, 76,* 3–9.

Peng, K., & Nisbett, R. E. (1999). Culture, dialectics, and reasoning about contradiction. *American Psychologist, 54,* 741–754.

Pennell, B.-E., Bowers, A., Carr, D., Chardoul, S., Cheung, G.-q., Dinkelmann, K., et al. (2004). The development and implementation of the National Comorbidity Survey Replication, the National Survey of American Life, and the National Latino and Asian American Survey. *International Journal of Methods in Psychiatric Research, 4*(13), 241–269.

Pérez, D. J., Fortuna, L., & Alegría, M. (2008). Prevalence and correlates of everyday discrimination among U.S. Latinos. *Journal of Community Psychology, 36,* 421–433.

Perez, W., & Padilla, A. M. (2000). Cultural orientation across three generations of Hispanic adolescents. *Hispanic Journal of Behavioral Sciences, 22,* 390–398.

Pérez-Stable, E. J., Nápoles-Springer, A., & Miramontes, J. M. (1997). The effects of ethnicity and language on medical outcomes of patients with hypertension or diabetes. *Medical Care, 35,* 1212–1219.

Perilla, J. L., Norris, F. H., & Lavizzo, E. A. (2002). Ethnicity, culture, and disaster response: Identifying and explaining ethnic differences in PTSD six months after Hurricane Andrew. *Journal of Social & Clinical Psychology, 21*(1), 20–45.

Perlmann, J. (2002). Second-generation transnationalism. In P. Levitt & M. C. Waters (Eds.), *The changing face of home: The transnational lives of the second generation* (pp. 216–220). New York: Russell Sage Foundation.

Perugini, M. (2005). Predictive models of implicit and explicit attitudes. *British Journal of Social Psychology, 44,* 29–45.

Pescosolido, B. A., Gardner, C. B., & Lubell, K. M. (1998). How people get into mental health services: Stories of choice, coercion and "muddling through." *Social Science & Medicine, 46*(2), 275–286.

Peterson, S. H., Wingood, G. M., DiClemente, R. J., Harrington, K., & Davies, S. (2007). Images of sexual stereotypes in rap videos and the health of African American female adolescents. *Journal of Woman's Health, 16,* 1157–1164.

Pettigrew, T. F. (1998). Intergroup contact theory. *Annual Review of Psychology, 48,* 65–85.

Pettigrew, T. F. (2004). Justice deferred a half century after *Brown v. Board of Education. American Psychologist, 59,* 521–529.

Pew Hispanic Center. (2006). *From 200 million to 300 million: The numbers behind population growth.* Washington, DC: Author.

Pham, T. B., & Harris, R. J. (2001). Acculturation strategies among Vietnamese-Americans. *International Journal of Intercultural Relations, 25,* 279–300.

Phinney, J. S. (1989). Stages of ethnic identity development in minority group adolescents. *The Journal of Early Adolescence, 9*(1), 34–49.

Phinney, J. S. (1990). Ethnic identity in adolescents and adults: Review of research. *Psychological Bulletin, 108,* 499–514.

Phinney, J. S. (1992). The multigroup ethnic identity measure: A new scale for use with diverse groups. *Journal of Adolescent Research, 7*(2), 156–176.

Phinney, J. S. (1993). Multigroup group identities: Differentiation, conflict, and integration. In J. Kroger (Ed.), *Discussions on ego identity* (pp. 47–73). Hillsdale, NJ: Lawrence Erlbaum.

Phinney, J. S. (1996). When we talk about American ethnic groups what do we mean? *American Psychologist, 51,* 918–927.

Phinney, J. S., & Chavira, V. (1992). Ethnic identity and self-esteem: An exploratory longitudinal study. *Journal of Adolescence, 15*(3), 271–281.

Phinney, J. S., Chavira, V., & Tate, J. D. (1993). The effect of ethnic threat on ethnic self-concept and own-group ratings. *Journal of Social Psychology, 133*(4), 469–478.

Phinney, J. S., Horenczyk, G., Liebkind, K., & Vedder, P. (2001). Ethnic identity, immigration, and well-being: An interactional perspective. *Journal of Social Issues, 57*(3), 493–510.

Phinney, J. S., Lochner, B. T., & Murphy, R. (1990). Ethnic identity development and psychological adjustment in adolescence. In A. R. Stiffman & L. E. Davis (Eds.), *Ethnic issues in adolescent mental health* (pp. 53–72). Thousand Oaks, CA: Sage.

Phinney, J. S., & Ong, A. D. (2002). Adolescent-parent disagreements and life satisfaction in families from Vietnamese- and European-American backgrounds. *International Journal of Behavioral Development, 26*(6), 556–561.

Phinney, J. S., & Ong, A. D. (2007). Conceptualization and measurement of ethnic identity: Current status and future directions. *Journal of Counseling Psychology, 54*(3), 271–281.

Phinney, J. S., Ong, A. D., & Madden, T. (2000). Cultural values and intergenerational value discrepancies in immigrant and non-immigrant families. *Child Development, 71*(2), 528–539.

Phinney, J. S., Romero, I., Nava, M., & Huang, D. (2001). The role of language, parents, and peers in ethnic identity among adolescents in immigrant families. *Journal of Youth and Adolescence, 30*(2), 135–153.

Phinney, J. S., & Rosenthal, D. A. (1992). Ethnic identity in adolescence: Process, context, and outcome. In G. R. Adams, T. P. Gullotta, & R. Montmayor (Eds.), *Advances in adolescent development: Vol. 4. Adolescent identity formation* (pp. 145–172). Thousand Oaks, CA: Sage.

Pike, F. B. (1992). *The United States and Latin America: Myths and stereotypes of civilization and nature.* Austin: University of Texas Press.

Plunkett, S. W., & Bamaca-Gomez, M. Y. (2003). The relationship between parenting, acculturation, and adolescent academics in Mexican-origin immigrant families in Los Angeles. *Hispanic Journal of Behavioral Sciences, 25*(2), 222–239.

Pole, N., Best, S. R., Metzler, T., & Marmar, C. R. (2005). Why are Hispanics at greater risk for PTSD? *Cultural Diversity & Ethnic Minority Psychology, 11*(2), 144–161.

Ponterotto, J. G., Casas, J. M., Suzuki, L. A., & Alexander, C. M. (2001). *Handbook of multicultural counseling* (2nd ed.). Thousand Oaks, CA: Sage.

Ponterotto, J. G., Gretchen, D., Utsey, S. O., Stracuzzi, T., & Saya, R., Jr. (2003). The Multigroup Ethnic Identity Measure (MEIM): Psychometric review and further validity testing. *Educational and Psychological Measurement, 63*(3), 502–515.

Ponterotto, J. G., & Park-Taylor, J. (2007). Racial and ethnic identity theory, measurement, and research in counseling psychology: Present status and future directions. *Journal of Counseling Psychology, 54*(3), 282–294.

Population Reference Bureau. (2002). Foreign-born make up growing segment of the U.S. Black population. *Population Today.* Available at http://www.prb.org/Articles/2002/ForeignBornMakeUpGrowingSegmentofUSBlackPopulation.aspx?p=1.

Portes, A. (1999). Immigration theory for a new century: Some problems and opportunities. In C. Hirschman, P. Kasinitz, & J. DeWind (Eds.), *The handbook of international migration: The American experience* (pp. 21–33). New York: Russell Sage Foundation.

Posner, S. F., Stewart, A. L., Marín, G., & Pérez-Stable, E. J. (2001). Factor variability of the Center for Epidemiological Studies-Depression Scale (CES-D) among urban Latinos. *Ethnicity & Health, 6,* 137–144.

Poston, W. C. (1990). The biracial identity development model: A needed addition. *Journal of Counseling & Development, 69*(2), 152–155.

Poverty rate up 3rd year in a row. (2004, August 27). *The Washington Post,* p. A01.

Powell-Hopson, D., & Hopson, D. S. (1988). Implications of doll color preferences among Black preschool children and White preschool children. *The Journal of Black Psychology, 14,* 57–63.

Proctor, D., & Dalaker, J. (2002, September). *Poverty in the United States: 2001.* Washington, DC: U.S. Census Bureau.

Pyke, K. D., & Johnson, D. L. (2003). Asian American women and racialized femininities: "Doing" gender across cultural worlds. *Gender & Society, 17*(1), 33–53.

Quintana, S. M. (1998). Children's developmental understanding of ethnicity and race. *Applied & Preventive Psychology, 7*(1), 27–45.

Quintana, S. M. (2007). Racial and ethnic identity: Developmental perspectives and research. *Journal of Counseling Psychology, 54*(3), 259–270.

Rainwater, L. (1970). *Behind ghetto walls: Black life in a federal slum.* Chicago: Aldine.

Ramirez, M., & Castaneda, A. (1974). *Cultural democracy and bicognitive developmental education.* New York: Academic Press.

Rankin, B. H., & Quane, J. M. (2000). Neighborhood poverty and the social isolation of inner-city African American families. *Social Forces, 79*(1), 139–164.

Read, J. G., & Gorman, B. K. (2006). Gender inequalities in US adult health: The interplay of race and ethnicity. *Social Science & Medicine, 62,* 1045–1065.

Redfield, R., Linton, R., & Herskovits, M. J. (1936). Memorandum on the study of acculturation. *American Anthropologist, 38,* 149–152.

Rehm, J., Ustun, T., Saxena, S., Nelson, C. B., Chatterji, S., Ivis, F., et al. (1999). On the development and psychometric testing of the WHO screening instrument to assess disablement in the general population. *International Journal of Methods in Psychiatric Research, 8,* 110–123.

Reichman, J. S. (1997). Language-specific response patterns and subjective assessment of health: A sociolinguistic analysis. *Hispanic Journal of Behavioral Sciences, 19,* 353–368.

Roberts, R. E., Phinney, J. S., Masse, L. C., Chen, Y. R., Roberts, C. R., & Romero, A. (1999). The structure of ethnic identity of young adolescents from diverse ethnocultural groups. *The Journal of Early Adolescence, 19*(3), 301–322.

Roberts, R. E., Vernon, S. W., & Rhoades, H. M. (1989). Effects of language and ethnic status on reliability and validity of the Center for Epidemiologic Studies-Depression Scale with psychiatric patients. *The Journal of Nervous and Mental Disease, 177,* 581–592.

Robins, L., & Regier, D. (Eds.). (1991). *Psychiatric disorders in America: The Epidemiologic Catchment Area study.* New York: Free Press.

Rodriguez, N., Myers, H. F., Mira, C. B., Flores, T., & Garcia-Hernandez, L. (2002). Development of the Multidimensional Acculturative Stress Inventory for adults of Mexican origin. *Psychological Assessment, 14,* 451–461.

Rogler, L. H. (1999a). Implementing cultural sensitivity in mental health research: Convergence and new directions. *Psychline, 3*(1), 5–11.

Rogler, L. H. (1999b). Methodological sources of cultural insensitivity in mental health research. *American Psychologist, 54,* 424–433.

Rogler, L. H., Cortes, D. E., & Malgady, R. G. (1991). Acculturation and mental health status among Hispanics. *American Psychologist, 46,* 585–597.

Rohner, R., & Pettengill, S. (1985). Perceived parental acceptance-rejection and parental control among Korean adolescents. *Child Development, 56,* 524–528.

Romero-Gwynn, E., Gwynn, D., Grivetti, L., McDonald, R., Stanford, G., Turner, B., et al. (1993). Dietary acculturation among Latinos of Mexican descent. *Nutrition Today, 28*(4), 5–12.

Romo, L. F., Kouyoumdjian, C., Nadeem, E., & Sigman, M. (2006). Promoting values of education in Latino mother-adolescent discussions about conflict and sexuality. In J. Denner & B. L. Guzman (Eds.), *Latina girls: Voices of adolescent strength in the United States* (pp. 59–76). New York: New York University Press.

Root, M. P. P. (1990). Resolving "other" status: Identity development of biracial individuals. *Women & Therapy, 9*(1), 185–205.

Root, M. P. P. (1992). Back to the drawing board: Methodological issues in research on multiracial people. In M. P. P. Root (Ed.), *Racially mixed people in America* (pp. 181–189). Newbury Park, CA: Sage.

Root, M. P. P. (1998). Multiracial Americans: Changing the face of Asian America. In N. W. S. Zane & E. Lee (Eds.), *Handbook of Asian American psychology* (1st ed., pp. 261–287). Thousand Oaks, CA: Sage.

Root, M. P. P. (2003). Racial identity development and persons of mixed race heritage. In M. P. P. Root & M. Kelley (Eds.), *Multiracial child resource book* (p. 41). Seattle, WA: Mavin Foundation.

Rosario, M., Schrimshaw, E. W., & Hunter, J. (2004). Ethnic/racial differences in the coming-out process of lesbian, gay, and bisexual youths: A comparison of sexual identity development over time. *Cultural Diversity & Ethnic Minority Psychology, 10*(3), 215–228.

Rosenblum, K. E., & Travis, T.-M. C. (2003). *The meaning of difference: American constructions of race, sex and gender, social class, and sexual orientation.* New York: McGraw-Hill.

Rosenheck, R., & Fontana, A. (1996). Race and outcome of treatment for veterans suffering from PTSD. *Journal of Traumatic Stress, 9,* 343–351.

Rosenthal, D., Ranieri, N., & Klimidis, S. (1996). Vietnamese adolescents in Australia: Relationships between perceptions of self and parental values, intergenerational conflict, and gender dissatisfaction. *International Journal of Psychology, 31*(2), 81–91.

Rossa, M. W., Dumka, L. E., Gonzales, N. A., & Knight, G. P. (2002). Cultural/ethnic issues and the prevention scientist in the 21st century. *Prevention & Treatment, 5,* 21–36.

Rotheram, M. J., & Phinney, J. S. (1987). Ethnic behavior patterns as an aspect of identity. In J. S. Phinney & M. J. Rotheram (Eds.), *Children's ethnic socialization: Pluralism and development* (pp. 210–218). Beverly Hills, CA: Sage.

Rothman, R. A. (2002). Structural inequality and social stratification. In R. A. Rothman (Ed.), *Inequality and stratification: Race, class, and gender* (4th ed., pp. 2–17). Upper Saddle River, NJ: Prentice Hall.

Rowatt, W. C., Franklin, L. M., & Cotton, M. (2005). Patterns and personality correlates of implicit and explicit attitudes toward Christians and Muslims. *Journal for the Scientific Study of Religion, 44,* 29–43.

Rudmin, F. W. (2003). "Critical history of the acculturation psychology of assimilation, separation, integration, and marginalization": Correction to Rudmin (2003). *Review of General Psychology, 7,* 250.

Rumbaut, R. G., & Portes, A. (2001). *Ethnicities: Children of immigrants in America.* Berkeley: University of California Press.

Ryan, W. (1972). *Blaming the victim.* New York: Vintage.

Sabogal, F., Marín, G., Otero-Sabogal, R., Marín, B. V., & Pérez-Stable, E. J. (1987). Hispanic familism and acculturation: What changes and what doesn't? *Hispanic Journal of Behavioral Sciences, 9,* 397–412.

Saéz-Santiago, E., & Bernal, G. (2003). Depression in ethnic minorities: Latinos and Latinas, African Americans, Asian Americans, and Native Americans. In G. Bernal, J. E. Trimble, A. K. Burlew, & F. T. L. Leong (Eds.), *Handbook of racial & ethnic minority psychology* (pp. 401–428). Thousand Oaks, CA: Sage.

Safren, S. A., Gonzalez, R. E., Horner, K. J., Leung, A. W., Heimberg, R. G., & Juster, H. R. (2000). Anxiety in ethnic minority youth: Methodological and conceptual issues and review of the literature. *Behavior Modification, 24,* 147–183.

Sam, D. L. (2006). Acculturation and health. In D. L. Sam & J. W. Berry (Eds.), *The Cambridge handbook of acculturation psychology* (pp. 452–468). Cambridge, MA: Cambridge University Press.

Sam, D. L., & Berry, J. W. (Eds.). (2006). *The Cambridge handbook of acculturation psychology.* Cambridge, MA: Cambridge University Press.

Sampson, E. E. (1999). *Dealing with differences: An introduction to the social psychology of prejudice.* Orlando, FL: Harcourt Brace.

Sanchez, J. I., & Fernandez, D. M. (1993). Acculturation stress among Hispanics: A bidimensional model of ethnic identification. *Journal of Applied Social Psychology, 23,* 654–668.

Sanders, R. G. W. (2002). The Black church: Bridge over troubled water. In J. L. Sanders & C. Bradley (Eds.), *Counseling African American families* (pp. 73–84). Alexandria, VA: American Counseling Association.

Sanders Thompson, V. L., Bazile, A., & Akbar, M. (2004). African Americans' perceptions of psychotherapy and psychotherapists. *Professional Psychology: Research and Practice, 35,* 19–26.

Santisteban, D. A., Suarez-Morales, L., Robbins, M. S., & Szapocznik, J. (2006). Brief strategic family therapy: Lessons learned in efficacy research and challenges to blending research and practice. *Family Process, 45*(2), 259–271.

Santos, S. J., Ortiz, A. M., Morales, A., & Rosales, M. (2007). The relationship between campus diversity, students' ethnic identity and college adjustment: A qualitative study. *Cultural Diversity & Ethnic Minority Psychology, 13,* 104–114.

Santrock, J. W. (2004). *Life span development* (10th ed.). Boston: McGraw-Hill.

Santrock, J. W. (2005). *A topical approach to life-span development.* (2nd ed.). New York: McGraw-Hill.

Savage, S. L., & Gauvain, M. (1998). Parental beliefs and children's everyday planning in European-American and Latino families. *Journal of Applied Developmental Psychology, 19,* 319–340.

Schaefer, R. T. (1996). *Racial and ethnic groups* (6th ed.). New York: HarperCollins.

Schaefer, R. T. (Ed.). (2008). *Encyclopedia of race, ethnicity, and society* (Vols. 1–3). Thousand Oaks, CA: Sage.

Schofield, J. W., & Hausmann, L. R. M. (2004). School desegregation and social science research. *American Psychologist, 59,* 538–546.

Schoon, I., Bynner, J., Joshi, H., Parsons, S., Wiggins, R. D., & Sacker, A. (2002). The influence, timing, and duration of risk experiences for the passage from childhood to midadulthood. *Child Development, 73*(5), 1486–1504.

Schraufnagel, T. J., Wagner, A. W., Miranda, J., Peter, P., & Roy-Byrne, M. (2006). Treating minority patients with depression and anxiety: What does the evidence tell us? *General Hospital Psychiatry, 28,* 27–36.

Schuman, H., Steeh, C., & Bobo, L. (1985). *Racial attitudes in America.* Cambridge, MA: Harvard University Press.

Sciacca, K., & Thompson, C. M. (1996). Program development and integrated treatment across systems for dual diagnosis: Mental illness, drug addiction and alcoholism, MIDAA. *Journal of Mental Health Administration, 23*(3), 288–297.

Sears, D. O., Fu, M., Henry, P. J., & Bui, K. (2003). The origins and persistence of ethnic identity among the "new immigrant" groups. *Social Psychology Quarterly, 66*(4), 419–437.

Seaton, E. K., & Taylor, R. D. (2003). Exploring familial processes in urban, low-income African-American families. *Journal of Family Issues, 24*(5), 627–644.

Segall, M. H., Lonner, W. J., & Berry, J. W. (1998). Cross-cultural psychology as a scholarly discipline: On the flowering of culture in behavioral research. *American Psychologist, 53,* 1101–1110.

Seligman, M. E. P., & Csikszentmihalyi, M. (2000). Positive psychology: An introduction. *American Psychologist, 55*(1), 5–14.

Serpell, R. (1979). How specific are perpetual skills? A cross-cultural study of pattern. *British Journal of Psychology, 70,* 365–380.

Serrano, E., & Anderson, J. (2003). Assessment of a refined short acculturation scale for Latino preteens in rural Colorado. *Hispanic Journal of Behavioral Sciences, 25,* 240–253.

Shavers-Hornaday, V. L., Lynch, C. F., Burmeister, L. F., & Torner, J. C. (1997). Why are African Americans under-represented in medical research studies? Impediments to participation. *Ethnicity & Health, 2*(1–2), 31–45.

Shaw, D., Winslow, E., & Flanagan, C. (1999). A prospective study of the effects of marital status and family relations on young children's adjustment among African American and European American families. *Child Development, 70*(3), 742–755.

Shelton, J. N., Richeson, J. A., Salvatore, J., & Trawalter, S. (2005). Ironic effects of racial bias during interracial interactions. *Psychological Science, 16,* 397–402.

Shi, L. (2001). The convergence of vulnerable characteristics and health insurance in the United States. *Social Science Medicine, 53*(4), 519–529.

Shih, M., Pittinsky, T. L., & Trahan, A. (2006). Domain-specific effects of stereotypes on performance. *Self and Identity, 5,* 1–14.

Shih, M., & Sanchez, D. T. (2005). Perspectives and research on the positive and negative implications of having multiple racial identities. *Psychological Bulletin, 131*(4), 569–591.

Shin, H. B., & Bruno, R. (2003). *Language use and English-speaking ability* (Census 2000 Brief C2KBR-29). Washington, DC: U.S. Census Bureau.

Shive, S. E., Ma, G. X., Tan, Y., Toubbeh, J. I., Parameswaran, L., & Halowich, J. (2007). Asian American subgroup differences in sources of health information and predictors of screening behavior. *California Journal of Health Promotion, 5*(2), 112–127.

Simon, C. E., Crowther, M., & Higgerson, H. K. (2007). The stage-specific role of spirituality among African American Christian women throughout the breast cancer experience. *Cultural Diversity & Ethnic Minority Psychology, 13,* 26–34.

Simons, R. L., Murry, V., McLoyd, V., Lin, K. H., Cutrona, C., & Conger, R. D. (2002). Discrimination, crime, ethnic identity, and parenting as correlates of depressive symptoms among African American children: A multilevel analysis. *Development and Psychopathology, 14*(2), 371–393.

Singelis, M. T. (1994). The measurement of independent and interdependent self-construals. *Personality and Social Psychology Bulletin, 20,* 580–591.

Smedley, B. D. (2008). Moving beyond access: Achieving equity in state health care reform. *Health Affairs, 27*(2), 447–455.

Smedley, B. D., Stith, A. Y., & Nelson, A. R. (Eds.). (2003). *Unequal treatment: Confronting racial and ethnic disparities in health care.* Washington, DC: National Academy Press.

Smetana, J., & Gaines, C. (1999). Adolescent-parent conflict in middle-class African American families. *Child Development, 70*(6), 1447–1463.

Smith, T. W. (1990). *Ethnic images* (GSS Topical Report No.19). Chicago: National Opinion Research Center.

Snowden, L. R., & Cheung, F. K. (1990). Use of inpatient mental services by members of ethnic minority groups. *American Psychologist, 45,* 347–355.

Snowden, L. R., & Hines, A. M. (1999). A scale to assess African American acculturation. *Journal of Black Psychology, 25,* 36–47.

Snowden, L. R., Masland, M., & Guerrero, R. (2007). Federal civil rights policy and mental health treatment access for persons with limited English proficiency. *American Psychologist, 62*(2), 109–117.

Snowden, L. R., & Thomas, K. (2000). Medicaid and African American outpatient mental health treatment. *Mental Health Services Research, 2,* 115–120.

Social Science Research Council. (1954). Acculturation: An exploratory formulation. *American Anthropologist, 56,* 973–1002.

Sodowsky, G. R., Lai, E. W., & Plake, B. S. (1991). Moderating effects of sociocultural variables on acculturation attitudes of Hispanics and Asian Americans. *Journal of Counseling & Development, 70,* 194–204.

Soldier, L. L. (1985). To soar with the eagles: Enculturation and acculturation of Indian children. *Childhood Education, 10,* 185–189.

Solomon, R. C., & Higgins, K. M. (1997). *A passion for wisdom: A very brief history of philosophy.* Oxford, UK: Oxford University Press.

Sperber, A. D., Devellis, R. F., & Boehlecke, B. (1994). Cross-cultural translation: Methodology and validation. *Journal of Cross-Cultural Psychology, 25,* 501–524.

Stanfield, J. H., & Dennis, R. M. (Eds.). (1993). *Race and ethnicity in research methods.* Newbury Park, CA: Sage.

Steele, C. M. (1997). A threat in the air: How stereotypes shape intellectual identity and performance. *American Psychologist, 52,* 613–629.

Steele, C. M., & Aronson, J. (1995). Stereotype threat and the intellectual test performance of African Americans. *Journal of Personality and Social Psychology, 69,* 797–811.

Stein, J., Nyamathi, A., & Kington, R. (1997). Change in AIDS risk behaviors among impoverished minority women after a community based cognitive-behavioral outreach program. *Journal of Community Psychology, 25,* 519–533.

Steinberg, L. (2001). We know some things: Parent-adolescent relationships in retrospect and prospect. *Journal of Research on Adolescence, 11,* 1–19.

Steinman, K. J., & Zimmerman, M. A. (2004). Religious activity and risk behavior among African American adolescents: Concurrent and developmental effects. *American Journal of Community Psychology, 33*(3/4), 151–161.

Stephenson, M. (2000). Development and validation of the Stephenson Multigroup Acculturation Scale (SMAS). *Psychological Assessment, 12,* 77–88.

Stern, M. P., Knapp, J. A., Hazuda, H. P., Haffner, S. M., Patterson, J. K., & Mitchell, B. D. (1991). Genetic and environmental determinants of type II diabetes in Mexican Americans: Is there a "descending limb" to the modernization/diabetes relationship? *Diabetes Care, 14,* 649–654.

Sternberg, R. J. (1985). *Beyond IQ: A triarchic theory of human intelligence.* New York: Cambridge University Press.

Sternberg, R. J. (2004). Culture and intelligence. *American Psychologist, 59,* 325–338.

Stevenson, H. W., Chen, C., & Uttal, D. H. (1990). Beliefs and achievement: A study of Black, White, and Hispanic children. *Child Development, 61,* 508–523.

Strasburg, J. (2002). Abercrombie & glitch: Asian Americans rip retailer for stereotypes on T-shirts. *San Francisco Chronicle,* p. A-1. Available at http://www.sfgate .com/cgi-bin/article.cgi?file=/c/a/2002/04/18/MN109646.DTL.

Sturgeon, J. (2005, January/February). *The many languages of medicine.* Retrieved April 29, 2005, from Unique Opportunities: The Physician's Resource at http://www.uoworks.com/articles/language.html.

Suárez-Orozco, C., & Suárez-Orozco, M. M. (1995). *Transformations: Migration, family life, and achievement motivation among Latino adolescents.* Stanford, CA: Stanford University Press.

Substance Abuse and Mental Health Services Administration. (2006). *Results from the 2005 National Survey on Drug Use and Health: National findings* (NSDUH Series H-30, DHHS Publication No. SMA 06-4194). Rockville, MD: Author.

Sudano, J. J., & Baker, D. W. (2006). Explaining US racial/ethnic disparities in health declines and mortality in late middle age: The roles of socioeconomic status, health behaviors, and health insurance. *Social Science & Medicine, 62*(4), 909–922.

Sue, D. W. (2003). *Overcoming our racism: The journey to liberation.* San Francisco: Jossey-Bass.

Sue, D. W. (2004). Whiteness and ethnocentric monoculturalism: Making the "invisible" visible. *American Psychologist, 59,* 761–769.

Sue, D. W., Capodilupo, C. M., Torino, G. C., Bucceri, J. M., Holder, A. M., Nadal, K. L., et al. (2007). Racial microaggressions in everyday life. *American Psychologist, 62,* 271–286.

Sue, D. W., Ivey, A. E., & Pedersen, P. B. (1996). *A theory of multicultural counseling and psychotherapy.* Pacific Grove, CA: Brooks/Cole.

Sue, D. W., & Sue, D. (1999). *Counseling the culturally different* (3rd ed.). New York: John Wiley.

Sue, D. W., & Sue, D. (2008). *Counseling the culturally diverse: Theory and practice.* Hoboken, NJ: John Wiley.

Sue, S. (1999). Science, ethnicity, and bias. *American Psychologist, 54,* 1070–1077.

Sue, S. (2006). Cultural competency: From philosophy to research and practice. *Journal of Community Psychology, 34*(2), 237–245.

Sue, S., Fujino, D., Hu, L., Takeuchi, D., & Zane, N. (1991). Community mental health services for ethnic minority groups: A test of the cultural responsiveness hypothesis. *Journal of Consulting and Clinical Psychology, 59,* 533–540.

Sue, S., & Okazaki, S. (1990). Asian-American educational achievements: A phenomenon in search of an explanation. *American Psychologist, 45,* 913–920.

Sue, S., Sue, D. W., Sue, L., & Takeuchi, D. T. (1998). Psychopathology among Asian Americans: A model minority? In P. Balls Organista, K. M. Chun, & G. Marín (Eds.), *Readings in ethnic psychology* (pp. 270–282). New York: Routledge.

Sue, S., Zane, N., Hall, G. C. N., & Berger, L. K. (2009). The case for cultural competence in psychotherapeutic interventions. *Annual Review of Psychology, 60,* 525–548.

Suinn, R. M., Rickard-Figueroa, K., Lew, S., & Vigil, P. (1987). Suinn-Lew Asian Self-Identity Acculturation Scale: An initial report. *Educational and Psychological Measurement, 47,* 401–407.

Suls, J., & Rothman, A. (2004). Evolution of the biopsychosocial model: Prospects and challenges for health psychology. *Health Psychology, 23,* 119–125.

Suzuki-Crumly, J., & Hyers, L. L. (2004). The relationship among ethnic identity, psychological well-being, and intergroup competence: An investigation of two biracial groups. *Cultural Diversity & Ethnic Minority Psychology, 10*(2), 137–150.

Swarns, R. L. (2004, August 29). "African-American" becomes a term for debate. *New York Times,* p. 01.

Szapocznik, J., & Kurtines, W. (1980). Acculturation, biculturalism and adjustment among Cuban-Americans. In A. M. Padilla (Ed.), *Acculturation: Theory, models and some new findings* (pp. 139–159). Boulder, CO: Westview.

Tajfel, H. (1981). *Human groups and social categories: Studies in social psychology.* Cambridge, UK: Cambridge University Press.

Takaki, R. T. (1979). *Iron cages: Race and culture in nineteenth century America.* Seattle, WA: University of Washington Press.

Talbot, M. (1997, November 30). Getting credit for being White. *The New York Times Magazine, 30,* 116–119.

Tam, V. C. W., & Detzner, D. F. (1998). Grandparents as a family resource in Chinese-American families. In H. I. McCubbin, E. A. Thompson, A. I. Thompson, & J. E. Fromer (Eds.), *Resiliency in Native American and immigrant families* (pp. 243–262). Thousand Oaks, CA: Sage.

Tang, C. S. K., Cheung, F. M. C., Chen, R., & Sun, X. (2002). Definition of violence against women: A comparative study in Chinese societies of Hong Kong, Taiwan, and the People's Republic of China. *Journal of Interpersonal Violence, 17*(6), 671–688.

Taylor, R. D., Casten, R., & Flickinger, S. M. (1993). Influence of kinship social support on the parenting experiences and the psychosocial adjustment of African-American adolescents. *Developmental Psychology, 29*(2), 382–388.

Taylor, S. (2009). *Health psychology* (7th ed.). New York: McGraw-Hill.

Thomas, W. I., & Znaniecki, F. (1918). *The Polish peasant in Europe and America.* Boston: R. Badger.

Torres, A. (1992). Nativity, gender, and earning discrimination. *Hispanic Journal of Behavioral Sciences, 14,* 134–143.

Torres, J. B., Solberg, V. S. H., & Carlstrom, A. H. (2002). The myth of sameness among Latino men and their machismo. *American Journal of Orthopsychiatry, 72*(2), 163–181.

Tran, C., & Des Jardins, K. (2000). Domestic violence in Vietnamese refugee and Korean immigrant communities. In J. L. Chin (Ed.), *Relationships among Asian American women* (pp. 71–96). Washington, DC: American Psychological Association.

Tran, Q. D., & Richey, C. A. (1997). Family functioning and psychological well-being in Vietnamese adolescents. *Journal of Sociology & Social Welfare, 24*(1), 41–61.

Triandis, H. C. (1990). Cross-cultural studies of individualism and collectivism. In J. J. Berman (Ed.), *Cross-cultural perspectives: Nebraska Symposium on Motivation, 1989* (pp. 41–133). Lincoln: University of Nebraska Press.

Triandis, H. C. (1994). *Culture and social behavior.* New York: McGraw-Hill.

Triandis, H. C. (1995). *Individualism and collectivism.* Boulder, CO: Westview.

Triandis, H. C. (2002). Subjective culture. In W. J. Lonner, D. L. Dinnel, S. A. Hayes, & D. N. Sattler (Eds.), *Online readings in psychology and culture* (Unit 15, Chapter 1). Available from Center for Cross-Cultural Research, Western Washington University, Bellingham, at http://www.wwu.edu/~culture.

Triandis, H. C., Bontempo, R., Villareal, M., Asai, M., & Lucca, N. (1988). Individualism and collectivism: Cross cultural perspectives on self-ingroup relationships. *Journal of Personality and Social Psychology, 59,* 1006–1020.

Triandis, H. C., & Gelfand, M. J. (1998). Converging measurement of horizontal and vertical individualism and collectivism. *Journal of Personality and Social Psychology, 74,* 118–128.

Trickett, E. J. (1996). A future for community psychology: The contexts of diversity and the diversity of contexts. *American Journal of Community Psychology, 24,* 209–234.

Trimble, J. E. (2007). Prolegomena for the connotation of construct use in the measurement of ethnic and racial identity. *Journal of Counseling Psychology, 54*(3), 247–258.

Tropp, L. R., Erkut, S., Coll, C. G., Alarcón, O., & Garcia, H. A. (1999). Psychological acculturation development of a new measure for Puerto Ricans on the U.S. mainland. *Educational and Psychological Measurement, 59*(2), 351–367.

Tseng, V., & Fuligni, A. J. (2000). Parent-adolescent language use and relationships among immigrant families with East Asian, Filipino, and Latin American backgrounds. *Journal of Marriage and Family, 62,* 465–476.

Tseng, W.-S. (2006). From peculiar psychiatric disorders through culture-bound syndromes to culture-related syndromes. *Transcultural Psychiatry, 43*(4), 554–576.

Tucker, J. A., Phillips, M. M., Murphy, J. G., & Raczynski, J. M. (2004). Behavioral epidemiology and health psychology. In T. J. Boll (Series Ed.) & R. G. Frank, A. Baum, & J. L. Wallander (Vol. Eds.), *Models and perspectives in health psychology: Vol. 3. Handbook of clinical health psychology* (pp. 435–464). Washington, DC: American Psychological Association.

Turner, S. M., DeMersr, S. T., Fox, H. R., & Reed, G. M. (2001). APA's guidelines for test users' qualifications: An executive summary. *American Psychologist, 56,* 1099–1113.

Twine, F. W., & Gallagher, C. (2008). The future of Whiteness: A map of the "third wave." *Ethnic and Racial Studies, 31*(1), 3–24.

Uba, L. (1994). *Asian Americans: Personality patterns, identity, and mental health.* New York: Guilford.

Umana-Taylor, A. J., Diversi, M., & Fine, M. A. (2002). Ethnic identity and self-esteem of Latino adolescents: Distinctions among the Latino populations. *Journal of Adolescent Research, 17*(3), 303–327.

Unger, J. B., Gallaher, P., Shakib, S., Ritt-Olson, A., Palmer, P. H., & Johnson, C. A. (2002). The AHIMSA acculturation scale: A new measure of acculturation for adolescents in a multicultural society. *Journal of Early Adolescence, 22,* 225–251.

U.S. Census Bureau. (2002). *Poverty in the United States: 2002.* Retrieved December 20, 2005, from http://www.census.gov/hhes/www/poverty/publications.html.

U.S. Census Bureau. (2006). *American Community Survey.* Retrieved July 3, 2008, from http://www.factfinder.census.gov.

U.S. Census Bureau. (2008). *Percent of the projected population by race and Hispanic origin for the United States: 2010 to 2050* (NP2008-T6). Retrieved January 30, 2009, from www.census.gov/ipc/www/usinterimproj/.

U.S. House of Representatives, Committee on Government Reform. (2004, January). *A case study in politics and science: Changes to the National Healthcare Disparities Report.* Retrieved April 22, 2009, from http://oversight.house. gov/features/politics_and_science/pdfs/pdf_politics_and_science_disparities_rep.pdf

Utsey, S. O., Chae, M. H., Brown, C. F., & Kelly, D. (2002). Effect of ethnic group membership on ethnic identity, race-related stress, and quality of life. *Cultural Diversity & Ethnic Minority Psychology, 8*(4), 366–377.

Vandiver, B. J. (2001). Psychological nigrescence revisited: Introduction and overview. *Journal of Multicultural Counseling and Development, 29*(3), 165–173.

Vandiver, B. J., Fhagen-Smith, P. E., Cokley, K. O., Cross, W. E., Jr., & Worrell, F. C. (2001). Cross's nigrescence model: From theory to scale to theory. *Journal of Multicultural Counseling and Development, 29*(3), 174–200.

Vanman, E. J., Saltz, J. L., Nathan, L. R., & Warren, J. A. (2004). Racial discrimination by low-prejudiced Whites: Facial movements as implicit measures of attitudes related to behavior. *Psychological Science, 15,* 711–714.

Vega, W., Warheit, G., Buhl-Autg, J., & Meinhardt, K. (1984). The prevalence of depressive symptoms among Mexican Americans and Anglos. *American Journal of Epidemiology, 120,* 592–607.

Vega, W. A., Gil, A. G., & Kolody, B. (2002). What do we know about Latino drug use? Methodological evaluation of state databases. *Hispanic Journal of Behavioral Sciences, 24,* 395–408.

Vijver, F. V., & Hambleton, R. K. (1996). Translating tests: Some practical guidelines. *European Psychologist, 1,* 88–99.

Wade, C., & Tavris, C. (2008). *Psychology* (9th ed.). Upper Saddle River, NJ: Pearson.

Waldinger, R. (2007). *Between here and there: How attached are Latino immigrants to their native country.* Washington, DC: Pew Hispanic Center.

Wallen, G. R., Feldman, R. H., & Anliker, J. (2002). Measuring acculturation among Central American women with the use of a brief language scale. *Journal of Immigrant Health, 4,* 95–102.

Wandersman, A., & Nation, M. (1998). Urban neighborhoods and mental health: Psychological contributions to understanding toxicity, resilience, and interventions. *American Psychologist, 53,* 635–646.

Wang, C., Abbott, L., Goodbody, A. K., Hui, W. Y., & Rausch, C. (1999). Development of a community-based diabetes management program for Pacific Islanders. *Diabetes Educator, 25*(5), 738–746.

Wang, P., Lane, M., Olfson, M., Pincus, K., & Kessler, R. C. (2005). Twelve-month use of mental health services in the United States: Results of the National Comorbidity Survey Replication. *Archives of General Psychiatry, 62,* 629–640.

Washington in brief. (2004, February 11). *The Washington Post*, p. A20.

Weaver, C. N. (2005). The changing image of Hispanic Americans. *Hispanic Journal of Behavioral Sciences, 27,* 337–354.

Weaver, C. N. (2007). The effects of contact on the prejudice between Hispanics and non-Hispanic Whites in the United States. *Hispanic Journal of Behavioral Sciences, 29,* 254–274.

Weaver, C. N. (2008). Social distance as a measure of prejudice among ethnic groups in the United States. *Journal of Applied Social Psychology, 38,* 779–795.

Webster, C. N. (1996). Hispanic and Anglo interviewer and respondent ethnicity and gender: The impact on survey response quality. *Journal of Marketing Research, 33,* 62–72.

Weinstein, R. S., Gregory, A., & Strambler, M. J. (2004). Intractable self-fulfilling prophecies fifty years after *Brown v. Board of Education. American Psychologist, 59,* 511–520.

Weiss, J. W., & Weiss, D. J. (2002). Recruiting Asian-American adolescents for behavioral surveys. *Journal of Child and Family Studies, 11*(2), 143–149.

Westermeyer, J., Callies, A., & Neider, J. (1990). Welfare status and psychological adjustment among 100 Hmong refugees. *Journal of Nervous and Mental Disease, 178,* 300–306.

Westra, L., & Lawson, B. E. (Eds.). (2001). *Faces of environmental racism: Confronting issues of global justice* (2nd ed.). Lanham, MD: Rowman & Littlefield.

Whaley, A. L. (2000). Sociocultural differences in the developmental consequences of the use of physical discipline during childhood for African Americans. *Cultural Diversity & Ethnic Minority Psychology, 6*(1), 5–12.

Whaley, A. L. (2001). Cultural mistrust: An important psychological construct for diagnosis and treatment of African Americans. *American Psychologist, 32,* 555–562.

Whaley, A. L. (2004). A two-stage method for the study of cultural bias in the diagnosis of schizophrenia in African Americans. *Journal of Black Psychology, 30*(2), 167–186.

Whaley, A. L., & Davis, K. E. (2007). Cultural competence and evidence-based practice in mental health services: A complementary perspective. *American Psychologist, 62,* 563–574.

Wheeler, D. L. (1997, December 12). 3 medical organizations embroiled in controversy over use of placebos in AIDS studies abroad. *The Chronicle of Higher Education*, pp. A15–A16.

Whitley, B. E., Jr., & Kite, M. E. (2006). *The psychology of prejudice and discrimination.* Belmont, CA: Thomson Wadsworth.

Wilbert, J. (1976). *Enculturation in Latin America.* Los Angeles: University of California, Los Angeles, Latin American Center.

Wilkes, R. E., & Valencia, H. (1989). Hispanics and Blacks in television commercials. *Journal of Advertising, 18,* 19–25.

Williams, C. B. (1999). Claiming a biracial identity: Resisting social constructions of race and culture. *Journal of Counseling & Development, 77,* 32–35.

Williams, D. R., & Collins, C. (1995). U.S. socioeconomic and racial differences in health: Patterns and explanations. *Annual Review of Sociology, 21,* 349–386.

Williams, D. R., Haile, R., Gonzalez, H. M., Neighbors, H., Baser, R., & Jackson, J. S. (2007). The mental health of Black Caribbean immigrants: Results from the National Survey of American Life. *American Journal of Public Health, 97*(1), 52–59.

Williams, D. R., Neighbors, H. W., & Jackson, J. S. (2003). Racial/ethnic discrimination and health: Findings from community studies. *American Journal of Public Health, 93,* 200–208.

Williams, L. (2006). *Neo soul: Taking soul food to a whole 'nutha level.* New York: Avery.

Wilson, W. J. (1974). The new Black sociology: Reflections on the "insiders" and "outsiders" controversy. In J. E. Blackwell & M. Janowitz (Eds.), *Black sociologists: Historical and contemporary perspectives.* Chicago: University of Chicago Press.

Wong, C. A., Eccles, J. S., & Sameroff, A. (2003). The influence of ethnic discrimination and ethnic identification on African American adolescents' school and socioemotional adjustment. *Journal of Personality, 71*(6), 1197–1232.

World Health Organization. (1948). *Constitution of the World Health Organization.* Geneva, Switzerland: World Health Organization Basic Documents.

Yap, P. M. (1974). *Comparative psychiatry: A theoretical framework.* Toronto, Canada: University of Toronto Press.

Yee, A. H., Fairchild, H. H., Weizmann, F., & Wyatt, G. E. (1993). Addressing psychology's problem with race. *American Psychologist, 48*(11), 1132–1140.

Yee, B. W. K., Huang, L. N., & Lew, A. (1998). Families: Life-span socialization in a cultural context. In L. C. Lee & N. W. S. Zane (Eds.), *Handbook of Asian American psychology* (1st ed., pp. 83–135). Thousand Oaks, CA: Sage.

Yick, A. G. (2000). Predictors of physical spousal/intimate violence in Chinese American families. *Journal of Family Violence, 15*(3), 249–267.

Ying, Y. (1990). Explanatory models of major depression and implications for help-seeking among immigrant Chinese-American women. *Culture, Medicine, and Psychiatry, 14,* 393–408.

Ying, Y. (1999). Strengthening intergenerational/intercultural ties in migrant families: A new intervention for parents. *Journal of Community Psychology, 27*(1), 89–96.

Yinger, J. (1988). Examining racial discrimination with fair housing audits. *New Directions for Program Evaluations, 37,* 47–62.

Yip, T., & Fuligni, A. J. (2002). Daily variation in ethnic identity, ethnic behaviors, and psychosocial well-being among American adolescents of Chinese descent. *Child Development, 73*(5), 1557–1572.

Youn, G., Knight, B., Jeong, H.-S., & Benton, D. (1999). Differences in familism values and caregiving outcomes among Korean, Korean American, and White American dementia caregivers. *Psychology and Aging, 14*(3), 355–364.

Zaff, J. F., Blount, R. L., Phillips, L., & Cohen, L. (2002). The role of ethnic identity and self-construal in coping among African American and Caucasian American seventh graders: An exploratory analysis of within-group variance. *Adolescence, 37*(148), 751–773.

Zane, N., Aoki, B., Ho, T., Huang, L., & Jang, M. (1998). Dosage-related changes in a culturally responsive prevention program for Asian American youth. *Drugs and Society, 12,* 105–125.

Zane, N., & Mak, W. (2003). Major approaches to the measurement of acculturation among ethnic minority populations: A content analysis and an alternative empirical strategy. In K. M. Chun, P. Balls Organista, & G. Marín (Eds.), *Acculturation: Advances in theory, measurement, and applied research* (pp. 39–60). Washington, DC: American Psychological Association.

Zane, N. W. S., Takeuchi, D. T., & Young, K. N. J. (Eds.). (1994). *Confronting issues of Asian and Pacific Islander Americans.* Thousand Oaks, CA: Sage.

Zea, M. C., Quezada, T., & Belgrave, F. Z. (1994). Latino cultural values: Their role in adjustment to disability. *Journal of Social Behavior and Personality, 9,* 185–200.

Zhang, A. Y., & Snowden, L. R. (1999). Ethnic characteristic of mental disorders in five communities nationwide. *Cultural Diversity & Ethnic Minority Psychology, 5,* 134–146.

Zhou, M. (1999). Segmental assimilation: Issues, controversies, and recent research on the new second generation. In C. Hirschman, P. Kasinitz, & J. DeWind (Eds.), *The handbook of international migration: The American experience* (pp. 196–211). New York: Russell Sage Foundation.

Zhou, Y., Dominici, F., & Louis, T. A. (2006). *Racial disparity in mortality rates in a sample of the U.S. Medicare population* (Working Paper 114). Baltimore: Johns Hopkins University, Department of Biostatistics. Available at http://www.bepress.com/jhubiostat/paper114/.

Ziegert, J. C., & Hanges, P. J. (2005). Employment discrimination: The role of implicit attitudes, motivation, and a climate for racial bias. *Journal of Applied Psychology, 90,* 553–562.

Zimmerman, M. A., Ramirez-Valles, J., Washienko, K. M., Walter, B., & Dyer, S. (1996). The development of a measure of enculturation for Native American youth. *American Journal of Community Psychology, 24,* 295(16).

Zuckerman, M. (1998). Some dubious premises in research and theory on racial differences: Scientific, social, and ethical issues. In P. Balls Organista, K. M. Chun, & G. Marín (Eds.), *Readings in ethnic psychology* (pp. 59–72). New York: Routledge.

PHOTO CREDITS

SUBJECT INDEX

Supporting researchers for more than 40 years

Research methods have always been at the core of SAGE's publishing program. Founder Sara Miller McCune published SAGE's first methods book, *Public Policy Evaluation*, in 1970. Soon after, she launched the *Quantitative Applications in the Social Sciences* series—affectionately known as the "little green books."

Always at the forefront of developing and supporting new approaches in methods, SAGE published early groundbreaking texts and journals in the fields of qualitative methods and evaluation.

Today, more than 40 years and two million little green books later, SAGE continues to push the boundaries with a growing list of more than 1,200 research methods books, journals, and reference works across the social, behavioral, and health sciences. Its imprints—Pine Forge Press, home of innovative textbooks in sociology, and Corwin, publisher of PreK–12 resources for teachers and administrators—broaden SAGE's range of offerings in methods. SAGE further extended its impact in 2008 when it acquired CQ Press and its best-selling and highly respected political science research methods list.

From qualitative, quantitative, and mixed methods to evaluation, SAGE is the essential resource for academics and practitioners looking for the latest methods by leading scholars.

For more information, visit **www.sagepub.com**.